Persuasion and Healing

Persuasion and Healing

A Comparative Study of Psychotherapy

THIRD EDITION

Jerome D. Frank, PH.D., M.D.

Julia B. Frank, M.D.

The Johns Hopkins University Press

BALTIMORE AND LONDON

Second printing, paperback, 1993

The Johns Hopkins University Press
2715 North Charles Street
Baltimore, Maryland 21218-4319
The Johns Hopkins Press Ltd., London

LIBRARY OF CONGRESS CATALOGING-IN-PUBLICATION DATA
Frank, Jerome D. (Jerome David), 1909–
    Persuasion and healing : a comparative study of
psychotherapy / Jerome D. Frank and Julia B. Frank. – 3rd ed.
        p.   cm.
    Includes bibliographical references (p.   ) and index.
    ISBN 0-8018-4067-8 (alk. paper)   ISBN 0-8018-4636-6 (pbk.)
    1. Psychotherapy.   I. Frank, Julia (Julia B.).   II. Title.
RC480.F67   1991
616.89′14–dc20   90-4847 CIP

A catalogue record for this book is available from the British Library.

To Paul R. McHugh, M.D.,

whose steadfast encouragement and support emboldened me to undertake this revision and sustained me until its completion

J.D.F.

Contents

Foreword

High on the list of medical achievements in the twentieth century is the increasing knowledge of the uniqueness of the human animal. This knowledge includes, first of all, an understanding of the special qualities of the brain — not just as the seat of consciousness but as the control mechanism for bodily functions and changes. It also involves the way attitudes, moods, and emotions, processed by the brain, can promote health or set the stage for illness.

The new scientific term for the interaction of the nervous system, the endocrine system, and the immune system is "psychoneuroimmunology," generally credited to Dr. Robert Ader, of the University of Rochester Medical School. But long before this term was devised, Jerome Frank was studying and writing about the complex interactions of mind and body. Few medical investigators have probed more thoroughly the reality of a belief system and its effects on the healing system than has Frank. His book, *Persuasion and Healing*, originally published in 1961, anticipated the principal findings of a multitude of later researchers who identified the pathways and biochemical reactions involved in the ability of the mind to affect physical states. What has given special distinction to Frank's work is a philosophical and sociological dimension that matches an understanding of the interactions between the individual and the outside world. It is not enough for the individual to overcome feelings of helplessness and despair with respect to illness; it is important for the individual to feel connected to the collective organism of society itself, called upon as it is to meet threats to human welfare and, indeed, to human survival. No one can be truly healthy, Frank believes, in an unhealthy world. No individual may have it within his or her power to overcome or expunge the malaises or misfortunes of society. But everyone has something important to contribute to the whole, and the radiating effects of that contribution are sometimes beyond calculation.

Persuasion and Healing, then, deals with an eternal theme but has a quintessentially modern value, especially in its revised and expanded form. It addresses itself squarely to the greatest need of our time, which is to shatter our feelings of helplessness about challenges that are personal or impersonal, in the immediate community or the outside world. For it is not enough to be told that we possess powers far beyond our conscious awareness; it is important to know the nature and reach of those powers and how to activate them. Not all prescriptions come in bottles. Jerome and Julia Frank's prescription for the individual approaching the twenty-first century is a highly accessible understanding of our mental and physical assets and how to put them to work. The discovery of self and of the pathways to our potentialities is the most exciting adventure on earth.

NORMAN COUSINS

Preface

The enterprise of psychotherapy is both timeless and constantly evolving. Successive editions of this book have recorded my understanding of the fundamental nature of psychotherapy over nearly fifty years of practice and research. Recent developments within the field and changes in my own conceptualizations have inspired me to undertake a second revision of this book. Since many use this as an introductory text, bringing it up to date for a new generation of readers seems desirable.

A multitude of conflicting theories and methods characterizes the current American psychotherapeutic scene. Despite their diversity, however, all psychotherapies attempt to relieve suffering and psychological disability by inducing changes in patients' attitudes and behavior. Thus, they share features not only with each other but also with many forms of persuasion and healing. This book attempts to identify and describe these common features by exploring healing in nonindustrialized societies, miracle cures, religious revivalism, and the so-called placebo response in medical practice and relevant experimental studies. Some major types of contemporary psychotherapy are then considered from the perspective these examples provide. The particular choice of therapies reflects my interests and those of my coauthor. To those readers whose favorite form of psychotherapy has been passed over, we can only offer apologies. We believe, however, that the features shared by the methods we describe are also important in those we have neglected.

Three major themes develop in the pages that follow. The first is that all psychotherapies involve a particular setting and a conceptual framework that specifies a relationship between healer and patient. Within this relationship, the task of the therapist — whatever his or her technique — is to clarify symptoms and problems, inspire hope, facilitate experiences of success or mastery, and stir the patient's emotions. The second theme is that the main effect of such activity is to alleviate the patients' sense of powerlessness to change themselves or their environment, a condition that may be termed *demoralization*. Features that combat demoralization and facilitate helpful changes in attitude and behavior appear in all forms of religious and secular healing in the West and in the healing methods of other cultures. The third theme is that psychotherapy may be more closely akin to rhetoric than to applied behavioral science, a position fraught with implications for how the subject should be practiced, studied, and taught.

The emphasis on shared features of psychotherapeutic patients and therapies has led to two common misunderstandings. The first is that the book promulgates the nihilistic view that psychotherapy is ineffective. Each school of psychotherapy embodies conceptual schemes and procedures that distinguish it from others. Since the trained psychotherapist's claim to status and recognition depends on the mastery of a special theory and technique, all therapists naturally stress the features that distinguish their work from others'. The presentation of evidence that much of the effectiveness of psychotherapy depends on attributes possessed by all its forms threatens the psychological security of those trained in specific approaches, and this may, in part, account for this widespread misinterpretation. To say that much of the healing and persuasive power of psychotherapy depends on features shared by all schools is by no means to assert that psychotherapy is ineffective. The question this book explores is not whether psychotherapy works; that goes without saying. Rather, the question is, what are the ingredients that account for the effectiveness of psychotherapy's many different forms?

A more understandable but equally erroneous misreading is that, since demoralization contributes to the distress of most patients and all therapeutic schools and methods combat demoralization, training in any particular theory or technique is superfluous. In psychotherapy anything goes.

This misinterpretation overlooks three important considerations, which, since they are scattered through the text, may be insufficiently emphasized in it. The first is that personal values, characteristics, and life experiences may make particular patients more amenable to one technique than to another. Patients who fail to profit from an existential approach may respond to a behavioral one, and vice versa.

The second consideration is that knowledge of the conceptualization and mastery of the method of at least one school of therapy heightens the therapist's sense of competence and thereby the patient's confidence in the therapist, a major source of the effectiveness of all psychotherapy.

Finally, evidence is accumulating that certain techniques may indeed prove to be more effective than others for specific syndromes — notably, exposure to the fear-inducing stimulus for situation-bound fears, and abreaction for posttraumatic stress disorders.

My position is not that technique is irrelevant to outcome. Rather, I maintain that, as developed in the text, the success of all techniques depends on the patient's sense of alliance with an actual or symbolic healer. This position implies that ideally therapists should select for each patient the therapy that accords, or can be brought to accord, with the patient's personal characteristics and view of the problem. Also implied is that therapists should seek to learn as many approaches as they find congenial and convincing. Creating a good therapeutic match may involve both educating the patient about the therapist's conceptual scheme and, if necessary, modifying the scheme to take into account the concepts the patient brings to therapy.

Though the basic conceptualizations of this edition are mine, the updating of particular applications to new forms of therapy has required the help of a younger collaborator. Fortunately, my daughter Julia (J.B.F.) was on hand to assume this role. She has been associated with this book from its inception. As a child she proposed titling the first edition "The Wonderful World of Psychiatry" — a suggestion that, though regretfully rejected, has lingered in memory. She copy-edited the second edition, and now, as a trained psychiatrist, has become a full collaborator in the third.

Readers familiar with the previous two editions will find the following major changes. Chapter 1 includes some discussion of descriptive diagnosis of mental illness. Chapter 2 greatly expands upon the role of demoralization in mental illness and its alleviation by the common features of all psychotherapies. Entirely new sections about psychotherapy as a form of rhetoric involving hermeneutics, and consideration of some limits of research from this perspective, appear in Chapter 3, along with some of the research studies formerly included in Chapter 7. Other case studies from the original Chapter 3 have been distributed throughout the text or omitted. Chapter 4 expands and updates the material about cults from earlier editions. The earlier discussion of thought reform has been omitted as no longer topical and as too tangential to the central theses. Chapter 6 pulls together and enlarges upon previous discussions of mind-body relationships and the role of psychotherapy in physical illness, topics that were formerly scattered throughout the text. Chapter 10 takes account of new developments in directive psychotherapy, especially cognitive and abreactive therapies. A new section on family therapy appears in Chapter 11. Chapter 12 de-emphasizes the asylum and incorporates much new material on the therapeutic community and community psychiatry.

One of the great pleasures of successful collaboration lies in discovering that separate ideas blend together so well that knowing who thought of what becomes impossible. Both J.B.F. and I worked on the basic outline of the new edition and decided what to include and what to leave out. As senior author, I take responsibility for the basic concepts and overall format of the book, while J.B.F. assumes responsibility for particular discussions of contemporary applications — specifically, the sections on *DSM III-R*, psychopharmacology, family therapy, milieu therapy, and community psychiatry. Her special expertise in posttraumatic stress disorders substantially shaped my thinking about abreactive therapies. Each of us worked on the entire text, removing implicit gender bias and polishing the organization and style.

JEROME D. FRANK

Acknowledgments

Let me first briefly recapitulate the contributors, living and dead, to the first two editions of this book, since their contributions continue to pervade the text, and my gratitude to them remains lively: John C. Whitehorn, M.D.†, director of the Department of Psychiatry, Johns Hopkins Medical School (1941–59), whose intellectual and administrative support was invaluable; Ralph W. Tyler, Ph.D., director of the Center for Advanced Study in the Behavioral Sciences, his staff, and my colleagues there during a seminal fellowship (1958–59); and, at the Johns Hopkins Medical School, professional colleagues Rudolf Hoehn-Saric, M.D., Stanley B. Imber, Ph.D., Otto Kernberg, M.D., Bernard Liberman, Ph.D., Earl K. Nash, Ph.D.†, Sashi Pande, M.D., and Anthony R. Stone, M.S.S.W.†.

Turning to the current edition, my essential debt is to Julia B. Frank, M.D., for her many specific contributions but especially for her cheerful willingness, in the midst of heavy family and professional duties, to share responsibility for this edition. Without her commitment, this revision would not have been undertaken, much less completed. I again gratefully acknowledge the continuing, loving support of Elizabeth K. Frank over so many years.

I wish to thank Everett Siegel, M.D., and H. Richard Warranch, Ph.D., for their helpful critical readings of the sections on evocative therapies and directive therapies, respectively, and Mr. Michael Sharp, who carefully read the entire manuscript and suggested useful stylistic changes. My coauthor joins me in acknowledging with thanks the bibliographical help of Sven Willenberger, Susan Herman, and Maruquel Castillo. Both of us also deeply appreciate the help of Wendy Harris and Penny Moudrianakis, our editors at the Johns Hopkins University Press.

The forbearance and unfailing good humor of my secretary, Mrs. Claire Mooney, has helped me through many stressful periods.

Grants from the Ford Foundation and the National Institutes of Mental Health supported in part the research described in the sections on expectations and the placebo response, preparation of patients for psychotherapy, and emotional arousal. I wish also to thank George W. Gorham, M.D., for a personal grant, part of which was used to defray expenses in connection with the preparation of this edition.

JEROME D. FRANK

Beyond the incalculable debt of a child to a loving parent, J.B.F. is deeply grateful to J.D.F. for the opportunity to work with him and for his acceptance of her as a full collaborator in revising this book. She wishes to thank Dr. David Drum and the staff of the Counselling and Mental Health Center of the University of Texas at Austin for allowing her to take leave to work on this project. She expects to spend the rest of her natural life working off the debt she owes to her husband, Mark Graber, both for his unstinting emotional and practical support over the past two years and for his careful review of the manuscript. Professor Graber claims credit for half the periods and none of the commas in the pages that follow.

JULIA B. FRANK

Persuasion and Healing

ONE

Psychotherapy in America Today

> They all crowded around it, panting, and asking, "But who
> has won?" This question the Dodo could not answer
> without a great deal of thought. . . . At last the Dodo said
> "*Everybody* has won, and *all* must have prizes."
>   — Lewis Carroll, *Alice's Adventures in Wonderland*

Throughout life, we are influenced by others' behavior toward us. Relationships with our fellows shape our behavior, attitudes, values, self-image, and world view and affect our sense of well-being. It is customary to classify different forms of personal influence in accordance with their settings and the role of the influencing figure. Thus we say that a person is brought up by parents in the family, educated by teachers in school, and led by officers in battle.

Attempts to relieve suffering and disability are usually labeled treatment, and every society trains some of its members to apply this form of influence. Treatment typically involves a personal relationship between healer and sufferer. Certain types of therapy rely primarily on the healer's ability to mobilize healing forces in the sufferer by psychological means. These forms of treatment may be generically termed psychotherapy.

Although psychotherapeutic methods have existed since time immemorial and a vast amount of accumulated experience supports a belief in their value, some of the most elementary questions about them remain

1

unanswered. Despite decades of effort, no one has shown convincingly that one therapeutic method is more effective than any other for the majority of psychological illnesses. This suggests that, for these conditions at any rate, the specific effects of particular healing methods may be overshadowed by therapeutically potent ingredients shared by all. The primary purpose of this book is to identify and clarify the features common to various forms of psychotherapy, in other cultures as well as in our own, on the assumption that their appearance in so many different guises is persuasive evidence of their therapeutic power. Thus, it seems appropriate to begin this undertaking with a definition of psychotherapy, followed by a brief consideration of its historical roots. We shall then examine its place in America today and consider, with a preliminary glance, research concerning its effects.

What Is Psychotherapy?

Since practically all forms of personal influence may affect a person's sense of well-being, the definition of psychotherapy is of necessity somewhat arbitrary. We shall consider as psychotherapy only those types of influence characterized by:

1. a healing agent, typically a person trained in a socially sanctioned method of healing believed to be effective by the sufferer and by at least some members of his or her social group. The healing agent need not be a professional. Other types include a fellow sufferer, a group of fellow sufferers with or without a trained leader, or even a book or audiotape invested by the sufferer with healing powers. Except where specifically indicated, the healing agents we shall consider are persons.
2. a sufferer who seeks relief from the healer
3. a healing relationship — that is, a circumscribed, more or less structured series of contacts between the healer and the sufferer in which the healer, often with the aid of a group, tries to bring about relief of symptoms. This relief is typically accompanied by changes in emotional state, attitudes, and behavior. Except in cases of involuntary treatment, all concerned believe the changes to be beneficial. Although physical and chemical adjuncts may be used, the healing influence is exercised primarily by words, acts, and rituals in which sufferer, healer, and sometimes a group participate jointly.

These three features are common not only to all forms of psychotherapy as the term is generally used but also to methods of healing in nonindustrialized societies, religious conversion, and even so-called brainwashing.[1] All of these activities involve systematic, time-limited contacts between a person in distress and someone who tries to reduce the distress by producing changes in the sufferer's feelings, attitudes, and behavior. By this definition, the administration of an inert medicine — a "placebo" — by a doctor to a patient also is a form of psychotherapy, since the placebo's effectiveness depends on its symbolization of the physician's healing function, which produces favorable changes in the patient's feelings and attitudes. Our search for the active ingredients of psychotherapy, then, includes exploration of these activities.

The Historical Roots of Psychotherapy

Since at least part of the efficacy of psychotherapeutic methods lies in the shared belief of the participants that these methods work, the predominant method will differ between societies and across historical epochs. Modern psychotherapies are rooted in three historical traditions of healing: the religiomagical, the rhetorical, and the empirical or naturalistic (Ehrenwald 1966). Religiomagical healing (see pp. 87–112), originating before recorded history, regards certain forms of suffering or of alienation from one's fellows as caused by some supernatural or magical event, such as the loss of one's soul, possession by an evil spirit, or a sorcerer's curse. Treatment consists of suitable rites conducted by a healer who combines the roles of priest and physician. These highly charged, emotional rites typically require the active participation of the sufferer and members of the family or social group. If successful, they undo the supernaturally or magically caused damage, thereby restoring the victim's health and reestablishing or strengthening his or her ties with the group. As we shall see, the religiomagical tradition is still influential, even in secularized Western society.

Some readers may be startled by our inclusion of rhetoric as an ancient doctrine of healing. Until recently, with the notable exception of Szasz (1988), it was seldom mentioned by writers on psychotherapy. For the Greeks, psychotherapy included epic, drama, philosophy (B. Simon 1978), and "noble" rhetoric. Rhetoric as therapy seems to have slipped from view for many centuries, only to attract increasing attention in recent years (Glaser 1980; Spillane 1987). Indeed, as considered more fully in Chapter 3, rhetoric and a related discipline, hermeneutics, may prove to have more in common with psychotherapy than either religion or empiricism.

1. For further discussion of the similarities between psychotherapy and "brainwashing," see Frank 1973, chap. 4.

The earliest surviving accounts of the principles of naturalistic healing appear in writings attributed to the Greek physician Hippocrates of
the fifth century B.C. Hippocrates viewed mental illnesses, like all illnesses, as phenomena that could be studied and treated empirically.
Though largely eclipsed in the Middle Ages, this view attained increasing prominence in the early nineteenth century and now, in the guise of
applied behavioral or psychological science, is the dominant one in the
Western world. While rhetorical healing implies symbolic and aesthetic
experiences addressed only to the soul or spirit, religiomagical and empirical therapies historically combined physical and psychological methods. The two spheres were not rigidly separated in Western conceptions
of disease or therapy until Descartes articulated the doctrine of mind-
body dualism in modern form.

The emergence of psychotherapy as a distinct form of healing probably began with the dramatic demonstration by Franz Anton Mesmer, in
the late eighteenth century, that he could cause the symptoms of certain
patients to disappear by putting them into a trance. Though his particular theories and methods were soon discredited, mesmerism was the
precursor of hypnotism, which quickly gained wide recognition as a
method of psychotherapy. Using hypnosis, Sigmund Freud and Joseph
Breuer discovered toward the end of the nineteenth century that many of
their patients' symptoms seemed to be symbolic attempts to express and
resolve chronic conflicts rooted in upsetting experiences of early life.
This led Freud to develop a form of treatment based on detailed exploration of patients' personal histories, with emotional reliving of childhood
experiences in the treatment setting. From the information thus gained,
Freud formed a theory of human nature and mental illness known as
psychoanalysis. His theory provides a framework for linking various
patterns of early experience and modes of thought to adult symptomatology, thereby supplying a rationale for therapy. Therapies derived from
psychoanalysis involve repeated, emotionally charged interactions with
a therapist who tries to increase the patient's awareness of more or less
unconscious feelings and attitudes, especially those formed in childhood.
Freud's trail-breaking achievement opened a rich field for innovations,
though many of his followers have moved so far from his teachings that
his influence is scarcely detectable.

Almost simultaneously with Freud, another early twentieth century
giant, I. P. Pavlov, initiated his monumental research on the laws governing the linking of autonomic responses to neutral environmental stimuli.
He demonstrated that he could make dogs "neurotic" by exposing them
to insoluble conflicts, and in his later years he applied his theory and
findings to human mental illness and its treatment. In the United States

Pavlov's ideas were seized on by the psychologist J. B. Watson. Together, their works provide the conceptual rationale for therapies that examine the immediate environmental determinants of patients' attitudes and behavior and systematically try to alter their responses.

The work of E. L. Thorndike further strengthened this second strand in the web of modern American psychotherapy. Thorndike's ingenious experiments showed that the behavior of cats could be shaped by the consequences associated with certain actions. This principle, which he termed the "law of effect," came into full flower with the research of B. F. Skinner, who applied it to education and psychotherapy under the name "behavior modification." In recent years behavioral methods have been vastly elaborated and extended by the incorporation of cognitive processes into their conceptual framework under the guise of internal behaviors. Reflecting their training, psychiatrists and psychiatric social workers have preferred Freudian and neo-Freudian conceptualizations and methods, while psychologists have concentrated on behavioral and cognitive approaches.

Most current empirically based theories of mental illness and its treatment represent various combinations, modifications, and extensions of concepts originating with Freud, Pavlov, and Skinner. Fortunately, despite differences in terminology, these conceptual schemes are not incompatible. Together, they supply scientifically respectable rationales for contemporary methods of psychotherapy. It remains possible, however, that the therapeutic effectiveness of these methods may depend to a large extent on implicit and unacknowledged religiomagical and rhetorical components.

In this connection, contemporary Western psychotherapies include a third approach, which questions the application of scientific concepts and methods to psychotherapy. These so-called existential therapies are based on philosophic doctrines. Granting that a person's behavior and subjective life are partly determined by the interplay of present and past environmental influences with genetically determined structures, these therapies stress that humans' unique spiritual dimension gives them ultimate freedom of choice (Frankl [1965] 1986). Anxiety, despair, and abnormal behaviors are viewed as reactions to or efforts to escape from the "existential predicament" that life is meaningless. Proponents of this approach maintain that a person has the capacity to find a purpose in life despite this realization. Humans both fashion their world and are shaped by it. The existential therapeutic interview is a free-flowing encounter that helps the patient face existential dilemmas directly, thereby gaining the power to relinquish psychopathological symptoms and achieve greater self-realization. While psychoanalytically and existentially based therapies have much in common, existential therapists' more explicit emphasis on a philosophy of existence brings their work closer to religiomagical and rhetorical forms of healing. Their stress on immediate experience is congenial to the rationale underlying many group and family therapies.

Until recently, dyadic forms of empirical therapy dominated the scene. This may be a historical accident, reflecting the absence of a compelling and scientifically grounded theory of group behavior and the fact that Freud, as a physician, was trained to treat patients in private. However, human beings are social creatures whose personalities, world views, and behavior are molded by the standards of the groups to which they belong. This has been implicitly recognized by all forms of religiomagical and rhetorical healing, which incorporate group rituals. In this country, after a slow start, group approaches have mushroomed (Yalom [1970] 1985), based on a variety of rationales that range from the scientific to the spiritual.

At this historical juncture, professionally conducted group therapies, most of them time-limited, seem to be making increasing inroads on the traditional two-person therapies conducted in private. Emphasis within psychiatry and psychology also seems to be shifting from open-ended, long-term interview treatment with rather ill-defined goals, for which psychoanalysis was the initial model, to time-limited therapies aimed at crisis management or the relief of specific symptoms through focused behavior change. Meanwhile, nonprofessionals are conducting all manner of alternative therapies (McGuire 1989). These approaches invoke a dizzying variety of theories of the etiology of illness and the sources of healing power. We shall shortly return for a closer look at contemporary psychotherapies.

Cultural Definitions of Mental Illness and Psychotherapy

Before proceeding further, we must wrestle briefly with a surprisingly thorny question: what is it that psychotherapy purports to treat? There are various paths into this conceptual briar patch, but no entirely satisfactory routes out. Perhaps because of our medical training, we start with the common-sense notion that treatment implies illness, and psychotherapies treat forms of illness known as mental illnesses. Forms of distress and disability that bring persons to healers in any culture are classified in terms of theories that are products of that culture (Kleinman and Good 1985). In contemporary America, the category "mental illness" is a grab bag that includes patients who display sufficiently prominent disturbances in communicative behavior, thoughts, and feelings that they or others are alarmed. These disturbances reflect various combinations of physical, psychological, and social factors.

The more bodily factors contribute to the etiology of a mental illness, the less the manifestations of that illness are influenced by culture and the more easily the illness can be diagnosed across cultures (Murphy 1976). Alzheimer's disease is essentially the same in Katmandu and Kalamazoo. Though some manifestations and the meanings attached to them may vary, most of the symptoms, the course, and the pathological findings of the disease will be the same in every society.

On the other hand, the attitudes and values of the surrounding culture heavily shape those mental illnesses whose etiology is prominently social or psychological. Cultural settings also largely determine how such conditions are diagnosed. Symptoms that in contemporary American society are viewed as manifestations of mental illness appropriately treated by psychotherapy (Gross 1978; Zilberfeld, 1983) may be classified in other times or places as appropriate responses to life's stresses, as evidence of spirit possession requiring exorcism, as wrongdoing requiring punishment, or as mere eccentricity.

In World War II, for example, Russian soldiers were never classified as having psychoneuroses, because the Russian army did not recognize this condition. Soldiers with what Americans would term psychoneurotic complaints were regarded either as malingerers, who were therefore subject to disciplinary action, or as medically ill and therefore to be treated by regular physicians. In the American army, by contrast, many commonplace reactions to the stresses of military life were initially regarded as signs of illness warranting discharge from the service. Today many of these same discharged soldiers would be promptly returned to duty.

Analogously, the current American diagnostic scheme includes the term "dependent personality disorder" to describe people who seem unable to function and maintain their well-being outside a significant relationship (American Psychiatric Association 1987). However, we do not recognize any "independent personality disorder." An American teenager going three thousand miles away from home to attend college is considered normal, but in a more closely knit society such determination to leave the family might be considered evidence of illness requiring treatment.

Exemplifying the impossibility of divorcing psychiatric diagnoses from cultural influences, the same behavior may seem pathological from one culturally determined moral position while appearing to be evidence of psychological strength from another. If an adolescent finds the values of society abhorrent and drops out of college to search for alternative values and lifestyles (including, perhaps, joining a religious cult or experimenting with psychedelic drugs), is the adolescent suffering from a personality disorder or displaying praiseworthy independence? What is the psychotherapist's proper role: to reinforce societal values by persuading such an adolescent to go back to school, or to encourage continuing rebellion against social pressures that hamper emotional growth?

Obviously, the answer depends on the particular case and circumstances, but these examples show that psychiatric diagnoses may conceal culturally influenced covert judgments about whether the person's behavior is pathological and whether the source of that behavior lies in the person or in the culture (Kleinman 1988). This issue is well illustrated by the American controversy surrounding the proposed diagnosis "self-defeating personality" for persons who seem to act contrary to their self-interest by avoiding pleasure, refusing help, and remaining in situations where they are abused or exploited (American Psychiatric Association 1987). As initially proposed, this diagnosis would have been applicable to a woman who refused to leave an abusive husband. Critics cogently pointed out that calling such behavior "illness" ignored the many social forces that are at work to keep women in such situations. Locating the problem in the victim, furthermore, implied that the victim's "illness" — not social and economic constraints — was what kept her in a destructive marriage. In such situations, offering "treatment" may be pejorative and may cause more appropriate interventions to be overlooked (Caplan 1987).

While in some instances the "illness" label seems prejudicial, in others it may be too forgiving. Americans have increasingly come to regard such conditions as alcoholism, drug abuse, and impulsive criminal behavior as illnesses requiring treatment rather than as manifestations of wickedness. This humanitarian development follows from the recognition that constitutional vulnerabilities may contribute to such behaviors and that some social deviants are trying to deal with the same internal conflicts and external stressors that confront persons who are consensually regarded as mentally ill. The only difference is that the offenders' efforts to cope take the form of socially destructive behavior.

Unfortunately, treatment based simply on the disease model does not work in such motivated behaviors as drinking. The illness model typically implies that the sufferer is the blameless victim of such impersonal forces as germs or bad genes, and that the doctor's responsibility is to provide a remedy. The patient's responsibility is limited to following the doctor's orders. Allowing the alcoholic to depend passively upon a professional for cure fails because he or she is not forced to assume responsibility for the drinking. More effective treatment, such as the form of psychotherapy embraced by Alcoholics Anonymous, invokes the idea of illness in order to relieve the alcoholic from fruitless feelings of guilt about lack of will power or past behavior. At the same time, the program makes the alcoholic responsible for the consequences of his or her drinking and for following the steps to recovery, which involve moral acts such as making amends to others and helping other alcoholics (Alcoholics Anonymous 1953).

Another cultural influence upon the definition of mental illness is the implicit theory of human nature and moral code underlying therapeutic techniques (London 1986). Variants of normal behavior and ordinary unhappiness become illnesses amenable to psychotherapy when a theory exists to explain them as such. For example, in classical psychoanalysis, homosexuality is a form of maldevelopment rooted in conflict and requires treatment. Yet many homosexuals consider their behavior to be normal and reject the label "illness." By calling people's attention to particular experiences or behaviors and by labeling these as signs of illness, publicity about mental health can create unwarranted anxieties, leading those who have not previously felt in need of help to seek it. To quote Schofield: "Case finding tends frequently to result in case making. . . . The individual who is dissatisfied with his work, unhappy in his social relationships, lacking in recreational skills . . . is not helped by sensitization to the notion that he is 'sick'" (1964, p. 27).

Similarly, the greater the number of treatment centers and the more widely they are known, the larger the number of persons seeking their services. To a large extent, the demand for psychotherapy keeps pace with the supply, and one gets the uneasy feeling that the supply may even create the demand. The German psychiatrist Karl Jaspers put it succinctly: "Therapeutic schools unwittingly foster the phenomena which they cure" (1964, p. 8). Psychotherapy will never suffer the predicament of comedian Victor Borge's uncle, who became despondent when he realized that he had discovered a cure for which there was no disease.

Cultural assumptions influence methods of healing as well as concepts of illness. For example, a perceptive Oriental psychiatrist suggests that the underlying value system of Western psychotherapy stresses interaction between the self and the outer world, in contrast with the Eastern emphasis on awareness as an end in itself. As a result, in the West everything worthwhile involves some form of action. A Westerner feels guilty simply sitting under a tree and savoring the springtime; a parent and a child cannot enjoy being with each other without doing something; and a helping relation such as psychotherapy must involve some goal-directed task. Thus in the West the measure of success of a therapeutic session is whether the patient has been productive, worked something through, advanced up a desensitization hierarchy, or the like, rather than whether the therapeutic encounter was an enriching one (Pande 1968).

The effects of such social variables as ethnicity, economic status, and education on the diagnosis and treatment of mental illness provide further evidence that these are culturally biased enterprises. Thirty years ago, Hollingshead and Redlich (1958) showed that lower-class or minority patients were more likely to receive directive treatment, often accompanied by medication. Patients who were better off or more educated, by contrast, were more likely to receive permissive forms of treatment stressing insight. These particular effects of social class on psychiatric care are somewhat less pervasive today (Mollica and Milic 1986), perhaps because insurance reimbursement policies (themselves culturally influenced) so powerfully affect access to care (Chodoff 1987) and because pharmacological and directive approaches are gaining in general popularity.

Having considered some aspects of the historical and cultural contexts of psychotherapy, we now turn to an overview of who receives it, who conducts it, and the settings in which it takes place in America today.

Who Receives Psychotherapy?

The thousands of Americans who undergo some form of psychotherapy suffer from diverse disorders that all have significant emotional or psychological components. For more than a decade, the American Psychiatric Association has been making a heroic effort to classify these disorders on the basis of culture-free, objectively determined characteristics. To this end it has issued repeated revisions of its *Diagnostic and Statistical Manual,* the latest being *DSM III-R* (American Psychiatric Association 1987). This classification scheme has had an enormous and justified impact on every aspect of psychiatric research and practice except psychotherapy.

DSM III-R is of limited helpfulness to psychotherapy because it classifies disorders phenomenologically — that is, according to what can be observed and measured. While its authors could not entirely ignore therapists' inferences or the subjective statements of patients, they gave great weight to bodily manifestations or to verifiable abnormal or destructive behaviors. This ostensibly "atheoretical" approach, however, constitutes a theory in itself — namely, that the meanings patients attach to their symptoms, the attitudes that may be behind the symptomatic behaviors, and the social and historical antecedents of a person's suffering are all epiphenomena, and as such are not central to the diagnosis. The task of psychotherapy, however, is to address these very concerns. A lengthy critique of *DSM III-R* (Wallace 1988) would draw us away from our main focus. Suffice it to note that *DSM III-R* provides a distorted picture of persons who receive or should receive psychotherapy. As we divide the universe of patients into categories we believe to be more relevant to psychotherapy, we shall, however, allude to the *DSM III-R* groups into which they may fall.

We propose to group those who receive psychotherapy into five rough categories: the psychotic, the neurotic or persistently disturbed, the shaken, the misbehaving, and the discontented. Psychotics (whose diagnoses correspond roughly to the *DSM III-R* classifications "schizophrenia," "delusional disorder," "organic mental disorder," "bipolar disorder," and "major depressive episode with psychotic features") are people whose mental experience does not correspond to ordinary reality. They experience delusions, hallucinations, paranoia, fragmentation of thought, and similar symptoms. They are usually significantly impaired in their ability to fulfill normal social roles when ill, though many also experience periods of normal functioning. Except for a brief period in American psychiatric history when some influential psychoanalysts considered some of these conditions to be treatable by analytic therapy, the major psychoses have generally been recognized as mental manifestations of neurophysiological abnormalities. Many have a significant genetic or constitutional component. Psychotic patients used to be confined in mental hospitals. Today, following a period of efforts to "de-institutionalize" the mentally ill, they may spend brief periods in the hospital but live wherever they can and receive their treatment in psychiatric clinics or community mental health centers. Because patients with severer forms of these conditions require a variety of services, they are underrepresented in private-practice settings.

While it has become clear after years of dedicated effort that psychotherapy by itself cannot cure most psychoses, it has also become clear that psychotherapy plays a part in their management. Psychotherapy can be used to support the morale of patients (and their families), help them handle stress, including the stresses caused by their illnesses, and facilitate rehabilitation (May 1976).

Psychotherapy plays a similar role for patients with other chronic organic diseases — for example, diabetes, epilepsy, and multiple sclerosis. Because emotional factors frequently contribute more than bodily damage to the distress and disability of patients with chronic disease, rehabilitative methods increasingly incorporate psychotherapeutic principles. Psychotherapy also benefits patients with such so-called psychosomatic illnesses as asthma, peptic ulcer, and eczema, in which definite disorders of body organs seem related to emotional distress.

The second category, neurosis, describes persons with persistent dysphoric moods, recurrent maladaptive patterns of behavior, physical complaints without discoverable disease, and the like. Physiological dysfunctions and genetic factors have been found in many of these conditions (which correspond loosely to the *DSM III-R* categories "depressive disorders," especially "dysthymia," "anxiety disorders," "somatoform disorders," "dissociative disorders," "eating disorders," and some of the "personality disorders"). These findings have engendered much research and some controversy over the relative merits of somatic treatments (especially psychopharmacological treatment) and psychotherapy for these disorders. Still, most neuroses involve psychological factors, especially early deprivations and traumas that distort the normal processes of maturation and learning. These lead to faulty coping strategies that perpetuate the patient's difficulties. Many consider psychotherapy in some form, alone or in conjunction with drugs, to be the most appropriate treatment for these conditions.

Failure to recognize the importance of psychological factors in patients who express personal problems through bodily complaints can lead to misdefinition of the problem as primarily medical or surgical, with resulting serious errors in choice of treatment. A striking example of this was the case of a student nurse who, after her jaw had been dislocated in the dentist's chair, suffered a severe spasm and was unable to close her mouth. For months she was subjected to drastic procedures, including surgical destruction of the hinge of the jaw and attempts to cut nerves to certain muscles (attempts that fortunately were unsuccessful). Finally her jaws were wired together — all to no avail. Only after the surgeons reached the end of their tether did they call in a psychiatrist. He discovered that her symptom was related to severe conflicts about her choice of career, whereupon her treatment shifted immediately from surgery to psychotherapy. This soon resolved the problem of the spasm and allowed the patient to focus on the real issue: how to cope with many family problems and manage her relations with an autocratic father who opposed her career choice.

Our colossal national appetite for mood-altering substances, ranging from prescribed medication to illicit drugs, suggests that blindness to the emotional and psychological dimensions of much somatic distress is a widespread cultural phenomenon. With more than a third of all adults reporting the use of either prescribed or over-the-counter psychotropic drugs over the course of a year (Parry et al. 1973), and uncounted numbers using both alcohol and "street drugs," our tendency to seek physical solutions for psychological problems has created a mammoth public health problem. In other cultures, distressed persons whom Americans would send for medical treatment might be candidates for religious or secular psychotherapy, or might not need treatment at all.

Because it is difficult to sort out the causes of neurotic conditions on the basis of symptoms alone, this group seems to evoke the most intense competition between psychopharmacologists and behavioral and dynamic psychotherapists. Some neurotic patients may be hospitalized for brief periods, but most are treated as outpatients in clinics, social service agencies, and private practitioners' offices. Many also receive nonprofessional psychotherapy in religious settings or in organizations devoted to primal therapy, est, dianetics, and the like.

The third category, the psychologically shaken ("adjustment disorder" and the "V" codes in *DSM III-R*), merges with the neuroses. It consists of persons who are unable to cope with aspects of their immediate life situations, including bereavement, marital disharmonies, misbehaving children, and crises that overtax their adaptive capacities (Caplan 1964; Rusk 1971). Relatively brief interventions usually suffice to restore emotional equilibrium. Since persons severely shaken by current life stresses can transiently manifest the entire gamut of neurotic and psychotic symptoms (Tyhurst 1957), and since all respond gratifyingly to any form of psychotherapy, they tend to fan the competitiveness between different therapeutic schools.

People in the fourth category, the misbehaving, come to the attention of psychotherapists because their behavior disturbs others but is attributed to psychological causes rather than to wickedness. Here belong "acting out" children and adolescents, abusive or irritating spouses, and addicts, alcoholics, and antisocial personalities. (Each of the last three subcategories appears in *DSM III-R*.) The popularity of psychotherapy in treating such problems waxes and wanes, and the enterprise is fraught with pitfalls. At times therapy is instituted to avoid criminal sanctions — for instance, when a spouse abuser is sent to family therapy rather than to jail. At other times, help is denied to transgressors who might benefit substantially.

As noted above, psychotherapy generally requires that therapist and patient share similar values and goals for treatment. Criminals or abusive partners, however, may have a coherent but deviant value system that permits or even sanctions the undesirable behavior, thereby defeating therapy. Alcoholics and addicts who are actively drinking or using drugs, similarly, justify their behavior as acceptable and view efforts to change it as an invasion of personal freedom. Sometimes the misbehaving person shares the values of the wider society (and the therapist) and may be amenable to psychotherapy. At other times, in order to be effective in changing the behavior, psychotherapy must focus explicitly on changing the person's value system, and may require such overtly coercive techniques as rewards and punishment, confinement (Vaillant 1975), or required attendance (Yochelson and Samenow 1977). Such approaches obviously present significant ethical problems, which we shall not pursue here except to say that the proper handling of criminal or deviant behavior requires the cooperation of the healing, legal, and corrective professions (Rosenheck, Frank, and Graber 1987).

The fifth category, the discontented, consists of members of the leisured or educated classes who struggle with problems of identity and alienation, often looking to psychotherapy to relieve spiritual unrest or the feeling of not getting enough out of life. Such people shun behavior therapies and gravitate instead to psychotherapies with well-articulated, strongly held rationales, such as Freudian or Jungian psychoanalysis and logotherapy. Some also flock to the quasi-religious movements mentioned earlier. Because existential despair is hard to categorize as an illness, its treatment is often not covered by health insurance. Though the social support for such treatment is threatened by reimbursement policies, one could argue that the need for it is increasing in the face of the erosion of traditional values and the rapidly changing conditions of contemporary life.

Patients in all these groups typically seek or are brought to psychotherapy because they have failed to fulfill others' expectations or their own. All experience various degrees of helplessness, hopelessness, confusion, and subjective incompetence. We propose to consider these and related feelings as manifestations of *demoralization*, a term that denotes the psychological state that responds to the elements shared by all psychotherapies (Frank 1974).

For completeness, we must also list among recipients of therapy psychotherapists-in-training, who are required to undergo the procedure as part of their education. Although these cannot be classified as patients, they are of some importance in the total scene. As trainees, they are likely to exhibit symptoms and treatment responses that accord with their therapists' beliefs (see Chapter 8). Their treatment, which may occupy a significant portion of an experienced clinician's time, thus tends to shape and reinforce the ideology of therapists who as educators are very influential in the field.

Who Conducts Psychotherapy?

As mentioned in the historical survey, the variety of psychotherapeutic practitioners at work today is almost as great as the range of persons they seek to help. Psychotherapists in the empirical tradition include a relatively small group who are specifically trained for this art, a much larger number of professional healers who practice psychotherapy (without labeling it as such) in connection with their healing or advisory activities, and a growing army of new types of professionals and nonprofessionals who receive various amounts of training. The largest group of professionals trained to conduct psychotherapy are clinical psychologists. Their ranks are supplemented by psychiatrists, social workers, and psychiatric nurses with psychotherapy skills. The practice of psychoanalysis, once restricted in the United States to physicians, now attracts members of all the established disciplines, and these would-be practitioners attend analytic institutes for postgraduate training.

Psychologists enter the field of psychotherapy through the scientific study of human thinking and behavior, and they supply most of the sophisticated research in this field. In such settings as hospitals and psychiatric clinics they carry out diagnostic tests and provide therapy. While psychologists are currently achieving more professional autonomy, in clinical settings they usually work under the more or less nominal supervision of psychiatrists. The major institutions in which they work independently are schools and universities. Increasing numbers, especially in the nation's larger cities, are going into independent private practice as both diagnosticians and therapists.

Psychiatric social workers are specialists within the helping profession of social work. Like clinical psychologists and psychiatric nurses in hospitals and clinics, they are members of treatment teams that, for legal reasons, work under psychiatric supervision. They also operate independently in social agencies, family agencies, marriage counseling centers, and so on, and as private practitioners. Psychiatric nurses with masters' degrees may be found in a similar range of settings, while nurses with diplomas and bachelors' degrees work under more direct medical supervision in hospitals and clinics.

Psychotherapy also forms part of the practice of many other professional groups. An indeterminate number of America's nonpsychiatric physicians and osteopaths use psychotherapy with many of their patients, often without recognizing it as such. To this list must be added such healers on the fringes of medicine as chiropractors, naturopaths, and the indigenous healers consulted by members of various ethnic groups. Their effectiveness, especially with emotionally disturbed persons, probably rests primarily on their intuitive use of psychotherapeutic principles. In addition to the healers associated with medicine, a wide variety of counselors and guides may use psychotherapeutic principles with their clientele. These include marriage counselors, family therapists (many of whom come from the established professions), rehabilitation and vocational counselors, parole officers, and clergy.

Members of established disciplines, moreover, are ceasing to monopolize the field. Because so many kinds of intervention can help people with a wide variety of symptoms, the excess of demand for personal help over the available supply has fostered a rapid proliferation of new training programs in psychotherapy for nonprofessionals. Many focus on a particular problem, such as substance abuse, or emphasize a particular modality, such as group or family therapy. Some of these programs provide graduate degrees or certificates of training, thereby creating such new subprofessions as registered family therapists, alcohol and drug abuse counselors, and mental health technicians.

Any review of psychotherapeutic practitioners would be incomplete without mentioning the thousands of religious healers who are either members of such established sects as Christian Science and New Thought or, on their fringes, cultists of all sorts, whose claim to healing powers rests solely on their own assertions. Though there is no way to count religious healers, they treat vast numbers of troubled people who are indistinguishable from those receiving secular forms of psychotherapy (see Chapter 5).

Moreover, people with a variety of physical, psychological, or social problems have banded together to form self-help organizations based on group techniques. Estimating the exact number of persons involved in the self-help movement is impossible, but clearly the number is huge. It may be larger than the whole mental health system (Powell 1987). The oldest surviving self-help organizations are Alcoholics Anonymous (Alcoholics Anonymous, 1953) and Recovery, Inc., and new ones continue to emerge. Some, like Recovery, Inc., have leadership-training programs and screen leaders for competence and reliability (Wechsler 1960; Galanter 1988). In addition, the sensitivity or encounter-group movement, though waning in popularity, still affords a wide variety of group experiences aimed at greater self-awareness, freedom of expression, heightened aesthetic awareness, and more open and intimate communication with others. While not described as therapeutic in the strict sense, the work of these groups obviously overlaps with that of psychotherapy. Encounter groups and self-help organizations are patronized by many persons who are indistinguishable from seekers of psychotherapy.

The settings in which psychotherapy or its equivalent is conducted also have multiplied. Community mental health centers financed by public funds, psychiatric units in general hospitals, and health maintenance organizations with psychotherapy services have been added to the traditional locales of mental hospitals, outpatient clinics, social service agencies, university counseling centers, and private offices. Encounter groups are conducted at "growth centers" such as Esalen, as well as in hotel rooms, meeting halls, and private homes. Self-help groups meet everywhere from hospitals to church basements.

Members of different helping professions tend to describe their psychotherapeutic activities in different terms. Medical and quasi-medical healers treat patients, psychiatric social workers do case work with clients, clergy offer pastoral counseling, group workers do group work. To attract practitioners and clients, and to stake the strongest possible claim on the economic resources apportioned for mental health (health insurance and public funding), each discipline tends to emphasize the special features of its approach, thereby creating the appearance of greater differences than actually exist.

All forms of psychotherapy have similarities that these "turf battles" may obscure. The distinction between different healers and advisers lies less in what they do than in the persons with whom they do it; this, in turn, depends largely on the settings in which they work. Certain settings sharply limit the kinds of persons who seek or receive psychotherapeutic help. Hospitals and related clinical settings tend to restrict themselves to patients who merit *DSM III-R* diagnoses such as schizophrenia, dementia, major and minor affective disorders, anxiety disorders, and substance abuse, with or without major adjustment problems. Persons using the services of social agencies tend to be struggling with economic, social, marital, or parental problems, with or without diagnosable disorders. The school psychologist inevitably deals with children with school problems, the prison psychologist or psychiatrist with offenders, and so on.

Other settings are open to all. These include self-help programs, centers for personal growth, and the offices of private practitioners. The referral channel a person happens to pick or the patient's belief about the cause of a particular problem partly determines who will conduct the treatment. The same patients might be treated by a psychiatrist, a psychologist, a psychiatric social worker, a clergyperson, or the untrained leader of a sensitivity group, depending on the size of their pocketbooks and where their feet carry them.

What Are the Effects of Psychotherapy?

The persistent popularity of psychotherapy and the ever-increasing investment of time, effort, and money in it indicate that both recipients and practitioners believe it does some good. Patients must believe that they will be helped or they would not continue to seek psychotherapy in such numbers, and psychotherapists of every persuasion have seen permanent and striking improvement in patients treated according to their method. Such popularity has stimulated a demand for research into every aspect of psychotherapy. Studies of the outcome of different treatments are particularly important because of their implications for training and funding. Psychotherapy research is a major activity of all graduate and postgraduate education programs, some free-standing, but most in university departments of psychology. Social work departments and a decreasing number of departments of psychiatry also conduct research in psychotherapy. Each year hundreds of doctoral and masters theses are added to the flood of data, along with articles and books by senior researchers.

Most would agree that the increase in knowledge of psychotherapy from this vast enterprise has not been commensurate with the investment of time, effort, and money and the sophistication of the researchers. Different studies often yield inconsistent findings, and most of the relationships found, even those reaching the conventional level of statistical significance, have been too weak to influence clinical practice. In fact, even the practitioners of those therapies that make the most plausible claims to being based on rigorous research admit that their work with patients is guided more by clinical experience than by scientific scholarship. As a recent survey of practicing psychotherapists concluded, "Therapists learn about therapy overwhelmingly from experience with clients and only rarely consult therapy research" (Cohen, Sargent, and Sechrest 1986, p. 194).

The few noncontroversial research findings in psychotherapy seem simply to confirm common sense. The most robust of these findings is that patients benefit more from any form of therapy than from being kept on a waiting list for an equivalent period of time (Lambert, Shapiro, and Bergin 1986). On the average, patients who receive therapy report greater improvement than about 80 percent of those who do not. Since many patients waiting for therapy continue to elicit and receive informal help and advice from family and friends, it seems reasonably safe to conclude that any systematic form of help guided by a definite rationale is more effective than unorganized, informal efforts.

Another well-established research finding that confirms common sense is that cognitive and behavior therapies designed to alleviate such particular symptoms as phobias relieve these symptoms more effectively than do open-ended exploratory or humanistic approaches (Shapiro and Shapiro 1987). This is hardly surprising. Among the focused therapies, however, none has yet consistently been shown to be more effective than any other.

In our present state of ignorance the most reasonable assumption, as already mentioned, is that all enduring forms of psychotherapy must do some good or they would disappear. While different therapies may have different effects on particular problems, it is likely that the similarity of improvement rates across the board reflects features that are common to them all. If this is so, it will be hard to tease out the unique contributions of different forms of treatment until we can identify the features they all share, along with the attributes of patients that respond to these elements.

We shall try to identify these shared, active ingredients by looking for features common to many different forms of interpersonal healing, including contemporary psychotherapies. Our exploration will lead us quite far afield and into some largely uncharted areas. Before setting out, however, let us identify home base more clearly by outlining in Chapter 2 a theoretical framework for psychotherapy.

Summary

In this chapter we have attempted a general definition of psychotherapy, briefly reviewed its historical roots, and described the types of patients, therapists, and settings that characterize psychotherapy in contemporary America. It appears that many thousands of troubled people of all sorts seek psychotherapy or have it thrust upon them. Moreover, psychotherapy's practitioners are almost as varied as its recipients. Cultural norms and world-views influence not only the definition of mental illness but also the nature of its treatment. Psychotherapies in societies or groups that have a primarily religious world-view are based on religiomagical theories, and healing rituals merge with religious rites. Consistent with their world-view, Western industrialized societies consider psychotherapy to be the systematic application of the scientific understanding of human nature to the treatment of the mentally ill.

The enduring popularity of psychotherapy is strong evidence that it does some good, yet extensive research efforts have produced little conclusive knowledge about the relative efficacy of its different forms. The failure to find differences in outcome between therapies reflects in part formidable methodological problems. However, it also suggests that the features common to all types of psychotherapy contribute as much, if not more, to the effectiveness of those therapies than do the characteristics that differentiate them.

TWO

A Conceptual Framework
for Psychotherapy

Alice knew it was the Rabbit coming to look for her, and
she trembled till she shook the house, quite forgetting that
she was now about a thousand times as large as the Rabbit
and had no reason to be afraid of it.

—*Alice's Adventures in Wonderland*

Describing features common to all forms of psychotherapy requires the
consideration of a wide variety of patterned personal and social interactions. To keep our bearings in this exploration, we need a general conceptual framework. Such a scheme should relate a person's inner life to
interactions with other persons and to his or her group allegiances. It
should suggest how certain kinds of distress might both arise from and
contribute to disturbed relationships with others, and how particular
types of interpersonal experience might help ameliorate both. This is
obviously a very big order. To handle it adequately we would have to
provide a complete theory of personality development and structure as
related to social and cultural influences, an enterprise beyond the scope
of this book. The following presentation attempts only to sketch a few
useful concepts for orientation purposes.

Mental Illness, Psychotherapy, and Interpersonal Stress

Although, as described in Chapter 1, the conditions for which psycho-therapy is sought or offered are protean, all can be viewed as temporary or persistent unsuccessful adaptations to stress. Everyone must deal with experiences that temporarily disturb equanimity and create tensions with others. The healthy person is able to handle most such experiences promptly and effectively. Others cannot. It is useful to think of all ill-nesses as "non-adapted" states (Stunkard 1961) characterized by dis-ability and distress.

Failures of adaptation imply an imbalance between the severity of an environmental stress and the person's susceptibility to it. Imbalances between stress and coping capacity may be due primarily to constitution-al defects or vulnerabilities. "Constitutional" vulnerabilities are built into the body structure, either genetically or through trauma occurring early enough in life to affect the subsequent development of the organ-ism. It is now well established that congenital factors, probably involving defective enzyme systems in the brain, reduce the adaptive capacity of many schizophrenic people. Sometimes the psychological effects of con-stitutional factors wax and wane — as in manic-depressive disorders. Problems that seem overwhelming to a person when he or she is de-pressed shrink to trivialities when the mood brightens. Constitutional weaknesses in coping capacity cannot be directly treated by psycho-therapy, though some may be helped by drugs. Psychotherapy can, how-ever, help impaired persons maintain their morale despite their hand-icaps.

At the other extreme, constitutional characteristics connoted by the term "stamina" (Thomas 1982) enable persons to withstand and even benefit from environmental strain. As has been said, heat that melts wax tempers steel. Despite the enormous popular health literature on the importance of avoiding stress, most moderate stresses in fact promote health. To use another analogy, life, like a violin string, is no good unless it is stretched. Some highly successful people may even seek stress to enjoy the triumph of mastering it. Sir Edmund Hillary, for example, felt impelled to climb Mount Everest simply because it was there.

Uncontrollable environmental stressors may overtax the adaptive capacities of almost anyone. Examples include the prisoner who finally yields to the prolonged tortures and deprivations of thought reform; the soldier who collapses after overwhelming battle stress; or the housewife with no reliable source of income, six young children, and a brutal alco-holic husband. Persistent adverse environmental conditions may limit psychotherapy's ability to relieve distress. However, since a person's attitudes and values affect the interpersonal environment, and psychotherapy can modify these attitudes, such limits are not absolute.

For most persons, responses to adversity are largely determined by psychological characteristics based primarily on life experiences. These characteristics include moral values, beliefs, and psychological defenses that determine the meanings the person attaches to the stressful event. Objectively similar family and social disturbances could produce an alcoholic, a criminal, an anxiety neurotic, or a priest. Divorce or bankruptcy may spell disaster to one person and relief to another. Similarly, a promotion is an invigorating challenge to someone who sees it as an opportunity to gain increased influence or power, but a demoralizing stress to someone who sees only the prospect of new worries or isolation from supportive colleagues.

In general, when a person knows how to cope with a particular stress, or when the stress is well defined and time-limited, it will seem a surmountable challenge. Examples of benign stress might be a broken leg or even a bereavement when the bereaved person knows appropriate rituals for assuaging grief. By contrast, stresses with demoralizing meanings lack a clear solution and are often expected to last indefinitely. Examples include chronic illness or persistent unemployment.

People's perception of the supportiveness of their social network may further affect their view of a stress as severe or manageable (Henderson 1981; Steinglass, Weisstaub, and Kaplan De-Nour 1988). Stresses that undermine a person's world-view and trust in others may be especially demoralizing. In his study of victims of a flash flood caused by a burst dam, for example, Kai Erikson (1978) noted that the trauma was more devastating because it could be attributed to human error and negligence rather than to an accident of fate.

When attempts to overcome the distress caused by adversity are ineffective, the person or the family may come to regard their disequilibrium as illness and seek expert help. By and large, persons who attribute their distress and disability to bodily causes turn to physicians; those who perceive their illnesses as related primarily to disturbed relations with others or to internal psychological conflicts gravitate toward psychotherapists. As we shall see, such persons have much in common with other victims of interpersonal stress — for example, the villager who consults a shaman about a curse, and the outcast on the verge of religious conversion.

Psychotherapy is commonly offered to those who seem basically intact yet are unable to handle usual environmental demands. Psychotherapists see mainly persons whom stress readily demoralizes — that is, persons who lack stamina or who attach ominous or malevolent meanings to events that others might interpret differently. This consideration brings us to what Cantril (1950) termed the "assumptive world,"[1] a useful concept for understanding the sources of distress and disability appropriately treated by psychotherapy.

The Assumptive World

Leading a successful life, even surviving, depends on the ability to predict future events from present ones, or at least the belief that one can do so (Kelly 1955). Since prediction is based on understanding, the need to make sense of events is as fundamental as the need for food or water.

Just as nature is said to abhor a physical vacuum, so the human mind abhors a vacuum of meaning. All human behavior reflects the need to make sense of the world. A major function of theology, for example, is to assign a divine purpose to all happenings, especially those that appear random or unjust; to "unscrew the inscrutable," as a minister is reported to have expressed it. Clinically, psychotic delusions reflect patients' desperate efforts to make sense out of their inexplicable experiences. Experimentally, if persons under hypnosis are instructed to perform a posthypnotic act on cue but to have amnesia for the instruction, they will always provide a rational explanation for even the most nonsensical behavior.

Like all fundamental needs, the need to attribute meanings to events probably has a neurophysiological base. Reviewing extensive studies of persons with split brains, a leading neurophysiologist concluded that our brains contain a special component, located in the dominant left hemisphere of right-handed humans, that he termed the "interpreter." This interpreter "instantly constructs a theory to explain why [any] behavior occurred" (Gazzaniga 1985). Our need to create a meaningful world is manifested by the automatic formation of certain assumptive systems or schemata (Goleman 1985) about ourselves, other persons, and the nonhuman environment. The totality of each person's assumptions may be conveniently termed his or her assumptive world.

Each person evaluates internal and external stimuli in the light of assumptions about what is dangerous, safe, important, unimportant, good, bad, and so on. These assumptions become organized into sets of highly structured, complex, interacting values, expectations, and images of self and others that are closely related to emotional states and feelings.

---

1. Cantril confined this term to the sphere of perceptions, but his discussion of the "assumptive world" seems to justify the broader use we have adopted. For example, he said: "The net result of our purposive actions is that we create for ourselves a set of assumptions which serve as guides and bases for future actions" (1950, p. 87).

Such psychological structures and processes shape, and in turn are shaped by, a person's perceptions and behavior.

Enduring assumptions become organized into attitudes with cognitive, affective, and behavioral components (Rokeach 1968). Attitudes have the potential to determine behavior — that is, interaction with the environment — though they may, of course, exist only as silent thoughts. The cognitive aspect of an attitude (the pilot) guides the behavior, while the affective part (the fuel) drives the engine. To take a simple example, an attitude about hats may lead a person to think about them, to buy one, or to avoid hat stores. What actually happens (the behavioral aspect) will depend on both the person's knowledge of hats (the cognitive aspect) and the strength of his or her feelings about hats — pleasure, distaste, and the like. Efforts to influence attitudes usually involve all three components, which are inseparable, though different therapeutic methods may emphasize one component over another. Especially pertinent here are attitudes concerning attributions of causality (Kelley 1967), because these strongly influence our feelings and our responses to events. If a man gets sick after eating fish, it makes a difference if he attributes his nausea to the market's having sold him spoiled fish or to his wife's trying to poison him.

In general, we tend to attribute our own behavior to external circumstances and the behavior of others to their internal motivations. A frequent goal of psychotherapy is to help patients recognize and accept responsibility for their difficulties. Patients' acknowledgment that they contribute to their own problems implies that they may also have the power and responsibility to overcome them. That is, such awareness can paradoxically increase a sense of "self-efficacy" (Bandura 1982) and the motivation to act. The first step in the program of Alcoholics Anonymous, for example, is for the person to acknowledge that drinking has become uncontrollable and to accept the label "alcoholic." Only then can the person take action to overcome the addiction.

The emotional components of attitudes are important as well. Attitudes connected with a sense of personal inadequacy and confusion or with the prediction of unfavorable outcome tend to generate such unpleasant emotions as anxiety and despair. Attitudes that give the person a sense of security and promise a better future engender feelings of hope, faith, and the like. As we shall see, these emotional states shape persons' ability to modify perceptions and behavior and largely determine their sense of well-being.

Attitudes range widely in scope. At one extreme would be attitudes connected with brushing one's teeth; at the other, attitudes concerning the nature of God. Attitudes also vary in their time orientation, some being concerned primarily with the past, some with the present, and some with the future. In addition, attitudes may be enduring or transient. A person's feelings about the attractiveness of a hat can usually be changed as easily as the hat itself, but this is not true for attitudes about the nature of God. Some attitudes are held only tentatively, others with firm conviction. The degree of subjective conviction need not parallel the persistence of an attitude — someone may be absolutely convinced that a hat is flattering one day and hideous the next — but generally conviction and tenacity vary together.

Different parts of the assumptive world exist at different levels of consciousness. Only a minute part is in awareness at any one time, and the relative accessibility of different aspects may differ greatly (Gazzaniga 1985). A woman may be clearly aware of her attitudes toward the nuclear arms race but oblivious of an unverbalized belief that one must be perfect to gain love. Yet the latter conviction may have considerably more effect on her behavior than the former. Unconscious assumptive systems are especially pertinent to psychotherapy because they profoundly influence behavior yet are especially resistant to change.

Attitudes vary in their degree of internal consistency. Disharmonies can exist between the cognitive, affective, and behavioral components of an attitude. Certain symptoms can be understood as expressions of such conflicts. For example, if a person cannot resist excessive handwashing, yet knows that this behavior is absurd, the feeling toward the act may be one of repulsion. Conflicts also exist between attitudes at both the conscious and the unconscious level. Conscious hatred of an enemy may arouse urges to fight that conflict with pacifistic convictions, and each side may gain strength from unconscious attitudes toward violence that developed in early life. Since internal conflicts are major sources of feelings of insecurity and other types of distress, humans devote much intellectual energy to maintaining the internal consistency of their assumptive worlds. Psychodynamic psychotherapies, in particular, are designed to help people resolve such conflicts.

The Formation of the Assumptive World
To deal with the world and enjoy life, a person's assumptive world must correspond more or less closely to conditions as they actually are. In the social realm, "actual" conditions are those validated by at least a few important others. People can maximize their chances for success and minimize failure only if they can accurately predict others' responses to their acts. Thus, everyone is strongly motivated to monitor the validity of his or her assumptions. Every act is both a consequence of a more or less explicit expectation and a test of its validity. If an act fails to produce predicted consequences, the person is in trouble. He or she must either

modify expectations or resort to maneuvers that conceal incorrect assumptions and evade or redefine their consequences. For the most part, these processes go on automatically and outside of awareness.

The validity of some aspects of the assumptive world can be checked directly against experience without being mediated by other people. For example, the test of the assumption that a glowing poker is hot is to touch it. Still, a person's most significant experiences are social ones, and most attitudes and values can be validated only by checking them against the behavior and opinions of other individuals, especially members of groups to which the person belongs or aspires to belong—his or her reference groups (Hyman and Singer 1968). The social comparison process (Festinger 1954), also termed consensual validation (Sullivan [1953] 1968), exerts strong pressure on individuals to harmonize their assumptive worlds with those of persons important to them. The overriding power of consensual validation explains how a person can feel and appear mentally quite healthy yet be involved in a highly deviant, destructive, or irrational group, such as the Nazi party or a Satanic cult.

An example of the power of the need to bolster one's own assumptions by persuading others to confirm them is the repeated observation that members of millennial religious sects start to proselytize only after their prophecies of the end of the world fail to materialize. Apparently they must convert others in order to maintain their own beliefs in the face of such devastating disconfirmation (Festinger, Riecken, and Schachter [1956] 1964).

Development of the assumptive world starts as soon as the infant enters into transactions with the environment. Such experiences lead the infant to form assumptions about the world. These coalesce into generalizations whose validity depends on three factors: the representativeness of the sample on which they are based, the accuracy of the information it provides (Imboden 1957), and the social world to which the infant belongs (Berger and Luckman 1966; Geertz 1973).

The infant, of course, has only very small samples to go on. This matters little with respect to the inanimate world, because its features are relatively homogeneous and supply clear, unambiguous information. One does not have to experience many chairs or shoes to reach valid generalizations about chairs and shoes, and a single experience with a lighted match suffices to produce a valid conclusion about some properties of fire.

The social world is more complex. People's messages are often ambiguous, and the child's sample—the immediate family in the first instance—may be far from typical. If the family group provides a rich repertoire of adaptive skills, treats the child as capable and good, and makes each member feel loved and wanted — in Bowlby's terms (1980), provides opportunities for secure attachment — the child's self-perception will likely be that of a competent, lovable person in a friendly, secure social world. Persons with such a history generally welcome new experiences, tackle them with confidence, and can easily modify their behavior and assumptive world according to the outcome.

The family environment may fall short of this ideal in many ways. Opportunities for certain experiences may not exist. The family may lack a father figure, or the child may not have adequate opportunities to play with other children. Thus, the child may fail to form certain important assumptive systems simply because he or she does not have a chance to develop them. A child who grows up without playmates, for example, may have problems making friends in school for want of knowledge about how to interpret the behavior of peers. He or she may misinterpret a temporary rebuff as complete rejection or be unduly disappointed because of unrealistic expectations based on wishful fantasies concerning how friends normally treat each other.

More serious difficulties occur if the parents are unloving or are inconsistent figures to whom the child can form only anxious attachments, thereby paving the way for a fear-ridden, insecure adulthood. Continued belittlement and rejection by others may lead to the conviction of being surrounded by a strange, hostile world: "I a stranger and afraid. / In a world I never made" (Housman 1922). People with these assumptive systems tend to avoid new experiences because they fear the worst from them.

The strategies people develop to resolve stress initially created by their families often bring temporary relief but lay the foundation for future trouble. The following example of a miniature neurosis illustrates how a person's solution to a childhood problem caused later difficulties. A scientist walking with some professional colleagues on the boardwalk at Atlantic City suddenly launched into an angry diatribe against the worthlessness of the merchandise in the curio shops. Although his remarks had some justification, the disproportionate intensity of his feelings aroused quizzical looks. Noting this, he became uncomfortable and began to wonder about it himself. He then suddenly remembered a long-forgotten childhood experience. At the age of seven he had spent a few days in Atlantic City with his mother and grandmother. To give his grandmother a birthday present, he emptied his piggy bank and bought her a cuckoo clock. Instead of being pleased, the grandmother angrily criticized his mother for letting him be so extravagant. As the grown man retold this story, he laughed and seemed relieved.

Let us describe this episode in theoretical terms. In giving a birthday present to his grandmother, the boy was acting on the assumption that she would be pleased. The unexpected failure of his prediction must have been most unpleasant for him. He probably felt resentment and anger at his grandmother as well as guilt for upsetting her and for the pain he had inadvertently caused his mother. He might even have been angry at his mother for letting him get into such a fix.

A young child obviously cannot resolve such feelings by "having it out" with the adults who caused them, but must resort to more oblique solutions. Our "patient" resorted to two common neurotic "mechanisms of defense" — repression and displacement (Brenner [1955] 1973). He blotted the unpleasant episode from awareness, and displaced the object of his angry feelings from his grandmother to the curio shops. This solution had two advantages: it afforded a less dangerous object for his anger than his grandmother, and it allowed him to relieve his guilt by blaming the shops instead of himself. Like all neurotic solutions, however, it also had drawbacks. The scientist was left with an overly negative evaluation of curio shops that was immune from correction through subsequent experience because he thereafter avoided them. He was also left with a definite, if trivial, psychic scar, in that curio shops continued to arouse an unpleasant feeling when circumstances again brought him in contact with them. By sharing his feelings with his peers, he was implicitly trying to validate them. Their quizzical looks, indicating they did not share his view, led him to examine himself for its source, and he discovered a past situation for which the feeling had been appropriate, By the same act, he realized that this situation no longer existed. That is, he gained insight into the inappropriateness of his attitude and thus was able to bring it into line with the attitude of his colleagues.

Note that the scientist's emotions were aroused both when his grandmother failed to confirm his assumption that curio shops were sources of pleasure, leading him to change his belief, and again years later when he reformulated his views on the basis of a different interaction, as shown by his discomfiture and laugh. It is worth noting, too, that the supportive, relaxed attitude of his colleagues made it relatively easy for him first to express his feelings, then to search himself for their source, and finally to offer a bit of self-revelation that explained and resolved them.

The family is only the first, although the most influential, of the many reference groups that shape a person's assumptive world. In the above example, the scientist's colleagues represented another of his reference groups. Each reference group transmits to the individual both idiosyncratic assumptions and values and those of the larger society. In the aggregate, these groups form a person's culture, which supplies many ready-made categories by which to label and evaluate the experiences generated by encounters with the world. The relative power of broad cultural assumptions depends on how well knit the culture is and on the extent to which its world-view permeates the lives of its members. The assumptive worlds of the members of an isolated tribe on a small Pacific atoll probably have more in common than do those of twentieth-century Americans.

A simple experiment demonstrates that members of a culture selectively perceive those stimuli that accord best with the culture's assumptive world. A group of Americans and a group of Mexicans were each shown two different pictures simultaneously, one to each eye. When a picture of a baseball player was shown to one eye and that of a bullfighter to the other, Americans tended to see the baseball player first, Mexicans the bullfighter (Cantril 1957).

Societies, like families, often contain built-in conflicts, or sources of stress, which create disharmonies in the assumptive worlds of their members. Often a society also contains institutionalized ways of resolving the stresses it creates. Societies that believe in witchcraft also have ways of counteracting witches' spells. Too often, however, no readily available institutionalized solution exists for a conflict engendered by discrepancies in a society's assumptive world. Americans, for example, are taught to be aggressive yet at the same time affable and considerate. Violence is simultaneously glorified in the mass media and condemned in personal relationships or in the encounters of daily life. American society offers no institutionally sanctioned way of resolving the confusion and guilt engendered by these conflicting social values. More significantly, children in our society may be exposed less to clearly conflicting values than to amorphous and constantly changing ones. Many factors contribute to this flux, including social and geographical mobility and multiple parenthood resulting from frequent divorces and remarriages. The confusion thus engendered is compounded by the shifting modes and morals of the larger society. Such a society hampers the formation of a solid sense of identity in its members. As a result, distress that brings people to psychotherapy today may arise less from internal conflict than from feelings of alienation and the loss of a sense of purpose, termed by Erik Erikson "identity diffusion" (1968).

The Stability of the Assumptive World in Relation to Psychotherapy

The aim of psychotherapy is to help people feel and function better by encouraging appropriate modifications in their assumptive worlds, thereby transforming the meanings of experiences to more favorable ones. What helps or hinders such changes? Assumptive systems, once established, tend to resist change for a variety of reasons. With increasing age, for example, new experiences lose their power to produce changes in established patterns of perception and behavior. Such inelasticity reflects in part the physiological changes concomitant with maturation. Moreover, as life goes on, new experiences are increasingly outweighed by the accumulation of previous ones.

Similarly, the reference groups against which persons test the validity of their assumptions inhibit change. Most such groups are not actually present, but exist as residues of past experiences that have been internalized. Internalized figures range from single individuals, such as "my father," to groups that exist only as concepts, such as "patriotic Americans" or "the scientific community." Because these constructs and the assumptions they engender are often unconscious and rooted in the past, they are not easily modified by present experience. Such internalized standards of reference are necessary for stable personality organization, and they help individuals withstand the pressures of groups to which they temporarily belong, even as they create resistance to potentially beneficial changes in attitudes.

Since a person relies on the assumptive world to make the universe predictable, any event or experience that is inconsistent with a person's expectations creates surprise or uncertainty. These feelings are not necessarily unpleasant. If the possible outcomes of the event include pleasant ones and the person feels able to cope with potential unpleasant ones — as, for example, at the start of a new love affair — uncertainty is accompanied by exhilaration. If, however, the most probable anticipated outcomes are unpleasant, the new experience may be tinged with fear or other unpleasant emotions, especially if the person lacks self-confidence.

In either case, the strength of the emotional impact of an unsettling experience seems to be related to the extent of change it requires in a person's assumptive world. The more crucial an attitude is to a person's security and the greater the change required, the deeper the emotional response when the attitude is challenged. Contrast the emotions accompanying the discovery that what one took to be a robin is really a bluebird with those accompanying a conversion from atheism to a transcendental religious belief.

Although changes in a person's assumptive world rarely if ever occur without a concomitant emotional reaction, simple emotional upheaval is seldom sufficient to produce major change. Even when being compelled to recognize an error causes distress, correction does not automatically follow. Such experiences may, however, motivate the individual to reexamine basic assumptions and seek more reliable guides to expectation.

Two of the mechanisms by which people strive to maintain their assumptions in the face of new experiences are especially relevant to mental patients: avoidance and confirmatory bias (Meichenbaum 1984). All people filter incoming information through assumptive systems that emphasize confirmatory experiences. Contradictory information is either ignored or quickly forgotten. Recognizing this, the conscientious scientist Charles Darwin made a special effort to write down instances that did not fit his hypotheses.

Information that threatens a person's psychic equilibrium may arise from such internal sources as memories or from the external world. Active avoidance of input from the internal world, called "repression" in Freudian terminology, is exemplified by the man who repressed his painful childhood experience with curio shops. Banishing an experience from consciousness prevents initially erroneous conclusions from being modified by subsequent experience. Repressed emotions or thoughts also reduce people's adaptive capacity and their sense of security. The mental effort required to keep repressed material from awareness depletes a person's resources for meeting current stresses. Moreover, repression is seldom perfect. Repressed emotions or thoughts are apt to erupt into consciousness attached to obviously inappropriate objects or at inappropriate times, in ways that may seem mysterious or frightening to the patient. In our example, the scientist was startled by the inappropriate intensity of his dislike of the shops. The sense of not being able to account for one's feelings or thoughts contributes to patients' common fear that they are going crazy.

Persons also seek to avoid external stimuli that might reawaken repressed material. Such avoidance deprives them of the chance to discover that previously traumatic situations may no longer hold any terrors. Someone who has been frightened by a snake in early life, for example, may continue to avoid snakes, precluding any new experiences with snakes that might assuage the fear. Psychotherapy, by persuading patients to face what they fear, enables corrective learning to take place.

Inappropriate attitudes are also perpetuated by confirmatory bias, which is often strengthened by social interaction. People typically elicit from others behavior that reinforces their own preconceptions. Friendliness tends to beget friendly responses, and anger, angry ones, thus confirming the assumptions underlying the person's initial act.

Confirmatory bias seems especially important in maintaining the assumptive worlds of persons with inadequate repertories of social behavior. Limited or inflexible people typically repeat the same behavior with everyone they meet, effectively "training" others to respond in ways that confirm their expectations. Patients tend to get caught in self-fulfilling prophecies (Merton 1957), leading to behavior that is both self-perpetuating and self-defeating. Being convinced that everyone is malevolent, for example, a paranoid patient will react to most persons in a surly, suspicious manner, thereby antagonizing even those who initially bear no ill will. Such negative reactions, in turn, reinforce the paranoid person's basic assumptions and stimulate further antagonistic behavior. Breaking these vicious circles by confronting patients with the discrepancies between their preconceptions and the world around them is another important goal of psychotherapy.

Since the assumptive worlds of many mental patients deviate from the general consensus of a society, one might think that their attitudes would be easier to change than those of well-adjusted persons. The reverse is true. Inaccurate or unrealistic assumptions lead people to experience frustrations and failures that generate feelings of impotence and bewilderment. A person in the grip of such emotions, whose sense of self-efficacy is weak, feels unable to control either external events or subjective feelings, and therefore fears new experiences. Such people, like Hamlet, prefer to bear the ills they have rather than fly to others they know not of.

Chronic frustrations, furthermore, elicit anger, resentment, and other unattractive emotions. Patients' awareness of these feelings and of their failure to live up to expectations may increase their sense of unworthiness. The patient's self-image as being different from and inferior to others creates a sense of alienation. This makes the patient less accessible to others, especially when feeling misunderstood, so he or she avoids potentially corrective social interactions. To such a person, the act of seeking psychotherapy may represent a public admission of inadequacy, a further source of resistance to change. In short, a healthy person seeks enriching new experiences, while a person preoccupied with merely surviving fearfully avoids them. As a result, the person who lacks a sense of self-efficacy may be more difficult to help than someone whose assumptive world is less out of joint.

Psychotherapy in all its forms aims to help patients modify troublesome attitudes. These attitudes may be quite circumscribed and specific, such as the fear of snakes, or very general, such as pervasive alienation or despair. In all cases, success in psychotherapy depends on influencing those attitudes that hamper the patient's ability to change.

To be effective, any therapy must first combat patients' demoralization and heighten their hopes of relief. All forms of psychotherapy do this implicitly, regardless of their explicit aims. In some instances, psychotherapy consists solely of supporting patients through crises until they can regain their previous state of equilibrium, changing only those attitudes related to the current situation. Progress in therapy, in turn, further shifts the balance toward the "welfare emotions" — for example, love, joy, and pride (Rado 1956). With luck, the process becomes self-enhancing.

Because major assumptive systems, especially unhealthy ones, are resistant to change, the changes produced directly by psychotherapy are usually minor. Fortunately, these often suffice. Small improvements in one assumptive system may initiate changes in many others. By enabling an individual to gain a more favorable perception of a boss, for example, psychotherapy may lead that person to treat the boss differently. This in turn may evoke changes in the boss's behavior that heighten the patient's self-confidence, initiating a widening circle of beneficial changes in the patient's assumptions about self and others.

To say that the central effect of most psychotherapy is to buffer crises and support morale does not disprove the claims made by many therapists that the effect of treatment is to promote personal growth. Personal growth is a rather nebulous concept, and what it means depends on the conceptualizations underlying the therapy in question. In terms of the conceptual framework offered here, "growth" would involve movement toward more accurate and realistic perceptions of oneself and others, including greater accessibility to one's own inner life, and behavior better suited to achieving personal goals. Personal growth can also imply increased self-acceptance and emotional security, with a resulting enhanced flexibility and spontaneity in dealings with others and a fuller measure of welfare emotions. Beyond these gains, psychotherapy may enable some patients to achieve a more coherent and satisfying philosophy of life.

Different schools of psychotherapy may focus primarily on emotions, cognition, or behavior. Since all attitudes involve all three components, however, the component a therapy emphasizes may be inconsequential. Thus, by definition, behavior therapies concentrate on modifying behavior, but many do so by manipulating imagery and producing emotional arousal. Interview therapies stress the communication of feelings and cognitive reorganization, but all assume that these will be reflected in behavioral change. Therapies that focus on eliciting intense emotional reactions assume that this is the preferred route to new insights and changed behavior.

Demoralization: The Common Characteristic of Persons in Psychotherapy

In Chapter 1 (p. 14) we proposed the term "demoralization" to characterize the state of mind of persons seeking psychotherapy. Dictionaries define *demoralize* as "to deprive a person of spirit, courage, to dishearten, bewilder, to throw a person into disorder or confusion." These terms well describe the state of candidates for psychotherapy, whatever their diagnostic label (deFigueiredo and Frank 1982; Frank 1974, 1985; Young 1988). Typically, they are conscious of having failed to meet their own expectations or those of others, or of being unable to cope with some pressing problem. They feel powerless to change the situation or themselves and cannot extricate themselves from their predicament. This situation has been conceptualized as a "crisis" if acute (Korchin 1975) and as the "social breakdown syndrome" if chronic (Gruenberg 1974) (see Chapter 12).

For many people the distress of a crisis or social breakdown is compounded by the feeling that they are somehow unique, that no one else has ever been through a similar experience, and that therefore no one really understands them. Some severely demoralized persons feel unable to control even their own feelings, and this gives rise to the fear of going crazy so often seen in those seeking psychotherapeutic help. Metaphorically, the demoralized person cowers in a spatiotemporal corner. Thus, he or she clings to a small round of habitual activities, avoids novelty and challenge, and fears making long-term plans. The state of demoralization, in short, is one of hopelessness, helplessness, and isolation in which the person is preoccupied with merely trying to survive.

Although some demoralized persons fight help-givers because they are so mistrustful, many actively seek out and respond readily to a helper; that is, they are in a state of heightened suggestibility. Such people enter treatment with a variety of symptoms. At one end of the spectrum are complaints directly related to demoralization, such as anxiety and depression. These are both the most common and the most responsive symptoms of patients in psychotherapy (Smith, Glass, and Miller 1980). Other dysphoric emotions, such as anger and resentment, also may be present. At the other end of the spectrum are symptoms that clearly are not caused by demoralization but that often have demoralizing consequences, for example, the cognitive deterioration of Alzheimer's disease or the mood swings of manic-depressive illness. Overall, demoralization may be a cause, a consequence, or both, of presenting symptoms, and its relative importance differs from patient to patient.

Persons with certain personality structures may successfully conceal their demoralization behind symptoms that seem quite unrelated. However, the underlying despair may erupt into consciousness if the symptom is removed while the person is still demoralized. The hypnotic removal of a hysterical paralysis, for example, has been known to precipitate suicidal depression.

One must add that not all demoralized people get into professional treatment and not all patients in psychotherapy are demoralized. Sometimes such patients as sociopaths or alcoholics are brought to treatment because their behavior demoralizes people around them. Uncounted numbers of people are too demoralized even to seek help. Many demoralized persons seek help outside the mental health system. Finally, of course, a small proportion of patients seek treatment for specific symptoms without being otherwise demoralized. An example would be the person who comes for help after hearing that behavior therapy can cure a phobia of heights.

Presenting symptoms relate to the underlying reasons that patients seek therapy in complex ways. At the beginning of treatment, symptoms take a high priority, but the presenting complaint may be merely the admission ticket — the basis of the patient's claim on the therapist's attention. Most people do not seek therapy solely because they hallucinate, fear snakes, or enjoy a few drinks too many. In fact, most people who are entitled to psychiatric diagnoses probably never come to professional attention. Epidemiological surveys always uncover large numbers of never-treated cases of mental illness among persons living in the community. Similarly, university researchers on psychotherapy can survey their classes and unearth students with phobias who never thought of seeking treatment until the researcher offered it.

The difficulty of relating diagnosis to the choice or intensity of treatment suggests that most patients are in therapy because, whatever their complaints, they or persons around them are also demoralized. Symptoms interact with demoralization in various ways. They may reduce a person's coping capacity, increasing vulnerability to demoralizing failures. Such symptoms as schizophrenic thought disorder, depressed mood, or compulsive ritual may cause patients to be defeated by problems of living that asymptomatic persons handle with ease. Furthermore, psychiatric symptoms contribute to demoralization by heightening the alienation of patients who feel their symptoms are shameful or beyond others' understanding. Finally, symptoms wax and wane with the degree of demoralization; thus, schizophrenic patients' thinking becomes more disorganized when they are anxious, and obsessive-compulsive patients become worse when they are also depressed.

Morale can be restored by removing crippling symptoms, and certain psychotherapeutic procedures may be differentially effective for particular symptoms. Conversely, to the extent that a patient's symptoms are expressions of demoralization, restoration of self-esteem by whatever means may cause the symptoms to subside. Successful psychotherapy may enable a patient to function more successfully even in the face of persisting symptoms. Examples are paranoid patients whose delusions remain unchanged but who have learned not to reveal them, or patients who no longer avoid phobic situations, although they still experience physiological symptoms of anxiety in them.

Evidence for the Demoralization Hypothesis

The demoralization hypothesis has never been directly tested, but supporting indirect evidence comes from several sources. Some confirmatory studies compare cohorts of persons who seek or have sought psychotherapy with those who have not. Studies of college students (Galassi and Galassi 1973), alumni out of college for twenty-five years (Vaillant 1972), and ordinary citizens in England and America (Kellner and Sheffield 1973) all showed a higher incidence or greater severity of social isolation, helplessness, or sense of failure or unworthiness — all symptoms of demoralization — among the treated than among the untreated.

The surveys of Bruce Dohrenwend and Barbara Link provide the strongest empirical support for the importance of demoralization as a common element of many types of psychopathology. These researchers devised a set of scales to determine the extent of psychiatric symptoms and clinical impairment in the general population (Dohrenwend et al. 1980). To their surprise, they found that eight of their scales correlated as highly with one another as their internal reliabilities would permit; that is, they all seemed to measure a single dimension. These scales included such features of demoralization as anxiety, sadness, hopelessness, and low self-esteem. According to the authors' criteria, about one-fourth of the persons in the population they surveyed appeared to be demoralized. Of these, about one-half were also clinically impaired (Link and Dohrenwend 1980). Most supportive of our hypothesis was the finding in a related study (Dohrenwend and Crandall 1970) that about four-fifths of clinically impaired outpatients had high scores on a scale that was later found to be highly correlated with the demoralization scales.

Surveys of reported emotional distress and perceived social support provide further indirect evidence for the demoralization hypothesis. A general population survey determined that persons who feel they have a supportive network are much less likely to be disturbed by severe environmental stresses than are persons who do not feel supported (Henderson 1981). This finding was confirmed in a prospective study of persons relocated from an isolated Israeli town to scattered locations throughout Israel. The researchers found that their subjects' perception of themselves as belonging to a supportive kinship network (though these kin were not directly present) correlated better with their psychosocial adjustment after the move than did the size of their actual friendship networks in the new settings (Steinglass, Weisstub, and Kaplan De-Nour 1988). Perceived emotional support from others either protects individuals from demoralization or reflects adequate morale. Galanter's study (1989) of members of a religious cult supports the first interpretation. Subjects in this study reported a sharp decline in anxiety, depression, and general emotional problems after joining the cult, a decline they attributed primarily to emotional support from other group members.

The demoralization hypothesis receives further support from evidence that many patients come to psychotherapy months or years after the onset of their symptoms. During this time they presumably try and fail to find relief by other methods. Patients did not seek treatment at one university hospital until six months to two years after their symptoms first appeared (Karasu 1982). A study of college students' use of a university counseling service similarly revealed that "the decision to actually use psychotherapy was likely to come only after ineffective attempts to cope with the problem oneself or with the help of a close friend or relative" (Farber and Geller 1977, p. 306). Alcoholics wait an average of five years after the first signs of pathological intoxication before seeking treatment (Mandell 1983), while persons with panic disorders endure their symptoms for twelve years on the average before seeking professional help (Shader, Goodman, and Gever 1982). In other words, people seek help not in response to the symptoms themselves but because their efforts to cope with the symptoms have failed.

The rapidity with which many patients improve in psychotherapy also indirectly supports the demoralization hypothesis. Early improvement is presumably a response to the reassuring aspects of the therapeutic situation rather than to any particular procedure. The mean number of therapeutic interviews in clinic settings is between five and six (Garfield 1986). Researchers usually interpret this finding as evidence that many patients who are in need of psychotherapy reject it. While this may be true of some, others stop because they have obtained symptomatic relief and no longer feel the need to continue. Unfortunately, patients who drop out of therapy early are not usually called back for reassessment. One study that did call them back found average symptomatic relief to be just as great in those who dropped out before the fourth session as in those who had received six months of therapy (Frank et al. 1959).

In a different study with similar implications, Sloane et al. (1975) reported that about three-fourths of psychiatric outpatients improved while on a waiting list. During this period, their only contact was an occasional telephone call from a research associate to ensure that they would wait for the assigned treatment. Apparently some patients gain relief from any contact with a therapeutic setting. Either they perceive the contact as therapy or they respond to the hope that they will soon be relieved of their symptoms.

Shared Components of Psychotherapies That Combat Demoralization

At this point it becomes necessary to ask the following question: In what sense can we legitimately refer to psychotherapy as a single entity rather than to different psychotherapies? At first glance, the question seems to answer itself. Scores of schools of psychotherapy exist, and the conditions that these psychotherapies purport to treat cover an enormous range. On closer inspection, however, certain aspects of the psychotherapeutic scene strongly suggest that the features shared by psychotherapies far outweigh their differences. Practitioners of all schools claim to be able to treat persons with similar conditions; each can report success with patients who have failed to respond to the methods of another. Since all can do this, however, the claims cancel each other out. That is, therapists using method A cure some patients who were not helped by method B, but those using method B also succeed after method A has failed. Moreover, in most comparative studies the degrees of improvement obtained by different methods do not differ significantly. In their comprehensive survey of psychotherapy-outcome research, Garfield and Bergin argued that "the equal outcomes phenomenon may be the most frequent and striking theme" (1986, p. 18). The obvious conclusion is that all therapies have some healing ingredients in common.

Using an analogy, on the one hand two such apparently different psychotherapies as psychoanalysis and systematic desensitization could be like penicillin and digitalis — totally different pharmacological agents suitable for totally different conditions. On the other hand, the active therapeutic ingredient of both could be the same, analogous to two aspirin-containing compounds marketed under different names. We believe the second alternative is closer to the truth.

To forestall misunderstanding, we wish to remind the reader that aspirin, though nonspecific, is not inert. Its active pharmacological principle reduces fever and alleviates aches and pains regardless of the specific illnesses with which they are associated. Similarly, the active principles of psychotherapy may be quite powerful, though not specific for particular symptoms or diseases.

Interest in the shared therapeutic components of all forms of psychotherapy (Beitman, Goldfried, and Norcross 1989) has surged in recent years. While various authors (Rosenzweig 1936; Marmor 1976; Karasu 1986; Torrey 1986) have described and grouped these common features differently, and none to our knowledge has explicitly linked them to combating demoralization, all conceptualizations, including our own, are mutually compatible. Our list of the features common to all effective psychotherapies, which follows, pertains to secular dyadic therapies conducted by professionals in contemporary America. We shall consider modifications required by group methods of healing, in their appropriate places.

In our view, all psychotherapies share at least four effective features.

An emotionally charged, confiding relationship with a helping person (often with the participation of a group). With a qualification to be mentioned presently, the therapeutic alliance (Luborsky 1976) is a necessary, and perhaps often a sufficient, condition for improvement in any kind of psychotherapy (Rogers 1957). As Sloane et al. found, "Successful patients rated the personal interaction with the therapist as the single most important part of their treatment" (1975, p. 225).

Patients are willing to depend on a therapist for help because they believe that the therapist is competent, genuinely cares about their welfare, and has no ulterior motives (Gurman 1977). This attitude has been characterized by one eminent psychotherapist as "therapeutic eros" (Seguin 1965). Caring in this sense does not necessarily imply approval, but rather a determination to persist in trying to help, no matter how desperate patients' conditions or how outrageous their behavior. The helping alliance implies the therapist's acceptance of the sufferer, if not for what he or she is, then for what he or she can become. The patient's dependence on the therapist is reinforced by the congruence of the therapist's approach with the patient's expectations, the therapist's socially sanctioned role as a healer, and the patient's knowledge that the therapist is an expert in a particular therapeutic method. Chapter 8 explores these points in more detail.

Thanks to humans' remarkable powers of symbolization, the creation and maintenance of a therapeutic relationship does not always require the therapist and patient to be in direct contact. If a symptom is clearly limited to specific times and places and the treatment procedure is equally specifiable, certain patients can successfully treat themselves by following a manual that carries a therapist's authority (Marks 1978). Actual contact with the therapist can be limited to the therapist's initial presentation of the program, sometimes supplemented by an occasional booster session (Marks 1987b).

In fact, judging from the insatiable and apparently growing demand for self-help books, many persons seem not to need a live therapist at all.

Self-help books may be especially useful for persons who would feel constrained by a physically present therapist. For them a book obviates such problems as embarrassment and preoccupation with the impression they may be making. To anticipate a bit, self-help books provide, to varying degrees, several common healing components of psychotherapies: stimulation of hope, a conceptual scheme linked to healing procedures, new information, and instructions to practice what has been learned.

To be sure, the brief life span of most of these books suggests that their effectiveness depends in part on their apparent novelty — that is, their ability to arouse hope in people for whom previous types of help have failed. On the other hand, the continuing sale of such books as Norman Vincent Peale's *Power of Positive Thinking* ([1952] 1985) and Kushner's *When Bad Things Happen to Good People* (1981) attests to the enduring power of a therapeutic relationship with a book that stands in for a person. In this sense, the Bible is the most enduring self-help book in our culture. As considered in Chapters 4 and 5, some persons in every culture establish a powerful healing relationship with a supernatural being or beings in various ways, including reading sacred texts or participating in rituals (see Chapter 5).

A healing setting. Most psychotherapeutic encounters transpire in special locales regarded as places of healing. In all societies, religious healing rites are conducted in temples or sacred groves. When the setting is a patient's home, purification rites transform it into a sacred place. Secular therapies typically take place in a therapist's office, a hospital, or a clinic. Many of these sites carry the aura of science. Both secular and religious healing sites are distinguished from the rest of the patients' surroundings by special attributes, including sharply delineated spatial and temporal boundaries.

Special settings have at least two therapeutic functions. First, they heighten the therapist's prestige and strengthen the patient's expectation of help by symbolizing the therapist's role as a healer. This occurs whether the setting is a clinic in a prestigious hospital or a private office complete with bookshelves, impressive desk, couch, and easy chair. Often the setting also includes such evidence of the therapist's training and competence as diplomas, citations, and pictures of his or her teachers and colleagues. Second, the setting provides safety. Within its protective walls patients know they can freely express feelings, dare to reveal aspects of themselves that they have concealed from others, and do whatever else the therapy prescribes. Patients can feel secure that no harm will come to them during the session, that they will not be held accountable for their behavior in it when they reemerge into the daily world, and that their revelations will remain confidential.

A rationale, conceptual scheme, or myth that provides a plausible explanation for the patient's symptoms and prescribes a ritual or procedure for resolving them. We have chosen the term "myth" to characterize theories of psychotherapy because such theories resemble myths in at least two ways: (1) they are imagination-catching formulations of recurrent and important human experiences; and (2) they cannot be proved empirically. Successes are taken as evidence of their validity (often erroneously), while failures are explained away. "No form of therapy has ever been initiated without a claim that it had unique therapeutic advantages. And no form of therapy has ever been abandoned because of its failure to live up to these claims" (Parloff, quoted in Hilts 1980). To our knowledge, no therapeutic school has voluntarily disbanded because empirical findings convinced its members that its rationale was wrong. Freud, a truly great myth maker, was literally correct when he characterized the Freudian instincts as "our mythology."

Therapeutic rationales and procedures acquire plausibility through their links to the dominant world-view of their particular culture. In the Middle Ages, therapeutic symbols drew their power from their association with Christian belief. Indigenous healing rituals in non-Western societies inevitably draw upon the cosmology of their particular group. Psychotherapies based on mystical or religious doctrines have never lost their appeal to the adherents of these doctrines.

In the contemporary United States, faith in science still seems to provide the predominant source of symbolic healing power. A symposium of proponents of leading therapeutic schools amusingly demonstrated this point. Each began by invoking symbols of science. One showed anatomical charts, another displayed polygraphic tracings, and a third referred to experimental work with mice. In each case the introductory material was related only tenuously to the description of therapy which followed.

Some schools of psychotherapy seek plausibility by linking their theory to a prestigious figure — in the past, Freud, Jung, Adler, and their disciples; more recently, B. F. Skinner, Carl Rogers, and Milton Erickson. The last two names remind us that, in the field of psychotherapy at least, science may be losing its glamour. Existential therapies that base their claims to plausibility on the writings of philosophers further illustrate this trend.

One would expect that a therapeutic rationale intended to combat demoralization would inspire hope. Religiously based psychotherapies all include rituals for enlisting the benevolent intervention of supernatural forces. Similarly, the rationales underlying most secular American psychotherapies incorporate an optimistic philosophy of human nature. These theories imply that human beings are naturally good. They maintain that aggression, cruelty, and other unattractive forms of human behavior generally result from past hurts, frustrations, or damaging environmental contingencies. Psychotherapies guided by these theories are meant to free patients from the consequences of these experiences, whether through increasing self-awareness, heightening the sense of mastery, or enhancing personal security. These therapies share the goal of enabling persons to overcome crippling or destructive emotions and behaviors and thereby lead fuller, more satisfying, and socially constructive lives.

Many psychotherapies imported from Europe — notably psychoanalytic and existential therapies in their various forms — are more pessimistic about human nature. Nevertheless, practitioners still construe their theories in the most optimistic light possible. For example, the Freudian view of the human psyche as essentially a battleground between Eros and Thanatos, with Thanatos winning in the end, could hardly be called cheerful. Therapeutically, however, psychoanalysis is redeemed by the faith that the truth shall make you free. Truth was Freud's god. Psychoanalysis, as the scientific search for truth, is supposed to enable humans to gain rational control of the base impulses of the Unconscious and thereby free themselves to pursue the prosocial, self-fulfilling goals of love and work.

Existentialist philosophies that stress the essential meaninglessness of existence are the most pessimistic of the world-views upon which psychotherapies are based. Existentialists manage to give this gloomy outlook a heroic twist, however, by viewing therapy as a process that enables a person to wrest a sense of purpose and meaning out of life.

A ritual or procedure that requires the active participation of both patient and therapist and that is believed by both to be the means of restoring the patient's health. The procedure serves as the vehicle for maintaining the therapeutic alliance and transmitting the therapist's influence. It also enhances the therapist's self-confidence by demonstrating mastery of a special set of skills. Procedures such as hypnosis, relaxation, or emotional flooding, in which the therapist alters the patient's subjective state, are especially impressive demonstrations of the therapist's power.

A not infrequent and easily overlooked function of therapeutic rituals is to provide a face-saving way for a patient to abandon a symptom or complaint without admitting that it was trivial or produced for some ulterior motive. The more spectacular the ritual, the greater its face-saving power. In consequence, one must be cautious in attributing a remission of symptoms to a particular maneuver. The procedure may simply serve as the occasion for a patient to relinquish symptoms he or she was ready to give up for other reasons.

The Functions of Myth and Ritual

Despite differences in specific content, all therapeutic myths and rituals have functions in common. They combat demoralization by strengthening the therapeutic relationship, inspiring expectations of help, providing new learning experiences, arousing the patient emotionally, enhancing a sense of mastery or self-efficacy, and affording opportunities for rehearsal and practice. Let us consider each of these briefly in turn.

Combating the patient's sense of alienation and strengthening the therapeutic relationship. Because a shared belief system is essential to the formation and maintenance of groups, the adherence of therapist and patient to the same therapeutic myth creates a powerful bond between them. Within this context, the therapist's continued acceptance of the patient after the patient has "confessed" combats the latter's demoralizing feelings of alienation. This is especially so if, as is usually the case, the therapist explicitly or implicitly represents a group. The ritual further serves to maintain the patient-therapist bond, especially over stretches when nothing much seems to be happening (see Chapter 8).

By giving the patient and therapist something to do together, the ritual sustains mutual interest. The chief problem of kindly but therapeutically untrained college professors in their otherwise successful treatment of college students (Strupp and Hadley 1979) was that the professors sometimes ran out of things to talk about, a predicament never reported by experienced therapists (Strupp, personal communication).

Inspiring and maintaining the patient's expectation of help. By inspiring expectations of help, myths and rituals keep the patient coming to treatment and are powerful morale builders and symptom relievers in themselves (Friedman 1963; Jacobson 1968). The arousal of hope, similarly, may account for the finding in several studies that "the best predictor of later benefits is . . . [the expectation] of early benefits expressed in the early sessions" (Luborsky 1976, p. 107). Sometimes merely the name of a therapeutic procedure mobilizes patients' hope of relief. This is at least a plausible interpretation of the finding that patients who received a standard relaxation sequence in response to their request for hypnosis showed more subjective and objective improvement if the word "hypnosis" was substituted for "relaxation" whenever possible (Lazarus 1973).

For therapy to be effective, patients must link hope for improvement to specific processes of therapy as well as to outcome (Imber et al. 1970; Wilkins 1979). This link can be taken for granted by purveyors of traditional therapies like psychoanalysis because most patients come to them already familiar with their procedures (Kadushin 1969). Practitioners of new or unfamiliar therapies regularly spend considerable time and effort in introducing patients to their particular therapeutic game and shaping the patients' expectations accordingly. Thus, an eyewitness report of the therapy of a prominent behavior therapist noted: "[During the orientation period] the therapist tells the patient at length about the power of the treatment method, pointing out that it has been successful with comparable patients and all but promising similar results for him too. [This approach] seems designed . . . to turn the patient's hopes for success into concrete expectations" (Klein et al. 1969, p. 262).

Along the same lines, a study of outpatient psychotherapy showed that patients who received a preliminary "role-induction interview," based on the "anticipatory socialization interview" of Orne and Wender (1968) and designed to coordinate the patients' expectations with what they would receive, had a better outcome than did controls who received the identical treatment but without preparation (Hoehn-Saric et al. 1964). This finding was replicated in another setting (Sloane et al. 1970).

The role-induction interview, by leading the patients to behave the way the therapists expected "good" patients to behave, made the patients more attractive to the therapists, thereby improving the patient-therapist relationship. Similarly, a pretherapy interview may improve the therapeutic alliance with socioeconomically disadvantaged patients, who may not fully share in the world-view of the dominant culture or who may have inappropriate expectations of treatment. Therapists for disadvantaged patients may also benefit from such preparation. In one study of treatment for disadvantaged people, if both the therapist and the patient were prepared, two-thirds of the patients reported improvement, as compared to one-half if only the patient or only the therapist was prepared, and only one-third if neither received a pretherapy interview (Jacobs et al. 1972).

Providing new learning experiences. In all forms of psychotherapy, the therapist is a teacher who provides new information in an interpersonal context that enables the patient to profit from it (Strupp 1986). Especially with children, some types of psychotherapy are virtually indistinguishable from corrective education. For expository purposes, it is useful to distinguish cognitive and experiential learning experiences in psychotherapy. Cognitive learning includes patients' awareness of the rules of the therapist's particular method, patients' identification of the psychological sources of their difficulties and the contingencies that maintain them (insight), alternative ways of conceptualizing problems, and the like. The therapist and, in group therapy, other patients also provide models who exemplify alternative values or ways of behaving (Bandura 1977).

Experiential learning in therapy involves patients' emotions. Emotions are stirred, for example, when patients experience discrepancies between aspects of their assumptive world and actuality. Group therapies confront members with discrepancies between the impression they think they are making and the actual impression they make. Awareness of these cognitive dissonances (Festinger 1957) creates a powerful incentive to change in directions suggested by the cognitive insights the patient is gaining simultaneously. Patients' emotions may also be aroused by transference reactions and by patients' attempts to change contingencies governing their behavior.

New experiences provided by therapy can enhance morale by showing patients potentially helpful alternative ways of looking at themselves and their problems. The more numerous and more intense the experiential, as opposed to the purely cognitive, components of learning, the more likely they are to produce changes in the patients' attitudes or behavior. It is a truism that intellectual insight alone is essentially powerless to effect change. The power of experiential learning brings us to the fourth therapeutic ingredient common to all therapeutic conceptualizations and rituals, emotional arousal (Greenberg and Safran 1989).

Arousing emotions. Emotional arousal is essential to therapeutic change in at least three ways. It supplies the motive power necessary to undertake and endure the suffering usually involved in attempts to change personal beliefs and behavior. As considered in Chapter 10, emotional arousal also seems to facilitate attitudinal change and enhance sensitivity to environmental influences. Unpleasant emotions, moreover, lead patients to search actively for relief. When this occurs in therapy, the patient naturally turns to the therapist. If the arousal is intense enough to be disorganizing, the patient's dependence on the therapist may increase still further. Intense emotional experiences, in addition, may break up old patterns of personality integration and facilitate the achievement of better ones.

Though emotional arousal contributes importantly to attitudinal change, many Western psychotherapies consider it a by-product of their procedures rather than a primary focus. Thus, insight-oriented therapies arouse patients' emotions by requiring them to relive emotionally traumatic past experiences; behavior therapies have the same effect by requiring patients to expose themselves in fantasy or reality to situations they fear. Other therapies, whose popularity seems to fluctuate, use procedures specifically designed to evoke emotion. Mesmerism and Freudian abreaction are recent historical examples. Procedures aimed at arousing intense emotions are currently flourishing under various labels (see Chapter 10).

From the perspective of the demoralization hypothesis, the therapeutic effect of intense emotional arousal may lie in its demonstration to patients that they can stand, at high intensity, emotions that they fear. Surviving an emotionally intense experience can directly strengthen patients' self-confidence and mastery. Such an experience may also encourage patients to enter into and cope successfully with situations they previously feared or avoided, further bolstering their morale.

Pleasant aesthetic stimuli also can facilitate therapeutic changes in attitude by arousing emotion. The religious-healing rituals of revival meetings and healing shrines provide a particularly potent mix of therapeutic aesthetic and emotional experiences (see Chapters 4 and 5).

At a more mundane level, emotions stirred by the arts and literature also seem to help patients change. Creative arts therapies involve dancing, making music, painting, sculpting, and writing as means of stirring patients emotionally and helping them discover both new sources of pleasure and new ways of relating to other persons. Passive aesthetic experiences such as attending concerts or poetry readings or visiting art museums often seem to have similar, though less intense, beneficial effects. Consideration of the many potential roles of the arts in promoting mental health would lead us too far afield. Their relevance to this discussion lies primarily in their ability to elicit healing emotions.

All emotionally arousing therapeutic procedures conducted by professionals include encouraging patients to reflect on the implications of these experiences for their lives. While emotional arousal potentiates attitudinal change, the person undergoing the experience must draw the appropriate conclusions for his or her behavior if the change is to endure (Lieberman, Yalom, and Miles 1973). This is an example of the importance of conceptually distinguishing between factors in therapy that facilitate or produce change and those that sustain it (Liberman 1978a).

Enhancing the patient's sense of mastery or self-efficacy. Self-esteem and personal security depend to a considerable degree on a sense of being able to understand and thereby exert some control both over the reactions of others toward oneself and over one's own inner states. The inability to control feelings, thoughts, and impulses is inherently demoralizing. Uncontrolled feelings also impede a person's ability to influence others by preempting attention from social interaction and distorting perceptions and behavior. The feeling of loss of control gives rise to anxiety and other emotions that aggravate and are aggravated by the specific symptoms or problems for which the person ostensibly has sought psychotherapy.

Even psychotic patients can benefit from regaining a sense of control over their symptoms, as was illustrated by an out-of-town schizophrenic patient who telephoned one of us (J.D.F.) while on a visit to Baltimore. The patient stated that she was psychotic, that her symptoms had been controlled by Stelazine, but that she was beginning to hallucinate and giggle. She feared she might be suffering a relapse. After establishing that the patient's dose of medication was adequate and that she was under considerable tension during her visit, I reassured her that her symptoms would probably subside after she returned home. About six weeks later the patient wrote to me: "After receiving your opinion I returned to good functioning again. Just to be reassured by a competent psychiatrist that I and Stelazine are in control of the situation is the best therapy possible for me!"

All schools of psychotherapy bolster the patient's sense of mastery (Liberman 1978b) or self-efficacy (Bandura 1977) in at least two ways: by providing the patient with a conceptual scheme that explains symptoms and supplies the rationale and procedure for overcoming them, and by providing occasions for the patient to experience success.

Since words are a human being's chief tool for analyzing and organizing experience, the conceptual schemes of all psychotherapies increase patients' sense of security and mastery by giving names to experiences that had seemed haphazard, confusing, or inexplicable. Once the unconscious or ineffable has been put into words, it loses much of its power to terrify. The capacity to use verbal reasoning to explore potential solutions to problems also increases people's sense of their options and enhances their sense of control. This effect has been termed the principle of Rumpelstiltskin (Torrey 1986), after the fairy tale in which the queen broke the wicked dwarf's power over her by guessing his name.

To be effective, interpretations, the primary means of transmitting the therapist's conceptual framework, need not be correct, only plausible. One therapist demonstrated this by offering six "all-purpose" interpretations to four patients in intensive psychotherapy. An example of such an interpretation is "You seem to live your life as though you are apologizing all the time." The same series of interpretations, spaced about a month apart, was given to all four patients, regardless of what they were reporting at the time. In twenty of these twenty-four instances, the patients responded with a drop in anxiety. All four patients experienced this move from the "preinterpreted" to the "postinterpreted" state at least once (Mendel 1964).

Experiences of success, a major source of enhanced self-efficacy, are implicit in all psychotherapeutic procedures. Verbally adept patients experience success from achieving new insights; behaviorally oriented patients, from carrying out increasingly anxiety-laden behaviors. As already mentioned, by demonstrating to patients that they can withstand at maximal intensity the emotions they fear, emotional-flooding techniques yield powerful experiences of success.

Furthermore, performances that patients attribute to their own efforts enhance self-esteem more strongly than do those they attribute to such external factors as medication or outside help. Recognizing this, psychotherapists of all schools seek to persuade patients that their progress results from their own efforts. Nondirective therapists disclaim any credit for patients' new insights, and directive ones stress that patients' gains depend on their ability to carry out the prescribed procedures. When applicable, teaching patients to produce their symptoms voluntarily is a particularly powerful way of convincing them that they are in control. Thus, coaching a patient to induce panic by hyperventilating (Clark, Salkovskis, and Chalkley 1985) may be a successful psychotherapeutic technique for panic attacks (see Chapter 6).

Unfortunately, however, humans are not all-powerful. All of us must face problems we cannot solve and endure sources of distress that no amount of effort can alleviate. In these circumstances, trying to convince patients to take responsibility for their troubles may be counterproductive or even disastrous. In the heyday of dynamic psychotherapy, therapists caused endless misery and disrupted whole families by insisting, for example, that neurologically damaged, autistic children were really suffering from emotional blocks for which their parents' behavior was responsible (see Chapter 11). Encouraging patients to take responsibility for their symptoms and problems in living enhances morale only when patients possess the ability to change them. Since experiences of success or failure depend not on the actual level of performance but on whether it exceeds or falls below the person's expectations (Frank 1935), when problems or symptoms are intractable, the appropriate goal of therapy must be to help the patient lower unrealistic expectations.

> In the acceptance of helplessness and hopelessness lies the hope of giving up impossible tasks and taking credit for what we endure. Paradoxically, the abandonment of hope often brings new freedom. [Bennett and Bennett 1984, p. 562]

Existential psychotherapists such as Viktor Frankl ([1965] 1986) express a similar view.

Providing opportunities for practice. A final morale-enhancing feature of all psychotherapies is that they provide opportunities and incentives for internalizing and reinforcing therapeutic gains through repeated testing both within and outside the therapeutic session.

As considered in Chapter 11, group therapies involve the same morale-building principles as individual ones, often to a greater degree. The presence of other patients and the emergence of processes specific to groups introduce additional ways of combating the alienation that accompanies demoralization. Groups provide a variety of opportunities for cognitive and experiential learning, and for practicing what has been learned. They may be more emotionally arousing than individual sessions, increasing the patient's chance of achieving a sense of mastery through weathering the stresses of group interactions. Finally, as social microcosms that resemble real life more closely than do individual interview situations, groups facilitate the transfer of what has been learned to daily living.

Summary

All illness can be viewed as a failure of adaptation, an imbalance between environmental stress and coping capacity. The ability to cope is determined by constitutional vulnerabilities and strengths on the one hand and by the favorable or unfavorable meanings persons attribute to events on the other. These meanings are determined by an organized set of assumptions, attitudes, or beliefs about the self and others that we have termed the assumptive world.

Some determinants of the formation of a person's assumptive world are described, especially the part played by reference groups. Healthy assumptive systems are internally harmonious and correspond closely to actual environmental conditions. Such assumptive systems lead to reliable, satisfactory social interactions and feelings of competence, inner security, and well-being, feelings that enable the person to modify assumptions readily when they are challenged by new experiences. Unhealthy assumptive systems are internally conflictual and do not accurately correspond to circumstances. They lead to experiences of frustration, failure, and alienation that paradoxically increase a person's resistance to changing in response to new experiences such as those provided by psychotherapy. People protect the stability of their assumptive worlds by means of avoidance and confirmatory bias.

Persistent failure to cope resulting from maladaptive assumptive systems leads to demoralization. We offer evidence for the hypothesis that demoralization is a major incentive for persons to seek or be offered psychotherapy.

Despite the stubbornness of maladaptive assumptive systems, the psychotherapist, as a socially sanctioned expert and healer and a symbolic member of the patient's reference groups, may be able to mobilize forces that are sufficiently powerful to combat demoralization and produce beneficial changes in the patient's assumptive world, thereby improving the patient's adaptation and bringing about a concomitant reduction in symptoms. The chapter concludes with a review of the features shared by all forms of psychotherapy that combat demoralization.

THREE

Psychotherapy, the Transformation of Meanings

<hr>

> "I can't tell you just now what the moral of that is, but I shall remember it in a bit."
> "Perhaps it hasn't one," Alice ventured to remark.
> "Tut, tut, child!" said the Duchess. "Everything's got a moral, if only you can find it."
> — *Alice's Adventures in Wonderland*

We have proposed the imprecise concept of demoralization to summarize the kinds of distress and disability that bring persons to psychotherapy, and have suggested that major sources of demoralization are the pathogenic meanings patients attribute to feelings and events in their lives. The Greek philosopher Epictetus put it succinctly: "Men are not moved by things but by the views which they take of them." Effective psychotherapies combat demoralization by persuading patients to transform these pathogenic meanings to ones that rekindle hope, enhance mastery, heighten self-esteem, and reintegrate patients with their groups.

The assertion that psychotherapy operates in the realm of meanings raises questions as to which intellectual disciplines are best suited to examining its processes. In the United States the study of psychotherapy has traditionally been within the purview of science — specifically, behavioral science. We submit that psychotherapy also properly falls within the domains of rhetoric, "the use of words to form attitudes or induce action" (Burke 1969, p. 41), and hermeneutics, the study of "understanding and of correct interpretation of what has been understood" (Gadamer 1982, p. xi).

In this chapter we shall consider certain values and limitations of viewing psychotherapy as an applied behavioral science, then briefly outline an alternate view of psychotherapy as a form of rhetoric best studied hermeneutically.

Psychotherapy as Applied Behavioral Science

The proper domain of science, traditionally defined, is the world of facts — that is, variables that can be specified objectively and that are independent of the meanings observers attach to them. Generalizations derived from the scientific study of facts in the material world are universally valid. Traditional scientific concepts and methods, however, are ill equipped to deal with meanings, which are individual and unique. The meaning a person attributes to an event depends on the immediate social context and the person's state at the time. The meaning of an event may differ, not only between persons but also to the same person over time (Meichenbaum 1986). Although two persons may rate themselves "5" on a scale of self-esteem, they may base their rating on different sources and therefore differ from each other in ways that the rating cannot capture. Furthermore, experimental subjects may differ in how they interpret researchers' efforts to manipulate such variables. As a result, even two identically designed studies may produce noncomparable results.

Though the personal and situational context of every event strongly influences how people identify, classify, and experience its meanings, this conclusion should not be taken to extremes. Within a single culture, especially within a single "interpretative community" (Fish 1982), different individuals tend to attribute the same meanings to particular events and respond to the same words with similar feelings. These regularities are sufficient to allow for the discovery of some predictable relationships within the realm of meanings, though the degree of predictability is far less than that discoverable in material processes.

Some influential researchers in psychology are well aware of this problem (Koch 1981). Indeed, a leading researcher in psychotherapy has stated: "The concern with finding, imposing and creating meanings . . . is a primary concern of current empirical efforts" (Meichenbaum 1986, p. 123). How far these efforts will go toward solving the problem of deriving valid generalizations from specific contextual determinants of meanings remains unknown.

Meanwhile, despite the popularity of nonscientific healing cults and the small but influential band of existential-humanist therapists, professional training schools typically consider psychotherapy to be an applied behavioral science based on the model of the physical sciences. The strengths and limitations of psychotherapy as an applied behavioral science therefore deserve further examination.

To evaluate systematically the scientific claims of every school of psychotherapy would be impossible. However, two prominent examples, psychoanalysis and behavior therapy, will serve to demonstrate the core problems of the analogy between psychotherapy and science.

Psychoanalysis was among the first psychotherapeutic disciplines to don the mantle of science (Brenner 1973). Whether the logical structure of psychoanalysis satisfies the scientific requirement that its hypotheses be falsifiable (Popper 1959) is a matter of lively philosophical debate (Grünbaum 1984). Classical analytic theory, in particular, seems formally constructed to withstand radical challenges to its postulates. For example, the analyst can interpret any particular statement by a patient in various ways, depending on whether or not the statement threatens the theory. Thus, a patient's acceptance of an interpretation confirms its validity, while rejection may be discounted as "resistance" rooted in the patient's distorted perceptions.

Even if the formal characteristics of psychoanalytic theory were scientifically sound, Freud's generalizations were based on very sparse data, his experience with a few dozen patients at most. Moreover, psychoanalytic data — the patient's so-called free associations — are heavily biased by the expectations the analyst wittingly or unwittingly conveys (Fish 1986). Scientifically valid, reproducible, and generalizable findings from research on psychoanalysis have been exceedingly modest (Wallerstein 1986), as would be expected given these limitations.

The claims of cognitive and behavior therapies to scientific respectability rest upon firmer ground. Researchers have obtained the data supporting cognitive and behavioral theories according to conventional scientific designs. In particular, they have developed scales that measure patients' symptoms, the processes of therapy, the outcome of treatment, and other variables, reporting their findings with due regard for validity and reliability. Such scales, which are applicable to many psychotherapies, have been particularly helpful in the related field of clinical psychopharmacological research. Behavior therapists have also led the way in devising detailed manuals that specify therapist behaviors in a wide range of therapies, including psychodynamic ones. These methodological advances facilitate rigorous comparisons between therapies (Lambert, Shapiro, and Bergin 1986).

Unfortunately, the first large-scale application of these new tools, a multicenter comparison of two psychotherapies for depression (Elkin et al. 1989), simply confirmed the findings of innumerable less well controlled studies. While both therapies produced significant improvement in the symptoms measured, differences between them, if any, were unimpressive.

How often the results of scientific experiments actually lead to therapeutic innovations, moreover, is uncertain. More commonly, a therapist devises a new approach on the basis of a clinical hunch and then proceeds to make it scientifically respectable by testing it experimentally. Even when an innovator does begin with laboratory data in developing a therapy, the therapy may be effective for reasons other than its scientific rationale. Thus, Wolpe (1958) derived his reciprocal inhibition therapy for phobias by analogizing relaxation in humans to eating behavior in cats. He observed that he could gradually extinguish a cat's conditioned avoidance response to an aversive stimulus by simultaneously presenting the animal with a stimulus that elicited a positive response incompatible with the response elicited by the aversive one. The aversive stimulus was progressively increased in stepwise fashion, but at each step was kept sufficiently weak to prevent inhibition of the animal's positive response. For example, after a hungry cat had been conditioned to fear the eating cage, the fear was overcome by bringing the food stepwise closer to the cage, and leaving it at each position until the cat resumed eating, until finally the cat again accepted food inside the cage.

Wolpe then devised a treatment for phobias based on the assumption that relaxation, like feeding, was incompatible with anxiety. Patients were trained to relax and imagine a hierarchy of progressively more fear-inducing scenes involving the phobic stimulus. They were instructed not to move to the next level of the hierarchy until they could remain relaxed at the current one, thus progressively extinguishing the fear of the object. Wolpe elaborated this basic model into treatment for many forms of anxiety.

Applying the results of animal experiments to humans, however, is perilous, for the difference between the symbolic processes of animals and human beings is a qualitative rather than a quantitative leap. Psychotherapy involves images and abstractions that are far more complex than those of even the most intelligent subhuman creatures. Thus, as discussed in Chapter 10, subsequent research on reciprocal inhibition has shown that a successful outcome requires neither relaxation nor the construction of hierarchies. As with other effective therapies for phobias, Wolpe's technique succeeds because its ritual persuades patients to remain in actual or imagined contact with the phobic situation long enough for the fear to subside (Klein et al. 1983; Marks 1987b). In other words, the success of this and other therapies for phobias depends to a considerable degree on their persuasiveness, to which the scientific rationale, valid or not, contributes.

Conventional scientific methods all require the exclusion of phenomena that can be neither measured nor controlled, another major limitation in studying psychotherapy, which is suffused with meanings. Focusing on what is scientifically demonstrable may deflect attention from the ability of psychotherapy to achieve such vaguely defined but potentially valuable goals as increasing emotional maturity. Methods of controlled research may also miss subtle changes that manifest themselves some time after therapy ends. Furthermore, the objectively defined conditions of a research protocol may convey different meanings to different patients. Without knowing what these meanings are, we may not be able to interpret some results.

For example, in the NIMH collaborative study of depression cited above (p. 55), four groups of patients matched for the severity of their depression received one of two forms of psychotherapy, a placebo with purely supportive therapy, or antidepressant medication. Patients in all groups knew that treatment would be terminated after sixteen weeks. Improvement was rated at four-week intervals. The three groups receiving active treatment all showed roughly the same degree of improvement at termination. Those on medication showed progressive improvement at each interval, but those receiving psychotherapy improved for up to eight weeks, then leveled off. The psychotherapy groups experienced another spurt of improvement between the twelfth and sixteenth weeks, thereby catching up with the subjects taking antidepressants (Elkin et al. 1989).

What is one to make of this intriguing finding? Without knowing what termination meant to different patients, one can only speculate. Five possibilities come readily to mind: (1) the effects of psychotherapy take longer to manifest themselves than do those of drugs; (2) patients reported improvement in order to justify to themselves the effort involved in completing the course of treatment, thereby reducing cognitive dissonance (Festinger 1957); (3) knowledge of impending termination caused those in psychotherapy to work harder in therapy during the last four weeks; (4) some patients found it necessary to tell themselves they had improved in order to fortify themselves for the discontinuance of treatment; and (5) some patients reported improvement so as not to disappoint their therapists. Furthermore, since improvement rates were expressed as group means, any or all of the possible meanings could have applied to different patients.

Serious flaws in design and methods have plagued most past research.

An obvious flaw has been reliance on measures of central tendency, which discern only differences between populations as a whole, thereby obscuring possible differences among individuals. Another deficiency has been the failure to describe treatments in sufficient detail to ensure that therapists ostensibly practicing the same form of therapy actually do so. Past research has also inadequately characterized patients in ways relevant to psychotherapy and has been deficient in developing criteria for evaluating outcome.

The design of the collaborative study of the treatment of depression (Elkin et al. 1989) shows that considerable progress has occurred in overcoming these methodological flaws. For example, it is now possible to measure patients' locus of control and level of conceptualization, two personal characteristics relevant to accessibility to different forms of therapy (see Chapter 8). As already mentioned, manuals for various forms of therapy have enhanced research therapists' uniformity in conducting these treatments. As progress along these lines continues, we confidently expect researchers to unearth hitherto elusive differences between the outcomes of different therapeutic procedures. Techniques as disparate as, let us say, psychoanalysis and cognitive therapy should eventually yield demonstrable differences in outcome on some measures for some patients.

Despite the difficulty of dealing scientifically with certain realms of meaning and the laboriousness of developing methodologically rigorous instruments and experimental designs, the scientific method has certain advantages as applied to psychotherapy. Studies that satisfy the requirements of the scientific method permit a precise statement of the probability that the results are not due to chance. If this probability is sufficiently great — the conventional cutoff point is 95 chances out of 100 — results provide a firm basis for important policy decisions. For example, controlled studies that measure symptom reduction immediately after treatment have made it possible to convince third-party payers of the validity and cost effectiveness of some forms of psychotherapy. Careful studies have also shown that psychotherapy can significantly reduce the overuse of medical facilities by encouraging some patients to redefine their somatic symptoms as psychological in origin (Rosen and Wiens 1979). Such research justifies social support for psychotherapy and increases therapists' accountability. On the other hand, since costly, open-ended, long-term therapies provide no better immediate relief of symptoms than do brief, structured ones, insurers are increasingly reluctant to pay for long-term treatments. Such discrimination may lead to the neglect of potentially valuable therapeutic programs or confine their application to persons who can afford them.

Overall, the application of scientific methods to psychotherapy has tidied things up. Failure to confirm a hypothesis by these methods, although not necessarily proof of falsity, provokes critical and often fruitful reexamination of the hypothesis, the method chosen to check it, or both (see Chapter 7). The continuing need to demonstrate the validity of therapeutic claims increases practitioners' intellectual and economic accountability. With respect to psychotherapy itself, the results of controlled research have raised useful questions and increased some therapists' confidence in what they do.

Throughout this book we cite research findings to support various points. We do so partly because in Western culture, statements gain credibility by being couched in the language of science. However, we remind the reader that the relationships cited, although statistically significant, typically account for only a small part of the variance. Although we have selected those findings that we believe to be most valid, a determined critic could find serious flaws or cite counterexamples for many if not most of them. Hence we present research findings, including our own, not as proofs but simply as supportive illustrations.

Bearing this caution in mind, we wish to call attention to research findings obtained by conventional scientific methods, findings that are pertinent to all forms of psychotherapy. These data illustrate the effects of contextual cues (including the experimenter's expectations) on subjects' interpretation of internal and external stimuli.

Contextual Influences on the Interpretation of Emotion

Most persons seeking psychotherapy are gripped by disturbing emotions. They may be depressed, anxious, or furious, apparently without adequate cause. In turn, the inexplicability of patients' experiences may lead to fears of insanity, thereby heightening their distress. Successful psychotherapy diminishes such feelings or causes them to disappear, primarily by helping patients resolve problems and frustrations but also by providing reassuring explanations for the feelings. An ingenious series of experiments suggests that such explanations may themselves alter patients' experience. These studies showed that the feelings persons experience or report in response to a small dose of adrenalin depend to some degree on contextual cues (Schachter 1965). The subjects, male college students, were told that the purpose of the experiment was to test the effects of a new drug, "suproxin," on vision. All were reassured regarding its harmlessness. One group was told the effects of the drug (which was actually adrenalin) — that it might make them feel tense, have a rapid pulse, experience a slight tremor, and so on. Let us call these the "informed" subjects. A second group — the "uninformed" — were told nothing about how the injection would make them feel or were misled about its effects. Thus, the students in the second group were unlikely to attribute their feelings of tension to the injection.

After receiving the injection, each subject was asked to wait a few minutes for the drug to take effect. While he waited, another apparent subject, who was actually an accomplice, entered the room and tried to create either a jovial or an angry atmosphere by acting out a carefully planned scenario. Joviality was created by his clowning, anger by his increasing irritation at an insulting questionnaire that both groups were asked to fill out. Half of those in both the informed and the uninformed group were subjected to the "anger" condition and half to the "amusement" condition. During this period subjects' behavior was observed through a one-way screen, and after it they rated themselves on scales of happiness and anger. The informed subjects neither showed nor reported any emotion in either condition. They knew that the injection caused their aroused state. The uninformed subjects, who had no explanation for their feelings, acted happy and reported feelings of happiness in the amusing situation and acted angry in the annoying one. (Subjects in the annoying situation did not report anger — probably because they found it hard to tell the experimenter, who might influence their course grade, that the experiment angered them.)

In short, the identical physiological state may be felt as anger, happiness, or no emotion at all, depending on how the person explains it. In the experiment, explanations were suggested by cues in the immediate situation. In real life, people would have, in addition, memories of past circumstances in which they had felt the same way to help them "explain" their current feelings. By implication, interpretations in psychotherapy may relieve patients' distress in part by relabeling their emotions to make them more understandable. For example, a therapist may interpret an employee's inexplicable uneasiness at work as anger at the employer, who is a stand-in for the patient's father, whereupon the uneasiness loses its terrors. Another example of the power of an interpretation is given on pp. 205–7.

Similar considerations may explain why patients who find therapy unpleasant nevertheless persist in it. Psychotherapy is always an emotionally charged experience, and the emotions are more often unpleasant than pleasant. To be sure, therapies include interludes of hope, optimism, even elation, but episodes of such unpleasant feelings as fear, anger, despair, and guilt are apt to be more frequent and more prolonged. Since these states are often precipitated by the therapist, one can ask why the patient continues in treatment. In light of Schachter's (1965) findings, the main reason may be that these emotions carry a therapeutic meaning, just as a patient will take a bitter medicine because he or she associates the bitterness with the medicine's curative power.

The overriding importance of the meaning of an experience also helps explain why pilgrims to healing shrines such as Lourdes seem so ready to bear the sufferings of their pilgrimage (see Chapter 5). In the context of the journey, their distress may have come to signify hope instead of despair.

The Demand Characteristics of the Experimental Situation

"Demand characteristics" are defined as "the cues . . . which communicate what is expected [of the subject] and what the experimenter hopes to find" (Orne 1969, p. 146). The behavior of hypnotized subjects provides a striking demonstration of the power of the demand characteristics of a situation. Research has shown that many of the "spontaneous" behaviors of hypnotized subjects are not direct manifestations of the hypnotic state, but expressions of the subject's concept of how a hypnotized person should behave (Orne 1970). In one experiment illustrating this point, half of a class of naive students were shown a demonstration in which the subject "spontaneously" (as the result of an earlier posthypnotic suggestion) showed "catalepsy of the dominant hand." The hypnotized subject did not show this sign for the other half of the class. A hypnotist who was ignorant of the experiment then hypnotized all the students. Most of those who had witnessed catalepsy of the dominant hand displayed it spontaneously in trance; none of the others did. Other studies have shown that sufficiently motivated, nonhypnotizable subjects can fake all of the traditional signs of hypnosis — for example, catalepsy and anesthesia to pain — so successfully that experienced hypnotists cannot tell them from the genuinely hypnotized.

The simulation studies also yield another observation that is germane to psychotherapy: hypnosis proves to be a kind of *folie à deux* in which the hypnotist and subject play complementary roles. Subjects act as though they are unable to resist, and hypnotists as if they are all-powerful. Unless each plays the appropriate reciprocal role, the situation breaks down, as was neatly illustrated by the inability of a highly experienced hypnotist to hypnotize an excellent hypnotic subject whom he believed to be a simulator. Apparently while giving suggestions as usual, he failed to play his role convincingly, with the result that the subject failed to enter a deep trance and finally became angry at the hypnotist (Orne, personal communication, 1989).

An implicit demand characteristic of both experiments and therapy is that giving a person a test, then applying any sort of procedure after which the test is repeated, conveys the expectation that scores on the second test will differ from those on the first. In therapy, scores on the second administration are expected to show "improvement." This may account for an undetermined amount of the improvement in patients' test scores after psychotherapy.

Expectations, Evaluation Apprehension, and Performance

Another line of research relevant to psychotherapy has explored the ways that subjects' apprehension about being evaluated may influence the outcome of an experiment. The basic protocol measured the behavior of two groups, those who acted as experimenters and those who served as subjects in the experiment, with a third person, the principal investigator, conducting the research (Rosenthal 1969). In one procedure the principal investigator told the experimenters to show subjects a series of ten photographs of people's faces and ask them to rate the degree of success or failure shown in the face, using a scale of +10 for extreme success and −10 for extreme failure. The photos had been selected so that on the average they were neutral with respect to this characteristic — that is, they had an average numerical score of zero.

The principal investigator gave the experimenters identical instructions for administering the test and identical instructions to read to their subjects. Experimenters were cautioned not to deviate from these instructions. The crucial point was that the experimenters were told that the purpose of the experiment was to see how well they could duplicate previously established results. Half were led to expect that their subjects would rate the photos as being of successful people (average rating +5) and half that their subjects would rate the photos as being of unsuccessful people (average rating −5).

Principal investigators repeatedly found that experimenters given the "success" expectation obtained consistently higher ratings from their subjects than did those given the "failure" expectation. The effect was far from trivial: overall, about two-thirds of the experimenters biased subjects in the direction of their expectations, and the same proportion of subjects made judgments confirming the experimenters' expectations. Visual or auditory cues, so slight that the experimenter was unaware of them, must have communicated the experimenter's expectations. The most startling finding was how rapidly the experimenters transmitted their expectations. The subjects' very first responses confirmed experimenters' expectations, indicating that the experimenter must have conveyed them while greeting and seating the subjects and reading them the instructions.

The greater the power, prestige, or status of the experimenter, the greater the biasing effect. With college students, if the experimenter's status was higher than the subject's, the biasing effect was almost four times greater than if subject and experimenter were on the same level.

The transmission of expectations probably plays an important part in psychotherapy. Therapists have certain expectations of how patients will act, and their behavior may influence patients to act in ways that confirm their expectations. In psychotherapy the therapist is in a superior power position because the patient seeks his or her help; in addition, the therapist usually possesses higher status by virtue of professional training and, with lower-class patients, higher education and socioeconomic level (see Chapter 8). These factors presumably magnify the biasing effect of the conscious or unconscious transmission of therapists' expectations.

Status relationships affect psychotherapy training and research as well as practice. The supervisor of the therapist-in-training has considerable power to determine the latter's rate of academic progress. Thus, these experiments suggest not only that therapists easily bias patients but also that supervisors may have the same effect on trainees.

Another set of findings pertinent to psychotherapy concerns the reciprocal relationship between an experimenter's expectations and the subject's performance over a series of trials. Subjects' performances in early trials have been found to influence experimenters' expectations, which in turn affect how subjects perform in later trials. The experiment that established this finding used accomplices as the first few subjects of a series. If the accomplices confirmed the experimenter's hypothesis, the experimenter's behavior toward subsequent naive subjects influenced them to further confirm the original expectation. If the accomplices deliberately disconfirmed the experimenter's hypothesis, the latter's behavior changed so that later, genuine subjects also disconfirmed it. When naive subjects were used throughout, expectancy effects were greater with those who participated later in the series than with those who were seen earlier. Apparently, subjects progressively shaped the experimenters' behavior, leading experimenters to emit increasingly effective cues.

These findings would support the hypothesis that the longer patients remain in treatment, the more they may be influenced by their therapists. Moreover, a patient's behavior in early interviews may cause the therapist's subsequent behavior to reinforce it. This tendency works in a patient's favor if his or her early behavior arouses a therapist's positive expectations, but it could well work against the patient who elicits a pessimistic prognosis. The disquieting possibility exists that a patient who makes an unfavorable first impression may induce antitherapeutic behavior in the therapist, which in turn may elicit further discouraging behavior from the patient. This quality of the therapeutic situation, analogous to the *folie à deux* between hypnotist and subject, may account for the prognostic power of a first interview. Both are examples of self-fulfilling prophecies (Merton 1948).

Beyond the patient's and therapist's mutual reinforcement of each other's expectations, "evaluation apprehension" (Rosenberg 1969; Weber and Cook 1972), is another powerful determinant of susceptibility to influence. Human subjects typically approach psychological experiments with the anxious expectation that the experimenter may draw from their performance some conclusion about their emotional adequacy, mental health, or the like. Similarly, many patients regard their psychotherapists with considerable evaluation apprehension, which may be reinforced by the therapist's taking a history and performing psychological examinations. Patients wonder what the therapist will find wrong, how serious it is, whether the therapist will form a poor opinion of them, and so on. Findings of psychological experiments concerning the effects of evaluation apprehension on subjects' performance are therefore especially relevant to psychotherapy.

In one such experiment, the principal investigator, using a modified replication of the photograph-judging design described above, created high evaluation apprehension in half the college student subjects by means of preliminary instructions that stated that prior research had shown that poor social perception is usually associated with psychopathology. Subjects were led to believe that performance on the social perception task could be used to determine which college students were clinically maladjusted. The ostensible purpose of the experiment was to replicate the previous results.

The investigator weakened evaluation apprehension in another group of subjects by telling them that the experimental task was an effort to collect preliminary data on social perception for use in a later study. Subjects were told that their responses would be used to establish a baseline for judging the effects of later experimental manipulations. To this end, data from all subjects would be averaged to obtain a measure of how subjects typically perform. Graduate-student experimenters, who had been informed that their subjects had been classified as either "success perceivers" or "failure perceivers" on the basis of personality test data collected earlier in the year, then put the subjects through the protocol. As in earlier experiments, overall, the experimenters biased the judgments of the subjects in the direction of their own expectations. The crucial finding, however, was that the experimenters' expectations affected only those subjects with high evaluation apprehension. The expectancy effect was nonexistent for subjects whose evaluation apprehension had been reduced.

The transmission of influence seems to be related to those character-istics of both subjects and experimenters that make them susceptible to evaluation apprehension. Still another photo-rating experiment showed that the higher the subjects' scores on a postexperimental test of anxiety, the more susceptible they were to directional cuing. Furthermore, the biasing effect of the experimenters correlated with their own scores on a test of social anxiety and need for social approval — that is, their own evaluation apprehension.

Indeed, at least among college students, the anxiety level of the princi-pal investigator also affects the experimenters' biasing effects. For exam-ple, in one elaborate study, several principal investigators were each given two assistants who carried out a standard photo-rating study with a group of subjects. The anxiety level of the principal investigators corre-lated positively with the biasing effect of their assistants, and, aston-ishingly, the correlation was higher than that between the research assis-tants' own anxiety level and their biasing effect. In other words, the assistants' anxiety level predicted subjects' responses less well than did the anxiety level of the principal investigators. Since the principal inves-tigators never came into contact with the subjects, the effect of their anxiety must have been transmitted through their assistants.

The potential relevance of these findings to psychotherapists-in-training is apparent. Trainees inevitably experience evaluation ap-prehension, which heightens their susceptibility to the influence of their supervisors, who are analogous to principal investigators. In other words, the findings suggest that the supervisor's own evaluation of a patient could affect the trainee's therapeutic results. We have already seen how a patient's behavior early in therapy may elicit behavior from the therapist which creates a self-fulfilling prophecy. Now we must add the possibility that the supervisor's prognosis, transmitted through the therapist-in-training, could have a similar effect.

These experiments demonstrate the important role played by the meanings of the experimental situation in determining subjects' experi-ence and behavior. Subjects' responses may be influenced as much by their own interpretation of a particular experiment as by the procedure being tested. In the interests of scientific objectivity, most psychological research, including research in psychotherapy, has systematically ig-nored subjects' beliefs about particular experiments. Since, as already mentioned, different persons may attribute different meanings to objec-tively similar situations, neglecting this determinant of subjects' re-sponses may well account for the generally low correlations found in psychotherapy research.

More important for our purposes is the finding that where research (however rigorous or well controlled) ignores meanings, it fails to convey the essence of the psychotherapeutic experience. A hypothetical example may help clarify the limits of the scientific method as applied to the meanings provided by a novel or a play. *Hamlet* could be studied quantitatively, according to the methods of science. One could analyze such objective features as the number of male and female characters, the relative proportion of scenes of violence to scenes of love — the number of such questions is limited only by the curiosity of the researcher. One could also use the scientific method to determine *Hamlet*'s impact upon various audiences by asking them to fill out rating scales, or by conducting structured interviews. Such information would have considerable value for some purposes. Audience surveys could enable producers to anticipate the size and composition of the audiences they expect, and a publisher could predict, within a definable margin of error, what the sales of a printed version might be.

No matter how extensive and sophisticated, however, such studies could not convey the experience of actually seeing *Hamlet*. The closest approximation to the actual experience would be to read the play. Short of this, a gifted essayist or critic such as Samuel Johnson might be able to convey the essence of the play to someone who had never seen it. By analogy, a psychotherapist who is also a gifted writer, such as Freud or Yalom (1989), may best convey aspects of the experience of therapy.

In the study of psychotherapy, as in the study of *Hamlet*, the application of the scientific method is insufficient, if not downright misguided, for many purposes. A more productive mode of analysis may derive from two respected and ancient disciplines concerned exclusively with meanings — rhetoric and hermeneutics.[1]

Psychotherapy and Rhetoric

Many persons regard rhetoric as a "failed science . . . the ignoble art of persuasion" (White 1985, p. 684). The term "rhetorician" conjures up images of demagogues who seek to sway audiences to gain their own ends, chiefly power or money, by invoking emotionally charged images and metaphors. As a result of these negative associations, the instructive similarities between rhetoric and psychotherapy have been ignored until recently. In fact, the similarities between psychotherapy and a more positive conception of rhetoric are striking.

In ancient Greece, therapeutic oratory based on rhetoric and linked

1. The following sections on rhetoric and hermeneutics are modified from Frank 1986 and Frank 1987.

to medicine was the functional equivalent of psychotherapy. The Greeks distinguished two forms of rhetoric, "noble" and "base," according to whether the rhetorician's goals were good or bad in the view of the person making the judgment. For Plato, noble or therapeutic rhetoric sought to produce in the soul *sophrosyne:* "a beautiful harmonic and rightful ordering of all the ingredients of psychic life, by strengthening will, reorganizing beliefs, or by eliciting new beliefs more noble than the old" (Spillane 1987, p. 217). The aims of psychotherapy, although more modest and circumscribed, can easily be subsumed under this definition.

Both psychotherapy and rhetoric operate in the realm of subjective states and interactions. The truths of science, which deals with controllable, repeatable, objective phenomena, are empirically demonstrable. The truths of both rhetoric and psychotherapy, however, are far less certain. Dialectics, a form of disciplined conversation, seeks to approach rhetorical truths. Similarly, the partial or total aim of all psychotherapeutic methods, many of which resemble dialectics, is to arrive at psychological truths. We shall not attempt to delve more deeply into the perennial issue of the nature of truth, except to point out that the methods of both psychotherapist and rhetorician purport only to approach, not to achieve, truth. That is, the truths of these disciplines are probable, not certain.

According to Aristotle, the rhetorician seeks to influence hearers by (1) evincing a personal character or *ethos* that will win the confidence of the listener; (2) engaging the listener's emotions; and (3) providing a truth, real or apparent, by argument. The following sections compare rhetoric and psychotherapy with respect to their practitioners, targets, goals, and methods in order to point out some implications for practice.

Practitioners

Both psychotherapists and rhetoricians gain their power to influence others through their ethos, the sources of which can be classified as personal or contextual.

Personal Sources. Personal sources must account for the marked differences in the effectiveness of individual rhetoricians and therapists with essentially equivalent training and expertise. These personal qualities, often referred to by such terms as "charisma" or "personal magnetism," are easy to recognize but hard to define. Among personal attributes contributing to charisma is the rhetorician's ability to sense and respond to the mood of the audience. This personal quality corresponds to the psychotherapist's sensitivity to the feelings of the individual patient. Rhetoricians place great emphasis on understanding the psychology of the target group. The orator, James Boyd White noted, "must always start by speaking the language of his or her audience, whatever it may be" (1985, p. 688). Furthermore, "orators must know what provokes anger, admiration, shame, and how different categories of hearers . . . are likely to react . . . because what is not strictly proof must pass as such" (*Encyclopaedia Britannica* 1972, 19:258). The rhetorician's eloquence resembles the therapist's ability to construct with the patient a convincing, meaningful narrative or story that explains the causes of the patient's symptoms or difficulties and suggests a collaborative procedure for overcoming them (McHugh and Slavney 1983). Therapists' steadfastness in the face of patients' emotional displays and overt or implicit manipulativeness, finally, seems analogous to rhetoricians' ability to withstand the hostility of their hearers.

Contextual Sources. Contextual features of the settings in which rhetoricians and psychotherapists operate reinforce the personal dimensions of their ethos. Politicians use symbols of office that signify power; evangelists draw upon symbols signifying that they are God's messengers. The main contextual reinforcers for Western psychotherapists are diplomas and certificates attesting to membership in an established profession such as psychiatry, psychology, or social work. Such professional roles imply that the therapist is trustworthy, competent, and interested primarily in the patient's welfare. Psychotherapists, according to the ethics of their profession, are dedicated to serving the interests of the patient.

The professional identification of many psychiatrists and psychologists implies that their power derives from science, an entity that for many Americans is the equivalent of God. While practitioners of existential-humanist therapies do not clothe themselves in the mantle of science, most of them acquire their ethos through membership in one of the established healing professions.

Therapists who see themselves as applied scientists may be unduly inhibited from making full use of a means of enhancing their persuasive power, a means not available to rhetoricians. This is the exhibition of symbols of healing, the most widespread of which are inert medications termed placebos. Placebos, the subject of Chapter 7, have become the occasion for a vast and controversial literature, particularly with respect to their ethical implications, but their power is undeniable.

Targets of Psychotherapists and Rhetoricians

Both psychotherapists and such rhetoricians as evangelists and demagogues seek to influence discontented or disconnected persons. Those who locate the sources of their difficulties primarily in themselves seek therapy from psychotherapists or salvation from evangelists. Those who blame such environmental factors as injustice and poverty are fair game for demagogues. The desire for relief from distressing states of mind or adverse circumstances makes all troubled persons susceptible to those who promise to help them. The appeal of all types of rhetoric is greatest in times, like the present, when many members of a society face social dislocation or economic hardship and have lost faith in the institutions and values that formerly provided a sense of social stability, cohesiveness, and common purpose.

A major difference between psychotherapy patients and other targets of rhetoric is that the recipients of psychotherapy are personalized, whether they be individuals or small groups. By contrast, the rhetorician or orator customarily seeks to influence persons in large groups. The psychotherapist exerts influence through private conversation; the rhetorician, through public discourse. Recently this difference has been blurred by television and radio. Psychotherapists on talk shows give their hearers the illusion of personal contact on a mass scale. More striking, each member of a mass television or radio audience may experience an evangelist's or politician's message as directed to him or her personally, without losing the psychological benefit of the feeling of belonging to a large, closely knit group.

The Goals of Influence

Both noble rhetoric and psychotherapy share the goal of enhancing the well-being of their targets. How practitioners of each discipline define this goal and the means they use to attain it, however, may differ considerably. Most psychotherapists offer their patients procedures that are meant to foster personal development or alleviate specific symptoms such as obsessions or panics. Secular rhetoricians, by contrast, urge their followers to attack specific grievances by demonstrations and other public action. Psychotherapists and rhetoricians of every kind, however, hold out the hope that the activities they recommend will lead to enduring improvement in personal well-being. A particularly striking example is the promise of eternal salvation that evangelists offer to those who join their cults.

Methods of Influence and Implications for Practice

Both rhetoricians and psychotherapists rely on the stimulation of emotions and on what rhetoricians term "argument" as methods for transforming meanings.

Emotional stimulation. Strong emotional appeals are the stock in trade of rhetoricians. These range from horrific visions of the enemy or hellfire to inspiring portrayals of the rewards to be gained by following the rhetorician's exhortations. Strong emotional appeals, reinforced by group contagion, can evoke extreme actions, including massacres and even suicides, as was seen in Jonestown. Behavioral changes following strong emotional arousal are usually temporary, however, unless their effects are irreversible, as in the example just cited. The duration of an appeal's effects seems to depend on repeated reinforcement through participation in a group that represents the changed values, as evangelists typically advocate.

Viewing psychotherapy from the perspective of rhetoric suggests that with some notable exceptions — for example, transactional analysis, primal therapy, and est — secular psychotherapists may not make sufficient deliberate use of emotionally intense procedures and follow-up groups. As discussed earlier, the success of all forms of psychotherapy depends on the patient's experiencing emotional arousal. Except in the treatment of posttraumatic stress disorders, considered in Chapter 10, and with some prominent exceptions (Janov 1971; Stampfl 1976; Marks 1978), Western psychotherapists shy away from deliberately arousing patients' emotions (Olden 1977). Emotional displays may make therapists uncomfortable, or emotion-eliciting procedures may appear incompatible with a rational, scientific approach. The power of rhetoric raises the possibility that wider deliberate use of such procedures could enhance the overall effectiveness of psychotherapy.

Moreover, although some schools of psychotherapy pressure their adherents to join follow-up groups, most do not incorporate such recommendations. More widespread use of follow-up groups might enhance the effectiveness of all psychotherapies and increase the number of patients in whom psychotherapy induces long-term changes. Indeed, self-help groups, which are a form of psychotherapy, already follow this principle (see Chapter 11).

Argument. The third component of rhetoric (in addition to ethos and emotional appeal) is argument. This term includes much more than logical appeal to reason; it encompasses all of the resources that can be used in a given culture to convince or persuade. Argument in rhetoric seems roughly analogous to therapeutic procedures in psychotherapy. The logotherapy of Viktor Frankl (1984) is the method of psychotherapy closest to rhetoric. The central aim of logotherapy is to persuade patients to transform the depressing or frightening meanings they have attached to certain experiences into positive ones. Its aims are similar to those of Beck's cognitive therapy described in Chapter 10.

Glaser (1980) made explicit some of the parallels between the methods of rhetoric and psychotherapy. Psychotherapists use many of the same devices as rhetoricians. These include vivid metaphors and sensory images that focus the patient's attention on ideas central to the therapeutic message and make the therapist's ideas more believable. Successful therapists do this intuitively, but many could profit from more deliberate efforts to improve their communication with patients along these lines. In this connection, neurolinguistic programming, for example, suggests ways of determining the preferred sensory modality of a patient's imagery — visual, auditory, tactile, olfactory, or gustatory — so that the therapist can use the same modality in his or her communications (Bandler and Grindler 1979).

Based on our limited understanding of rhetoric as revealed in this superficial and sketchy account, we venture the following comparisons of the aims and methods of psychotherapy and rhetoric. Both seek to indoctrinate their listeners into their own assumptive worlds. This is an overt goal of all rhetoricians and many psychotherapists, though for some of the latter, indoctrination may be subtle and indirect. Rhetorical procedures are particularly effective in arousing hope, combating alienation, and stirring emotions. On the other hand, since most rhetoricians deliberately discourage reflection, rhetorical encounters rarely, if ever, result in new learning, nor do they provide opportunities for practice. Rhetorical interventions probably do not enhance a person's sense of mastery as an individual, although they could have this effect by promoting the hearer's sense of membership in a powerful group.

Psychotherapy and Hermeneutics: The Patient as a Text

Insofar as the psychotherapist seeks to understand and interpret the meaning of the patient's communications, psychotherapy bears interesting resemblances to hermeneutics or exegesis, disciplines concerned with discovering the intended meaning of religious and other texts (McHugh and Slavney 1983). Like patients' histories, most texts are short on facts by which the exegete could verify the validity of interpretations. A patient's history, moreover, typically invites multiple interpretations. It therefore resembles a text that "may yield a number of very different interpretations according to the exegetical presuppositions and techniques applied to it" (*Encyclopaedia Britannica* 1986, 4:629).

Pursuing the analogy further, the therapist does not construct a purely personal interpretation of a patient's history. Rather, healer and patient attempt to develop a mutual understanding of the significance of the experiences the patient reports. As an authority on hermeneutics writes, "If understanding always means coming to an understanding, then it always involves two different participants. . . . The criterion of textual understanding is not recovery of the author's meaning but discovery of a common meaning, one that is shared with the interpreter. Such a meaning never depends exclusively on the author any more than it does on the interpreter" (Weinsheimer 1988, p. 178). Shared meanings are inevitably indeterminate, given the many factors brought to the encounter by both parties and their possible combinations. In medicine as well as psychiatry, diagnosis and treatment have been described as forms of mutual interpretation between healer and patient. Kleinman (1980) characterizes diagnosis as a process of negotiation between patient and physician to come to an agreement on the cognitive ordering of the patient's illness by labeling, classifying, and explaining. Other medical theorists emphasize the way the physician listens for the assumptions and principles by which the patient creates the reality in which he or she lives (Budd and Zimmerman 1986) and for the conceptual structure that supports the patient's perception of his or her problems (Evans et al. 1986).

To the extent that they cannot be directly observed, patients' symptoms and personal difficulties must be discovered through their reports. Of course, these reports — the patient's "history" — are not impartial statements of facts but are colored to an indeterminate degree by distortions of memory, the impression the patient seeks to make on the therapist, and many other influences. In this regard, the ambiguity of language constitutes an irreducible source of variability in the interpretation of these accounts. An authority on legal rhetoric made the point clearly: "A plain meaning approach breaks down in the face of the reality of disagreement among equally competent speakers of the same language" (Levinson 1982, p. 379).

The patient's history may be usefully conceptualized as an "apologia" that creates "an image of a life course . . . which selects, abstracts, and distorts in such a way as to provide the patient with a view of himself that he or she can usefully expound in current situations" (Goffman 1959, p. 133). The patient can continually modify his or her apologia in response to the demand character of the treatment situation (Orne 1969).

In psychotherapy the apologia characteristically emphasizes anxiety- and stress-producing encounters that account for the patient's demoralization. As already noted, this demoralization is typically intensified by patients' inability to make sense of what they are currently experiencing. In other words, one of the most demoralizing aspects of the apologia is frequently the lack of a coherent plot that explains why the experiences occurred. In other instances, the plot may be coherent but destructive, as when patients attribute all of their difficulties to personal inadequacy or to the malevolence of others. The psychotherapist must collaborate with the patient to construct a new plot (Hillman 1983; McHugh and Slavney 1983), preferably one that sustains a better self-image. The relative contributions of therapist and patient to this enterprise depend both on how "directive" the school of the therapist is and on the intelligence and sophistication of the patient.

The construction of a mutually satisfactory story involves what has been termed the hermeneutic circle (Jaspers 1963). Each experience both gains significance by reference to its place in the whole story and contributes to the meaning of the story overall. The overall meaning, in turn, directs attention to new items that may then alter the meaning of the whole. As a result, "validation proceeds in a cumulative fashion through mutual reinforcement of criteria which taken in isolation would not be decisive, but whose convergence makes them plausible and, in some cases, probable and even convincing" (Ricoeur 1977, p. 866). This process has no objective end point. As Jaspers put it, "A final 'terra firma' is never reached" (1963, p. 357).

Interpretations play an important part in molding the patient's story into a coherent plot. Therapists who see themselves as applied behavioral scientists assume that the therapeutic power of an interpretation depends on how closely it approximates objective truth. Comparison of psychotherapy with hermeneutics suggests, rather, that the criterion of the "truth" of a psychotherapeutic interpretation, as of a religious text, is its plausibility. The "truest" interpretation would be one that is most satisfying or that makes the most sense to the particular person or interpretative community.

In psychotherapy, the patient is the ultimate judge of the truth of an interpretation. The therapist's power to convince the patient of the validity of an interpretation depends on many factors. These include the ability of the interpretation to make sense out of the material the patient has offered, the terms in which it is expressed, the patient's confidence in the therapist, and perhaps most important, the interpretation's fruitfulness — its beneficial consequences for the patient's ability to function and for the patient's sense of well-being. Examples are given elsewhere of the remarkable power of interpretation to lift a chronic recurrent depression (pp. 205–7) and reduce patients' anxiety and heighten their sense of mastery in panic states (pp. 127–28) and ambulatory schizophrenia (p. 48).

To be effective, interpretations must be couched in terms that catch and hold the patient's attention. Vivid imagery and metaphor are helpful in this respect. Much of the therapeutic power of psychoanalysis and of Jung's individual psychotherapy lies in their extraordinarily evocative imagery. Who can forget the Ego struggling to tame the wild horses of the Id, or the Jungian archetypes?

Finally, a therapeutic plot must offer the prospect of a happy ending. It must hold out the hope that if the patient accepts the changes in assumptions, perceptions, and behaviors that the plot incorporates, he or she will experience less distress, enhanced self-worth, and greater effectiveness in dealing with the vicissitudes of life and greater ability to tolerate failure without loss of self-esteem.

Summary

We have contrasted psychotherapy as an applied behavioral science — the dominant view among professionals — with the view that it is a form of rhetoric that relies on the methods of hermeneutics. To be sure, the findings of conventional scientific methods applied to psychotherapy have influenced reimbursement policies, deepened knowledge of the effects of psychoactive drugs, and enhanced our understanding of some features of psychotherapy. Scientific methods, however, deal poorly with the meanings of the therapeutic situation. These meanings partly determine therapists' influence and patients' productions and contribute to the healing power of therapy. Psychotherapy may be better understood by reference to its similarities to rhetoric, including sources of influence, targets, and the methods of persuasion used. Viewing the patient's reports as meaningful stories to be interpreted and modified in collaboration with the therapist casts light on the therapeutic process.

FOUR

Religious Revivalism and Cults

Alice laughed. "There's no use trying," she said: "One *can't* believe impossible things."

"I daresay you haven't had much practice," said the Queen. "When I was your age, I always did it for half-an-hour a day. Why, sometimes I've believed as many as six impossible things before breakfast."

— Lewis Carroll, *Through the Looking Glass*

In this chapter and the next we shall consider forms of spiritual and bodily healing that spring from the third — religiomagical — root of psychotherapy. This chapter focuses on spiritual healing, the ways in which cults and revival meetings may produce beneficial changes in attitudes and behavior. The next chapter explores the religiomagical healing of bodily complaints. Given the intimate relation of mental and bodily states, these are artificial distinctions made primarily to facilitate exposition.

Participants in all forms of religiomagical healing share an unshakable conviction. They believe that suitable rituals enable humans to enter special states of consciousness in which they can directly experience and invoke the aid of powerful supernatural forces or personalities. These phenomena are difficult to consider dispassionately because they raise controversial issues involving others' deepest convictions and may require discussion of behaviors that offend large segments of the population. Members of Hare Krishna, for example, shave their heads, dress bizarrely, and chant in public places; followers of Rajneesh practice sexual freedom; and members of the Unification Church allow Sun Myung Moon to select their marital partners.

Moreover, religiomagical experiences cannot be verified or disproved by objective criteria. As a result, observers' biases can easily influence the selection of data reported, even the terms used to describe cult members. For example, Delgado (1977) spoke of a "cult indoctrinee syndrome" and considered indoctrinees to be victims of a traumatic neurosis, while Levine (1981) asserted: "Cults do not adversely affect their members clinically any more than any other intense, dedicated, demanding movement" (p. 534). These are not inconsistent factual statements to be proven or disproven, but value judgments about what is healthy and what is not.

Both authors of this book were raised in a secular family in a secular culture, and neither has enjoyed a transcendental experience. Hence, we shall not presume to evaluate the validity of spiritual healing nor to delve into the many profound metaphysical questions these phenomena raise. We are interested only in the methods that cults and revivalists use to change peoples' attitudes and the determinants of the effectiveness of these methods. We ignore as irrelevant to our present purposes many questions about the desirability of the attitudinal changes, the moral implications of the methods, and the validity of transcendental experiences and of the world-views underlying them.

Revivalism in Cultural Context

Slade (1979) estimated that there are between one thousand and three thousand major and minor religious cults in the United States, with a total membership of about three million people. The current popularity of zealous cults with messianic goals may be one consequence of the confusion and anxiety created by the conditions of modern life. These conditions include the threat of annihilation posed by weapons of mass destruction and environmental pollution. Another psychologically destructive force is the decline of the communal value systems and institutions that once provided a sense of hope and conviction that life has meaning. Traditional religions seem to be losing their hold, and science, on which so many placed great hopes, appears more and more as a false god luring humankind to destruction. Not only has science failed to satisfy the needs met by religion, it cannot even tame the monsters it has created. Surveys show declining popular confidence in all political institutions, and the suspicion is growing that we may have reached the limits of social and economic progress.

Under these circumstances, increasing numbers of people turn to the supernatural for reassurance. Some look inward, seeking mystical experiences through meditation or mind-altering drugs. A growing number turn to astrology, numerology, and other pseudosciences for guidance. Still others seek to maintain or regain their sense of security by attending revival meetings or adhering to messianic religious sects. These sects, which promise their adherents experiences of direct communion with supernatural forces, flourish especially under social conditions of misery and frustration. For example, voodoo, whose adherents seek to experience possession by deities, is the dominant religion of a people largely "doomed to a life without one moment's relief from the most desperate, nerve-wracking struggle to eke out daily subsistence" (Deren 1953, p. 165). Indeed, Huxley (1959) speculated that the physiological disorders created by starvation and disease might facilitate hallucinatory religious experiences.

Though the evidence is inconclusive, there seems to be a tendency for evangelistic sects in affluent societies to flourish more among the economically or socially underprivileged. When believers rise in the economic and social scale and gain increased opportunities for worldly satisfactions, they tend to leave the sects. Furthermore, as demonstrated by the evolution of Quakerism and Methodism, when members become more able to join the social mainstream, the rituals of the sects themselves tend to become less dramatically emotional and their beliefs less militant.

The ecstasies of evangelical religions provide outlets for pent-up emotional tensions, offer relief from the impoverishment and monotony of daily life, and gratify important psychological needs. A common source of their appeal is the belief in an afterworld where the oppressed will find everlasting joy and the roles of oppressor and oppressed will be reversed. The ecstatic experience of union with God is a sign that the convert is "saved," to be taken as evidence of the intercession of infinitely powerful forces on the person's behalf. In these ways revivalistic religions may help their adherents maintain a sense of personal integration in the face of widespread and enduring frustrations.

Conversion Experiences and Revival Meetings

Religious conversion may occur as an undramatic reawakening and reaffirmation of previously held but dormant religious beliefs, as an end result of a slow maturational process, or as the result of an abrupt shift in assumptive systems precipitated by a mystical experience. The mystical experience may be unexpected; more typically it occurs while a person is participating in religious group rituals or during solitary but fervent meditation and prayer. Our interest is confined to conversions characterized by drastic and far-reaching psychic upheavals, usually accompanied by strong emotion, sometimes leading to permanent changes in attitude and behavior (James [1936] 1989).

In Western societies, conversions occur most commonly during revival meetings or during the initiation ritual of a cult. Both typically involve the efforts of a charismatic leader. To be sure, most of the attenders at revival meetings are believers who go there to reinforce their faith, not to be converted to a different one. Often, however, potential converts form a significant proportion of the audience, much like those who visit a cult for the first time.

The arrival of an evangelist who plans to hold a revival meeting in town is typically preceded by a build-up through publicity and sermons by acolytes. These preliminaries create some anticipatory excitement, arouse latent feelings of guilt, and promise relief through salvation. The meetings themselves are highly emotional events that bypass or overwhelm participants' critical capacities.

Revivalists try to arouse feelings of sin, guilt, and fear in their hearers by harping on their wickedness and on the dire punishments that await those who do not repent. Some persons respond to these exhortations with emotional confessions of sin and repentance, thereby contributing to the group contagion created by the evangelist's dramatic pleas, threats, and exhortations. A particularly powerful source of contagion is the singing of gospel hymns by the entire congregation, led by a choir and soloists. Billy Graham's revivals sometimes had a choir of fifteen hundred (Argyle 1958). The emotional excitation causes susceptible persons to produce such manifestations of dissociation as "speaking in tongues," shaking, and convulsions, similar to signs of "possession" in non-Christian religions such as voodoo (Sargant 1957).

The hymn singing and the revivalists' sermons conjure up images of the bliss that awaits the converted. The relative emphasis on the contrapuntal themes of salvation and damnation varies considerably with different evangelists and at different periods of history. Great evangelists of previous eras, such as Jonathan Edwards and John Wesley, dwelt on the horrors of damnation (Sargant 1957), while some modern evangelistic movements, such as the Salvation Army, stress the joys of salvation: "It is the rejoicing, singing, irrepressible happiness of the Salvationist which often makes him such a powerful savior of other men" (Begbie 1909, p. 19).

The deep concern that the revivalist and the congregation show for the penitent's welfare further enhances the process of conversion. General William Booth, the founder of the Salvation Army, declared that "the first vital step in saving outcasts consists in making them feel that some decent human being cares enough for them to take an interest in the question whether they are to rise or to sink" (quoted by James [1936] 1989, p. 34).

Cults

A cult is "a relatively stable, transcendentally oriented group surrounding a powerful central figure who influences his or her followers in a direction that deviates strongly from that of the dominant culture" (Deutsch 1980). This definition excludes groups that do not possess all of these features — for example, est (Rhinehart 1976), which does not claim links to the supernatural, or A.A., in which the role of the central figure is weak and many of the values promulgated are those of the wider society. Even this rather narrow definition covers an enormous range of doctrines of spiritual healing. Cults also differ widely in the activities or rituals they prescribe to enable members to enter mystical and other healing states of consciousness. These range from calm meditation to strenuous exercises pursued to the point of exhaustion, such as the Dynamic Meditation of Bhagwan Shree Rajneesh (Gordon 1987).

The rituals of some cults include ingestion of substances that promote mystical experiences. On the basis of extensive clinical experience, for example, Grof asserted that with sufficiently high doses, "the experience of death and rebirth, union with the universe or God, encounters with demonic appearances, or the reliving of 'past incarnations' observed in LSD sessions appear to be phenomenologically indistinguishable from similar descriptions in the sacred scriptures of the great religions of the world" (1975, p. 14).

Cults also differ widely in the extent to which their rituals and other activities occupy the lives of their members. Cults whose members live in the larger community may require only that adherents frequently attend meetings for worship, while some residential cults may demand members' participation in prescribed activities throughout their waking hours. These activities may include dancing, chanting, prayer, various forms of meditation, and long hours of listening to expositions of the cult's doctrines by the leader or selected disciples.

Members of many cults are expected to promote or support the cult by begging, proselytizing, making and selling objects, or farming. These activities strengthen adherence to the cult's doctrines, foster submission to the leader, cement ties among the cult's members, and accentuate the separateness between them and people in the mainstream of society.

The boundaries between cults and the wider society differ markedly in permeability. Some, such as those around the charismatic sects of major religions, are virtually nonexistent. Thus, most "born again" Christians act in ways that are essentially indistinguishable from those of the general population. At the other extreme, the social barriers walling off some cults from society are insurmountable. An example would be the Manson family, whose members committed crimes reprehensible by any civilized standards. Most cults function between these extremes. Members distinguish themselves from their neighbors by behaviors that, while not antisocial, often violate the implicit values or behavioral standards of the community. Examples include behaviors such as total subservience to the cult leader or participation in orgiastic rites.

Cults typically require that potential members undergo a period of initiation before they are accepted as members. The initiation procedure of one of the best-studied cults, the Unification Church, consists of three workshops of increasing duration. During this period, potential members spend more and more time in the cult's residential center, receiving various forms of indoctrination and participating in the cult's activities. After these sessions, candidates must formally apply for membership. At least half of the participants in these probationary activities are members of the cult who offer an enormous amount of personalized, loving support (Galanter 1989). Critics label these activities "brainwashing," an unjustifiably pejorative term. To be sure, potential members are subjected to strong psychological pressures, but these do not include incarceration or physical abuse, crucial aspects of all forcible indoctrinations.

Personal Characteristics of Leaders

The personal qualities of the successful evangelist or cult leader cannot be authoritatively described. Probably all have a deep religious conviction and great organizing ability, in addition to such rhetorical skills as a capacity for communicating vivid, intense emotional experiences and a sensitivity to audience response. Personal prestige also may contribute to an evangelist's success. Billy Graham, for example, gained a higher percentage of conversions during his English tour than did his assistants.

Genuine religious faith appears to be compatible with irregular lifestyles, financial unscrupulousness, and even psychosis. At least two contemporary cult leaders, Jim Jones and Bhagwan Shree Rajneesh, became clinically paranoid (Gordon 1987). Indeed, some of history's great religious leaders, such as Joan of Arc, might be considered psychotic by today's standards. The delusions and hallucinations of such figures, however, must have been couched in terms that gained them wide cultural acceptance. In any case, years of absolute subservience and adulation by followers, coupled with the intense hostility of the surrounding community, would be enough to threaten the psychological equilibrium even of cult leaders who were not originally unstable.

Personal Sources of Susceptibility to Conversion

There is little firm knowledge concerning the social and personal factors that might heighten susceptibility to conversion. For converts and cult members who have had a religious upbringing, conversion is more a resurgence of dormant attitudes than a shift to totally new ones. A close previous relationship with a charismatic religious figure can usually be found in the lives of persons whose conversion experiences occur in isolation (Weininger 1955).

Personal attributes related to general susceptibility to influence also may play a role, particularly in cases where conversion involves an abrupt shift in a person's assumptive world. Thus, hysterics, persons with low self-esteem, and those who fear social disapproval seem to be good targets for evangelists or cult leaders. Surveys of both the Divine Light Mission and the Unification Church showed that 30–40 percent of members had sought professional help, and 6–9 percent had been hospitalized before joining (Galanter 1982).

Christensen (1963), Linn and Schwarz (1958), and Salzman (1953) offered confirmatory evidence that highly emotional or even frankly psychopathological states may precede religious conversion. Salzman regarded these states as disintegrating experiences; the others saw them as reintegrating ones. All conceptualized them as regression to an infantile state. These observations all concerned patients seen in psychoanalysis, so they may overemphasize the pathological dimensions of converts' susceptibility.

The passionate skeptic may be as susceptible to conversion as the believer. Many persons at revival meetings have become suddenly converted while in a state of high indignation at what is happening. Sargant commented: "The best way to avoid possession, conversion, and all similar conditions is to avoid getting emotionally involved in the proceedings" (1957, p. 109).

Adolescence is the age of highest susceptibility to sudden conversions. This transitional period of life, at least in the West, is characterized by internal and external conflicts. The former reflect the upwelling of sexual and aggressive feelings, the latter involve efforts to establish an independent identity by resisting or attacking authorities. Thus, many teenagers at times experience the feelings of anger, guilt, and isolation that characterize the preconversion state. Such alienation may make the support and promised spiritual harmony of a cult irresistibly attractive.

Within our frame of reference, we would characterize the period before religious conversion as one of severe demoralization. This may be so intense that the person becomes confused and attributes inner experiences to the outer world, entering a state of transient psychosis. Dominant affects include despair, hatred, resentment, and helpless fury, often directed by youngsters toward a parent or parent-substitute. The candidate for conversion may be tormented by self-doubts and guilt and feels cut off from or abandoned by God. In addition, many feel estranged from other people. The person in such a state longs to submit to an all-powerful, benevolent figure who can give absolution and restore order to his or her assumptive world. At the moment of conversion the convert feels closer to God and confident of divine favor. This experience is intensely emotional and may be followed by a sense of inner joy and peace.

The Effects of Cults and Revival Meetings

The Frequency and Duration of Conversions

The effectiveness of revivalist services varies. Charismatic evangelists and cult leaders differ in their ability to obtain conversions, and the conversions they obtain vary in permanence. At one extreme is the libertine who becomes a monk; at the other are persons who "make a decision for Christ" at a revival meeting but are quite themselves again the next morning.

According to Argyle (1958), only 2–5 percent of the audience at Billy Graham's revival meetings make a decision for Christ, and only about half of these converts are active a year later. Of these, about 15 percent — less than 1 percent of the initial audience — remain permanently converted. This statistical analysis might suggest that revival meetings are woefully ineffective compared to psychotherapy, until one remembers that for the tiny proportion of permanent converts, a session lasting only a few hours produces profound and widespread beneficial changes in their assumptive worlds. These changes last the remainder of their lives, an achievement that is ordinarily beyond the reach of any equally brief secular psychotherapy.

The effectiveness of revivalistic services also varies in different epochs. Though no precise figures are available, Wesley's percentage of conversions was probably higher than Graham's. God's wrath was more vivid in eighteenth-century England than in twentieth-century America. Moreover, Wesley recognized the importance of a like-minded group in sustaining the assumptive world of its members. Hence he placed great stress on continuing class meetings to consolidate and strengthen the new world-view. He divided his converts into groups of not more than twelve, and had them meet weekly under an appointed leader. Problems relating to their conversion and their future mode of life were discussed in agreed secrecy. The leader kept close watch for evidence of backsliding, and members who "grew cold and gave way to the sins which had long easily beset them" (Sargant 1957, p. 220) were expelled from both the classes and the Methodist Society.

The incidence and duration of conversions obtained by cults should be greater than those of modern revival meetings, since the exposure is much longer and potential converts are separated from their outside personal contacts during the initiation period. According to Galanter's study of the Unification Church (1989), 29 percent of initial attenders at an initiation workshop completed the twenty-one-day sequence and 9 percent eventually joined the church. Those who joined had weaker outside personal ties than those who did not.

The duration of a conversion probably depends on the extent to which converts' perception of a changed relationship with supernatural forces entails changes in their self-image, image of others, and patterns of social participation. The invocation of supernatural forces to support certain attitudes may promote personality integration by resolving some intrapsychic conflicts. The convert's sense of self-worth may be enhanced, though paradoxically coupled with a new sense of humility. The paradox is only apparent, however, for it is hard to conceive of a greater source of inner strength and personal security than the conviction that one has direct access to benevolent supernatural powers.

Conversion also affects a person's social perceptions. Sometimes the convert comes to love and admire those previously held in contempt or anger, such as a long-suffering spouse or parent. Alternatively, converts may shun or proselytize people they once admired and emulated. In either case, the convert often forsakes previous haunts and cronies and joins forces with other converts living a different lifestyle.

Positive Clinical Effects

The proportion of long-term conversions achieved by cults and revival meetings is an inadequate measure of their effects. Such a criterion ignores evidence that many people regard participation in a revival meeting or cult as a rewarding personal experience, however temporary.

Moreover, from a clinical perspective, religious conversion is one of the few effective available treatments for certain pathological behaviors, such as drug and alcohol abuse, gambling, and sexual deviations. In contrast to most psychopathological symptoms, which are distressing from the start, these addictions are initially pleasurable. Though such behaviors frequently disturb the person's intimates, the addict typically does not experience distress until he or she becomes unable to abstain despite a strong wish to do so. By invoking belief and reliance on a higher power and mobilizing strong group pressure, cults may create a motivation strong enough to break the stranglehold of alcohol, drugs (Galanter 1982), or deviant sexual behavior (Pattison and Pattison 1980). They may also provide the continuing support needed to maintain the recovering addict's improvement.

Negative Effects of Cults

As havens from life's stresses, transcendental cults attract a significant proportion of psychologically fragile persons. Though many of these display signs of psychopathology, it is difficult to determine the extent to which cult activities actually cause their symptoms. Levine (1981) found that of fifty-seven disturbed cult members, only fifteen had decompensated while in the groups being observed. Membership in the cults did not adversely affect the remaining thirty-six. He concluded that the incidence of psychological casualties in transcendental cults is no greater than that caused by any intense group experience. Other sorts of cults, such as Satanic ones, are much more clearly harmful, but presumably they represent only a small proportion of the total number.

Cult leaders are not as accountable to external controls as mainstream professionals are. Those who become paranoid or who are ethically corrupt may do their followers great harm, including ruining them financially, exploiting them sexually, and, should the cult be dissolved or betrayed by the leader, leaving members adrift without the means to function in the wider society.

Persons who leave a cult, whatever their reasons for going, may suffer distress from having to move from a closely knit, strongly supportive environment in which all decisions are made for them and all activities prescribed into a world where they have to make their own decisions and establish their own relationships. This reentry problem causes some former cult members to experience loneliness, depression, indecisiveness, and a blurring of mental acuity. Under stress, some slip into the trancelike states that they experienced in the cult (Singer 1979). How enduring, widespread, or serious such manifestations are cannot be determined, since the information has been obtained primarily from those former cult members who sought help. One study of fifty current or former cult members concluded that no data "suggested that any of these subjects are unable or even limited in their ability to make sound judgments and legal decisions as related to their persons and property" (Ungerleider and Wellisch 1979).

The major negative effects experienced by members of transcendental cults arise from their total subservience to the cult's leadership and doctrines when these conflict with the values and behavioral standards of the outside world. This negative feature is specific to cults; in many other intense healing group experiences similar results are achieved without alienating participants from their original communities.

During periods of active involvement, cult activities may not disturb cult members but may bother the wider community. Such activities as panhandling in airports and shopping malls or the mass marriages conducted by Reverend Moon between strangers who are members of the Unification Church (Galanter 1989) may not disturb those who participate but may create tensions with other persons. These tensions, in turn, may adversely affect the behavior of cult members.

More disturbing are the rifts that cults cause between cult members, especially young ones, and their families. Thus, children raised in cults may be deeply distressed during the process of maturing and choosing their own lifestyles when these choices involve leaving the group. They may be considered damned or fallen and cut off from continuing contact with their former friends and even from close family members.

Conversely, the rage and anguish of parents of children lost to cults whose doctrines and practices they abhor must resemble that felt by parents of early Christians who left home to follow Christ. Under the spell of such emotions, some families have resorted to "deprogrammers" to try to reclaim their erring children. Deprogramming consists of "a set of techniques for removing persons from new religious groups and involving them in a rigorous and even coercive resocialization process in an attempt to get them to renounce their beliefs and accept more traditional ones" (Richardson 1980, p. 19). The methods of deprogrammers have included such drastic measures as kidnapping and incarceration.

The success of these methods is limited. A study of twenty current or former cult members who had undergone deprogramming revealed that eleven had returned to their cults; of the remaining nine who did not return, six subsequently became deprogrammers themselves. All but one of those in whom deprogramming failed had been in their cult for a year or more, while all of those who renounced the cult had been members for less than a year (Ungerleider and Wellisch 1979). It is not easy to undo a conversion that has been reinforced for a year. One wonders, too, if the high percentage of successfully deprogrammed persons who become deprogrammers themselves reflects a need to reinforce their new world-view by seeking to convert others (Festinger, Riecken, and Schachter [1956] 1964).

Discussion and Summary

Revival meetings and cults share most of the characteristics of secular psychotherapies that help produce and maintain beneficial changes in attitudes and behavior, as described in Chapter 2. Successful instances of both psychotherapy and spiritual healing reduce psychologically caused suffering, increase self-esteem, and foster a sense of mastery in persons who seek their ministrations. Followers of rhetoricians, evangelists, and cult leaders enhance their sense of mastery vicariously, through identification with the power of the leader and group. Paradoxically, members achieve this identification by surrendering control of their decisions and behavior to the group and its leader. For patients in psychotherapy who alter their belief systems, the psychotherapeutic experience is analogous to a partial, gradually occurring conversion in which the role of submission to authority is much less well defined.

Psychotherapies resemble revival meetings in that the values they promote are shared and supported by large segments of the communities in which they operate. By definition, this is not true of cults. However, when enough people accept a countercultural belief system, the movement is no longer a cult but becomes an established religion. Examples that come to mind are Christianity, the Seventh Day Adventists, and the Church of the Latter Day Saints.

Psychotherapists, like rhetoricians, evangelists, and cult leaders, operate in special settings containing symbols that reinforce the belief systems underlying their activities. With important exceptions, however, psychotherapists ordinarily do not deliberately attempt to mobilize the intense emotions or the group support that rhetoricians and cult leaders foster.

The targets of revivalists, cult leaders, and psychotherapists are all often in a similar state of demoralization. Confusion, guilt, or frustration springing from personal characteristics or social conditions seems to heighten the attractiveness and enhance the effectiveness of revivalistic religions and cults. Such demoralization increases a person's susceptibility to emotionally charged methods of influence that arouse hope by offering detailed guides to behavior based on an inclusive, infallible assumptive world.

Revivalists and leaders of transcendental cults differ from psychotherapists in their access to a potent force for change. This is their firm belief in the existence of beneficent transcendental forces that can be directly experienced through appropriate rituals. Submission to an evangelist or cult leader as the channel for supernatural forces creates a more powerful sense of mastery than submission to a secular leader, especially for those participants who have the joyous experience of being "saved." Shared belief in supernatural powers and shared rituals for invoking them, furthermore, forge particularly strong bonds between the leader and the members of these groups and among the members themselves. Rituals that include confessions, enabling members to share each other's private thoughts and feelings and to forgive each other's secret transgressions, further strengthen these bonds.

Rhetoricians and most psychotherapists have not traditionally stressed ongoing group participation to reinforce the changes they engender in patients' attitudes and behavior. Though revivalists may be equally shortsighted, cults are particularly effective in supporting and maintaining the new belief systems their methods create. Current schools of psychotherapy are becoming more aware of the importance of continuing group reinforcement. Various schools of psychoanalysis encourage their members to continue attending their institutes indefinitely, and follow-up groups are an integral part of programs for alcoholics and addicts as well as for persons in primal therapy (Janov 1970) and reevaluation counseling (Jackins 1978), among others.

Though mental health professionals practicing psychotherapy in their offices can evoke only pale shadows of the emotional states and group pressures evoked by evangelists and cult leaders, they may deploy several forces for change that these others minimize or lack. Many psychotherapists derive considerable symbolic power from their link to science. Those in medical settings have access to powerfully effective remedies such as drugs to enhance their psychological healing powers. Since most psychotherapies aim to reintegrate patients into the wider society, or at least some portion of it, ordinary social involvement sometimes maintains the changes they have induced, even in the absence of ongoing group pressure. Finally, and most important, therapists are typically skilled in mobilizing persons' cognitive ability to identify and resolve problems. Though emotions and aesthetic sensibility are crucial parts of human experience, humans' critical intelligence is still their greatest mental resource and a powerful healing force.

FIVE

Religiomagical Healing

<hr>

> "I can't believe *that*," said Alice.
> "Can't you?" the Queen said in a pitying tone. "Try
> again; draw a long breath, and shut your eyes."
> — *Through the Looking Glass*

Religiomagical rituals are major forms of healing in nonindustrialized
societies and provide the foundation for faith healing in our own.
Though we have chosen to distinguish such activities from revivalism
and transcendental cults, this separation is largely arbitrary. Some revival meetings and cult activities include identified healing rituals. Even
when revivalists and cult leaders do not directly promote healing, their
results largely overlap those of faith healers and shamans. The psychological changes produced by religious conversion or by joining a cult may
improve persons' physical health, and a successful healing ritual benefits
participants both psychologically and physically.

Examination of religious healing across cultures illuminates certain
aspects of human functioning that are relevant to psychotherapy. Methods of supernatural healing highlight the close interplay between assumptive systems and emotional states and the intimate relation of both
to health and illness. Healing rituals also bring out the parallels between
inner disorganization and disturbed relations with one's group, and illustrate the healing power of patterned interactions of patient, healer, and
group within the framework of an internally consistent assumptive
world. Finally, certain properties of healing rituals in nonindustrialized

societies resemble naturalistic methods of psychotherapy in ways that may serve to increase our understanding of both.

The view that supernatural forces can cause and cure illness stretches back to furthest antiquity. Such beliefs continue to be important, though often in attenuated form, in most modern cultures. Patients who come from ethnic groups that harbor beliefs in supernaturalism may attribute their illness to supernatural forces more often than they are willing to admit to physicians. Three patients seen in the psychiatric clinic of a teaching hospital, a veritable citadel of scientific medicine, come to mind. None was in any sense psychotic. One, born in Sicily, sheepishly confessed that he believed his nervousness and restlessness were caused by the evil eye, incurred because he had flirted with someone else's girl. Another, raised in Appalachia, attributed her severe anxiety to a fortuneteller's prophecy that her father was about to die. She firmly believed in vampires and was convinced that her grandmother was a witch. The third, a devout Catholic, was more than half convinced that her two miscarriages were God's punishment for having divorced her first husband and married a Protestant.

Belief in supernatural forces, moreover, is found throughout the educational spectrum. A highly respected black physician once confided to one of us that when doctors were unable to relieve her foot pain, she was finally cured by a voodoo practitioner. Indeed, supernaturalism seems to be enjoying a resurgence in all sectors of American society, as shown by the growing interest among educated people in astrology, tarot cards, *I Ching*, and the like, as well as by the popularity of consciousness-altering drugs and charismatic religious sects.

Practitioners of biomedicine generally refuse to take seriously the evidence that healing can occur through procedures involving the paranormal or supernatural. In seeking to maintain objectivity, we shall try to navigate between the Scylla of scornful skepticism and the Charybdis of gullibility. Too much skepticism may blind the observer to genuine phenomena that cannot be verified by standard scientific methods, while a too eager readiness to believe may lead to the acceptance of such flagrant frauds as Filipino "psychic surgery" (Krippner and Villoldo 1976; Frank 1978b).

Religiomagical healing methods differ with regard to the particular theories of the supernatural they invoke, whether they dominate a society or are believed only by deviant groups, and the social acceptance and status of the healers. We shall consider primarily public and socially sanctioned rituals based on the transcendental belief system of a total society or of a respectable and numerically significant portion of it. The term "religious" seems applicable to such rites, though few readers of this book will share the particular beliefs that underlie most of them.

Religious healing practices in nonindustrialized societies, as in industrialized ones, exist side by side with naturalistic treatment involving medicines, manipulations, and surgery (Feierman 1985; Kleinman 1980). In all cultures religious healing is most often applied to illnesses that have important emotional components — the conditions for which secular psychotherapies also often seem appropriate. Despite the differences in their theoretical foundations, religious and naturalistic healing methods have much in common. Furthermore, both types of healing have persisted through the ages, suggesting that their common elements account for some part of their common effects. In this chapter we shall search for these common features in the religious healing methods of a few nonindustrialized societies, a great contemporary shrine of miraculous healing, and even a modern hospital.

Although the characteristics to be discussed are widespread, they are not universal. The cross-cultural diversity of healing methods is very great, and exceptions can be found to any generalization (Kiev 1964; Morley and Wallis 1979). The examples we offer are not meant to prove a line of argument (which would require consideration of negative instances) but simply to support and illustrate it.

Illnesses in Nonindustrialized Societies

Societies outside the industrialized world regard illness as a misfortune involving the entire person, including disturbed relations with the spirit realm and with other members of the community. Although these societies recognize different kinds of illness, their classifications often do not resemble those of Western medicine. In particular, non-Western societies may not distinguish sharply between mental and bodily illness, or between natural and supernatural causes of illness. Supernatural causes may be described as soul loss, possession by an evil spirit, the magical insertion of a harmful body by a sorcerer, or the machinations of offended or malicious ancestral ghosts. Patients may believe that some witting or unwitting transgression against the supernatural world has made them vulnerable to such calamities, or that they have incurred the enmity of a sorcerer or someone who has employed a sorcerer. Believers may ascribe their illness to personal transgressions or to the transgressions of a kinsperson.

Although all societies recognize that certain illnesses have natural causes, this does not exclude the ultimate role of supernatural forces. A broken leg may be recognized as caused by a fall from a tree, but the cause of the fall may have been an evil thought or a witch's curse.

Because of the precariousness of life among people in impoverished societies, many diseases represent a great threat to the patient, and the longer the illness lasts, the greater the threat becomes. In societies subsisting on a marginal level, illness is a threat to the group as well as to the invalid. Disease prevents the invalid from making a full contribution to the group's support and diverts from group purposes the energies of those who provide care. In such a context, every illness presumably engenders anxiety, despair, and similar emotions, which mount as cure is delayed. Thus, whatever their underlying pathological condition, the subjects of healing rituals experience emotions that aggravate their distress and disability. The invalid is in conflict internally and is out of harmony with the group. The group must chose between abandoning the ill member by completing the process of extrusion or making strenuous efforts to promote healing and restore the person to useful community membership.

The relationship between emotional distress and physical functioning is epitomized by the so-called taboo death. This disaster can befall members of certain cultures, and may have a counterpart in industrialized societies. Taboo death apparently results from noxious emotional states related to assumptive systems about supernatural forces — in particular, forces that influence the victim's relations with others.

Anthropological literature contains anecdotes of persons who, on learning that they have been cursed or have inadvertently broken a taboo, go into a state of panic and die in a few hours (Webster 1942). In none of these cases can such mundane causes of rapid death as overwhelming infection be entirely excluded. The *post hoc* nature of the explanations that attribute death to supernatural or emotional forces must not be overlooked. Indeed, in groups where this type of death occurs, practically all illness and death is attributed to the victim's having been cursed. Nevertheless, the process has been observed in sufficient detail in different tribes to give substantial support to the explanation that emotional factors may be a proximal cause of death.

The most convincing examples are those in which someone at the point of death from a curse rapidly recovers when the spell is broken by a more powerful one, as in the following anecdote, which can be multiplied many times:

> Some years ago my father, who lived in Kenya, employed a Kikuyu garden "boy," of whom we were all fond. Njombo was gay, cheerful and in the prime of life. He was paying goats to purchase a wife and looking forward

to marriage and a bit of land of his own. One day we noticed he was beginning to lose weight and looked pinched and miserable. We dosed him with all the usual medicines to no avail. Then we persuaded him, much against his will, to go into a hospital. Three weeks later he was back with a note from the doctor: "There is nothing wrong with this man except that he has made up his mind to die."

After that Njombo took to his bed, a heap of skins, and refused all food and drink. He shrank to nothing and at last went into a coma. Nothing we could do or say would strike a spark, and all seemed to be up with him.

As a last resort, my father went to the local chief and threatened him with all sorts of dreadful penalties if he did not take action to save Njombo's life. This was largely bluff, but the chief fell for it. That evening we saw a man with a bag of stoppered gourds entering Njombo's hut. We did not interfere, and no doubt a goat was slaughtered. Next morning, Njombo allowed us to feed him a little beef tea. From that moment he started to rally — the will to live was restored. We asked no questions, but learned some time later that Njombo had had a serious quarrel over the girl and that his rival had cursed him. Only when the curse was removed could he hope to survive. [Huxley 1959, p. 19]

Presumably, Njombo was aware of the ministrations of the shaman, though he appeared comatose to his employers.

In certain societies, group attitudes may reinforce the victim's expectation of death. For example, in the Murngin, a North Australian tribe, when the theft of a man's soul becomes general knowledge, he and his tribe collaborate in hastening his demise. Having lost his soul, he is already "half dead." Since his soul is in neither this world nor the next, he is a danger to himself as a spiritual entity and also to his tribe. All believe that his soul, not having been properly laid away, is likely to cause illness and death among his kin. All normal social activity with the man ceases, and he is left alone. Shortly before he dies, the group returns to him under the guidance of a ceremonial leader to perform mourning rites. The purpose of this ritual is "to cut him off entirely from the ordinary world and ultimately place him . . . in . . . the . . . world . . . of the dead." Concomitantly, the victim recognizes his change of status. "The wounded feudist killed by magic dances his totem dance to . . . insure his immediate passage to the totem well. . . . His effort is not to live but to die." As Warner concluded, "If all a man's near kin, . . . business associates, friends, and all other members of the society, should suddenly withdraw themselves because of some dramatic circumstance . . . looking at the man as one already dead, and then after some little time perform over him a sacred ceremony believed with certainty to guide him out of the land of the living . . . the enormous suggestive power of this twofold movement of the community . . . can be somewhat understood by ourselves" (1937, pp. 241–42).

In calling attention to the interpersonal forces involved in taboo death, we do not mean to minimize the importance of intrapsychic ones. Although the foregoing account stresses the role of group influences, the individual's emotional state is probably the major source of such a decline. The person's distress reflects the conviction, grounded in a shared belief system, of having lost his or her soul. In this example, the group's withdrawal reinforces this conviction. Conceivably, however, the victim might have died despite others' loving care if sufficiently convinced that the situation was hopeless.

Work with animals has generated plausible speculations about the physiological mechanism of death in these cases. Cannon's work (1957) supported the hypothesis that terror produces prolonged adrenal overexcitation, a state analogous to lethal surgical shock. Citing studies of physiological changes in wild rats who give up and die when placed in a stressful situation after their whiskers have been clipped, Richter (1957) speculated that the lethal emotional state is one of helplessness more than terror. In this model, the mechanism of death is stoppage of the heart from overactivity of the vagus nerve. Although these findings can be explained without assumptions about the rats' mental state (Hughes, Stein, and Lynch 1978), Richter's speculation strengthens the parallel between this phenomenon in wild rats and aspects of taboo deaths in humans, particularly the prompt recovery even at the point of death if the stress is suddenly removed. Since patients who believe themselves cursed may refuse food and drink, dehydration and malnutrition may contribute to taboo deaths (Barber 1961a), especially among people whose nutritional status is already marginal. Each hypothesis is plausible, and each may account for a particular variety of emotionally caused death — terror and adrenal failure for the rapid form, if it occurs, and dehydration or vagal overactivity induced by despair for the slower variety.

In all cultures, the conviction that one's predicament is hopeless may cause or hasten disintegration and death. In our own society, for example, the death rate of the aged shortly after admission to state mental hospitals is unduly high. Frequently, autopsy reveals no adequate cause of death, raising the possibility that some of these deaths result from hopelessness aggravated by abandonment by the patient's group. Similarly, schizophrenic people have been known to go into panic states in which they exhaust themselves and die. Since the advent of antipsychotic drugs, such states have become very rare. In the past, however, "acute exhaustive psychosis" (Adland 1947) usually occurred in conjunction with the patient's admission to the hospital — that is, at the moment when the family withdrew and the person felt abandoned. Sometimes it could be successfully interrupted if a member of the treatment staff succeeded in making contact with the patient and in getting across, by one means or another, the message that someone still cared.

The "give-up-itis" reaction described in Americans imprisoned by the Japanese and Koreans during past wars implicates a similar interaction of hopelessness and group isolation in producing death. A former prisoner of war described the phenomenon well. He listed the major factors that had to be dealt with to survive as "the initial shock and subsequent depression induced by being taken prisoner by Oriental people; the feeling of being deserted and abandoned by one's own people; the severe deprivation of food, warmth, clothes, living comforts, and sense of respectability; the constant intimidation and physical beatings from the captors; loss of self-respect and the respect of others; the day-to-day uncertainty of livelihood and the vague indeterminable unknown future date of deliverance" (Nardini 1952, p. 244). This list places physical and psychological threats on the same footing. Under these circumstances, "occasionally an individual would . . . lose interest in himself and his future, which was reflected in quiet or sullen withdrawal from the group, filth of body and clothes, trading of food for cigarettes, slowing of work rate . . . and an expressed attitude of not giving a damn. . . . If this attitude were not met with firm resistance . . . death inevitably resulted" (Nardini 1952, p. 245).

This is clearly a description of hopelessness. Combating such despair involved "forced hot soap-and-water bathing, shaving and delousing, special appetizing food, obtaining a few days rest in camp . . . a mixture of kindly sympathetic interest and anger-inducing attitudes. Victory was assured with the first sign of a smile or evidence of pique" (Nardini 1952, p. 245). Apparently, both provocative and nurturant behaviors can successfully raise morale. As another observer reported: "One of the best ways to get a man on his feet initially was to make him so mad, by goading, prodding, or blows, that he tried to get up and beat you. If you could manage this, the man invariably got well" (C. L. Anderson, quoted in Kinkead 1959, p. 149). Thus, any emotional stimulus, whether pleasant or not, may relieve lethal despair if it succeeds in breaking through the victims' isolation, demonstrates that others care, and implies that these persons may aid in their own recovery.

The Role of the Healer in Nonindustrialized Societies

While certain emotional states activated by personal assumptive systems interacting with group forces may contribute to disintegration and death, others contribute to healing. These states play a major role in the religious healing rituals of nonindustrialized societies. Such rituals, which grow directly out of the tribe's world-view, are usually conducted by a healer or shaman. They also typically involve the active participation of the patient and members of the family and tribe.

The society's assumptive world explains why the powers of the healer are accepted as genuine. The routes for becoming a healer vary greatly. In certain cultures, persons acquire healing powers, sometimes involuntarily, through personal and private mystical experiences, while in others, as in the Kwakiutl, they undergo an elaborate training course analogous to medical training in the West (Prince 1968). Another way of acquiring shamanistic powers is through inheritance, which calls to mind the frequency of physician dynasties in all societies.

In some groups, healers may be those who have recovered from serious illnesses themselves. Burmese society recognizes two types of shamans. One type, recruited from those with pathological symptoms, only propitiates harmful supernatural spirits. Shamans of the second type — exorcists or members of religiomagical sects — claim the power to control such spirits (Spiro 1967). The Burmese example points to at least two sources of a healer's ability to inspire a patient's confidence: having successfully overcome similar problems (which should also strengthen rapport) and being a member of a culturally valued healing sect. In our own culture, the analyzed psychoanalyst partakes of both (Henry 1966).

The social status of healers varies widely across cultures, reflecting both the nature of their training and the prestige of the conceptual scheme underlying their powers. Kwakiutl shamans, for example, are highly regarded, while other societies treat healers as deviants with little prestige, except when their healing powers are invoked.

Highly prestigious healers may suffer accompanying risk. In the United States, physicians, who are the practitioners with highest status, may be forced to pay enormous malpractice settlements after mistakes or unsuccessful treatment. In other cultures, failure to cure may require the payment of an indemnity or even the death of the shaman.

Healers are usually adept at distinguishing those illnesses they can treat successfully from the ones that are beyond their powers. Rejecting patients with whom they are likely to fail enables them to maintain a reputation for success. Such a reputation, by arousing favorable expectations in the patient and the group, undoubtedly enhances their healing power.

The remarkable autobiography of Quesalid, a Kwakiutl shaman (Lévi-Strauss 1958; quotes from pp. 193, 194, 196, translated by E. K. Frank), illustrates the importance of others' attitudes in determining both the healer's effectiveness and his or her own self-evaluation. Quesalid claimed that he entered training motivated by skepticism concerning the shaman's powers and by the desire to expose them. (Like many converts, he may later have exaggerated his former skepticism.) The training included learning to master various arts of deception, especially the technique of spitting out a bit of down covered with blood at the right moment, to represent the magical extraction of the foreign body that had made the patient ill.

Knowing that he was in training, a family called him in to treat a patient, and he was brilliantly successful. Quesalid attributed the cure to psychological factors: "the patient believed strongly in his dream about me." What shook Quesalid's skepticism was a visit to a neighboring Koskimo tribe, in which the shamans simply spit a little saliva into their hands and dared to pretend that this was the illness. To find out "what is the power of these shamans, if it is real or if they only pretend to be shamans," he asked and received permission to try his method on a person in whom this technique had failed. Again the patient said she was cured. Apparently some forms of healing were more fraudulent than others. This presented Quesalid with a problem that is "not without parallel in the development of modern science: Two systems, both known to be inadequate, nevertheless, [when] compared with each other appear to differ in value both logically and experimentally. In what frame of reference should they be judged?"

The Koskimo shamans were "covered with shame" because they had been discredited in the eyes of their compatriots. Assailed by self-doubts, they tried hard to ferret out Quesalid's secrets, to no avail. Finally, one of the most eminent challenged him to a healing duel, and Quesalid again succeeded where the other failed. Two interesting consequences followed. The old shaman, fearful of dying of shame and unable to get Quesalid to reveal his secrets, vanished the same night, leaving all his relatives "sick at heart." When he returned after a year, he was insane, and he died three years later. Quesalid, although he continued to expose impostors and was full of scorn for the profession, remained uncertain about whether there are real shamans or not: "Only once have I seen a shaman who treated patients by suction and I was never able to find out if he was a real shaman or a faker. For this reason only, I believe that he was a shaman. He did not allow those he had cured to pay him. And truly I never once saw him laugh." At the end it is unclear whether Quesalid considers himself to be a real shaman: "He pursues his calling with conscience . . . is proud of his successes and . . . defends heatedly against all rival schools the technique of the bloodstained down whose deceptive nature he seems completely to have lost sight of, and which he had scoffed at so much in the beginning." Quesalid's skepticism is not strong enough to withstand his own successes and the belief of his group in his powers.

The Healing Ceremony in Nonindustrialized Societies

Healing in nonindustrialized societies uses both individual and group methods. The healer conducts some procedures with the patient alone, analogous to the pattern of Western medicine. Like Western physicians, the healer makes a diagnosis by performing certain acts and then offers a remedy, which may be a medication or the performance of suitable maneuvers. The healing power of these procedures probably lies in patients' expectation of help, based on their belief that the healer has special powers derived from the ability to communicate with the spirit world. Other forms of traditional healing involve a prolonged relationship between healer-shaman and patient, a procedure analogous in some ways to long-term psychotherapy (Field 1955).

Another type of traditional healing that bears on psychotherapy is the group healing ceremonial. Such rituals are not undertaken lightly. Usually they occur only after simpler methods have failed. Similarly, in the West, patients are often not referred for psychiatric treatment until other procedures have failed to relieve their suffering. Thus, both the psychotherapy patient and the subject of a healing ritual are apt to be discouraged about their condition, though still hoping for relief.

Group ceremonials are intense, time-limited efforts to cure specific illnesses. Typically they involve members of the patient's family and community, with or without the invocation of ancestral or other spirits. While such rites cast little if any light on certain features that are presumed to be important in long-term individual psychotherapy, for instance, the development and examination of transference reactions between patient and therapist, they throw certain other aspects into relief by compressing them in time. These ceremonies highlight the role of group and cultural factors in healing. Group and family therapists recognize the importance of such forces, which are also present implicitly in individual therapy, though often underestimated.

Detailed consideration of a particular healing ceremony affords some insight into the nature of communal healing. A vivid example is Gillin's description of the treatment of *espanto* in a sixty-three-year-old Guatemalan Indian woman (1948, quotes from pp. 389, 391, 394). Guatemalan Indians consider *espanto*, which an American psychiatrist would probably diagnose as a form of agitated depression, to be a manifestation of soul loss. This was the woman's eighth attack.

The treatment began with a diagnostic session attended not only by the patient but also by her husband, a male friend, and two anthropologists. The healer felt the woman's pulse while looking her in the eye, then confirmed that she was suffering from *espanto*. He then told her in a calm, authoritative manner that she had lost her soul near the river when she saw her husband foolishly lose his money to a loose woman. He then urged her to tell the whole story. After a brief period of reluctance, the patient "loosed a flood of words telling of her life frustrations and anxieties." During her recital "the curer . . . nodded noncommittally, but permissively, keeping his eyes fixed on her face. Then he said that it was good that she should tell him of her life." Finally, they went over the precipitating incident of the latest attack in detail. She and her husband were passing near the spot where he had been deceived by the loose woman. She upbraided him, and he struck her with a rock.

The curer then told the woman he was confident she could be cured and proceeded to outline in detail the preparations she would have to make for the curing session four days later. She was responsible for these preparations, which involved procuring and preparing certain medications, persuading a woman friend or kinsperson to be her "servant" during the preparatory period and healing session, preparing a feast, and persuading one of the six chiefs of the village to participate with the medicine man in the ceremony.

The ceremony itself began at four in the afternoon and lasted until five the next morning. Before the healer arrived, the house and the house altar, a Christian symbol, had been decorated with pine boughs. In Christianized societies, incompatibilities between the assumptive systems underlying healing rituals and Christian beliefs may create embarrassing problems. Healing rituals, which typically strive to bring various conflicting elements of the patient's world into harmony, may mix the symbols of both traditions and actively promote a truce between the divergent belief systems, as will be seen below.

Numerous invited guests and participants had assembled. Once they were all present, the healer made his entrance, shook hands all around, and checked the preparations carefully. Then came a period of light refreshment and social chitchat. This apparently helped organize a social group around the patient and relaxed tensions.

After dusk, the healer, the chief, and others of the group went off to church, apparently to appease the Christian deities in advance, since "recovery of a soul involves dealing with renegade saints and familiar spirits certainly not approved of by God Almighty." When they returned, a large meal was served. The patient did not eat, but was complimented by all present on her food. Then the healer carried out a long series of rituals. He made wax dolls of the chief of evil spirits and his wife, and appealed to them for the return of the patient's soul. Next he elaborately massaged the patient with whole eggs, which were believed to absorb some of the sickness from her body. The curer, the chief, two male helpers, and the ever-present anthropologists then took the eggs and a variety of paraphernalia, including gifts for the evil spirits, to the place where the patient had lost her soul. There, the healer pleaded with various spirits to restore her soul to her.

On their return they were met at the door by the patient, who showed an intense desire to know whether the mission had been successful. The curer spoke noncommittal but comforting words. This was followed by much praying by the healer and the chief before the house altar and a special ground altar set up outside, and by rites to purify and sanctify the house. Some of these activities were devoted to explaining to the household patron saint why it was necessary to deal with evil spirits. The ceremony came to a climax at about two in the morning. The patient, naked except for a small loin cloth, went outside. Before the audience, the healer sprayed her entire body with a highly alcoholic magic fluid that had been prepared during the ritual. Then she had to sit, naked and shivering, in the cold air for about ten minutes. Finally, she drank about a pint of the fluid. All then returned indoors; the patient lay down in front of the altar, and the healer massaged her vigorously and systematically with the eggs, then with one of his sandals. She then arose, put on her clothes, lay down on the rustic platform bed, and was covered with blankets. By this time she was thoroughly relaxed.

Finally, the healer broke the six eggs used in the massage one by one into a bowl of water. As he watched their swirling whites, he reviewed the history of the patient's eight *espantos*, pointing out the "proofs" in the eggs. The sinking of the eggs to the bottom of the bowl showed that all the previous *espantos* had been cured and that the present symptoms would shortly disappear. The healer "pronounced the cure finished. The patient roused herself briefly on the bed and shouted hoarsely, 'That is right.' Then she sank back into a deep snoring sleep." This ended the ceremony and everyone left except the patient's immediate family.

The patient had a high fever for the following few days. This did not concern the healer, whose position was that everyone died sooner or later anyway, and if the patient died, it was better for her to die with her soul than without it. He refused to see her again, as his work was done. One of the anthropologists treated her with antibiotics, and she made a good recovery from both the fever and the depression. Gillin noted that for the four weeks he was able to observe her "she seemed to have developed a new personality. . . . The hypochondriacal complaints, nagging of her husband and relatives, withdrawal from her social contacts, and anxiety symptoms all disappeared."

This example illustrates certain points about religious healing ceremonies which, if not universal, are at least widely applicable. The theory of illness and healing and the healing method itself are integral parts of a culture's assumptive world. They supply the patient with a conceptual framework for making sense out of chaotic and mysterious feelings, and suggest a plan of action. This helps the person gain a sense of direction and mastery and resolve inner conflicts. As has been said about another magical cure,

> That the mythology of the shaman does not correspond to objective reality does not matter. The patient believes in it and belongs to a society that believes in it. The protecting spirits, the evil spirits, the supernatural monsters and magical monsters are elements of a coherent system which are the basis of the natives' concept of the universe. The patient accepts them, or rather she has never doubted them. What she does not accept are the incomprehensible and arbitrary pains which represent an element foreign to her system but which the shaman, by invoking the myth, will replace in a whole in which everything has its proper place. [Lévi-Strauss 1958, p. 217; translated by E. K. Frank]

The shaman's activities validate the patient's belief in the supernatural. In this example, the healer's manner in the diagnostic interview, especially his revelation to the patient of an undisclosed event that he presumably learned about through magic, established his access to supernatural forces. In other rituals the shaman may start by reciting the circumstances surrounding the "call" or by citing examples of previous cures, to which others present may add confirmation. While the shaman may resort to legerdemain, as in the case of the Kwakiutl, most authorities agree that this is not regarded as trickery, even when the audience knows how it is done. Those present seem to give emotional assent to the proposition that the bloody bit of cotton is the patient's illness and has been extracted from the body, while at another level they know perfectly well that it is only a piece of cotton. Partakers of communion may be in a similar state of mind. To them, the bread and wine are in one sense the body and blood of Christ, while in another they are just bread and wine. In any case, a curing ritual reinforces the image of the healer as a powerful ally in a patient's struggle with the malign forces that have engendered the illness.

In the struggle with the forces of evil, the shaman may risk his or her own soul. Fox (1964) described titanic battles between doctors and evil spirits in Cochiti therapy, during which, according to a doctor, "we are more scared than [the lay participants]. The witches are out to get us" (p. 185). Heightening the emotional intensity of the ritual may increase its therapeutic power by implying that the shaman has sufficient confidence to risk the danger; this not only increases the patient's confidence but also conveys the message that the healer cares enough to risk personal safety on behalf of the sufferer.

A conceptual scheme is validated and reinforced by the rituals it prescribes. In the above example, the healer's examination of the eggs swirling in the water served this purpose as he pointed out to the assembled group the "proofs" of the patient's previous illnesses. Failure of the ritual to cure the patient, moreover, does not shake the underlying world-view. Even had the patient in the example died, the ceremony would have been regarded as successful in restoring her soul. In Western medicine, similarly, physicians' and patients' faith in the power of science may survive any particular instance of failure, as illustrated by the famous quip, "The operation was a success but the patient died."

Rituals often involve a preparatory period, which creates a dramatic break in the usual routine of daily activities. In the above case of *espanto*, preparation for the ritual jolted the patient out of her usual routines, heightened her sense of personal importance by letting her have a "servant," and rallied family and group forces to her aid. In addition, like the rest of the ritual, the preparatory tasks gave the patient a means of actively combating her illness. Such activity in itself powerfully allays anxiety and boosts hopes of cure. The patient's family, as well as respected representatives of the tribe, convey their concern through their participation. Since they represent a healthy group, the patient's associates are not likely to reinforce pathological trends. In the West, by contrast, hospitalization, and particularly placement in a mental hospital, may have the opposite effect, surrounding patients with people who confirm their most despairing or pathological attitudes.

The healing ritual both heightens the patient's sense of self-worth and increases the merit of all participants. The patient is the focus of the group's attention and, by implication, is worthy of the invocation of supernatural forces. Moreover, all participants' activities have a strongly altruistic quality. The group helps the patient by performing parts of the ritual, interceding with the powers that have presumably been offended, and defending the patient to them. Sometimes, as in our example, the patient also performs services for the group such as preparing a feast. Mutual performance of services cements the tie between patient and group. Such activities may also help counteract morbid self-absorption and enhance self-worth by demonstrating that the patient can still be of use to others.

In those ceremonies that involve confession, atonement, and forgiveness, the gaining of merit is especially apparent. The fact that confession is required for cure implies a close link between illness and transgression. Impersonal forms of confession and repentance, as in some Christian liturgies, also serve the purpose of general purification.

Some healing rituals elicit confessions of specific personal transgressions based on a detailed review of the patient's past history, with special emphasis on the events surrounding the onset of illness. These events are expressed or interpreted in terms of the tribe's assumptive world. In addition to evoking confessions, this procedure brings the patient's vague, chaotic, conflicting, and mysterious feelings to the center of attention and places them within a self-consistent conceptual system. Thus they are "realized in an order and on a level which permits them to unfold freely and leads to their resolution" (Lévi-Strauss 1958, p. 219; translated by E. K. Frank).

Naming something is the first step toward controlling it, for "naming a sin is to recall it, to give it form and substance, so that the officiating medicine man can deal with it in the prescribed manner. No vague announcement of sinfulness suffices; each sin that has been committed must be specified. Sometimes when the patient can think of nothing serious done by him he will confess imaginary sins" (Webster 1942, p. 311).

As in the example cited, the shaman's technique in eliciting this type of confession may be another way of demonstrating exceptional powers. That is, the shaman warns the patient that the spirits have already disclosed the true facts and that they cannot be hidden. As the patient confesses, the shaman confirms that this is what was already known and urges the patient to confess further. Often the other participants jog the patient's memory or bring up episodes in which they too transgressed, or even crimes ostensibly unrelated to the patient's illness. In this way the process further cements the group, and participants other than the patient may gain virtue from it. The confession may be followed by intercession with the spirit world on behalf of the patient by the whole group as well as by the healer, heightening the patient's hope that forgiveness will be forthcoming.

Thus, confession may have many implications. It helps the patient make sense of the illness, counteracts the consciousness of sin, brings the person into closer relationship with the group, impresses all participants with the healer's powers, and improves the relationship of all concerned with the spirit world. In these ways it counteracts the patient's anxiety, strengthens self-esteem, and helps resolve conflicts.

Healing ceremonies are highly charged emotional events. As mentioned earlier, a shaman may act out a life-and-death struggle between the shaman's own spirit and the evil spirit that has possessed the patient. The patient may vividly reenact past experiences or act out the struggles of spirit forces. The emotional excitement may be intensified by rhythmic music, chanting, and dancing. The patient often becomes exhausted, especially when the general excitement is enhanced by some strong physical shock. Recall that in our example the patient was sprayed with an alcoholic liquid that gave her a bad chill.

Finally, many rituals have a strong aesthetic appeal that soothes and inspires those involved. The setting may be specially decorated for the occasion; participants may costume themselves elaborately, perform stylized dances, draw sand paintings, and the like. Since these activities have symbolic meanings, they also represent tangible reinforcements of the conceptual organization the ritual endeavors to impose on the patient's inchoate suffering. The participation of the whole group, either actively or as attentive spectators, fosters group solidarity.

In short, shamanistic healing invokes a conceptual framework that promotes harmony among patient, healer, group, and the world of the supernatural. An emotionally stirring group healing ceremony raises patients' expectations of cure, helps them harmonize inner conflicts, and reintegrates them with their group and the spirit world. The total process combats demoralization and strengthens the sufferers' sense of self-worth.

Lourdes and Religious Healing in the Western World

From its inception, Christianity has included belief in the possibility of healing through divine intervention. Starting with the healing miracles of Christ, this form of curing has persisted through the centuries. Today, healing sects like Christian Science and shrines of miraculous healing have millions of devotees. The rituals of these groups and places share many features with religious healing in nonindustrialized societies. Examining these parallels furthers our search for the common elements of all symbolic forms of influence, including psychotherapy. The great modern shrine of Lourdes is a particularly fruitful example to discuss because the cures of severe illness that have occurred there have been exceptionally well described and have received careful critical scrutiny.

The history of Lourdes, starting with the visions of Bernadette Soubirous in 1858, is too well known to require retelling here (Cranston [1955] 1957). In light of subsequent developments, it is curious that the apparition that told Bernadette where to dig for the spring said nothing about its healing powers. Nevertheless, miraculous cures following immersion in the spring were soon reported, and today four to five million pilgrims, of whom tens of thousands are sick, visit Lourdes every year (Marnham 1980).

The world-view supporting Lourdes, like the beliefs underlying tribal religious healing, is an all-inclusive one shared by almost all the pilgrims to the shrine. While cures are regarded as validations of this assumptive system, failures cannot shake it. Those who seek help at Lourdes have usually been sick a long time and have failed to respond to medical remedies. Like the tribespeople who undergo a healing ritual, most are close to despair. Being chronic invalids, they have had to withdraw from most or all of their community activities and have become burdens to their families. Their activities have become routinized and constricted, their lives bleak and monotonous, and they have nothing to anticipate but further suffering and death.

The decision to make the pilgrimage to Lourdes profoundly changes all this. The preparatory period is a dramatic break in routine. Collecting funds for the journey, arranging for medical examinations, and making the travel plans requires the cooperative effort of members of the patient's family and the wider community. Often the patient's church congregation contributes financial aid. Prayers and masses are offered for the invalid. Members of the family, and often the patient's physician or a priest, may join the pilgrimage to Lourdes. Their presence is tangible evidence of the interest of the family and the larger group in the patient's welfare. Pilgrims from many communities may travel together. As they near the shrine, religious ceremonies occur while the train is en route and at every stop. In short, the preparatory period is emotionally stirring, brings the patient from the periphery of a group to its center, and enhances the expectation of help. In this connection it is interesting that, except in the case of the original cures, Lourdes has failed to heal those who live in its vicinity. The emotional excitement connected with the preparatory period and journey to the shrine may be essential for healing to occur.

When sufferers arrive at Lourdes after an exhausting, even life-endangering journey, their expectation of help receives further support.

According to Cranston, patients are plunged into "a city of pilgrims, and they are everywhere; people who have come from the four corners of the earth with but one purpose: prayer, and healing for themselves or for their loved ones. . . . One is surrounded by them, and steeped in their atmosphere every moment of existence in Lourdes" ([1955] 1957, p. 31). Everyone hopes to witness or experience a miraculous cure. Accounts of previous cures are on every tongue, and the pilgrim sees the votive offerings and the piles of discarded crutches of those who have been healed. Thus, the ritual begins with a validation of the shrine's power that is analogous to the shaman's review of previous cures in tribal healing rites.

The pilgrims' days are filled with religious services and trips to the Grotto, where they are immersed in the ice-cold spring. Every afternoon all the pilgrims and invalids present at Lourdes — usually forty or fifty thousand — gather at the Esplanade in front of the shrine for the procession that climaxes each day's activities. The bedridden are placed nearest the shrine, those who can sit up are behind them, the ambulatory invalids behind them, while the hordes of visitors fill the rest of the space. An eyewitness account well conveys the enormous emotional and aesthetic impact of the procession:

> At four the bells begin to peal — the Procession begins to form. The priests in their varied robes assemble at the Grotto. . . . The Bishop appears with the monstrance under the sacred canopy. The loud-speakers open up. A great hymn rolls out, the huge crowd joining in unison, magnificently. The Procession begins its long, impressive way down one side and up the other of the sunny Esplanade. First the Children of Mary, young girls in blue capes, white veils . . . then forty or fifty priests in black cassocks . . . other priests in white surplices . . . then come the Bishops in purple . . . and finally the officiating Archbishop in his white and gold robes under the golden canopy. Bringing up the rear large numbers of men and women of the different pilgrimages, Sisters, Nurses, members of various religious organizations; last of all the doctors. . . . Hymns, prayers, fervent, unceasing. In the Square the sick line up in two rows. . . . Every few feet, in front of them, kneeling priests with arms outstretched praying earnestly, leading the responses. Nurses and orderlies on their knees, praying too. . . . Ardor mounts as the Blessed Sacrament approaches. Prayers gather intensity. . . . The Bishop leaves the shelter of the canopy, carrying the monstrance. The Sacred Host is raised above each sick one. The great crowd falls to its knees. All arms are outstretched in one vast cry to Heaven. As far as one can see in any direction, people are on their knees, praying. [Cranston (1955) 1957, pp. 36–37]

The results of this tremendous outpouring of emotion and faith are mixed. While the great majority of the sick do not experience a cure, most of the pilgrims seem to benefit psychologically from the experience. Like participation in healing rituals in nonindustrialized societies, the pilgrimage is regarded as conferring merit in itself, and the whole atmosphere of Lourdes is spiritually uplifting. The altruism of all involved is especially worthy of note. Physicians, *brancardiers* (stretcher-bearers), and helpers of all sorts give their time and efforts freely, and throughout the ceremonies the emphasis is on self-forgetfulness and devotion to the welfare of others. The pilgrims pray for the sick, and the sick pray for each other, not themselves. The words attributed to an old pilgrim may well be true: "Of the uncured none despair. All go away filled with hope and a new feeling of strength. The trip to Lourdes is never made in vain" (Cranston [1955] 1957, p. 127).

The evidence that an occasional cure of advanced organic disease does occur at Lourdes is as strong as that for any other phenomenon accepted as true. The reported frequency of such cures varies widely, depending on the criteria used. The piles of crutches attest that many sufferers achieve improved functioning, at least temporarily. In many of these cases, however, the improvement probably reflects heightened morale, enabling a person to function better in the face of an unchanged organic handicap. Fully documented cures of unquestionable and gross organic disease are extremely infrequent — probably no more frequent than similar ones occurring in secular settings.

In the century of the shrine's existence, fewer than a hundred cures have passed the stringent tests required for the Church to declare them miraculous. This figure may greatly underestimate the number of cures, as many convincing cases lack the extensive documentary support needed to qualify for official recognition. Nevertheless, even several thousand persons cured of organic diseases would represent only a minuscule fraction of those who have made the pilgrimage. As a sympathetic student of spiritual healing wrote, "There is probably no stream in Britain which could not boast of as high a proportion of cures as the stream at Lourdes if patients came in the same numbers and in the same psychological state of expectant excitement" (Weatherhead 1951, p. 153).

Although they are remarkably strengthened and accelerated, the processes by which cures occur at Lourdes do not seem to differ in kind from those involved in normal healing. Careful reading of the reports reveals that healing occurs over time, not instantaneously, as is often claimed (West 1957). It is true that the consciousness of cure is often (not always) sudden and may be accompanied by immediate improvement in function — those who are paralyzed walk, those who are blind see, and those who have been unable to retain food suddenly regain their appetites. However, as in ordinary healing, actual tissue repair takes hours, days, or weeks, and persons who have lost weight require the usual period of time to regain it. Moreover, gaps of specialized tissues such as skin are not miraculously restored, but are filled by scars. No one has regrown an amputated limb at Lourdes.

Cures at Lourdes involve the person's total personality, not merely the body. The healed, whatever they were like before their recovery, are said to be possessed of a remarkable serenity and a desire to be of service to others.

Rivers of ink have been spilled in controversy over whether or not the cures at Lourdes are genuine. Much of this debate reflects the erroneous assumption that acceptance or rejection of such phenomena requires belief or disbelief in miracles or in the Catholic faith. Actually, many devout Catholics reject modern miracles, and many contemporary skeptics acknowledge some Lourdes cures as genuine. The world is full of phenomena that cannot be explained by present cosmologies.

Inexplicable cures of serious organic disease occur in everyday medical practice. Every physician has either personally treated or heard about patients who mysteriously recovered from a seemingly fatal illness. Two surgeons assembled from the literature 176 cases of unquestionable cancer that regressed without adequate treatment (Everson and Cole 1966). While regression does not necessarily imply cure, about half the patients studied were well two years or more after their cancer was diagnosed, and about one-eighth were followed for ten years or more without recurrence. Unfortunately, the authors did not mention the possible role of psychological factors. Had these remissions occurred after a visit to Lourdes, they would have been regarded by many as miraculous.

Since no physician sees enough of these remissions to acquire a sufficient sample for scientific study, and since the remissions cannot be explained by current medical theories, the fascinating questions they raise have been neglected. Depending on one's theoretical predilections, one may believe in the miraculousness of all, none, or only a certain class of recoveries from diagnosed fatal illness. The mere occurrence of such recoveries leaves the question of their cause completely open.

Our review of healing in nonindustrialized societies suggests that these cases and the cures at Lourdes may be related to the sufferers' emotional state. The conditions under which cures occur at Lourdes and the types of people who seem most apt to experience them support this view. Although cures may occur en route to Lourdes, on the return journey, or even months later, most occur at the shrine and at the moments of greatest emotional intensity and spiritual fervor — while taking communion, during immersion in the spring, or when the host is raised over the sick at the passing of the sacrament during the procession. Though persons who have been cured include the deserving and the sinful, believers and apparent skeptics, they tend to have one common characteristic: they are "almost invariably simple people — the poor and the humble; people who do not interpose a strong intellect between themselves and the Higher Power" (Cranston [1955] 1957, p. 125). That is, pilgrims who are healed are not detached or critical. It is generally agreed that persons who remain entirely unmoved by the ceremonies do not experience cures.

The skeptics who are healed, moreover, typically have a devout parent or spouse. This suggests that their skepticism was a reaction-formation against an underlying desire to believe, or at least that the pilgrimage involved emotional conflict. In this connection, all cured skeptics have become ardent believers.

A point of considerable theoretical interest is that the emotions aroused by Lourdes, or by the healing rituals described earlier, may be unpleasant as well as intense. The sufferings of a debilitated invalid in a prolonged healing ritual or on the long trip to Lourdes are often severe, yet their effect is usually beneficial. This supports the claim that the effects of strong emotions depend on their meaning or context — that is, on how the person interprets them (see Chapter 3). Intense emotional arousal occurring in a setting of hopelessness and progressive isolation from usual sources of support may contribute to a patient's death, as in the example of "acute exhaustive psychosis" mentioned above (pp. 92–93). The same arousal experienced in a setting of massive human and supernatural encouragement — that is, in a context of hope — can be healing.

Studies of the faith-healing ceremonies of fundamentalist cults in the United States reinforce this conclusion. A typical faith-healing session occurs at the end of a regular church service. The healer begins with an impassioned recounting of biblical examples, then describes how he or she was healed by prayer and faith. Members of the congregation may chime in with similar testimonials. The healer then asks anyone with a problem to approach the altar. While the healer anoints and prays over each sufferer, elders of the congregation may lay healing hands on the suppliant and join in praying aloud for the person's recovery. The expectant, emotionally charged atmosphere is enhanced by loud prayers from members of the congregation. Healer and members of the congregation may speak in tongues, believed by the sect to signify possession by a supernatural power (Ness and Wintrob 1981).

In the following two studies of faith-healing ceremonies, we must stress that the primary data were reports of persons who claimed to have been healed. Such reports are subject to distortion because interviewees were motivated to convince the examiners of the validity of their faith by reporting a cure.

Viewed with appropriate caution, the findings of the two studies are nevertheless of interest. One, based on interviews with almost 200 persons (half members of charismatic groups like the one just described and half members of groups primarily using meditation), showed that the attenders at healing ceremonies reported significantly higher levels of physical and general well-being when compared with a matched group of patients in primary medical care (Glik 1986).

The other study described 71 healings reported by forty-three members of charismatic fundamentalist sects (Pattison, Lapins, and Doerr 1973). The researchers found that 62 of the recoveries occurred in the course of a healing ceremony, about half of them suddenly. Fifty involved moderately severe or life-threatening illness. Although the great majority of subjects reported no residual symptoms, the sense of being healed was related to participation in the healing ceremony, not to a perceived change in symptomatology. Consistent with the findings of the Lourdes study, these authors conclude that the primary function of faith healing is less to reduce symptomatology than to provide ego integration for the individual and social integration for the subculture by reconfirming the subculture's belief system.

In short, faith-healing ceremonies in both industrialized and nonindustrialized societies involve a climactic union of the patient, the family, the larger group, and the supernatural world by means of a dramatic, emotionally charged, aesthetically rich ritual that expresses and reinforces a shared ideology. Similar forces may also contribute to the healing that occurs in more typical medical settings. Let us imagine how a modern university hospital might look to anthropologists from Mars studying healing shrines in an industrialized society. They would learn that the local medical school is reputed to be a site of amazing cures, and they would eventually ferret out the chaplain's office and the chapel, tangible vestiges of a belief system still widely held but clearly secondary to a faith in Science. They would be impressed with the massive buildings through which pilgrims seeking health were continually streaming. Inside these buildings they would find a complex structure in which certain areas were open to the public and other areas — laboratories, operating rooms, radiotherapy suites, and intensive-care units — were reserved exclusively for the performance of arcane healing rituals by members of the staff. These special-purpose rooms contain spectacular machines that beep and gurgle and flash or emit immensely powerful but invisible rays, impressively evoking the healing power of Science. Those who tend and control these machines speak a special language that is unintelligible to the layperson and prominently display on their person healing amulets and charms, such as reflex hammers, stethoscopes, and ophthalmoscopes. All are expected to dedicate themselves to the service of the shrine, regardless of personal hardship or interference with other satisfactions of life. The operating rooms are the holy of holies where the most dramatic and difficult healing rituals are conducted. Even the priests can enter only after donning special costumes and undergoing purification rites known as scrubbing. So jealously guarded are the mysteries of the operating room that patients are rendered unconscious before they are allowed to enter them.

In evaluating the reports of the cures that occur in such a shrine, anthropologists might be as impressed with the features that mobilize the patient's expectant faith as with the staff's rationale for the treatments administered. The patient suffering from a threatening symptom approaches the hospital with a mixture of apprehension and hope that generates a special susceptibility to psychological influences. After performing a careful evaluation, which involves eliciting the patient's experience (the history) and using various kinds of touch (the physical exam), the physician provides an explanation of the illness and the procedures the patient is to undergo, both of which are based on a belief system that patient and physician share. Such explanations replace confusion and helplessness with clarity and hope. Family and friends convey their interest and support through visits and letters. The patient enjoys the attention of healers of high status within his or her own culture who for the time being are dedicated to the patient's welfare. In extreme cases — for example, open heart surgery — the climax of treatment is an expensive and impressive operation in which the surgeon stops the patient's heart, repairs it, and starts it again. The surgeon literally kills and then resurrects the patient. Few faith healers can make an equal demonstration of their healing power.

Other Forms of Nonmedical Healing

Lourdes is only one example of nonmedical healing in the West. An adequate survey of this phenomenon would have to include other religious healing institutions such as Christian Science, various secular therapies, and individual practitioners with idiosyncratic theories. Inglis (1965) classified nonmedical healing into three categories, progressively more distant from scientific medicine: those emphasizing the body, such

as herbalism, homeopathy, chiropractic, and osteopathy; those emphasizing the mind, such as psychotherapy, hypnotherapy, and autosugges-
tion; and those stressing the spirit, such as Christian Science and spiritual healing. Secular practitioners of unorthodox medicine in America
(Gevitz 1988) probably treat many more persons than do physicians.

Secular and religious healing sects are astonishingly popular. An old
survey (Reed 1932) documented the existence of some 36,000 sectarian
practitioners, excluding esoteric and local cults, which equaled almost
one-fourth of the total number of medical practitioners at that time.
Patients paid at least $125,000,000 annually for their services. One phy-
sician found that 43 percent of his private patients and 26 percent of his
clinic patients had patronized a cult during the three months preceding
their visits to him. There is no reason to believe that the popularity of
either religious or secular nonmedical healing has diminished over the
intervening decades. In fact, it may well have increased, as suggested
both by the popularity of small religious healing cults and the fabulous
profits of stores selling hosts of completely unsubstantiated remedies for
ailments of every kind (Deutsch 1977).

All alternative forms of healing share the ability to arouse patients'
expectations of help, a quality highly relevant to psychotherapy. Patients' anticipation of cure derives from at least two discernible sources.
The first is the personal magnetism of the healer, including the healer's
faith in his or her power. After interviewing many such healers, one
investigator wrote: "The vast majority of the sectarians sincerely believe
in the efficacy of their practices. . . . the writer has talked to [chiroprac-
tors] whose faith was . . . nothing short of evangelistic, whose sincerity
could no more be questioned than that of Persia's 'whirling dervishes'"
(Reed 1932, pp. 109–10). Peddlers of obviously worthless nostrums and
gadgets may be equally successful, however, which indicates that a healer
need not necessarily believe in the efficacy of a particular method to be
able to convince others of its power.

Another source of patients' faith is the ideology of the healer or sect.
Such rationales, however absurd to others, help sufferers make sense of
their illnesses and treatment procedures, and define the healer as a trans-
mitter or controller of impressive healing forces. In this respect the
fringe healer, like the orthodox physician, is analogous to the shaman.
Unorthodox healers frequently claim they have discovered new and potent scientific principles of healing and back up their pretensions with an
elaborate scientific-sounding patter, often adding an imposing array of
equipment complete with dials, flashing lights, and sound effects.

The apparent success of healing methods based on different or incompatible ideologies and methods compels the conclusion that the healing

power of faith resides in the patient's state of mind, not in the validity of a particular theoretical scheme or technique. At the risk of laboring this point, we cite an experiment testing the role of faith in the treatment of three severely ill, bed-ridden women (Rehder 1955). One had chronic inflammation of the gallbladder with stones, the second had failed to recuperate from a major abdominal operation and was practically a skeleton, and the third was dying of widespread cancer. The physician first permitted a prominent local faith healer to try to cure them in absentia without the patients' knowledge. Nothing happened. Then he told the patients about the faith healer, built up their expectations over several days, and finally assured them that the healer would be treating them from a distance at a certain time the next day. In fact, the physician chose an hour at which he was sure the healer would *not* be working. At the suggested time, all three patients improved quickly and dramatically. The second was permanently cured. The other two were not, but showed striking temporary responses. The cancer patient, who was severely anemic and whose tissues had become waterlogged, promptly excreted all the accumulated fluid, recovered from her anemia, and regained sufficient strength to go home and resume her household duties. She remained virtually symptom free until her death. The gallbladder patient lost her symptoms, went home, and had no recurrence for several years. The benefit these three patients derived from their false belief that the healer was treating them from a distance is strong evidence that "expectant trust" (Weatherhead 1951, p. 26) can be a powerful healing force in itself.

We cannot conclude this review of nonmedical healing without mentioning the possibility that some individuals, like Quesalid, may have a gift of healing that defies scientific explanation. Such a gift resembles the charisma of certain political leaders. Nor can we rule out the possibility, for which the evidence is quite persuasive, that some healers serve as a kind of conduit for a healing power in the universe. This power, often called the life force, must be called supernatural for want of a better term (Oursler 1957). That is, curative forces may exist that cannot be conceptually incorporated into the secular cosmology that dominates Western scientific thinking. Many will reject the notion out-of-hand on this account. Others are ever mindful of Hamlet's admonition to Horatio and prefer to keep an open mind.

Summary

This review of religiomagical and nonmedical healing highlights the profound influence of emotions on health. Anxiety and despair can be lethal; confidence and hope, life-giving. The dominant assumptive world of Western society, which rejects nonmaterial causation, has great difficulty incorporating the curative influence of mind on body and therefore tends to underestimate its importance.

The healing techniques reviewed in this chapter all share the ability to arouse the patient's hope, bolster self-esteem, stir emotion, and strengthen the patient's ties with a supportive group. All involve a healer on whom the patient depends for help and who holds out the hope of relief. The patient's expectations of cure are raised by the healer's personal attributes, by his or her culturally determined healing role, or, typically, by both. The role of the healer may be distinct or diffused, as at Lourdes, where it resides in participating priests.

All forms of healing are based on a conceptual scheme consistent with the patient's assumptive world. The scheme prescribes a set of activities and helps sufferers make sense out of inchoate feelings, thereby heightening their sense of mastery. Most participants believe that religiomagical healing rituals mobilize supernatural healing forces on the patient's behalf. Often these rites require patients to make detailed confessions and are followed by atonement and reacceptance into the group. Many rituals also stress mutual service, which counteracts the patient's morbid self-preoccupation, strengthens self-esteem by demonstrating that the patient can do something for others, and, like confession, cements the bonds between patient and group. Confession and mutual service contribute to the feeling that the performance of the healing ritual confers merit in itself. If the patient is not cured, he or she often feels more virtuous. If the patient is cured, this may be taken as a mark of divine favor, permanently enhancing his or her personal and social value. Such enhanced status may also help maintain the cure, for relapse implies that the patient is letting the group down. Finally, in religious healing, relief of suffering is accompanied not only by a profound change in the patient's feelings about self and others but also by a strengthening of previous assumptive systems or, sometimes, conversion to new ones.

SIX

Mind and Body
in Psychotherapy

They roused him with muffins — they roused him with ice —
They roused him with mustard and cress —
They roused him with jam and judicious advice —
They set him conundrums to guess.
— Lewis Carroll, *The Hunting of the Snark*

The bodily healing that may occur at religious shrines or during a tribal ceremonial challenges the belief — fundamental to much of Western medicine — that mind and body are independent, largely unrelated entities. By contrast, the holistic or cybernetic model of mind-body interaction regards the individual as a psychobiological unit that is integrated with the physical and social environment. A perturbation in any part of the system shakes the whole. Illness is a disturbance of the whole person in which pathogenic forces are greater than regenerative ones, and healing is the restoration of a healthy equilibrium, either spontaneously or through outside intervention (Gordon 1980). Thus the holistic view encompasses both the principles of scientific medicine and the healing phenomena discussed in previous chapters.

In holistic thinking, interdependent physical and psychological processes interact in complex ways. Physical processes may influence psychological ones directly, through their effects on the brain, or indirectly, by virtue of their meaning to the patient. The model encompasses psychotherapy, in the sense that equilibrium may be restored not only by such physical treatments as drugs or surgery but also by symbolic manipulations or social interventions that mobilize natural healing forces within the patient. This broad conception of health and illness encourages us to look closely at the influence of bodily states on mental life and at the role of psychotherapy as a form of medical treatment.

In this chapter we shall look first at the direct and symbolic effects of physical influences on mental life — notably, drugs and injuries. Following this, we shall turn to a consideration of the pathogenic psychological factors in chronic disease, including the influence of stressful life experiences, personal characteristics, and family attitudes. We shall then shift our focus to some healing mental states apparently linked to personality traits and to symbolic interventions that may enhance them. These interventions range from simple education to psychotherapy, including psychotherapies that involve bodily manipulation.

Drugs and Psychotherapy

The cognitive and behavioral changes induced by psychotropic substances illuminate the effects of physical processes on mental life. Chemicals ranging from prescribed medications to self-administered drugs can induce all sorts of psychopathological states in human beings. Lactate in vulnerable individuals induces panic attacks (Liebowitz et al. 1984), amphetamines produce paranoid psychoses indistinguishable from schizophrenia (Snyder 1974), reserpine can cause depression severe enough to require hospitalization (Lipton, DiMascio, and Killam 1978), and so forth. Conversely, drugs can substantially relieve many abnormal states, including panic attacks, depression, and mania.

The psychopharmacological revolution has profoundly influenced psychotherapy. As noted in Chapter 1, in conditions such as schizophrenia and mania, the availability of effective drugs has relegated psychotherapy to the status of adjunctive treatment. In other areas, such as the treatment of depression or panic, the relative roles of drugs and psychotherapy are still being determined.

Of greatest interest to us in our efforts to understand the basic elements of psychotherapy are the ways in which psychotherapy and medication may function together. These interactions may be either symbolic or directly related to the drugs' physical effects on the brain. Klerman (1972) reviewed the possible models for characterizing the interaction of medication and psychotherapy in the treatment of depression. These models include the possibility that drug treatment undermines psychotherapy by relieving the symptoms that motivate a patient to "work," that psychotherapy and drugs make independent contributions to healing, or that they enhance each other. Klerman's informed best judgment is that medication enhances psychotherapy mainly by facilitating the nonspecific aspects of treatment. Thus, drugs "contribute to the optimism of both therapist and patient by demonstrating that symptom control is feasible and reducing fear of relapse" (p. 89).

Patients may also attach negative meanings to medication. In particular, the administration of drugs may convince patients that their symptoms are beyond voluntary control. Such an interpretation may stimulate feelings of helplessness and produce overdependence on the drug and the prescribing physician. *Sybil* (Schreiber 1973), the best-selling description of the psychotherapy of a multiple personality, illustrates the problem well. In this account, the psychiatrist initially uses pentothal to facilitate the emergence of her patient's separate selves, but finds that this technique makes Sybil unhealthily dependent. Concerned about possible chemical dependency, the doctor substitutes hypnosis for medication. By teaching Sybil that she can exert some personal control over her symptoms, this step helps her feel strong enough to begin to work toward gradual resolution of her traumatic memories.

The treatment of patients with chronic pain provides another, more general example of some of the antitherapeutic effects of giving medication for subjective distress. Patients with chronic pain frequently become both physically and psychologically dependent on narcotics, drugs that often become progressively less effective over time in providing relief. Treating this difficult problem involves both persuading patients (and their significant others) to focus attention away from the pain and restoring sufferers' sense of being in control of themselves through techniques such as self-hypnosis (Spiegel and Spiegel 1978). When successful, this approach may end drug dependence and enhance patients' interpersonal functioning and psychological well-being, even if the disease causing the pain is unimproved.

Of course, withholding medication from patients who need it may be as demoralizing as giving medication to those who do not. The decision to conduct psychotherapy rather than to prescribe medication implies to patients that they should be able to master their symptoms voluntarily. Under these circumstances, when patients with such intractable conditions as chronic psychosis or severe depression fail to improve, they may experience feelings of self-blame and failure that can aggravate the original complaint.

Beyond the medication-responsiveness of particular illnesses and the general implications of choosing drugs or psychotherapy, patients' personality traits may influence the meanings they attach to medication (see Chapter 8). In consequence, therapists must consider the symbolic as well as the pharmacological effects of drugs when prescribing them.

Certain drugs have specific effects that may enhance patients' progress in psychotherapy. Antidepressants, in particular, seem to correct abnormalities in the neurotransmitter systems for coping with stress, thereby rendering patients more amenable to psychotherapeutic influence. The mechanisms by which these drugs enhance psychotherapy include their effects on attention and concentration, access to memory, and promoting an adequate but not overwhelming level of emotional arousal.

Drug treatment may improve the poor concentration that typically accompanies severe depression, making it possible for patients to absorb therapists' words or instructions. Moreover, the ability to focus attention at will may enhance people's sense of control over their thoughts or experience, a powerfully therapeutic effect in itself.

The effects of antidepressants on memory are less well established. Sternberg and Jarvik (1976) found that these drugs impair short-term memory in normal subjects but enhance it in depressed ones. While their laboratory studies revealed no drug effects on long-term memory, meaningful personal memories may differ from memories measurable by standardized tests. Thus, van der Kolk (1983) reported that after taking the antidepressant phenelzine, some patients with posttraumatic stress disorder unexpectedly experienced floods of previously inaccessible memories.

Similarly, Beck (1976) noted that therapeutic exploration of a person's life history is counterproductive in severe depression, because such patients can recall only the feelings and events that confirm the depressive world-view. After medication (or cognitive intervention) relieves the depressive symptoms, patients may be capable of more productive self-exploration, either because they have a broader spectrum of memories available to them or because their interpretations of what they do remember are more balanced. In his personal memoir *A Season in Hell*, for example, Percy Knauth (1975) described the experience of protracted depression. Although he credited his symptomatic improvement entirely to medication, he felt fully healed only after recapturing memories of the loving aspect of a past relationship that had seemed futile and bitter when recalled during his illness.

The treatment of posttraumatic stress disorder highlights the beneficial effects of drugs on emotional arousal. Severely traumatized patients may repress all conscious memory of their experience, and become panicky when made to recall it (Kolb 1987). This unpleasant hyperarousal causes them to struggle ever harder to avoid thinking of the traumatic event. Several studies have suggested that antidepressants may make patients more amenable to psychotherapy by moderating their level of arousal. Heightening arousal may facilitate learning in patients who are lethargic or relatively unresponsive to their environment (Weingartner et al. 1981). Conversely, drugs that moderate arousal may make it possible for traumatized patients to allow their memories to come to conscious awareness (Davidson, Kudler, and Smith 1990), a necessary prelude to examining and perhaps changing attitudes shaped by the traumatic experience (Friedman 1988).

Cultural hostility toward certain drugs limits their use in psychotherapy. Antidepressants and anxiolytics, drugs that normalize dysfunction, are becoming acceptable, but little attention has been paid to the potentially beneficial use of substances that induce abnormal states of consciousness. For example, the hallucinogen LSD in small to moderate doses seems to enhance sensory experience and bring vivid memories to awareness (Grof 1975). These functions might be useful to heighten the emotional arousal necessary for attitudinal change or to make forgotten experiences more available for therapeutic influence. However, after a few experiments in which LSD was used to give pleasure and rekindle hope in despairing alcoholics (Kurland et al. 1971), this line of investigation was abandoned (Bliss 1988). Widespread prejudice against "psychotropic hedonism" (Klerman 1972) may be as much to blame as concern over the unreliability of the drug's effects.

In sum, the effects of medication are but one proof that neurophysiological processes are deeply implicated in mental life. In addition to their symbolic meanings, drugs may facilitate or initiate healing processes in the brain that manifest themselves in patients' feelings, cognition, and behavior, processes that in turn may be influenced by psychotherapy.

Psychological Effects of Bodily Injuries

The direct effects of drugs upon mental life often overshadow their indirect or symbolic ones. Examination of the psychological sequelae of injuries throws the powerful symbolic aspects of bodily changes into sharper relief.

The human body is fraught with meanings. Indeed, our subjective sense of our bodies is a symbolic one that evolves during childhood and corresponds only loosely to the body's actual organization. Because of the symbolism attached to the body and its functions, actual tissue damage is only one of many factors that may influence patients' responses to mutilation or injury. Others include the nature of the injuring agent, the situational context, the kind of disfigurement, and the culturally and personally determined meanings of the body part involved.

An accidental injury, for example, will have quite a different meaning from one deliberately inflicted during torture. Similarly, various investigators have described differences in the quality and degree of pain caused by battle wounds, which signify escape from danger; pain from surgery for illness, which signifies the presence of danger (Beecher 1956); and experimental pain, which is unrelated to danger (see Chapter 7). Some injuries may be experienced as benevolent — for example, those from surgical procedures to promote health, relieve pain, or enhance appearance.

The context of an injury influences not only the pain patients experience but also their distress over any resulting disfigurement. Hair loss or scars that follow treatments for cancer, a profoundly threatening illness, may be as disturbing to patients as their primary disease. On the other hand, mutilating initiation rites or self-injury to attain spiritual benefits may produce scars of high personal and social value.

Mutilation in the service of personal or cultural goals compellingly illustrates the power of body symbolism. The process begins with an emotional state that either instigates self-mutilation or assents to mutilation by others (Favazza 1987). Psychological changes follow the bodily ones. Such changes range from simple relief of tension, as in many wrist-cutters, to complex alterations in self-image and role identification. Persons who mutilate themselves while in delusional states may seek idiosyncratic, symbolic ends, as when patients castrate themselves or enucleate their eyes to assuage guilt over sexual thoughts or impulses. Less dramatic examples include mutilation to enhance appearance, such as mammoplasty in the West or lip-stretching among the Ubangi. Sex-change operations are a drastic form of mutilation that influences role identification. A more commonplace example is circumcision, which changes a person from an outsider to an initiate of a closely knit ethnic or religious group.

Psychological Implications of Chronic Illness

The meanings we attach to our body and its functions are also evident in people's responses to illness. Chronic illnesses, in particular, may have profoundly negative meanings, which in turn exacerbate the physical manifestations of disease. As we have said, the state of demoralization is one of confusion and perceived loss of control over environmental contingencies, and is associated with feelings of helplessness, hopelessness, and lowered self-esteem. By their very nature, chronic diseases are demoralizing. Such illnesses cause patients to reduce or abandon normal social and economic roles, depriving them of their usual spheres of satisfaction and competence. When patients and their families organize daily life around the illness and its treatment, they may lose social contacts important to sustaining morale. Faced with uncertainty about how the disease will progress, the patient may feel hopeless about ever feeling or functioning well. Such demoralization is intensified if significant others defend against their own anxiety and distress by withdrawing emotional or material support.

An "experiment of nature" during World War II vividly illustrates the contribution of demoralization to disability and suffering in chronic disease (Frank 1946). The subjects were soldiers who continued to complain of symptoms after several months of hospitalization for schistosomiasis. Out of fifty men, only two felt well and forty-three reported being anxious, resentful, or confused. The soldiers were well fed and well housed, and they did not feel very sick. Though all eventually recovered, interviews suggested that their destructive mental state may have prolonged their distress. Three sources of demoralization emerged:

1. *Perceived threat to survival.* Thirty-two expected to die or be chronic invalids; only two were convinced that they were cured.

2. *Ambiguity.* While the physicians were trying to reassure the patients that their illness was not serious, the radio on the ward, controlled by the army's Information and Education section, was describing schistosomiasis in the most alarming terms to discourage swimming in infected streams. As one patient said, "Either the doctors or the radio are screwed up about something. I suppose the doctors are right, but then I suppose the doctors write the radio programs."

3. *A feeling that nobody in charge was concerned about their welfare.* The patients were subject to inconsistent disposition policies. One group might be evacuated to the United States and the next sent back to active duty. The physicians, too, were uncertain about the course of the disease. A vicious circle developed — patients' fears increased their symptoms, making the doctors more confused and discouraged. Feeling frustrated, the doctors tended to become impatient and avoidant, and the patients' alienation increased. As one man said, "I tell them something and they pass it off as though it didn't exist. I feel I might as well be talking to myself."

The literature on renal failure further illustrates the demoralizing effects of serious illness and the interaction between demoralization and the progression or slowing of disease. As the kidneys fail, various toxic substances usually excreted in the urine accumulate in the body. These toxins cause a host of physical complications, such as anemia, bleeding, and poor healing. Renal patients generally feel fatigued and unwell, leading them to curtail usual activities. The management of the illness requires severe dietary restrictions and changes in lifestyle. Eventually, the toxic products must be cleansed from the blood by dialysis, which may require the patient to lie attached to a machine for several hours several times a week.

Given the demoralizing impact of these conditions, it is not surprising that renal patients display high rates of depression (Levy 1981). Suicide, the manifestation of extreme hopelessness and isolation, occurs in almost 5 percent of dialysis patients. On the other hand, complications decrease and survival is prolonged in patients who learn to dialyze themselves at home (Abram, Moore, and Westervelt 1971). Presumably, mastering the technique of dialysis requires that patients learn more about the nature of their illness, which in turn combats confusion and feelings of loss of control. Furthermore, the patient who dialyzes at home can minimize the disruption of usual activities. He or she becomes an active collaborator in treatment rather than a passive and ignorant recipient of uncomfortable procedures performed by others. While home dialysis has physical advantages such as increased frequency of treatment and decreased exposure to hospital-based infections, its effect upon the patients' morale may contribute substantially to its beneficial impact on the course of the illness.

The current epidemic of acquired immune-deficiency syndrome (AIDS) provides the most dramatic example of the demoralizing effect of chronic disease. As is well known, AIDS preferentially afflicts homosexual men and intravenous drug abusers, two groups already vulnerable to social alienation. Public fear of contagion is extreme, and victims of the disease, even in the asymptomatic carrier state, are liable to loss of employment, housing, and insurance, along with extrusion by their families and friends.

Though research into the effects of noxious psychosocial conditions upon the physical manifestations of AIDS is not yet available, certain observations suggest that these effects are likely to be significant. Many patients who are infected with the causal virus develop a syndrome of fatigue, sweats, and swollen glands called the "AIDS-related complex," or ARC, but do not have the full-blown disease. Such patients are often deeply anxious and self-scrutinizing about their health. They appear in offices and clinics with all manner of symptoms that cannot be linked to a particular cause. Similar anxiety and protean physical complaints can be found in asymptomatic carriers of the virus and even in uninfected members of high-risk groups who suffer only from fear of AIDS. The striking presence of ARC-type symptoms among these "worried well" suggests that psychosocial factors undermining morale may exacerbate the manifestations of the disease.

Conversely, the preliminary findings of an ongoing study of long-surviving AIDS patients indicate that such persons have marked psychological resilience and coping skills (Solomon et al. 1987), including a capacity to find meaning in their experience and the ability to maintain a hopeful outlook. These findings support the likelihood that the psychological state of patients with AIDS may significantly influence the course, if not the final outcome, of the disease.

So far we have described some of the direct and symbolic effects of physical processes on mental life. An examination of the role of psychological factors in exacerbating or ameliorating bodily illness completes our exploration of the mind-body loop.

Stressful Life Experiences, Temperament, and Family Environment in Physical Illness

Epidemiological and clinical studies have explored the pathogenic effects of adverse psychological states. These states include the consequences of life events, temperamental qualities associated with vulnerability to particular illnesses, and qualities of the family environment that may contribute to illness in certain members.

With respect to life events, epidemiologists have found higher rates of illness and death in recently bereaved persons than in matched controls (Parkes, Benjamin, and Fitgerald 1969), in clinical psychiatric illnesses of many kinds (Tsuang, Woolson, and Fleming 1980), and in people reporting high rates of recent stressful life changes. One research group went so far as to conclude that "the linkage of mental factors to mortality [is] of an order of magnitude sufficient to warrant consideration of these factors as leading causes of death" (Markush et al. 1977).

Taken together, these studies strongly support our thesis that symbolic processes can have a major impact on physical condition. As noted in Chapter 2, it is not life events alone but the negative meanings patients attach to them which seem pathogenic. In a study of 100 Chinese immigrants, for example, researchers found that events considered benign by some observers were associated with illness when subjects perceived them as stressful. Conversely, when such apparently overwhelming stresses as poverty, bereavement, or alcoholic spouses were not associated with illness, subjects did not report them as stressful (Hinkle et al.

1957). One possible interpretation of this finding is that the relationship between perceived stress and illness is an artifact; that is, that informants remember events as stressful because they were temporally associated with illness. More recent studies of life events and physical illness (Miller 1988), however, tend to confirm that stress increases vulnerability to illness more than illness influences persons' perceptions of events.

Clinical reports spanning thirty years confirm epidemiological evidence that life experiences, particularly demoralizing ones, may profoundly affect the course of chronic illness.

In an early study, Imboden et al. (1959) compared eight patients who had recovered from brucellosis within two or three months of infection with sixteen who still complained of fatigue, headache, nervousness, and vague aches and pains after one year. The two groups were no different in medical findings at onset or time of reexamination. Life history and personality, however, differed significantly between the sixteen who were still ill and the eight who had recovered. More of the persistently symptomatic subjects reported psychologically traumatic events in early life (69 percent versus 25 percent) or a seriously disturbed life situation within one year before or after the acute infection (69 percent versus 25 percent). The symptomatic group also scored significantly higher on an index of morale loss derived from a standard personality test.

Since this was a retrospective study, the experience of chronic illness might explain the low morale of the symptomatic group. A few years later, knowledge of an approaching influenza epidemic made possible a prospective study to test this interpretation. The morale-loss scale was administered to the personnel of a military installation before the epidemic struck. Of the 600 persons who took the test, 26 contracted influenza. Of these, 14 recovered in an average of eight days, while 12 remained symptomatic for at least three weeks. Again, the initial attack, judged by a variety of tests, was equally severe in both groups. However, the slow recoverers scored significantly higher on the morale-loss scale before they became ill (Cluff, Canter, and Imboden 1966).

Clinical observations about the noxious effects of demoralization are further supported by research into the effects of "learned helplessness" in animals (Abramson, Seligman, and Teasdale 1978). The term "learned helplessness" connotes an animal's failure to use a plainly available escape from a noxious stimulus after previously being in a situation where escape from similar harm was impossible. Extended to humans, the concept refers to repeated experiences of noncontingency between behavior and its consequences.

Using variations of the learned-helplessness paradigm, many animal studies demonstrate that perceived loss of control, rather than a continuing noxious stimulus, is associated with increased rates of cardiovascular disease, decreased resistance to tumor or infection, ulcers, and other serious conditions (Rodin 1986). These effects are exacerbated in animals kept isolated from one another.

In humans, illnesses that do not respond promptly to treatment give rise to feelings of helplessness. The results of the animal experiments encourage the speculation that such feelings, engendered by personal characteristics or prior experiences of failure or powerlessness, may in turn contribute to physical complications and deterioration.

Other personal characteristics also have been found to affect susceptibility to illnesses. Thus, a low threshold for anger and hostility, a characteristic of the so-called Type A personality, is a risk factor for heart attacks (Williams 1989), and a different constellation of personality characteristics has been related to cancer. Bahnson and Bahnson (1969) found that cancer patients, compared both to patients with other illnesses and to healthy people, tend to repress or deny such unpleasant affects as depression, anxiety, and hostility. Under a façade of cheerful competence, they feel isolated and overwhelmed by life's difficulties. This sense of isolation is consistent with the finding that cancer patients have a greater tendency than others to report painful and destructive interpersonal emotional experiences before the age of seven (LeShan 1965/1966).

One must exercise caution in evaluating such retrospective, clinical studies, in which many variables are uncontrolled and are subject to distortions based on the patients' current state. However, a prospective study by Thomas and Dzubinski (1974) indirectly confirmed LeShan's work. These researchers gave 914 male medical students graduating between 1948 and 1964 a variety of tests, including a questionnaire measuring closeness to parents. By 1973, 26 of the students had developed malignant tumors. Of these, the 20 on whom complete data were available had scored significantly lower as a group on a closeness-to-parents scale ($p \leq .01$) than did a group matched by age, sex, and class who were still in good health.

Such findings are consistent with the findings of the studies of personality traits and early losses. Personal history and habitual modes of thought or action influence persons' levels of optimism, motivation to exercise control over their environment, or perception of events as beyond their control. Thus, a child who lost a parent early in life and never found adequate substitute attachments might be predisposed toward feelings of helplessness which over time become his or her habitual reaction to environmental events.

Persons' current social environment, especially their interactions with family members, also may exert profound effects on both their morale and their physical state. A study of family interaction in renal patients demonstrated that patients' rates of complications and adherence to treatment correlated with the degree to which their families were disruptive or accepting. Patients from families that were hostile, chaotic, and hopeless did significantly worse than those whose most intimate social contacts were more positive (Steidl et al. 1980).

Similarly, studies of families of diabetic and asthmatic children have shown that children who frequently relapse or become symptomatic come from families in which roles are blurred, members react to demands for change with tension or avoidance, and conflicts are not readily resolved. Though family members may not seem overtly depressed or demoralized, these qualities limit members' flexibility and capacity for change and increase their vulnerability to stress (Minuchin et al. 1979) (see p. 124).

Mastery, Hope, and Psychotherapy in Physical Illness

The many links between adverse psychosocial factors and physical illness suggest that positive attitudes may exert a beneficial effect on physical health. Indeed, the influence of positive emotional states upon physical disease has been noted since antiquity and forms the basis of all forms of psychological healing (see Chapters 4, 5, and 7). In the era of scientific medicine, the emphasis on the search for specific treatments for specific conditions has tended to discount the role of these factors, though they may be of life-and-death significance. Just as habitual negative attitudes may contribute to susceptibility to heart disease and cancer, so positive ones may enhance resistance and recovery.

In this section we shall discuss some of the psychological responses to chronic illness that may mitigate its effects. Like negative responses, positive ones derive primarily from patients' personality traits and habitual attitudes toward life's vicissitudes. Positive responses may be enhanced, however, by the symbolic interventions of education and psychotherapy, including purely verbal therapies and those that use relaxation or bodily manipulation to promote positive mental states.

As we have noted, anecdotal evidence suggests that temperamentally determined positive states of mind may extend the lives of AIDS patients. Similarly, just as panic may considerably increase the chances of dying following a heart attack (see pp. 127–28), an optimistic attitude may contribute to survival. A study by Hackett and Cassem (1975) showed that patients' psychological defenses affected the rate of complications, including sudden death, following myocardial infarction. Patients who appeared to deny the seriousness of their condition had smoother recoveries and a better rate of survival than patients who responded with despair. Though seemingly irrational, patients who refused to recognize the ominous meaning of their symptoms apparently created a positive self-fulfilling prophecy that reduced, though it did not eliminate, their vulnerability to dire complications.

In this connection, several studies have shown that a complex set of positive attitudes correlates with the speed of healing following certain operations. Thus, Mason et al. (1969) interviewed ninety-eight patients facing surgery for detached retina and rated their trust in the surgeon, optimism about outcome, confidence in ability to cope regardless of outcome, and preparedness to accept the bad with the good. From these factors, they generated an "acceptance" score that had a 0.61 correlation with patients' independently rated speed of healing. Using the same scale in a study of patients before open heart surgery, Mills et al. (1975) found a similar correlation between acceptance and a factor that measured decreased requirements for pain medication postoperatively, a lower rate of unspecified complications, and fewer days in the hospital. More striking, the mortality of the sickest patients at three months correlated more highly with the patients' preoperative acceptance than with the initial severity of their cardiac condition.

The findings in these correlational studies do not exclude the possibility that patients' positive attitudes and improved outcome both reflect a common factor such as general vitality. Studies of the effects of healers' words and ministrations provide stronger evidence that positive attitudes engendered by aspects of a therapeutic environment may be healing. We have considered this subject in our discussion of religiomagical healing (Chapters 4 and 5). It plays no less a role in scientific medicine.

The beneficial impact of favorable psychological factors on chronic illness accounts for the rapid growth of a variety of self-help organizations for patients with conditions ranging from terminal cancer to herpes. Professional recognition of these factors also provides a rationale for offering psychotherapy as part of medical treatment. Many studies have documented that a variety of mental health interventions can reduce patients' use of medical services (Jones and Vischi 1979). Two of the many possible explanations of these findings are especially relevant to our concerns. Psychotherapy may lead some patients to attribute certain complaints to psychological stresses rather than to bodily disease. Patients may also be less inclined to pursue medical care after finding that mental health personnel are willing to talk with them about personal concerns instead of focusing exclusively on diagnosing and treating bodily pathology.

Hypnosis, a long-established and widely used form of treatment, warrants special attention as a symbolic intervention with important healing effects on both mind and body (Orne and Dingus 1989). The psychological effects of hypnosis include bringing buried memories to consciousness, causing persons to regress to earlier psychological states, and anesthetizing pain. Hypnosis may induce other therapeutically beneficial states of consciousness. Simonton and Simonton (1975), for example, have used guided imagery facilitated by hypnosis to treat cancer, with modestly positive results.

Hypnotic procedures favorably affect those bodily systems that are most reactive to psychological inputs — notably, the cardiovascular, gastrointestinal, and respiratory systems and the skin (Crasilneck and Hall 1985). The well-authenticated hypnotic cure of warts is particularly noteworthy for our purposes because warts are caused by identifiable viruses. Apparently, hypnotic suggestion can induce immunological changes in the skin that combat these viruses. More remarkable is the finding that this procedure can cause warts to disappear on one side of the body only (Sinclair-Gieben and Chalmers 1959).

Not all healing symbolic interventions are clearly recognized for what they are. Many medical treatments succeed because of their psychological rather than their physical effects. Physicians are often unaware of how faith in the theoretical bases of their treatments — whether justified or not — contributes to their success by enhancing their own confidence and inducing positive attitudes in patients. The theories of physicians, who are the designated healers in a society oriented toward science, are often no more or less true than the mythical explanations of more traditional cultures. Only a small proportion of medical and surgical remedies have been scientifically validated. One study of thirty-six innovative surgical procedures, for example, showed that fewer than half were successful and only one-third were improvements over standard procedures (Mosteller 1981).

Furthermore, medical practice has always been swayed by fads based on erroneous theories (Thomas 1981). In the 1920s, thousands of teeth and tonsils and miles of intestines were removed in an effort to eliminate supposed sources of "focal infection," which was believed to cause all sorts of ills. These operations would not have been so popular had they not relieved symptoms in a sizable number of those on whom they were performed. Presumably, the key to their effectiveness was their plausibility to both physicians and patients.

Physicians may foster therapeutic attitudes in many ways. A variety of prospective, controlled studies have demonstrated the positive effects of information and support in such conditions as heart attacks and recovery from operations (Mumford, Schlesinger, and Glass 1982). These studies have shown that simple, brief psychological interventions may favorably affect physical outcome; prolonged, complex psychotherapy is not usually required.

Norman Cousins provides an anecdote that vividly illustrates how an ill person's mental state may be potentially lethal and how someone else may readily counteract it simply by offering a plausible and encouraging explanation for what the person is experiencing:

> In the fall of 1982, I saw an ambulance in front of the clubhouse of one of the golf courses in West Los Angeles. I went over to the ambulance and saw a man on a stretcher alongside the vehicle. He had suffered a heart attack while playing golf. The paramedics, working systematically and methodically, were attending to their duties, connecting him to a portable cardiograph monitor, which they placed at the foot of the stretcher, hooking him up to an oxygen tank, inserting a plug in his arm to facilitate intravenous ministrations.
>
> No one was talking to the man. He was ashen and trembling. I looked at the cardiograph monitor. It revealed what is termed a tachycardia — a runaway heart rate. The intervals on the monitor were irregular. I also looked at the paramedics, who, true to their training, were efficiently attending to the various emergency procedures. But no one was attending to the patient's panic, which was potentially lethal.
>
> I put my hand on his shoulder. "Sir," I said, "You've got a great heart."
>
> He opened his eyes and turned toward me. "Why do you say that?" he asked in a low voice.
>
> In Oliver Wendell Holmes' phrase I "rounded the sharp corners of the truth" with my reply.
>
> "Sir," I said, "I've been looking at your cardiograph, and I can see that you're going to be all right. You're in very good hands. In a few minutes, you'll be in one of the world's best hospitals. You're going to be just fine.
>
> "Are you sure?" he asked.
>
> "Certainly. It's a very hot day and you are probably dehydrated. The electrical impulses to the heart can be disrupted when that happens. Don't worry. You'll be all right."
>
> In less than a minute, the cardiograph showed unmistakable evidence of a slowing down of the heartbeat. The gaps between the tall lines began to widen; the rhythm began to be less irregular. I looked at the man's face; the color began to return. He propped up his head with his arms and looked around; he was taking an interest in what was happening.

I felt no remorse at having skirted the truth. What he needed — as much as the oxygen — was reassurance. He needed to be lifted out of his panic. [Cousins 1983, pp. 203–4]

An effectively reassuring explanation simultaneously promotes patients' feelings of mastery and offers hope of recovery. Though these two factors are inextricably linked, it is convenient to consider them separately. Rodin and Langer (1977), for example, compared a group of nursing home residents who were encouraged to trust in the staff to care for them with a group who were urged to plan and carry out their own activities. Immediately after the study, the subjects in the control-enhancing condition scored higher on self-esteem and well-being, relative to controls. More striking, eighteen months later the subjects who had been given increased control over self-care and daily activities had a lower death rate than the control group. These findings are consistent with the improved course of illness observed in patients who dialyzed themselves at home compared with those who were treated in the hospital (see p. 120).

Mastery is equally important in counteracting less dire bodily states such as the hyperarousal characteristic of panic attacks. Much systematic investigation has increased our understanding of the metabolic derangements associated with panic attacks, and from these data "biological psychiatrists" have concluded that this disorder requires pharmacological treatment. Cognitive and behavior-oriented therapists, however, have amassed well-controlled data to show that particular psychological treatments alone can reduce the disability associated with panic attacks and diminish the frequency and severity of episodes in patients without significant depression (Klosko et al. 1990; Marks 1987a). Apparently, the key to successful psychological treatment is to alter the meaning of the experience. Since panic attacks are often accompanied by a fear of dying, if patients can be convinced that their symptoms are both harmless and self-limited, they can stop avoiding the situations that evoke the attacks and resume their usual activities. The panic attacks may then cease after sufficiently prolonged exposure to the conditions that evoked them. Various psychotherapeutic techniques can alter the meaning of panic attacks, including systematic cognitive restructuring (Barlow et al. 1989), self-exposure therapy (Marks, 1987a), and panic control treatment (Klosko et al. 1990). In addition, patients can be taught to bring on their symptoms through hyperventilation and then trained in respiratory control to forestall panic (Clark, Salkovskis, and Chalkley 1985).

As these examples illustrate, an explanation linked to a voluntary activity that restores patients' feelings of control over their bodies and inspires their hopes can alleviate physiologically based symptoms. Medical and surgical procedures can elicit similar beneficial psychological responses because, in addition to their direct physical effects, they invoke the healing powers of Science. The therapeutic effect of hope aroused by medical and surgical remedies – the placebo effect – is sufficiently important in psychotherapy to warrant separate discussion (see Chapter 7).

Recognition of the inseparable links between mind and body raises fascinating questions about the mechanisms that link these two spheres of human functioning. This topic has been well reviewed by others (Reiser 1984). Without wandering too far afield, we may at least note that psychological processes have been shown to affect neurotransmitters, the chemical messengers by which nerve cells communicate with and regulate each other. These substances in turn affect both mental life and a host of physical processes in health and disease. In particular, neurotransmitters subserve the functions of the autonomic nervous system, which regulates cardiac rhythm, blood pressure, gastric acid secretion, motility of the gut, and other visceral functions.

An ingenious experiment by Luparello et al. (1970) illustrates the susceptibility of the autonomic nervous system to symbolic influence. In this study, under double-blind conditions, asthmatics were given a bronchodilator or a bronchoconstrictor to inhale. Some were led to expect that the inhalant would produce its pharmacological effect, while others were told that it would produce its opposite. The effect of the dilator on airway resistance, which is autonomically regulated, was about twice as great when the expectation coincided with the bronchodilator's pharmacological action as when expectation and action were opposed. A similar though weaker result was found for the bronchoconstrictor.

Neurotransmitters also influence the processes of immunity, either through the regulation of hormones or through direct effects upon immune cells (Schleifer et al. 1985).

Thus, the beneficial role of psychological factors and of psychotherapy in physical disease has been most widely studied in autonomically regulated cardiovascular, pulmonary, and gastrointestinal disease, and in diseases involving immune functions. Among the latter are infections, cancer, and autoimmune disease (Cousins 1989; Rhodes, Ford, and Dickstein 1989).

The Induction of Favorable Mental States through Bodily Manipulations and Exercises

We have considered therapeutic interactions of mental and bodily states from the standpoint of mental states and various symbolic interventions that benefit the body. We shall now reverse our perspective to consider briefly the induction of therapeutic mental states by means of bodily manipulations and exercises.

Such interventions, which have been elaborated by certain schools of therapy, fall into at least two categories: those meant to release bottled-up emotions and those meant to induce healing states of consciousness. With a few notable exceptions, professionally trained Western psychotherapists have avoided these methods for effecting psychological changes. This oversight may reflect a culturally biased perception of all bodily contact as either erotic or aggressive. Such bias robs therapists of powerful means of relieving tension and enhancing rapport that are widely used in other cultures (Torrey 1972).

In recent years, some unorthodox or nonprofessional therapists have reawakened interest in these methods. Leaders of sensitivity or encounter groups, for example, encourage a variety of exercises involving psychologically liberating or consoling bodily contact. Chiropractic may be the most widely accepted form of psychotherapeutic physical manipulation in our society. Though chiropractors weave elaborate theories to justify their interventions as specific for the physical ailments for which patients consult them, a large part of their success results from their ability to physically induce states of relaxation and from the inherent symbolism of their bodily procedures.

The powerful symbolic implications of bodily manipulation may account in part for the psychological effects of therapies such as bioenergetics (Lowen 1975). Bioenergetic theory asserts that patients' muscular tensions "embody" early childhood conflicts between the urge to perform certain acts and external prohibitions against them. For example, a child who is forbidden to cry may tighten certain facial muscles to inhibit this response. Eventually these muscles become locked into a state of chronic tenseness. The therapist, by suitable bodily manipulations (or by persuading the patient to forcefully express certain emotions), precipitates a discharge of the pent-up feelings, often with a reemergence of the early memories. When successful, such procedures enhance the patient's spontaneity and provide fruitful material for psychotherapy. Using a different rationale and bodily manipulations, structural integration (Rolf 1977) can achieve the same beneficial recovery of early traumatic memories (Schutz and Turner 1976).

Bodily exercises related to relaxation, either self-conducted or guided by others, can induce profound changes in psychological state. With sufficient training, persons can induce healing states of consciousness as well as transcendental experiences in themselves through various relaxation and meditation exercises (Benson and Proctor 1984). Corresponding examples from the secular realm are guided imagery, biofeedback, deep relaxation (Benson 1975), and hypnosis.

While none of these psychophysiological techniques is specific for any class of mental or physical illness, continuing refinement of our understanding of mind-body interaction may someday lead to the development of symbolic techniques with specific activity against particular disease states. Jaffe and Bresler (1980), for example, have suggested that the left hemisphere, which is specialized for verbal language, has an overriding influence over the voluntary motor system, while the right hemisphere, being specialized for metaphorical thinking and imagery, has a powerful effect on the autonomic nervous system. Thus, they speculate that therapies that encourage patients to develop and modify personally meaningful images of healing in conjunction with relaxation hold particular promise for the treatment of diseases in which the autonomic nervous system plays a role.

Summary

In this chapter we have drawn upon epidemiological and clinical studies of mind-body interaction to illustrate the role of physical processes in shaping mental life, and the power of psychological processes in regulating physical functioning. Physical interventions such as medications play a major role in alleviating many conditions once considered treatable only by psychotherapy. In addition, medications have symbolic and direct effects that are relevant to psychotherapy. The spectrum of patients' responses to injuries further illustrates the many symbolic aspects of bodily function and their effects on mental life. The symbolism we attach to our bodies also manifests itself in the meanings we attach to chronic illnesses, meanings that may in turn exacerbate the course of these conditions.

Conversely, psychological processes and psychological interventions affect bodily functions. Negative emotional factors such as reactions to stress, vulnerable temperament, or an adverse family environment can precipitate or exacerbate disease. Efforts to improve the psychological state of patients by increasing their sense of control, combating confusion, and supporting hope may improve health either by improving self-care and adherence to treatment or by directly influencing somatic processes. We close with a brief mention of ways that bodily manipulation may function as a form of healing symbolic intervention.

SEVEN

The Placebo Response and the Role of Expectations in Medical and Psychological Treatment

"I know *something* interesting is sure to happen," she said to herself, "whenever I eat or drink anything: so I'll just see what this bottle does."

— *Alice's Adventures in Wonderland*

Having roamed quite far afield in the search for information relevant to psychotherapy, we are now in a position to examine features of contemporary psychotherapy in the United States, our main concern. We shall start with a universal feature of successful psychotherapies, their ability to arouse the patient's expectation of help. Humans are time-binding creatures, so assumptions about the future have a powerful effect on their present state. Hope may have been an evolutionary requirement for human survival (Tiger 1979), as suggested by the legend of Pandora's box. As we saw in Chapters 5 and 6, hopelessness can retard recovery or even hasten death, while the mobilization of hope plays an important part in many forms of healing in both nonindustrialized societies and our own. Favorable expectations generate feelings of optimism, energy, and well-being and may actually promote healing, especially of those illnesses that have a large psychological or emotional component.

Hope has been defined as the perceived possibility of achieving a goal (Stotland 1969). It is aroused by cues in the immediate situation associated with progress toward a goal in the past and is strengthened by evidence of progress toward the goal. Most patients seeking treatment hope to obtain relief by following the therapist's prescription, whether it is a medication or a course of action. In either case patients look to the therapist to heal them. To be sure, all forms of psychotherapy try, directly or indirectly, to enhance the patient's feeling of mastery over self and environment, and thereby to facilitate greater self-reliance and initiative. However, unless the patient hopes that the therapist can be helpful, he or she will not come to therapy at all. Moreover, faith in the therapist may be healing in itself. This chapter considers two types of observations concerning patients' hopes and the outcome of treatment: the effects of inert medications or placebos in both medical treatment and psychotherapy, and the importance in psychotherapy of bringing the patient's expectations into line with what he or she will actually experience.

The Placebo Response

Physicians have always known that their ability to inspire expectant trust in a patient partially determines the success of treatment. Until recently this knowledge, like that obtained from anthropological studies, rested on uncontrolled observations and clinical impressions, so it was impossible to define in any systematic way the sources and limits of the effects of hope on different kinds of patients and their illnesses. The problem has been to domesticate the question, as it were, to lure it away from the bedside into the laboratory, where the factors involved could be systematically manipulated and their effects sorted out.

Fortunately, one form of medical treatment makes this possible, since its effectiveness rests solely on its ability to mobilize the patient's expectation of help. This is the use of a "placebo" — a pharmacologically inert substance that the doctor administers to a patient to relieve distress when, for one reason or another, the doctor does not wish to use an active medication. Thus the doctor may use a placebo rather than a sedative in treating a patient's chronic insomnia, to avoid the danger of addiction. Since a placebo is pharmacologically inert, its beneficial effects must lie in its symbolic power. The most likely supposition is that it gains its potency by being a tangible symbol of the physician's role as healer. In our society, the physician validates his or her power by prescribing medication, just as a shaman validates a treatment by spitting out a bit of bloodstained down at the proper moment.

In this connection it may be worthwhile to recall that until this century most medications prescribed by physicians were pharmacologically inert, if not actually harmful. As Oliver Wendell Holmes wrote, if most of the drugs of his day "could be sunk to the bottom of the sea, it would be all the better for mankind, — and all the worse for the fishes" (Holmes [1860] 1911, p. 203). That is, physicians were prescribing placebos or worse without knowing it. In a sense, the "history of medical treatment until relatively recently is the history of the placebo effect" (Shapiro 1959, p. 303). Despite their inadvertent reliance on placebos, physicians maintained an honored reputation as successful healers, which suggests that these remedies were often effective. Yet a physician who today knowingly prescribes a placebo may feel a little guilty. The act seems to imply deception of the patient, which is hard to reconcile with the physician's professional role. *Placebo* is Latin for "I shall please," and the dictionary defines a placebo as "a substance having no pharmacological effect but given merely to satisfy a patient who supposes it to be a medicine" (*Random House Dictionary of the English Language* 1966). The word "merely" is the stumbling block, since it implies that a placebo does nothing but satisfy the patient. Perhaps because of this implication, the conditions determining the effects of placebo administration failed for a long while to receive the careful attention they deserve.

The study of patients' reactions to pharmacologically inert medication makes possible an investigation of the effects of patients' expectations, mediated by the doctor-patient relationship, on their physical and emotional states. A cursory look at the present state of knowledge of some effects and determinants of placebo administration is therefore pertinent to our concerns (White, Tursky, and Schwartz 1985).

Placebos exert their effects primarily through symbolization of the physician's healing powers. The expectations conveyed by the physician in prescribing medication can be sufficiently powerful to reverse the pharmacological action of some drugs. For example, the drug ipecac is an emetic that usually halts normal stomach contractions shortly after it is ingested. The patient then experiences nausea. By having a patient swallow a balloon, which is inflated in the stomach and hooked to the proper equipment, a physician can directly observe these changes in stomach motility. A pregnant patient suffering from excessive vomiting showed the normal cessation of stomach contractions followed by nausea and vomiting after receiving a dose of ipecac. When the same medication was given to her through a tube, so that she did not know what it was, with strong assurances that it would cure her vomiting, gastric contractions started up at the same interval after its administration that they would normally have stopped, and simultaneously the patient's nausea ceased (Wolf 1950).

Demonstrations of placebos' ability to heal certain kinds of tissue damage offer further proof of their marked physiological effects. One can treat warts, for example, by painting them with a brightly colored but inert dye and telling the patient that the warts will be gone when the color wears off. Like hypnosis (see p. 126), this placebo treatment is as effective as any other remedy, including surgical excision. It works equally well on previously untreated patients and on those who have been unsuccessfully treated by other means (Barber 1961b).

Placebo treatment can also activate healing of more severely damaged tissues, especially when the damage seems related to physiological changes connected with unfavorable emotional states. In one study of patients hospitalized with peptic ulcers, for example, 70 percent showed "excellent results lasting over a period of one year" when the doctor gave them an injection of distilled water and assured them that it was a new medicine that would cure them. The control group, which received the same injection from a nurse with the information that it was an experimental medication of undetermined effectiveness, showed a remission rate of only 25 percent (Volgyesi 1954).

The symbolic meaning of medication may not always be favorable (see pp. 115–16). Some patients fear drugs and distrust doctors. In these patients a placebo may produce severe untoward physiological reactions, including nausea, diarrhea, and skin eruptions (Wolf and Pinsky 1954).

If medication can have strong placebo effects, one would expect surgical operations to involve even stronger ones. Compared to persons seeking medical treatment, most of those about to undergo surgery are more apprehensive, and are more dependent on the surgeon; the patient literally places his or her life in the surgeon's hands. Furthermore, because they are dramatic acts, operations are expected to produce immediate cures.

The placebo component of surgical procedures is most apparent in surgery of the heart, an organ highly susceptible to emotional influences. The marked placebo component of cardiovascular surgery was first shown by a study of mammary artery ligation. This procedure was supposed to increase blood supply to the heart, thereby relieving heart pain caused by impaired blood supply. When first introduced, this operation yielded marked symptomatic relief in about 40 percent of patients. It even increased the amount of exercise patients could endure before changes appeared in their electrocardiograms. In the days before the legal requirements of full disclosure and informed consent, one investigator performed the full operation on every other patient in a series and a mock operation on the alternates. The mock operation, which involved giving anesthesia and incising the chest without touching the artery, proved to be just as effective as the real one (Beecher 1961).

Similar psychological processes may account for some portion of the pain relief achieved by the coronary artery bypass operations that are currently in vogue. We do not deny that bypassing occlusions of the left anterior descending artery or multiple occlusions reduces mortality and improves function (Killip 1988), but the popularity of other, less effective procedures suggests that bypass operations also evoke significant placebo responses. The rationale for this operation is entirely convincing: occlusion of a coronary artery deprives the heart muscle of needed oxygen and nutrients, causing pain. Bypassing the occluded segment with a portion of the patient's vein is supposed to restore circulation and relieve the pain. Spectacular relief of pain was once obtained even with procedures now considered inadequate. In an early review, Ross (1976) found that symptomatic improvement does not necessarily reflect objectively measured improvement in function. It is likely that many patients improve in response to the physician's ability to provide a plausible explanation of their symptoms and of how surgery will bring relief, coupled with the expectant faith mobilized by preparation for surgery.

Many studies have consistently shown the power of placebos to relieve pain. Placebos are associated with at least 50 percent reduction of pain in about one-third of patients suffering from a wide variety of traumatic and postoperative pain. The powerful analgesic morphine produces similar relief in only three-fourths of patients, so this is an impressive showing (Evans 1985).

Since placebos are pharmacologically inert, they must exert their beneficial effect primarily through relief of apprehension and other emotional states. Beecher (1956) has termed these the processing aspects of pain, which aggravate the pain experience. An example of the contribution of emotional states to the pain experience is afforded by Beecher's finding that about 90 percent of civilians after surgical operations complained of pain severe enough to request a narcotic, as compared with only about one-quarter of a group of combat soldiers who were evacuated from the Anzio Beachhead because of battle wounds that had caused comparable tissue damage. For the soldiers, a wound meant highly welcome escape from imminent danger of death, while the civilians had no such comfort (Beecher 1956).

An analogous finding is that, compared with their pain-reducing ability in patients with illness or wounds, placebos relieve experimentally produced pain in only 3–15 percent of subjects, depending on the method used to induce pain (Evans 1974). Clinical pain, as a sign that something may be wrong, arouses apprehension. Experimental pain causes little if any anxiety in most subjects because they know the pain's source and how to stop it.

When the source of pain is independent of the patient's emotional condition, the relief afforded by a placebo tends to be transient, although it may last as long as that produced by analgesics. When the emotional state produced by the placebo also improves the physiological disorder producing the pain, the effect may be enduring, as in the peptic ulcer patients described above.

Some Determinants of the Placebo Response

The determinants of the placebo response are complex. Rickels (1967) listed fourteen features of neurotic outpatients and eight of physicians that may affect the placebo response. Many of these are fleeting, difficult to define, and differ from one clinic and its patients to another. Furthermore, these features interact with the patient's state at the time and with the contextual aspects of the situation in which the placebo is administered, including the patient's relationship to the physician (Jospe 1978), so a patient may respond differently to a placebo at different times. Properties of the immediate situation seem to predominate, as suggested by the finding that only a small percentage of medical and surgical patients showed a consistent positive response to placebos (Lasagna et al. 1954).

The situation-bound nature of placebo responsiveness was neatly demonstrated by a study in which obstetrical patients were given a placebo to reduce pain from three different causes — labor pains, afterpains, and self-induced pain caused by contracting muscles whose blood supply had been cut off by a tourniquet. In all three situations the placebo produced more relief of pain than occurred in a control group not receiving placebos, but the number of patients in whom the placebo caused the same reduction in pain from all three causes was no greater than would be expected by chance. That is, although the placebo relieved pain on the average, whether it did so for a given patient on a particular occasion seemed to depend more on an interaction between the momentary state of the patient and the specific source of the pain than on enduring personality attributes (Liberman 1964).

Despite the preponderance of the immediate situation in determining response to placebos, some studies have shown that persons with certain personality traits consistently respond more positively to placebos than do others. In general, the placebo reactors tend to be anxious, can let themselves depend on others for help, and can readily accept others in their socially defined roles. In a study of patients with surgical pain, placebo responders tended to be more dependent, emotionally reactive, and conventional, while the nonreactors were more likely to be isolated and mistrustful (Lasagna et al. 1954). The characteristics of placebo responders are consistent with the results of studies in which patients who improved more in response to placebo or medication than to psychotherapy had an external "locus of control" (see Chapter 8, pp. 170–72).

Occasionally, a patient who expresses strong distrust of doctors reacts positively to a placebo. A diabetic who was a trained nurse, for example, was the despair of her physicians because of her refusal to take her medicines and her constant diatribes against them. Yet, in the very midst of her rebelliousness she showed a striking relief of abdominal pain following a physician's injection of distilled water. Her response suggests that her attitude might have been an overcompensation for strong feelings of dependency, as if she were longing to accept help but could not admit it. The analogy to "skeptics" who benefit from a pilgrimage to Lourdes is obvious (see p. 107).

Since all medical and surgical procedures combine the remedy's physical properties and the meanings associated with its administration, a strict evaluation of the physical potency of any remedy requires that its effects be compared to those of a substance whose effects are purely psychological. Such validation is the goal of the double-blind clinical trial, in which either the agent being tested or an inert placebo is administered in such a way that neither physician nor patient knows which one the patient is receiving.

The Placebo Response and Psychotherapy

Because of the usefulness of the double-blind placebo design for determining the effectiveness of different medications, researchers in psychotherapy have been tempted to use it to evaluate the relative power of different forms of psychotherapy. Such a design also seems to meet the demands of third-party payers for evidence that at least some forms of psychotherapy are effective enough to warrant reimbursement. Accordingly, many studies have compared specific psychotherapeutic techniques with a "placebo" psychotherapy — that is, a procedure that conveys the therapist's attention, inspires the patient's hopes, and possesses other properties shared by all psychotherapies, but lacks the specific therapeutic components of the technique under investigation. Unfortunately, the apparent simplicity of this design conceals a host of formidable conceptual and methodological difficulties (Parloff 1986).

In addition to the complexity of the determinants of placebo responsiveness in general, placebo-psychotherapy comparison studies present the problem of assuring that they are truly double blind — that is, that neither the patient nor the therapist can surmise which is the "real" therapy. If the therapist suspects which is the placebo, he or she will probably expect it to be less effective, thereby unwittingly influencing the results. As we saw in Chapter 3, experimental subjects seem to sense and respond to experimenters' expectations despite the experimenter's best efforts. Patients, because of their evaluation apprehension, would be expected to be especially susceptible to this source of contamination.

Above all, the finding that a particular form of psychotherapy relieves some symptoms more effectively than a placebo, while of interest to reimbursement agencies, tells us nothing about the nature of the effective psychological components of the therapy. Indeed, the whole purpose of the placebo control design is to rule out these components in evaluating the effects of chemotherapies: "By using placebo groups, psychotherapy researchers have paradoxically searched for psychological causes with tactics that were specifically developed in chemotherapy research to rule out all psychological causes" (Wilkins 1984, p. 571).

Despite these limitations, the placebo control design has shown some promise for evaluating those therapies that rely on a specific technique to eliminate a particular symptom, such as desensitization for performance anxiety (Paul 1966). The difference between the amount of improvement following therapy and that following the placebo psychotherapy condition indicates the extent to which factors other than the expectation of help and other feelings aroused by all therapies contribute to the therapy's results. This is true, however, only if the placebo psychotherapy arouses these feelings as strongly as the therapy with which it is being compared. Otherwise, the apparent superiority of the experimental therapy could still be due to its superior ability to arouse positive expectations in the patient and the therapist.

At this point, rather than continue to enumerate the problems inherent in the double-blind placebo design for evaluating various psychotherapies, we shall turn to a more promising use of placebos in psychotherapy research, which is to explore determinants and effects of patients' positive expectations. As already indicated, a placebo is itself a form of psychotherapy (Frank 1983). The term is misleading in its implication that the pill itself is therapeutic; on the contrary, like all psychotherapies, its power depends on its symbolic message. By conveying that the physician cares about the patient's welfare and is competent, the placebo arouses hope. It can also enhance the patient's feelings of mastery. As one writer put it, it changes the patient's self-image from victim to coper (Bootzin 1985).

Placebos lack a major ingredient of psychotherapy: opportunities for new learning. Rather, placebos implicitly teach the wrong thing — namely, that the medication is what enables the patient to cope. As a result, the patient may relapse if the placebo is discontinued. A placebo may, however, induce enduring improvement if it enables the patient to approach problems with increased self-confidence. This may in turn facilitate other self-sustaining changes.

In any case, psychiatric outpatients respond positively to placebos about as frequently as do medical patients whose disorders have an emotional component. In five separate studies involving a total of fifty-six patients, an average of 55 percent reported significant improvement from placebos (Gliedman et al. 1958).

Some years ago, in order to explore the question of the contributions to symptomatic improvement of the patient's hope for relief as aroused by a placebo, the senior author and his colleagues studied the responses of psychiatric outpatients, diagnosed as suffering from a psychoneurosis or personality disorder, to the administration of an inert pill (Frank 1978a). The sample consisted of fifty-four white patients from eighteen to fifty-five years old. All patients received a routine evaluation interview on their first clinic visit. On their second visit one week later they were given a symptom checklist on which they indicated which symptoms they had and how distressing they were, and a mood self-rating scale. After this a psychologist administered some personality tests and tests of autonomic function over a period lasting about one and a half hours. The symptom checklist and mood scale were then repeated, and the patients were given a placebo described as a new pill not yet on the market, but known to be nontoxic and helpful to patients with similar complaints. The patients were then given more tests for about half an hour, after which they again filled out a symptom checklist and mood scale.

The patients were asked to continue taking the medication, and to return after one and two weeks, at which times the measures of symptoms and mood were repeated. The studies showed that, whatever the interval between the initial and later measures, the overall decrease in symptoms and improvement in mood for the group as a whole was statistically significant, and more patients improved than became worse.

The temporal course of the mean discomfort score, derived from the symptom checklist, is illustrated in Figure 1, which contains data from the twenty-eight patients we were able to persuade to return after a

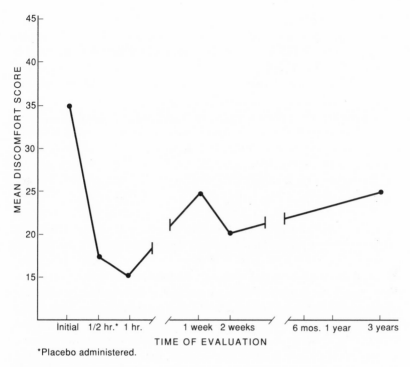

Figure 1.
Change in Mean Discomfort Scores in Placebo Patients Returning over a
Three-Year Period ($N = 28$)

three-year interval. Decreases in discomfort scores indicate improvement. Note that most of the drop in mean discomfort occurred even
before the administration of the placebo. Discomfort increased slightly
on the average over the two weeks during which patients continued to
take the placebo, then apparently dropped to about the same level that
was measured three years later.

More detailed analysis of the data revealed that diminution in the
symptoms of anxiety and depression accounted for most of the symptomatic improvement. This accords with the finding of the well-
designed NIMH collaborative study of the treatment of depression that
a placebo-attention therapy was as effective as two different forms of
psychotherapy in alleviating depression, at least during the sixteen weeks
of therapy (Elkin et al. 1989) (see p. 56). Similarly, a review of studies of
systematic desensitization concludes that creditable placebos "are as
effective as systematic desensitization in producing durable reduction of

maladaptive fear" (Bootzin and Lick 1979, p. 853). The findings of the placebo study are also consistent with Beecher's (1955) observation, mentioned above, that the ability of placebos to relieve pain after surgical operations lies in the placebos' success in combating the apprehension aroused by pain. In this, as in most other respects, psychiatric patients do not differ from the rest of us.

In some patients in the placebo study, the leveling-off of the average discomfort score may have been due in part to a statistical artifact known as regression to the mean, but for reasons that would lead us too far afield to consider, this was probably not the main factor. Probably more significant is that patients seek help when they are in a crisis; hence, the average distress of any group of patients would be expected to diminish over time as they regained emotional equilibrium and the crisis receded into the past. Anxiety and depression, the most placebo-responsive symptoms, are also the most common emotional responses to crisis.

Several mutually compatible explanations may be invoked to account for the remarkably prompt and extensive initial drop in reported discomfort. One is that some patients may exaggerate their complaints initially to dramatize their desire for help and then minimize them later in response to the demand character of the therapeutic situation. Furthermore, if the same scale, in this case a symptom checklist, is administered before and after any intervention, the implicit expectation is that the score will change, and in a treatment setting the expected direction would be toward improvement.

Another explanation for the prompt improvement in reported discomfort is that the patients' initial symptoms may have been aggravated by the evaluation apprehension induced by circumstances surrounding a first visit to a psychiatric clinic. At such a moment, patients are apprehensive about what the interview will be like, what will be found, whether they will be judged insane, and the like. The failure of these fears to be confirmed may in itself produce considerable relief.

Finally, a significant factor was the staff's attention and interest as conveyed by the testing as well as by the administration of the pill. The great importance of staff attitudes in producing symptom relief has been demonstrated with both hospitalized and ambulatory psychiatric patients. When tranquilizing drugs were first introduced into mental hospitals, for example, it soon became clear that a large part of their effectiveness resulted from the hopes they inspired in the staff, who had previously viewed their function as largely custodial. By producing symptomatic improvement in patients formerly deemed hopeless, tranquilizers probably set in motion a chain of therapeutic interactions. The rekindling of the staff's therapeutic interest would favorably affect the attitudes of all the patients on a ward, including those who, as controls, received placebos instead of active medication. In addition to being beneficial in themselves, the patients' improved attitudes would increase their desire to please the staff by showing improvement, and this would further inspire the staff. As a result, for a while patients on placebos in double-blind studies improved almost as much as those on tranquilizers. The behavior of delinquent boys in a training school improved equally upon administration of placebos or tranquilizers, presumably for the same reasons (Molling et al. 1962). Similarly, the mere introduction of a research project into a mental hospital ward is followed by considerable improvement in patients, even when no medications are given. One reason may be that research introduces structure and order into a previously largely unstructured environment, which in itself relieves anxiety (Rashkis 1960). Probably as important, however, is the fact that participation in a research project combats staff apathy and increases their interest in patients' progress (Frank 1952).

This supposition is supported by studies of psychiatric outpatients. In the investigation discussed earlier (Frank 1978a), patients filled out a symptom checklist at the beginning of the experimental session, then after taking a series of tests but before receiving the placebo, and again after receiving the placebo. Most of the improvement in symptoms occurred during the testing period before the administration of the pill (see Figure 1), as if the patients were responding to the interest and attention of the research staff.

This finding has been confirmed by a large-scale double-blind study of the effects of various drugs on chronic psychiatric outpatients with a variety of diagnoses. All these patients complained of anxiety but were considered unsuitable candidates for psychotherapy (Lowinger and Dobie 1969). The first group of patients were initially rated on several scales, given the medication or placebo, and told to return in a month, when they would be retested. In an effort to get more data and increase the effectiveness of the drugs, a later group of patients were tested after two weeks, as well as after a month, and received double doses of the drug or the placebo. The second group showed about twice as great a response both to active drugs and placebos as did the first. It appears likely that the greater response of the second group reflected the greater attention these patients received. Another possible determinant of the results was that the psychiatrists expected more improvement and paid more attention to the patients who received the double dose of medication (a double dose would increase the likelihood of toxic side effects).

Taken together, these studies suggest that physicians' expectations may strongly affect patients' responses to medication. These expectations may sharpen both the physicians' and the patients' perceptions of differences in the latter's reactions to medicine and placebos while increasing the patients' responsiveness to both by raising hopes.

There is considerable evidence, which we shall now sample, that with psychiatric as with medical patients, aspects of the immediate situation play a larger part in placebo responsiveness than do enduring personality traits. For one thing, the same patient may respond differently to a placebo at different times or under different conditions of discomfort-producing stress. In our 1978 study, for example, we re-administered placebos to some patients who had responded favorably to the first administration but had suffered some relapse at the time of their return three years later. The lower line in Figure 2 shows what happened. (We shall consider the upper line shortly [p. 148].)

The group as a whole showed an *average* drop in discomfort of almost exactly the same degree as it had three years previously. Astonishing, however, was the complete lack of correlation between the responsiveness of individual patients on the two occasions; some who showed a strong response the first time failed to respond the second time, and vice versa. Nor were there any strong relations between patients' scores on our measures of personality and autonomic functions and their responses to placebos (Frank 1978a). Responders were somewhat more likely than nonresponders to take vitamins and aspirins regularly, to be more outgoing, to participate more in organizations, and to be less cautious. These findings, which accord with those reported for medical and surgical patients, suggest that responders expect medicines to help them, are better integrated socially, and are less mistrustful than nonresponders.

The relation of placebo responsiveness of a group of schizophrenic patients to their subsequent clinical course (Hankoff, Freedman, and Engelhardt 1958) supports this supposition. Thirty-three who appeared at a follow-up clinic for a routine check-up shortly after their discharge from a state hospital were given placebos for three weeks. Their response was a remarkably good prognosticator of whether they would have to go back to the hospital or not. Of those who had to return within thirty days, not one responded favorably, while of those who remained well enough to stay out of the hospital, four-fifths had felt better after receiving the placebo. Placebo responsiveness may have been an indicator of the ability of these patients to trust their fellow humans as represented by the clinic physicians, an ability related to their capacity to adjust to the world outside the hospital.

A final bit of evidence relating placebo responsiveness to the propensity to have faith in a physician emerged from a study in which psycho-

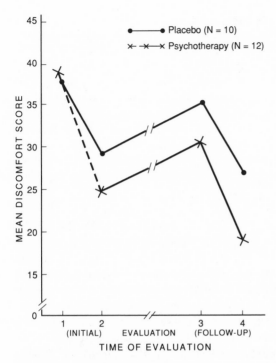

Figure 2.
Average Discomfort Scores of Psychiatric Outpatients Receiving
Psychotherapy and Placebos

Note: The interval between 1 and 2 is one week in the placebo study, six months in
the psychotherapy study. The interval between 2 and 3 is three years in both studies.
The interval between 3 and 4 is one week in the placebo study, two weeks in the
psychotherapy study.

neurotic adult outpatients were given a placebo and told precisely what it
was (Park and Covi 1965). The exact instructions were: "Many people
with your kind of condition have also been helped by what are sometimes
called sugar pills, and we feel that a so-called sugar pill may help you, too.
Do you know what a sugar pill is? A sugar pill is a pill with no medicine in
it at all. I think this pill will help you as it has helped so many others. Are
you willing to try this pill?" Patients were told to take the pill three times
a day for a week, after which a final recommendation for treatment would
be made. Of the fourteen patients who returned (the fifteenth was dis-
suaded by her husband's ridicule of taking an inactive pill), all reported
improvement. This astonishingly high success rate may have been in part

a reflection of the promise of specific treatment after a week on placebos. Of more interest for our purpose was the fact that patients who were sure in their own minds that the pill was a placebo or, conversely, that it was an active medication, reported significantly more relief of distress than those who had doubts. Those who were certain either way linked their certainty to their conviction that the doctor was trying to help them. Thus, one patient who was sure the pill was inactive feared becoming addicted to medication and thought the doctor had given her an inactive pill to protect her. Another connected active medication with her mother's suicidal gestures and felt the doctor had given her an inert pill for moral support. These findings with psychiatric patients are consistent with those reported for medical and surgical ones.

The ability of placebos to produce symptomatic relief under some circumstances should not be regarded as justification for their widespread use. In addition to the obvious consideration that this would cause placebos to lose their effectiveness and would damage patients' faith in the medical profession, the use of placebos has several serious drawbacks (Bok 1974). Insofar as the doctor feels that he or she is deceiving a patient by administering a placebo, this could undermine the doctor-patient relationship. If a patient showed a good response, the doctor might feel contemptuous of the patient as gullible; a patient's failure to respond might indicate that he or she had lost some faith in the doctor. Finally, the very power of the placebo makes it dangerous, for it may relieve distress caused by serious disease. This could lead to neglect of diagnostic studies that would reveal the condition and result in failure to give adequate treatment.

Psychotherapy and the Expectation of Help

If expectant trust contributes importantly to the success of all forms of medical treatment, it should play at least as important a role in psychotherapy. As Freud recognized, "Expectation colored by hope and faith is an effective force with which we have to reckon . . . in all our attempts at treatment and cure" (Freud 1953, p. 289). This being the case, some of the effects of psychotherapy should be similar to those produced by a placebo (Rosenthal and Frank 1956).

This possibility was first addressed in an exploratory study of three forms of psychotherapy with psychiatric outpatients drawn from the same outpatient population as in the placebo study described above (Frank 1978a) and assigned at random to one of the three types of treatment: individual therapy, in which patients were seen for one hour once a week; group therapy, in which groups of five to seven patients were seen for one and a half hours a week; and minimal contact therapy, in which patients were seen for not more than half an hour once every two weeks. The first two therapies differed from the third in the amount of treatment contact involved. They differed from each other in that patients were treated singly in one therapy and in a group in the other.

The treatments were conducted by three second-year psychiatric residents, each of whom had six patients in each form of treatment. The design called for each patient to receive six months of treatment. Although this goal was not quite achieved, it was reasonably approximated (Frank et al. 1959).

Criteria of improvement were chosen that, in one form or another, are used by all the healing arts: increased comfort (using the symptom checklist of the placebo study) and increased social effectiveness (Parloff, Kelman, and Frank 1954). Changes in social effectiveness were determined by means of a structured interview and patients were scored on a scale consisting of such items as overdependence, overindependence, officiousness, isolation, impulsiveness, and caution.

Patients were evaluated at the end of the experimental period of treatment and six months, eighteen months, and five years later. No effort was made to control patients' treatment experiences during the follow-up period. It was possible to examine thirty of the fifty-four treated patients at all three reevaluations.

The findings of the study suggest that improvement in discomfort and in social effectiveness depend to some extent on different processes, a supposition that gains support from the statistically insignificant correlations between changes in these measures. A closer look reveals two clues to the nature of these differences. Improvement in social effectiveness during the six months of the experiment was related to the amount of treatment contact, in that persons receiving individual or group treatment responded to the same degree, while those in minimal treatment did not improve. By contrast, minimal treatment was followed by as much average decrease in discomfort as the other two treatments produced.

The other clue is that, while changes in discomfort showed no consistent trend during the follow-up period, on the average, patients continued to improve progressively in social effectiveness; indeed, the average improvement between six months and five years was about twice as great as that during the initial six-month period.

The fact that improvement in social effectiveness seemed related to the amount of therapeutic contact and continued to progress thereafter suggests that some sort of learning process was involved. A reduction in discomfort, on the other hand, seemed to be a response to the positive expectations engendered by any form of treatment.

The same factors may be involved in the prompt relief of discomfort produced by psychotherapy and placebos. Support for this conjecture is given in Figure 2, which shows the average response to a two-week trial on placebos of twelve patients in the psychotherapy study who had shown some recurrence of symptoms two to three years after the initial study. As can be seen, the drop in average discomfort score in response to placebos after two weeks closely resembles the drop after six months of psychotherapy. The declines in average discomfort from each treatment remain similar at follow-up.

In view of the widely held belief that symptom relief is transient, it may be surprising to see that the average discomfort score remained low throughout the follow-up period. Some possible reasons for the persistence of this relief have been considered with reference to the placebo response. As suggested earlier, relief of symptoms by whatever means enhances the patient's self-confidence and leads to a general increase in effectiveness. As one writer put it, "If the patient believes strongly in a cure . . . by his very belief he at once obtains sufficient moral support to *face all his problems* with some degree of equanimity" (Kraines 1943, p. 135; italics in the original). Greater success in solving problems of living, in turn, results in increased satisfaction and diminished frustration, further ameliorating distress.

The expectations that patients bring to therapy are often quite vague and at variance with the actual therapeutic experience. A patient will probably not remain in therapy or profit from it unless his or her expectations are soon brought into line with what actually transpires. Since psychotherapy is such a powerful influencing situation, the patient typically accepts the conditions implicitly or explicitly set by the therapist. With respect to the frequency of the therapeutic contacts, for example, an eminent psychoanalyst pointed out that when psychoanalysis was transplanted from Europe to America, the frequency of sessions soon dropped from six times a week to five, then to three or even fewer. There is no reason to think that this reduction depended on differences in the severity of illness between European and American patients, and the writer suggested that it was probably a reflection of the increasing demands on the therapists' time created by the growing number of patients seeking help. Yet, "in actual duration of treatment, in terms of months or years, the patient going five times a week takes about as long to be cured as the patient going three times" (Thompson 1950, p. 235). Several decades later, the authors of a review of other forms of therapy concluded that "once weekly sessions are as beneficial for patients as more frequent sessions" (Orlinksy and Howard 1986, p. 315).

Of course, treatment contact cannot be attenuated indefinitely without reducing its effectiveness. For example, in the comparison of three psychotherapies described above (pp. 146–47), patients who received minimal therapy, which consisted of not more than half an hour every two weeks, reported less improvement in social effectiveness than patients who were seen once a week in group or individual therapy. However, the optimal frequency of contact has yet to be determined (Orlinsky and Howard 1986).

As with the frequency of sessions, the total duration of therapeutic contact seems to depend heavily on the expectations of the therapist. Thus, practitioners of long-term therapy, such as psychoanalysts, find that their patients take months or years to respond, while practitioners of forms of time-limited therapy, even therapy limited to a single session, obtain good results within their time frames (Talmon 1990).

These observations suggest that patients comply with therapists' expectations of how long therapy should take, a supposition that gains support from a comparison of time-limited with open-ended group therapy of patients with peptic ulcers (Chappell et al. 1936). In this study, one of two matched groups of clients at a university counseling center was offered treatment without a time limit. Members of the control group were told they could have twenty interviews over a ten-week period. The patients who were given a time limit started to improve after the seventh interview (patients in the control group showed no change at this point) and reported as much gain at the end of twenty interviews as the controls reported after an average of thirty-seven interviews. Moreover, both groups maintained their rate of improvement equally well during a follow-up period averaging twelve months. These results, obtained with client-centered therapy, were replicated at another clinic using an Adlerian approach (Shlien, Mosak, and Dreikurs 1962).

Such findings do not rule out the possibility that some patients may benefit more from long-term than from short-term therapy. Indeed, Orlinsky and Howard (1986) found that two-thirds of more than 100 measures of improvement yielded a positive correlation between outcome and length of therapy across all outcome measures. However, this result may itself be biased by the predilections of the evaluators, as suggested by the finding that the relationship between the duration of treatment and outcome was lowest for patients' self-evaluations and highest for evaluations made by therapists and independent clinicians. Could it be that patients wished to spend less time in therapy than therapists?

The Preparation of Patients for Psychotherapy:
The Role-Induction Interview

To the extent that expectations of patient and therapist affect the outcome of treatment, the more congruent these are, the better the outcome of treatment should be. This leads us to a consideration of the preparation of patients for therapy.

Psychiatrists in hospital settings have long been concerned with the failure of nonpsychiatric physicians to prepare their patients adequately for psychiatric treatment. Too often the patient experiences referral to a psychiatrist as a "brush-off," a sign that the physician believes the patient's complaints to be imaginary, is tired of hearing them, or has despaired of being helpful. This attitude is epitomized by one note on a patient's chart: "Refer to the psychiatric service as a last resort."

Patients prepared, or rather ill-prepared, in this fashion arrive at the psychiatrist's office humiliated, confused, and apprehensive. Furthermore, they characteristically expect that, as in medical treatment, they will tell the psychotherapist their symptoms and the therapist will give them medicine or advice (Riessman, Cohen, and Peari 1964). That is, their expectations of psychotherapy are likely to be highly discrepant from what actually occurs.

Therapists who work in hospital clinics share the impression that a major reason why patients drop out of treatment is that they do not know what is supposed to be going on or how it can help them. Being in awe of the therapist, they politely answer all questions, and the therapist thinks everything is going well; but all this time the patients are secretly wondering what psychotherapy is all about, until suddenly they quit without warning.

Psychotherapists, therefore, urge their referring sources to prepare patients properly for a consultation by informing them of its purpose and what it will be like. In addition, most mental health clinics put the patient through some sort of intake procedure. Traditionally this consists of one or more interviews with a social worker, the purpose of which is to determine the patient's suitability for psychotherapy and to prepare the patient for it. Implicitly, the intake interview may also heighten the importance of the psychotherapist and psychotherapy in the patient's eyes by appearing to be a probationary period in which the patient's worthiness to receive this form of treatment is determined. In this sense it may not be too far-fetched to liken the intake procedure to the preparatory rites undergone by suppliants at faith-healing shrines, with the intake interviewer in the role of acolyte and the therapist as high priest.

In the first therapeutic sessions, the experienced therapist usually reviews with the patient how he or she expects the patient to act, what the patient can expect of the therapist, and what the goals of treatment are. One detailed study of psychotherapy as a social system, based on content analyses of recorded interviews with neurotic patients consulting therapists in office practice, determined that 20–50 percent of both patients' and therapists' remarks in the first three sessions were concerned with clarifying "the primary role system," as the authors termed it. As the patients learned their roles, communication by both patient and therapist about the primary role system dropped off to 8 percent (Lennard and Bernstein 1960).

As these findings suggest, therapists in all schools do a considerable amount of role induction at the beginning of the therapeutic contact, coupled with implicit or explicit communications aimed at enhancing the patient's positive expectations of treatment. Psychoanalysts, for example, go to some pains to explain the "basic rule" of free association. Although some analysts explicitly avoid any promise of therapeutic benefit, this expectation is implicit in the analyst's accepting the patient for treatment. It is not credible that the analyst would be willing to devote so much time and effort to the patient, or would let the patient undertake such an expensive and wearisome task, unless the analyst believed some good would result.

Practitioners of cognitive, behavioral, and other forms of time-limited therapy, who have no time to waste, explicitly instruct new patients about the therapeutic task and goals in such a way as to strengthen their expectations. A group of mental health experts who were permitted to observe two prominent behavior therapists at work for five days reported that during the orientation period

> the therapist tells the patient at length about the power of the treatment method, pointing out that it has been successful with comparable patients and all but promising similar results for him too. The patient . . . is given a straightforward rationale for the way in which the specific treatment procedures will "remove" his symptoms. . . . The explicit positive and authoritarian manner in which the therapist approaches the patients seems destined, if not designed, to establish the therapist as a powerful figure and turn the patient's hopes for success into concrete expectations. [Klein et al. 1969]

These observations led the senior author's research team to devise an "anticipatory socialization interview" (Orne and Wender 1968) or "role-induction interview" (Hoehn-Saric et al. 1964) to prepare clinic patients for their role in the psychotherapeutic process. Forty psychiatric outpatients who were judged suitable for psychotherapy, but who had not had extensive previous treatment, were offered psychotherapy by four second- or third-year psychiatric residents. The residents were told to treat the patients as they usually would, except that they were not required to commit themselves to more than four months of treatment. As far as they were concerned, the patients were like any other outpatients, except that they had had one preliminary contact with the research staff.

A senior psychiatrist, who did not participate in the patient's therapy, conducted the initial evaluation interview and gave half the patients a role-induction interview at its close. To the patient, this was simply part of the initial evaluation. The purpose of the role-induction interview was to try to tailor the patient's expectations to fit what would actually occur and also to help him or her behave in accordance with the therapist's image of a good patient. As a group, patients receiving the role-induction interview showed more appropriate behavior in therapy and had a better outcome than those who were not given this interview. These findings have been replicated in other settings (Sloane et al. 1970; Yalom et al. 1967).

In conclusion, it should be emphasized that the mobilization of the patient's hopes, including tailoring expectations to what will actually occur, accounts for only some of the benefits of therapy, particularly the relief of the psychic and somatic manifestations of anxiety and depression. Since these states of mind contribute to the distress and disability of most psychiatric illnesses, however, combating them by the arousal of hope, as well as by other means, is a component of all successful psychotherapies.

Summary

Experimental studies of the effects of the administration of inert medications by physicians demonstrate that the alleviation of anxiety and the arousal of hope through this means — the so-called placebo response — commonly produces considerable symptomatic relief and may promote healing of some types of tissue damage. The relief may be enduring. Since all medical and surgical procedures arouse patients' hopes, the placebo response is an integral component of all types of treatment.

Although persons who are predisposed to trust others and to accept socially defined symbols of healing are most likely to respond favorably, the placebo response seems to depend primarily on interactions between the patient's momentary state and aspects of the immediate situation, including especially the attention and interest of the healer.

The relief of anxiety and depression in psychiatric outpatients by psychotherapy closely resembles the placebo response, suggesting that the same factors may be involved. Psychotherapeutic success depends in part on a congruence between the expectations a patient brings to treatment and what actually occurs; hence, shaping these expectations by means of instructions or a preliminary role-induction interview enhances the effectiveness of short-term psychotherapy.

EIGHT

The Psychotherapist and the Patient

"She's *my* prisoner, you know!" the Red Knight said
at last.
"Yes but then *I* came and rescued her!" the White
Knight replied.

— *Through the Looking Glass*

Having looked at patients' expectations of psychotherapy, we now turn
to those characteristics of patients, therapists, and their interaction that
affect the psychotherapeutic process. Although the therapeutic relationship and therapeutic procedures obviously affect each other, it is convenient to consider them separately. This chapter focuses on the relationship, Chapters 9 and 10 on procedures.

The success of all methods and schools of psychotherapy depends on
the patients' conviction that the therapist cares about them and is competent to help. Determinants of this state of mind include the socioeconomic positions of the therapist and the patient, the therapist's
training and experience, and personal qualities of both parties. These
factors interact as part of a dynamic system, the therapeutic relationship.

The material that follows comes from interview or psychodynamic
forms of psychotherapy as practiced by professionally trained persons in
offices, clinics, and hospitals. Reflecting our own background and experience, we will focus primarily on treatment by professionals, especially

psychiatrists and psychologists, though these are only partly representative of the entire field.

Studies of the relative importance of relationship and procedure in psychotherapy run the gamut between two logical extremes. Existential-humanist psychotherapists claim that the therapist's capacity to "merge" with the patient (Havens 1974) is the essential ingredient of therapeutic success. Some behavior therapists, on the other hand, maintain that the procedure is all that matters, at least for such problems as reducing fear. A self-help manual may be as effective for many phobic patients as a live therapist (see pp. 226–27).

While most therapists do not adhere to either extreme, behavior therapists typically regard a working relationship between patient and therapist as a precondition but not a cause of change. Hence, behaviorists rarely study or discuss the determinants or effects of the therapeutic relationship (Wilson and Evans 1977). Others, including the present authors, find the weight of evidence to be that the therapeutic bond itself is a major source of success in treatment (Orlinsky and Howard 1986). At the same time, we acknowledge that some patients with some symptoms may respond to automated therapies, just as some patients benefit from self-help books.

The Sociocultural Status of Psychotherapists and Patients

In all cultures, psychotherapeutic success depends in part on patients' confidence that the therapist possesses healing knowledge and skills. As noted earlier, culturally specific beliefs and symbols of the therapist's curative powers shape a patient's perceptions and expectations even before the two meet. In nonindustrialized societies the shaman's training is universally regarded as proof of healing powers. In the West, similarly, the various training programs for therapists validate their healing abilities for particular groups of prospective patients.

The shamans, however, have an advantage over their Western counterparts in that they represent and transmit the unified, all-encompassing world-view of their society. Because industrialized societies are pluralistic, no trained psychotherapist can be sure of general acceptance. Psychiatrists, in particular, suffer from a mixed public image (Gabbard and Gabbard 1987). Perhaps reflecting a dual heritage from religion and medicine, psychiatrists may be invested with attributes of both shaman and physician, leading to overvaluation in some respects and undervaluation in others. Some persons regard a psychiatrist as the possessor of unusual wisdom and, at times, almost magical powers. At parties, guests may speak half-seriously of their fear that a psychiatrist will read their minds. Some patients expect their psychiatrist to resolve lifelong problems in a few sessions. The ability gently to disabuse them of their exalted expectations without destroying their confidence is an important psychiatric skill.

Patients and the public derogate psychiatrists as well. Psychiatrists are the butt of endless jokes, are the target of much irritation, and are viewed by many, including quite a few medical colleagues, as near-quacks who promise much but perform little. Thus, with some patients the psychiatrist's initial task may be to overcome skepticism rather than to find a way of climbing down gracefully from a pedestal.

While contemporary psychotherapists cannot count on acceptance by all patients, pluralistic tolerance of a considerable variety of assumptive systems affords a multitude of routes to mental health. Patients can achieve personal integration by adhering to values that are not widely shared and without having to achieve harmonious relationships with any particular group. Those who reject such widely held values as conformity and social prestige can usually find therapists who share their views. Moreover, Americans place a high value on obedience to the dictates of one's own best self. The therapist who helps a patient achieve greater inner freedom and self-fulfillment, even at the expense of conformity, may in fact be advocating an important, shared social value. Patients who achieve these goals may gain in respect and admiration from a few others what is lost in general popularity.

On the negative side, in a complex, industrialized society, psychotherapists and patients may differ widely in ethnicity, education, and socioeconomic class. These disparities create a host of problems. Class differences have been the most widely studied, though educational, ethnic, religious, and racial differences between therapist and patient may be equally important. In particular, interview therapies developed for middle- and upper-class patients often fail to meet the expectations and needs of lower-class ones. Surveys over the years have consistently shown that the lower the socioeconomic status of patients, the less likely they are to accept or remain in conventional interview or psychodynamic therapy (Garfield 1986). Much thought and effort has been expended on the development of approaches that can bridge the gap between therapists and patients of different backgrounds.

Though many lower-class patients reject psychotherapy because they cannot afford it or relate to it, those who do remain in treatment respond at least as well as patients of higher socioeconomic status (Frank et al. 1957; Garfield 1986). Several possible explanations come to mind. The lower-class patient's determination in overcoming severe obstacles in order to make repeated clinic visits implies strong motivation. Moreover, a difference in class does not always imply a communication gap. Many lower-class patients have middle-class values. For some, the therapist may represent a group to which they aspire to belong. For others, the handicap of class difference may be more than overcome by the therapist's prestige. A high-status figure who simply listens receptively may raise patients' morale and be powerfully therapeutic, especially for those who have never had such an experience before.

The therapeutic power of sympathetic listening by a prestigious figure may explain the cure of a lower-class Korean woman who suffered from the monosymptomatic delusion that her nose was growing bigger and would eventually grow over her mouth. Afraid that others could see this, she progressively restricted her activities until she was practically housebound. She consulted a plastic surgeon, who of course referred her to a psychiatric clinic. There, a medical student and then a psychiatrist listened to her complaints for about an hour and a half. She left unconvinced, still insisting on an operation for her nose. A week later, however, she called the medical student to tell him that she felt much better and was resuming outside activities, because "the nose was only a little thing." A follow-up phone call eight months later revealed that she had continued to progress. When asked what had helped her, she replied: "I loved Dr. _____ [the medical student]. He had a feeling I wanted to talk, and he let me talk." It is highly unlikely that she had ever before received so much sympathetic attention from a person of high status.

The Training of Psychotherapists

The demand for psychotherapy is so great that psychotherapists trained in the traditional disciplines of psychiatry, psychology, and social work cannot begin to serve everyone who needs or wants such help. Laypeople or paraprofessionals of all sorts have flourishing psychotherapy practices. These healers range from those with minimal training or experience, such as many leaders of encounter groups, to highly trained mental health counselors (Rioch 1967). Students, indigenous helpers, psychiatric aides, and fellow patients have been enlisted to help, among others, the chronically ill, hospitalized patients, the clientele of community mental health centers, and persons contemplating suicide. All report good results. No one type of training or background seems to foster therapeutic ethos more effectively than another. Among those who have had professional training, moreover, psychiatrists, psychologists, and social workers seem to do equally well.

Some would argue that lay and professional therapists achieve similar results because much of the subject matter taught to professionals is irrelevant to psychotherapy. A more charitable hypothesis, and one probably nearer the truth, is that with most patients, success depends primarily on the therapist's ability to establish a therapeutic relationship, an ability that is taught equally well in the training programs of all disciplines.

Indeed, to the extent that persons seeking psychotherapy are demoralized, they may respond to anyone with a modicum of human warmth, common sense, some sensitivity, and a desire to help. Regardless of their training, healers may be effective if they are able to combat patients' demoralization, mobilize their expectation of help, and shore up or restore their self-confidence.

Though therapists with different training may achieve similar results, it would be wrong to conclude that training in psychotherapy is unnecessary. The content of therapeutic procedures should not be confused with their functions. Most training programs emphasize particular conceptual schemes and associated techniques. These include behavior therapies, group therapies, and a variety of interview approaches. By teaching particular skills, all training programs indirectly enhance the trainee's ability to maintain a therapeutic attitude. In particular, they strengthen the novice's self-confidence through mastery of a procedure, induction into a professional role and status, and support of like-minded colleagues. The mastery of one or more therapies through training creates and maintains the therapist's confidence, which in turn may be a therapeutic factor that enhances patients' expectations of help. Sustaining the therapist's confidence is especially valuable in the face of inevitable failures. As one young trainee put it, "Even if the patient doesn't get better, you know you're doing the right thing."

A brief look at psychoanalytic training, the longest established and probably the most arduous form of therapist education, highlights the positive and negative effects of systematically grounding therapists in a body of theory and technique. Those who undergo this training come from the ranks of other psychotherapeutic professions, and some of their self-confidence as healers remains linked to the prestige of their original disciplines. However, as time goes on, their confidence rests more and more firmly on the group identification provided by the training program of the psychoanalytic institute.

In its classical form, psychoanalysis involves frequent sessions over a period of months or years. The patient lies on a couch with the analyst out of sight and says whatever comes to mind. As the patient reviews and relives important early experiences, the analyst becomes a stand-in for parental and other important figures in the patient's life. This role may provoke strong emotional reactions, which the therapist interprets back to the patient.

The training methods of analytic institutes emphasize maximal participation of the trainee or "candidate" — a term not without significance, as we shall see. Typically, the program includes didactic work and carefully supervised treatment of several cases according to the method. The core of the training, however, is the therapist's "training analysis," in which he or she becomes the patient of a senior analyst.

Psychoanalytic training is prolonged, laborious, and expensive. It lasts at least four years and costs thousands of dollars. Young therapists willingly make these sacrifices for a number of reasons. Practical considerations such as prestige and the guarantee of referrals on completion of training undoubtedly influence some. For others, the appeal of analytic theories themselves may be the compelling factor. Other psychological theories may explain certain aspects of human functioning more satisfactorily or be more easily verifiable, but none approaches psychoanalysis in scope or intellectual fascination. Moreover, many analytic concepts have been incorporated not only into other explanations of mental illness and its treatment but also into all aspects of America's cultural and intellectual life. Mastery of psychoanalysis gives the candidate the satisfaction of being thoroughly familiar with theories that others know only indirectly or incompletely.

Whether the theory's attractiveness accounts for the appeal of psychoanalysis is uncertain. The power of the training procedure is probably equally significant. The analytic institute is a tight little island in which the candidate comes into continual formal and informal contact with other trainees and the teaching staff, all of whom represent a consistent viewpoint. Above all, as a form of indoctrination, the training analysis profoundly influences candidates' attitudes toward the whole enterprise.

The avowed purpose of the training analysis is to familiarize the candidate with the method through direct experience. The procedure is intended to make the trainee a better therapist by enhancing self-knowledge, resolving or at least mitigating certain emotional conflicts and vulnerabilities, and enabling the person to guard against the effects of those that remain. The training analysis supposedly helps the candidate become more objective and more sensitive to and tolerant of patients' attitudes and feelings. This is believed necessary because prolonged psychotherapy often creates a highly charged emotional relationship between patient and therapist. Unless the therapist is emotionally secure and able to identify personal feelings and motives, his or her reactions may adversely affect patients.

The training analysis influences the candidate's personality. The analysand repeatedly reviews current thoughts and feelings in relation to his or her life history, which the analyst consistently interprets in accordance with the institute's particular brand of analytic theory. Since the candidate must take the initiative in these intensely personal revelations, the method fosters improvisation and participation. Training analyses last several years, during which some material is reviewed repeatedly. Such engagement and repetition are important in producing attitudinal change. Furthermore, the training analysis is not complete until the candidate produces thoughts, memories, and feelings in a form that confirms the doctrine of the institute. As a leading psychoanalyst noted, "It is scarcely to be expected that a student who has spent years under the artificial . . . conditions of a training analysis and whose professional career depends on overcoming 'resistance' to the satisfaction of his training analyst, can be in a favorable position to defend his scientific integrity against the analyst's theory and practice" (Glover 1952, p. 403).

At this point the full significance of the term "candidate" becomes clear. The ultimate criterion for acceptance into membership in an analytic institute is completion of the training analysis. No matter how heavy a candidate's investment of time, effort, and money, participation in the education program does not by itself guarantee membership; for the candidate to become a member, he or she must personally respond to the training analysis. This requirement provides a powerful incentive for candidates to conform to and accept the institute's particular model of human behavior (Greben 1982).

The trainee's colleagues, who also are in the process of becoming indoctrinated, further reinforce the conceptual scheme. The more deeply candidates immerse themselves in their training, the more they tend to confine their professional and social contacts to one another. This self-selection both fosters and reflects the development of a common body of shared experience and the acquisition of a specialized vocabulary, the terms of which are fully grasped only by members of the same school. The cohesiveness of each group is heightened by the competition of rival analytic groups and the hostility of large segments of other professions, especially medicine.

Like other specialists, analysts continue to associate with their own group after they finish training. This seems to preserve the conceptual scheme in a fashion similar to Wesley's classes, especially since members who come to doubt the theory usually drift out of the group. Finally, public adherence to certain methods and doctrines that the trainee has made important sacrifices to master creates strong incentives for belief. In these circumstances, the trainee's abandonment of his or her position would entail severe cognitive dissonance (Festinger 1957).

Such training has both positive and negative effects on the therapist's ability to enter into a therapeutic alliance with patients, and on his or her ability to persist in the face of difficulties. The effect of analytic training on the therapist's ability to form relationships depends in part on the candidate's education and personality before enrollment. For example, the personality changes fostered by the training analysis may improve the therapeutic ability of physicians whose previous experience has taught them to view patients as specimens of disease rather than as persons. Indeed, greater self-awareness and self-acceptance may enable therapists of any background to dispense with self-protective maneuvers and relate to patients in a more personal and accepting way. On the other hand, the cultivation of objectivity and self-awareness may reduce the therapeutic efficacy of those who are already aloof, passive, or overly introspective. Analytic training may entice such therapists across the thin line between objectivity and coldness, self-awareness and morbid introspection, tolerance and indifference.

A therapist's thorough indoctrination in any theory, including psychoanalysis, has other mixed consequences for practice. Indoctrination may increase the therapist's capacity to inspire patients' hope and confidence. A therapist who is convinced by personal experience of the validity of a particular method may be powerfully effective in persuading patients that they too will benefit. Moreover, psychoanalysis resembles many other theories of healing in providing explanations for lack of progress that protect its core beliefs from disproof and its practitioners from despair. Patients who do not improve may be showing "resistance," and their criticism of the therapist may be dismissed as "negative transference." Since treatment is open-ended, the analyst can always believe that further sessions might have made the therapy effective. In certain cases, such persistence can in fact transform failures into successes. In general, commitment to the theory keeps the therapist willing to take on new patients even after disappointments with others, and willing to try multiple techniques within the theory if one particular one is not effective.

Analytic institutes have contributed to overall progress in the field of mental science. Their support has enabled analysts to persist in trailbreaking explorations of the human psyche in the face of widespread and often vehement opposition. Despite early exclusion from the ranks of academic medicine — with concomitant lack of status, financial insecurity, and lack of access to students — the analysts persisted. Their theory and its derivatives have had an invigorating and liberating influence not only on psychiatry but also on all intellectual disciplines concerned with human beings and on many forms of creative activity.

Nevertheless, an overemphasis on training and theory can also be harmful to patients and therapists. On a very pragmatic level, the expenses and sacrifices of prolonged study increase the costs of therapeutic services and force many therapists into private practice. This leads to a disproportionate expenditure of therapeutic effort on a small segment of the patient population.

From another standpoint, the confidence instilled by intensive training and maintained by group support may foster dogmatism and rigidity. Highly trained therapists often prefer to restrict their practice to patients who fit their particular training, excluding many others. Behaviorists may ignore patients whose suffering does not take the form of a discrete symptom. Psychoanalysts typically prefer to treat young, verbal, and emotionally responsive patients who might do as well in many less costly and arduous therapies. By limiting themselves to a narrow range of patients and rigidly adhering to a particular theory, therapists may avoid challenging experiences that are conducive to professional growth. Rationalizing therapeutic failures in order to preserve a theory, furthermore, may lead therapists to blame patients for their failure to improve. Especially when this is done covertly, by ignoring or disconfirming the patient's point of view, such behavior may increase the person's confusion, sense of failure, and demoralization.

Finally, psychoanalysis, like other broad theories, has fostered interest in certain areas at the expense of others that may be equally important. In particular, although theoretically recognizing the importance of biological factors in mental illness, analysts in their writings have stressed psychological factors and given inadequate weight to the role of biologically based assets and liabilities. They have also stressed the role of personal life experiences, especially in childhood, to the relative neglect of the current context of patients' behavior and of sociocultural forces.

Being all-inclusive, psychoanalysis, like many other therapeutic rationales, has great persuasive power. Many of its postulates, however, are not susceptible to empirical verification. Analytic theories do evolve and change in the light of experience, but these changes consist primarily of elaborations, accretions, and shifts in emphasis. The critical scrutiny applied within the confines of the institute is limited in scope (Greben 1982). No training institute has yet disbanded because it concluded that its theory was inferior to that of another school.

On balance, we would argue that professional training of psycho-therapists is important to their success, but that its value has been over-estimated. Indeed, the success of various subprofessions of therapists, in which training is typically much shorter than that of the classical disci-plines, suggests that the minimum theoretical knowledge needed to be an effective therapist is far less than has previously been recognized.

An ingenious study of psychodynamic therapy involving college stu-dents illustrates the difficulty of clearly identifying the contribution of training to therapeutic success. The study compared the results of trained professionals with those of untrained professors who were chosen for their interest in helping students (Strupp and Hadley 1979). Both groups were relatively ineffective in treating hostile patients who had poor egos. In the sample as a whole, the professionals achieved no greater average improvement than the untrained therapists. The trained therapists, however, did "impressively better" with highly motivated patients who readily formed a therapeutic alliance (Strupp 1986, p. 517). The chief problem of the kindly but therapeutically untrained college professors was that they sometimes ran out of things to talk about. This predicament was never reported by the experienced therapists (Strupp, personal communication).

Beyond training, experience seems to be a crucial determinant of therapeutic competence. Despite dissenting voices (Klein and Rabkin 1984), the weight of evidence suggests that experienced therapists, re-gardless of their special training, get better results than novices (Beutler, Crago, and Arizmendi 1986, pp. 283–87). One explanation could be that therapists whose patients do poorly are more likely to leave the field before achieving seniority. More probably, experience correlates with success because psychotherapy is an art that improves with practice. Indeed, most training programs include as much apprentice practice as theoretical grounding, so professionally trained therapists typically en-ter practice with more experience than lay practitioners.

Experience has particularly strong effects on the quality of the thera-peutic relationship. A study of taped interviews revealed that the psycho-therapeutic relationships developed by experienced practitioners from different schools were more similar than those created by experts and novices from the same school (Fiedler 1953). The relationships fostered by the expert therapists, furthermore, were more like the "ideal" thera-peutic relationship than those created by nonexperts. The ideal thera-peutic relationship was determined simply by asking four experts from different schools to describe it. These experts emphasized therapists' complete participation in patients' communication, and their ability to understand and share patients' feelings. Apparently, experience overcomes doctrinal differences. This finding was confirmed by another study, which showed that patients treated by therapists from different schools attributed their improvement to the different methods used but described their relationships with their therapists in similar terms (Heine 1953). The patients' descriptions were very similar to the practitioners' views of the ideal therapeutic relationship.

One training program has focused exclusively on the cultivation of a therapeutic relationship. It tries to enhance the trainee's ability to be empathic, genuine, and warm — the postulated essential qualities of a healing attitude — through the study of tapes of interviews, role-playing with other trainees, and working with patients under close supervision, all of which are followed by group discussions (Truax and Carkhufff 1967).

In recent years, research has become more sophisticated in assessing simultaneously the contribution of the therapeutic relationship and of specific techniques to successful outcome. In particular, researchers have created manuals of procedure that specify and operationalize aspects of the therapeutic process. These manuals permit experimenters to measure how closely the therapist adheres to the procedure and how this adherence relates to the therapeutic outcome. Findings to date suggest that the outcome depends on a complex interaction between adherence to the technique and personal properties of therapists and patients (Luborsky et al. 1986; Strupp 1988).

Thus, a study of time-limited, dynamic psychotherapy showed that adherence to the manual was related to a good outcome overall, but that a subgroup of therapists who adhered most closely to the manual also had the worst outcomes (Strupp 1988). These therapists described themselves as self-controlling and self-blaming, were judged to display the least warmth and friendliness, and elicited the highest levels of hostility from their patients.

In any case, with most patients and therapists, a good therapeutic relationship and adherence to a technique reinforce each other. Both the therapist's adherence to the treatment manual and a good outcome may be facilitated by qualities in the patient that enable the therapist to "maintain the integrity of the therapeutic approach" (Docherty 1985, p. 634). A therapist probably finds it easier to adhere to the manual with a patient who welcomes and is responsive to the therapist's procedures than with a patient who resists them.

Furthermore, the therapist's adherence to a particular technique provides both therapist and patient with a feeling of security and demonstrates the therapist's competence. This in turn enhances the patient's faith in the therapist, strengthening willingness to cooperate and making it easier for the therapist to stick to the procedure.

Backgrounds and Personal Characteristics of Psychotherapists

Turning from the training and experience of psychotherapists to aspects of their backgrounds and personalities, we find several clues that psychotherapists may be self-selected for their sensitivity to certain kinds of human distress. For example, an extensive interview and questionnaire survey of psychotherapists in three large American cities revealed that, compared with the population at large, children of Jewish immigrants from Eastern European cities were highly overrepresented in the therapeutic professions. Psychiatrists, psychologists, and social workers were all socially mobile as well as more politically liberal and less religious than their parents. Beyond the specifically Jewish cultural value placed on language and on understanding interpersonal processes (Herz and Rosen 1982), persons whose own ties to traditional values are in flux may be predisposed to empathize with others who have problems of personal adjustment (Henry 1977).

Indeed, the choice of a career in psychotherapy has sometimes been a way of solving the therapist's personal problems. Some members of the early generations of psychotherapists, especially in the psychoanalytic tradition, clearly had troubled lives (Maeder 1989). This gave rise to the quip that one doesn't have to be crazy to be a psychiatrist — but it helps. Personal vulnerability may motivate and enable a person to heal others, an insight embodied in the Greek myth of the centaur Chiron: Chiron, the teacher of Aesculapius, suffered from a wound that never healed. We may recall that some shamans are or have been mentally ill (see Chapter 4). A person's own wounds may enhance the ability to empathize with the sufferings of others. In addition, the healer who has been cured may serve as a model and a source of hope to the sufferer.

The therapist's personal suffering, however, is not inevitably helpful; troubled therapists have been known to exploit patients in the service of their own needs, with predictably disastrous results. Nor is there any evidence that psychotherapists who have undergone therapy themselves are more successful than those who have not (Greenberg and Staller 1981).

A psychotherapist's success depends in part on his or her genuine concern for the patient's welfare. One influential existential psychiatrist even insists that the therapist should be willing to "risk his own existence in the struggle for the freedom of his partner's" (Binswanger 1956, p. 148). This attitude recalls those shamans who risk their souls in certain healing rituals (see p. 100). Other things being equal, therapists probably invest more effort in patients whom they like and respect, if not for what they are, then for what they can become. Freud expressed this clearly in his first publication on psychotherapy: "[Psychoanalysis] presupposes in [the physician] . . . a personal concern for the patients. . . . I cannot imagine bringing myself to delve into the psychical mechanism of a hysteria in anyone who struck me as low-minded and repellent, and who, on closer acquaintance, would not be capable of arousing human sympathy" (Breuer and Freud 1957, p. 265). In short, psychotherapists' personal predilections may influence their choice of patients and their relative success with different types (Rogow 1970). Recognizing this, some psychiatrists will not attempt to treat alcoholics, while others avoid hysteric patients; some believe they do especially well with depressed patients, while others regard their forte as persons with schizophrenia.

Research provides support for the claim that personal qualities of therapists make appreciable contributions to their success. A repeated finding is that success rates of therapists differ widely and that these differences seem to depend more on the therapist than on the type of treatment (Luborsky et al. 1986). A study of encounter groups, which are sufficiently similar to therapy groups to justify extending this finding to them, illustrates the point. Analyzing the success rates of at least two therapists from each of several therapeutic schools, Lieberman, Yalom, and Miles (1973) found that the best and the worst outcomes were obtained by therapists belonging to the same school. In a retrospective review of 150 women treated by sixteen male and ten female therapists, Orlinsky and Howard (1980) extended this finding to individual therapy. They found that two-thirds of the patients of the most successful therapists were much improved and none were worse, while for the least successful therapists only one-third of the patients were much improved and one-third were worse. This finding suggests that effectiveness is primarily a quality of the therapist, not of a particular technique.

Our understanding of personal qualities of therapists that account for differences in therapeutic success, however, has not progressed beyond the empathy, warmth, and genuineness that Rogers and his school (Truax and Carkhuff 1967) found helpful with neurotic patients. More recent studies of the interpersonal treatment of depression (Rounsaville et al. 1987) partly confirm the importance of these qualities, which also resemble the "active personal participation" that has been described as contributing to therapists' success with schizophrenic patients (Dent 1978; Whitehorn and Betz 1975).

While research on therapist variables has produced interesting findings, the essence of some therapists' healing power may have eluded scientific definition. Every age produces great healers who are typically dismissed as quacks by their conservative brethren, but who nevertheless are often astoundingly effective. Some proceed to create schools based on the doctrines they devised to explain their healing ability, chiropractic being a notable example. The founder of such a method typically discovers his or her healing power before evolving a theory to explain it. Many founders of schools of psychotherapy seem to be similarly gifted, and they obtain better results than most of their disciples.

Healing ability, like musical talent, may well be a widely but unevenly distributed quality. No amount of training can make a tone-deaf person into a musician. Given a modicum of musical talent and sufficient determination, however, anyone can become a passable performer, though not a virtuoso. The same may hold true for psychotherapeutic talent. Thus, while some healers may need little training, many persons can learn to be better therapists through formal study.

Personal Attributes of Patients

The personal qualities and attitudes that patients bring to psychotherapy seem to have a greater effect on their response to therapy than does the technique their therapist uses. Patients' own world-views or personal attributes predispose them to accept some therapeutic conceptualizations and procedures more readily than others. For example, a practical-minded engineer with a fear of flying might respond best to the concrete formulations and rituals of a behavior therapist. A philosophy student with similar symptoms, on the other hand, might benefit more from an existential therapist who linked fear of flying to fear of death and helped cure the student by means of the therapeutic encounter.

In general, the research findings concerning responsiveness to interview psychotherapies confirm what common sense predicts: the better a person's overall emotional health, the more likely it is that he or she will benefit from psychotherapy. For example, Rounsaville, Weissman, and Prusoff (1981) administered a structured prognostic interview to depressed outpatients after their first session of interpersonal therapy and found that those with the best general level of functioning improved the most in symptoms and social functioning during treatment. These patients also participated most fully in the processes of this form of therapy, a result that supports the surmise that the relationship between therapists' adherence to a therapeutic manual and favorable outcome reflects mainly the greater ease of maintaining therapeutic purity with responsive patients.

Also predicted by common sense is the finding that interpersonal responsiveness influences accessibility to psychotherapy. In civilian life, most of the stresses that bring persons to psychotherapy involve such interpersonal disturbances as family or work-related conflicts or losses. A study of interpersonal therapy for depression found that patients whose depression could be linked to stresses of this kind did better than those whose symptoms did not seem related to obvious external pressures (Prusoff et al. 1980).[1] Apparently, psychotherapy works best for patients who are significantly affected by their personal relationships. This finding may explain, in part, the preponderance of women among seekers of psychotherapy, since women may be particularly influenced by the quality of their interpersonal relationships (Miller 1976).

In general, psychotherapy seems most helpful to people who have some capacity and willingness to enter into close relationships with others. Thus, persons who participate in group activities and are generally socially successful seem to do better than antagonistic, mistrustful loners and nomads. The authors of a small pilot study found that patients who had a close, confidential relationship with a family member or friend did better in brief psychotherapy than those who lacked such support (Stone, Imber, and Frank 1966). Along the same lines, Strupp suggested that patients' ability to benefit from psychotherapy requires their experiences with their own parents to have been sufficiently rewarding to permit them to develop "the capacity to profit from and change as a result of the forces operating in a 'good' human relationship" (1976, p. 99).

A person's emotional reactivity also correlates with both interpersonal responsiveness and suitability for psychotherapy. Patients who seek psychotherapy report a great range of distress. Some are absolutely desperate, and most are sufficiently troubled that they wish relief and are open to any helpful influence, though some show little evidence of emotional tension. Emotional arousal, as we have already noted, seems to be

1. Beyond the role of interpersonal reactivity as a character trait, the presence of precipitating stress may predict a favorable response to therapy because stress induces a whole range of transient symptoms that are overdiagnosed as evidence of illness. In this connection, the manifestations of emotional turmoil seen in disaster victims encompass a wide range of neurotic symptoms (Bolin 1988) that may subside spontaneously or with prompt supportive help (Titchener 1988). Analogously, a considerable proportion of those patients whose distress is linked to environmental pressures may need only a little help to regain their emotional equilibrium, and whatever brand of psychotherapy the therapist uses receives credit for this outcome.

both a facilitator and a concomitant of attitudinal change (see pp. 46–47), and distressing emotional arousal may motivate patients to engage in psychotherapy.

In this connection, the patients who are most refractory to treatment seem to have nothing in common except a lack of distress. For example, antisocial personalities are among the most difficult patients to treat. Such people may be forced into treatment as a consequence of their misbehavior, but most seem to be relatively content with their lifestyles. To form a therapeutic relationship with such persons, the healer must create or unearth some source of distress or otherwise convince them that they need to change. As Kubie wrote years ago, "Without a full-hearted acknowledgment of the sense of illness a patient can go through only the motions of treatment" (1936, p. 140). The difficulty of treating persons who are not in distress brings to mind the efforts of cult leaders and revivalists to arouse painful emotions such as fear and guilt. Some persons can be motivated to change only by being incarcerated in a mental hospital or prison, with release depending on appropriate changes in their behavior and attitudes (Vaillant 1975).

To be suitable for interview therapies, moreover, patients must not only be in distress but must also be able to experience and relate their emotional states to psychological problems. Patients who recognize their feelings, express them in psychological terms, and relate their distress to interpersonal problems tend to stay in psychotherapy longer and do much better than "alexithymic" patients, who experience and express emotions indirectly, through bodily symptoms (Sifneos, Apfel-Savitz, and Frankel 1977). The latter simply lack the language in which psychotherapy is conducted. In some, absorption with bodily complaints also represents an attempt to retreat from involvement with others. Such patients have great difficulty relating closely to a therapist.

Conversely, when linked to interpersonal issues, complaints of anxiety or other psychic symptoms imply both responsiveness to others and a willingness to risk humiliating self-revelation. The ability to experience and reveal feelings often implies that a person can learn to trust a psychotherapist and has some motivation to change. Openness or self-relatedness has been found to be the personality attribute most consistently related to a positive outcome of therapy (Orlinsky and Howard 1986).

In a series of experimental and statistical studies, Schachter (1959) beautifully demonstrated the close relationships that exist between the degree of expressed anxiety, dependency on others, and acceptance of psychotherapy. In one of them, female college students were led to expect a painful shock after a ten-minute delay. They were then given the choice of waiting with other students in a similar predicament or staying by themselves. Schachter simultaneously ascertained their level of anxiety by asking them to rate how they felt about receiving a shock and by giving them a chance to withdraw from the experiment if they wished to do so. The anxiety of those who withdrew was greater than that of those who stayed. Actually, the experiment terminated before the shock was administered.

Schachter found that the desire to be with others was related to the expressed degree of anxiety. Subjects who were the only or the firstborn child in a family reported more anxiety than children who were later in the birth order. Moreover, firstborn subjects with high anxiety had a stronger desire to be with others than later-born subjects with the same degree of anxiety.

Schachter then analyzed the statistics of a nearby Veterans Administration mental hygiene clinic. He found that patients who were firstborn or only children accepted psychotherapy more readily and stayed in therapy longer once they accepted it than did those who were later-born. Patients in the first group were, however, no "sicker" than those in the second; that is, ordinal position in the family was unrelated to the degree of psychological disturbance. A plausible explanation that relates the experimental study to the statistical review is that firstborn children tend to be more dependent on others to relieve their distress than are later-born siblings. Parents are both more inexperienced and more anxious with firstborn children than with subsequent offspring; moreover, they are able to give the first child undivided attention. Thus, parents may be overprotective of the first child and/or they may handle the child inconsistently, both of which patterns would, on theoretical grounds, be expected to increase dependency. We may tentatively conclude that dependency is related both to a susceptibility to anxiety and to the acceptance of psychotherapy. That all three qualities may relate to the order of birth is a fascinating finding that opens interesting vistas for further study.

So far we have considered personality traits that are related to accessibility to interview psychotherapies in general. A personality attribute that is termed "locus of control" (Rotter 1966) seems to influence relative responsiveness to different forms of psychotherapy. Persons with a predominantly internal locus of control tend to attribute favorable or unfavorable life events to their own efforts or to enduring personal characteristics. In contrast, persons with a predominantly external locus of control attribute life events primarily to chance, fate, or powerful others.

The locus of control concept applies to psychotherapy. In one complex study (Liberman 1978b), outpatients in brief psychotherapy performed a series of therapy-linked tasks designed to show that their per-

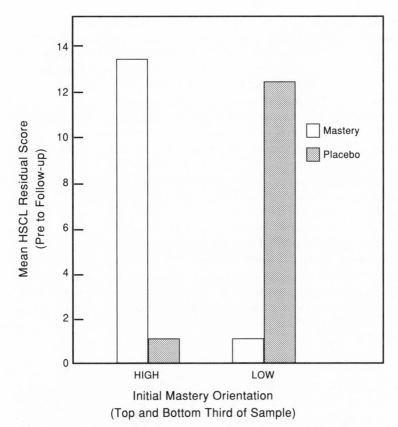

Figure 3.
High and Low Mastery Orientation and Response to Mastery and
Placebo Conditions

Note: The higher the mean HSCL Residual Score, the greater the improvement (Frank
et al. 1978, pp. 57–59).

formance progressively improved. Half of the patients were led to
attribute this improvement to their own efforts (an internal source) and
half to a placebo pill (an external source). At the start of the experiment,
patients rated themselves on a symptom checklist, and an interviewer,
using a structured questionnaire, rated them on their sense of mastery, a
concept similar to locus of control.

Figure 3 shows the degree of symptomatic improvement on the symptom checklist (HSCL) three months after the end of the experiment. For
patients who attributed improved task performance to their own efforts,
those who were rated as having a high sense of mastery reported signifi-

cantly more symptomatic improvement than those with a low sense of mastery. Conversely, for patients who attributed improved task performance to the pill, those who were rated as having a low sense of mastery reported more improvement than those with a high sense of mastery (Liberman 1978b). This finding suggests that placebo responsiveness (see Chapter 7) is related to external locus of control.

Simons et al. (1985) provided further indirect support for the importance of locus of control in determining psychiatric patients' responses to psychotherapy and medication. They compared the effects of imipramine versus cognitive therapy in depressed patients who differed in "learned resourcefulness," a concept closely related to both mastery and locus of control. Although medication and cognitive therapy were equally effective overall in relieving depression, patients who scored high on learned resourcefulness did relatively better in cognitive therapy, while low scorers did relatively better on imipramine.

Finally, a review of several studies of psychotherapy that classified patients in terms of locus of control or similar concepts reported that externals had better outcomes with structured, directive psychotherapies, while internals gained more from nondirective, unstructured therapies (Foon 1987).

The Therapeutic Dyad

So far we have considered therapists and patients largely independently of each other. In previous chapters we briefly reviewed the importance of the therapist's being caring, competent, without ulterior motives (Chapter 2), and possessing personal characteristics and trappings that would contribute to his or her credibility in the eyes of patients — his or her ethos, to use a term from rhetoric (Chapter 3). In this chapter we have considered some sociocultural background factors and personal qualities of the patient and the therapist that affect the therapeutic encounter.

It is now time to recall that the therapy situation is an evolving dynamic system comprising patient, therapist, and therapeutic procedure. The properties of this system are determined by the interaction of these three components (Lennard and Bernstein 1960), as well as by features of the broader context in which therapy transpires. Our primary focus will be on the patient-therapist relationship — also labeled the therapeutic bond (Orlinsky and Howard 1986), the therapeutic relationship (Strupp and Binder 1984), and the helping alliance (Luborsky 1984) — as both the vehicle of psychotherapy and the major determinant of its outcome. A bit of empirical support for the overriding importance of the therapeutic relationship is the finding (with a large cohort of male methadone addicts treated by nine therapists using three different forms of psychotherapy) that the patients' perception of the favorableness of the alliance, obtained after the third interview, correlated significantly with outcomes after six months both across therapies and within each therapist's case load (Luborsky et al. 1986). The items comprising the helping-alliance questionnaire addressed how well the patients thought the therapists understood their problems and were able to help them.

When therapy is viewed as a system, the relevance of personal attributes of patients to their responses to psychotherapy may lie primarily in the impression these attributes make on the therapist. This impression, in turn, affects the therapist's behavior toward the patient. Several types of evidence support this statement. One consists of the relation often found between a favorable therapeutic outcome and the therapist's and patient's positive feelings toward each other. We have already quoted Freud's statement that he could not imagine himself analyzing patients who failed to arouse some human sympathy, a statement consistent with a quantitative study that revealed substantial correlations between clinic therapists' retrospective ratings of outcome and their feelings of warmth and liking for their patients (Strupp et al. 1963). Similarly, the study described earlier (pp. 151–52) on the preparation of patients for psychotherapy found that "attractive" patients improved more after four months of therapy than "unattractive" ones. The rating of attractiveness was a global judgment made by the initial interviewer (not the patient's therapist) and turned out to be based primarily on youth, intelligence, education, and occupational level. Presumably therapists, too, would find these qualities attractive (Schofield 1964). Not all attractive patients did well, however, nor did all unattractive ones do poorly, confirming the obvious fact that the impression made by the patient is not the only determinant of therapeutic outcome.

With respect to the patients' perception of the therapeutic system, a major study determined that successful patients in both interview and behavior therapy "rated the personal interaction with the therapist as the single most important factor in their treatment" (Sloane et al. 1975, p. 225). Those who reported higher levels of warmth, empathy, or genuineness in their therapists also tended to report greater improvement.

Findings such as these have encouraged researchers in psychotherapy to look for similarities and dissimilarities between patients and therapists that might affect the therapeutic outcome. In their study of women in therapy, for example, Orlinsky and Howard (1980) found that the differential success rate of therapists appeared to be due primarily to particular patient and therapist combinations rather than to properties of the patient or therapist alone. Although the sex of the therapist made no difference overall, young single women benefited more from female therapists, which suggests that they may have considered men somewhat threatening. Conversely, the only female patients who did better with male therapists were parents without partners. Perhaps the therapist represented to them a potential new partner.

Demographic variables such as age and sex provide only indirect clues about which features of patients and therapists relate directly to therapeutic success. More promising are studies of therapists' and patients' conceptual levels and values.

The level of conceptualization may prove relevant to the matching of patients, therapists, and therapies (Carr 1970). Although no conclusive findings have emerged, the weight of evidence is that persons who conceptualize at relatively concrete levels respond best to structured therapies in a structured environment. Furthermore, studies of psychiatric outpatients treated by medical students, college students treated by counselors, and delinquents in a community treatment project all revealed that patients whose conceptual level was similar to that of their therapists improved more than those for whom there was a mismatch (Posthuma and Carr 1975).

Studies of the similarities and differences in patients' and therapists' values as related to improvement have yielded several thought-provoking findings. A study that measured certain values of psychoanalytic candidates and their patients, for example, revealed that the values of each therapist resembled those of his or her own patients more than those of the patients seen by the other therapists, and that each saw more improvement the more the patient's values resembled his or her own (Welkowitz, Cohen, and Ortmeyer 1967).

This study also brought out the interactive aspect of therapy, in that the resemblance of patients' and therapists' values seemed to be at least partly a consequence of the therapeutic interaction. That is, since most patients were arbitrarily assigned to their therapists, the similarity in values could not have been the result of selection bias. Moreover, there was a low but significantly positive correlation between the length of treatment before the patients' values were tested and the degree of their similarity to those of the therapist; the similarity of values between patient and therapist tended to increase with the length of the treatment.

This hint that improvement is accompanied by a convergence of certain values of therapist and patient has received support from other studies (Beutler 1981). No two studies have investigated the same values or used the same scales for determining them, so one cannot be more specific, but a couple of examples illustrate this point. A study of outpatients compared ratings of therapists and their patients on the values of sex, aggression, and authority at the beginning and end of therapy. These comparisons revealed a positive correlation between ratings of improvement and a shift in the patients' values toward those of the therapists (Rosenthal 1955). However, since the therapists' values were measured only once, it was not possible to determine whether their values also changed.

One ingenious investigation of intensive psychotherapy with outpatients repeatedly measured patients' and therapists' attitudes toward certain key persons in the patients' lives. It revealed that the convergence of therapists' and patients' attitudes during therapy was due to a movement of the therapists' attitudes as well as the patients'. As might have been expected, the patients shifted more than the therapists (Pande and Gart 1968). This finding is a reminder of the imbalance of power in the therapeutic relationship, to which we shall return shortly.

Before examining the issue of power in therapy, we wish to emphasize that many contextual factors in addition to demographic features, levels of conceptualization, and value orientations of patient and therapist influence the outcome of therapeutic encounters. Since these factors usually are not included in designs of therapeutic research — in fact, researchers may not even be aware of their existence — they may well account for the generally low level of the relationships found among the variables under study.

The existence of such unrecognized contextual factors is suggested by certain unexpected findings of the role-induction study described earlier (pp. 151–52). The patients in that study were initially evaluated by one of two interviewers who never saw them again, after which the patients were randomly assigned for treatment to four therapists. One of the initial interviewers was older and had a higher academic rank than the other and was the project director. The patients he interviewed did less well in therapy than those of the junior interviewer. At least two mutually compatible explanations come to mind, one possibly affecting the therapeutically relevant attitudes of the patients, the other the attitudes of the therapists. The patients may have experienced more of a comedown when transferred to a psychiatric resident if they had first seen the senior rather than the junior interviewer. The therapists knew which initial interviewer had interviewed each of their patients. Since only the senior interviewer had any control over the careers of the residents, perhaps their evaluation apprehension (pp. 63–64) led them to be more constrained with his patients.

The latter speculation is consistent with the fact that the resident who obtained the best results was a foreigner with a career already established in his home country, while the one with the poorest results felt that he was being unfavorably evaluated by the project director. In addition, the most successful resident believed in short-term therapy and enjoyed participation in the study; the least successful one felt exploited and did not believe in short-term treatment.

In short, the therapists' feelings about the initial interviewers and about the project itself seemed to affect their therapeutic success, presumably by influencing their behavior in the therapeutic encounter.

These reminders of the subtle and indirect ways in which the attitudes of a therapist may be transmitted to a patient call to mind the experimental findings concerning the transmission of influence from experimenter to subject in psychological experiments (Chapter 3).

The Power Imbalance in the Therapeutic Encounter

If experimenters exert power over subjects in psychological experiments — often unwittingly — psychotherapists presumably exert at least as much power over patients. The therapist's ascendancy has several sources. Especially in cities, persons often choose psychotherapists on the recommendation of friends who have been helped by them (Kadushin 1969). These persons arrive at the office door already predisposed to submit to the therapist. This attitude is reinforced by the therapist's ethos as derived from a socially validated form of training, leading to professional credentials that imply both competence and trustworthiness. In consequence, patients expect the therapist to relieve their suffering and disabilities. Since the forms of suffering amenable to psychotherapy usually involve disturbed interpersonal relations, patients often implicitly expect therapists to be allies in their struggles with others. Such an expectation would contribute to patients' willingness to depend on the therapist.

As discussed earlier, an important additional determinant of the therapist's power position is the patient's evaluation apprehension. If the therapist is in training, his or her own evaluation apprehension increases the likelihood that the supervisor's expectations also affect the patients' productions. Finally, in long-term therapy, the patient and therapist progressively shape each other's behavior, with the patient increasingly fulfilling the therapist's expectations, which were determined by the patient's behavior in the early interviews.

Proponents of most culturally established psychotherapies seldom discuss the issue of a power imbalance between therapist and patient. Practitioners of these therapies need not concern themselves with establishing their ascendancy in the therapeutic encounter; it is simply taken for granted. Practitioners of innovative therapies, however, may not be so fortunate.

In the early days of psychoanalysis, before its procedures had achieved their culturally induced symbolic power, the analyst might find it necessary to impress the patient by other means. This is illustrated by Freud's example of the patient who fails to shut the door to the waiting room when the waiting room is empty. He pointed out that this omission

> throws light upon the relation of this patient to the physician. He is one of the great number of those who seek authority, who want to be dazzled, intimidated. Perhaps he had inquired by telephone as to what time he had best call, he had prepared himself to come on a crowd of suppliants. . . . He now enters an empty waiting room which is, moreover, most modestly furnished, and he is disappointed. He must demand reparation from the physician for the wasted respect that he has tendered him, and so he omits to close the door between the reception room and the office. . . . He would also be quite unmannerly and supercilious during the consultation if his presumption were not at once restrained by a sharp reminder. [Freud 1920, pp. 212–13]

In terms of this discussion, Freud interpreted the patient's behavior as expressing unwillingness or at least hesitation to accept his ascendancy and sought to restore this position by means of a brusque command.

When the patient is in the presence of a professionally credentialed psychotherapist, his or her image of the therapist as a help-giver and authority figure is reinforced by certain culturally established symbols. Patients automatically identify a clinic or hospital office with the healing activities of the institution (Wilmer 1962). The private office of the psychiatrist who maintains identity as a physician contains such familiar medical trappings as the framed diploma and license, examining table, stethoscope, ophthalmoscope, reflex hammer, and doctor's white coat. Psychoanalysts, whose medical identification has been weakened, have developed special symbols of their healing art. These include heavily laden bookcases, couch with easy chair, and usually a large photograph of the leader of their particular school gazing benignly but impressively on the proceedings.

Psychologists may establish their expertise and thereby strengthen their ascendancy by putting their patients through an elaborate battery of personality tests. While psychiatric social workers and nonprofessional therapists lack specific symbols of professional competence, they partake of the prestige of the institutions or agencies in which they work. In any case, once therapy has started, the personal qualities and behavior of the therapist outweigh the symbols of the culturally established therapeutic role in mobilizing patients' favorable expectations.

It would appear that a therapist cannot avoid biasing the patient's performance in accordance with the therapist's own expectations. Although many psychotherapists recognize the crucial importance of this source of bias, therapists of psychoanalytic and other nondirective types of therapy have claimed that they do not influence the patient. Freud implied this when he characterized the psychoanalyst as a mirror. Freud's disconcerting discovery that some analysands fabricated infantile memories to fit his theories shook this view. The widespread finding that patients dream in imagery that accords with their therapists' theories (p. 194) and the experiments just reviewed would seem to make it even more untenable.

Several studies of psychotherapy itself provide clinching evidence that therapists bias their patients' productions, however unintentionally. One study revealed that psychotherapists tend to approve or discourage statements by patients that are related to their own personality characteristics. Twelve psychotherapists of parents in a child guidance clinic were rated by the research staff, on the basis of prolonged social and personal contacts, with respect to their ability to express hostility directly and their need for approval. Those who could express their hostility directly were more likely to make an encouraging response after a hostile statement by a patient than were those who could not give vent to their hostility or those who sought approval. The patients responded to the therapists' leads. Encouraging responses were followed by a continuation of hostile responses 92 percent of the time, discouraging ones only 43 percent of the time. In this study, most of the therapist's encouraging or discouraging responses were fairly obvious, but there was no relation between their obviousness and their effectiveness. A subtle sign of approval, such as reflecting the patient's feeling, had the same effect as open encouragement, and simply ignoring the hostile content of a patient's remark had the same discouraging effect as suggesting a change in topic (Bandura, Lipsher, and Miller 1960).

Psychotherapists influence patients' productions by such subtle expressions of approval or disapproval that the therapist may not even be aware of them. This conclusion is strongly suggested by an analysis of a treatment record, published as an example of "nondirective therapy," in which the therapist supposedly simply encouraged the patient to speak by taking a supportive attitude and without influencing the patient's productions in any way. Two startling findings emerged. The therapist's responses could be reliably categorized without difficulty as approving or disapproving; that is, the therapist was conveying his attitudes unwittingly. Furthermore, this implicit approval or disapproval strongly influenced the patient's productions. Statements in categories disapproved by the therapist fell from 45 percent of the total number of statements in the second hour to 5 percent in the eighth, while over approximately the same period statements in approved categories rose from 1 percent to 45 percent (Murray and Jacobson 1971).

This finding was confirmed by a detailed analysis of the statements of Carl Rogers, the initial promulgator of nondirective therapy, and a patient of his in long-term therapy. The researchers selected nine classes of the patient's verbal behavior. They found that, despite his theoretical position that the therapist must offer warmth and empathy nonselectively to whatever the client says, Dr. Rogers responded selectively by increased empathy, warmth, or directiveness to five of the categories but not to the other four. Of the five categories that were systematically reinforced, four showed changes in the predicted direction over time; of the four others, three neither increased nor decreased (Truax and Carkuff 1967). Since this was a correlational study, it leaves unclear who was influencing whom and how much; that is, each might have been causing the other to give reinforcing responses.

The findings of these two studies, although fragmentary, support the assumption that patients in therapy respond to cues from the therapist in a fashion similar to the way college student research subjects respond to experimenters. To be sure, the findings concern changes only in patients' conscious verbal responses. To what extent such responses correspond to what the patients actually feel remains unknown. It should be added, however, that one's attitudes are probably affected by one's own words. Most people cannot indefinitely tolerate the cognitive dissonance created by discrepancy between their words and their underlying attitudes, and under some circumstances the attitudes may yield. Furthermore, a technique of influence of which the person is not fully aware may be especially effective because it provides no target for resistance.

In pursuing the question of the power relations in the therapeutic encounter, we acknowledge that our views may be biased by our being physicians. It may be that the power relationship between patient and psychotherapist differs in important ways from that between patient and physician. An obvious difference, for example, is that the physician assumes a degree of responsibility for the welfare of the patient's body which the nonmedical psychotherapist does not. We regard the physician-patient relationship as the standard against which the psychotherapeutic relationship must be compared, acknowledging that readers with different professional backgrounds may legitimately reach other conclusions.

The issue of power in psychotherapy is obfuscated by the currently popular use of terms borrowed from business and law, a trend undoubtedly influenced by the growing role of third-party payers who analogize psychotherapy to a contract for the provision of services. Psychotherapists are called providers, patients are labeled consumers of a product called mental health care, and their interactions are guided by a therapeutic contract specifying the obligations and rewards of both parties.

While this conceptualization may be useful for many purposes (Menninger and Holzman 1973), its basic flaw is the assumption that, like participants in a business deal, both parties to the therapeutic contract are free, autonomous agents. A person can, of course, enter into a valid contract that places restrictions on his or her freedom, but its validity depends on the assumption the contractor is a free agent. The freedom of one of the parties to a psychotherapeutic contract, the patient, is always compromised to varying degrees by suffering, disability, or such mental states as anxiety, depression, and thought disorders that warp judgment. As a result, the therapeutic relationship "must be conducted in such a way that the patient's 'wounded humanity' is recognized even as his moral worth is affirmed" (Slavney and McHugh, 1987, p. 98). To this extent the relationship is a fiduciary one, based not so much on bargaining guided by considerations of self-interest as on trust.

Furthermore, the patient's vulnerability as well as his or her possibly impaired judgment places on the therapist responsibilities that distinguish the therapeutic relationship from, for example, that of lawyer and client. To the extent that the patient's ability to reach autonomous decisions is impaired, the therapist must be paternalistic, but only to maximize the patient's potential for autonomy (Komrad 1983). Achieving this requires the therapist to act in such a way as to provide the basis for the patient to form a secure attachment, a prerequisite for summoning the courage to change (Jones 1983).

Above all, the therapist is not relieved of responsibility when the patient violates the terms of the contract, if this violation endangers the patient's welfare. Almost every psychiatrist sooner or later has to face such a situation. This point may be illustrated by an experience of the senior author. The patient was an emotionally stormy young man who at one point in the therapist's judgment presented a suicidal risk. This was on a Friday afternoon. The patient agreed to the therapist's request that he phone in the next morning to report on how he felt. He failed to do so, and after several hours the therapist tried to reach him by phone. When many attempts yielded only a busy signal, the therapist, fearing that the patient had taken the phone off the hook, went to the patient's apartment, only to find the door locked. Failing to get a response to knocks and somewhat alarmed by this time, the therapist decided to call the police to break into the apartment, which proved to be empty. It turned out that the patient had left for the weekend without notifying the therapist, and the "busy" signal had been caused by a malfunctioning telephone. When the patient returned and the therapist told him what had happened, the patient insisted on paying for the damaged door, thereby indirectly reassuring the therapist that his action had not harmed the therapeutic relationship and may have strengthened it.

Professionalism implies adherence to well-defined expectations of conduct, enforced by legal sanctions. All professional therapists must scrupulously avoid exploiting patients for their own gratification. Along with training in technique, enforced ethical standards may be one of the few important distinctions between professional and nonprofessional therapists. Medically trained therapists, in particular, have a responsibility for patients' welfare that extends beyond the treatment sessions, as in the example just cited. By contrast, the leader of an encounter group may disavow responsibility for the consequences of participation, even though such groups may be harmful to some persons (see Chapter 11). In a recent court decision, a pastoral counselor was specifically absolved from the responsibility to prevent a client's suicide (Griffith, Adams, and Young 1988). A physician in the same case would have had both the responsibility to prevent the suicide and the legal authority to hospitalize the person to prevent self-harm.

A Note on Telepathy and Psychotherapy

One cannot conclude consideration of the psychotherapeutic relationship without mentioning a controversial form of therapist-patient communication — namely, telepathy. Telepathy falls into the category of "psi" phenomena, along with extrasensory perception, clairvoyance, precognition, psychokinesis, and other paranormal phenomena. Such occurrences have been accepted as valid and reported extensively for millennia throughout the world, yet many persons still maintain that they do not really exist. This skepticism is understandable on many grounds. Like transcendental religious experiences and faith healing, psi phenomena do not obey the laws of time, space, and energy of everyday reality and cannot be explained by the concepts of Western cosmology. If they exist, it must be in a different realm, termed by some "clairvoyant reality" (LeShan 1974). In consequence, Western scientists are motivated to dismiss not only anecdotal but also research evidence of their existence. Above all, professional magicians have been able to convincingly fake many demonstrations of psi phenomena (Randi 1980). As Filipino psychic surgery has shown, fraud can bring great financial rewards (Frank 1983), so temptations to perpetrate fraud are great.

Hence it is not surprising that telepathy, a psi phenomenon directly relevant to psychotherapy, is not even mentioned in the standard handbook of research on psychotherapy (Garfield and Bergin 1986). Yet the literature of psychoanalysis abounds with anecdotes of apparent telepathic communication between analysts and patients, usually discovered through analysis of a patient's dreams that suggest that he or she had picked up an unspoken preoccupation of the analyst. Such events seem facilitated not when patient and analyst are in particularly good rapport, as one might expect, but when, as in the example cited by Freud (1964), they are drifting apart. At such times the telepathic experience seems to result from the patient's desperate effort to recapture the analyst's attention. Although these occurrences bear the imprimatur of such luminaries as Freud and Jung (Eisenbud 1970), anecdotal reports never convince the skeptic, because they contain too many potential sources of error. Mere multiplication of erroneous observations does not make them true.

Research findings face similar obstacles to acceptance. Telepathic communication in dreams has been demonstrated by increasingly rigorous and sophisticated research studies (Krippner and Ullman 1970). Also relevant are studies reporting telepathic transmission to an awake person placed in a condition of relaxation in a dimly lit room, with patterned visual, auditory, and tactile stimuli excluded, the "Ganzfeld" condition (Honorton 1977). As researchers freely acknowledge, however, telepathic sensitivity fluctuates capriciously in the same person and may be influenced by the immediate state of the relationship between the sender and the receiver.

The degree of correspondence between the message sent and the one received also varies widely, and is typically only approximate. As a result, findings of research in telepathy can seldom be reliably replicated, so grounds for rejecting any particular report can always be found. An additional reason for skepticism is that many investigators of parapsychological phenomena are so eager to prove their existence on philosophical grounds that their reports may reflect witting or unwitting bias.

As with transcendental religious experiences, moreover, neither of the present authors, with the dubious exception cited below, has ever personally experienced telepathy. Nevertheless, after giving full weight to these sources of misgiving, consideration of the enormous amount of supportive data found throughout the world has satisfied us that the evidence for telepathy, at any rate, is as convincing as the evidence for most phenomena that are accepted as real.

An experience of one of us (J.D.F.) made vivid the problems telepathy presents for research. I served as receiver in a simplified Ganzfeld design in which the sender in another room chose one of four pictures by consulting a table of random numbers, and at periodic intervals tried to transmit the picture by staring at and thinking about it. At the same time I freely associated into a tape recorder, to which the sender listened. At the end of the experiment I was shown the four pictures and was asked to choose which the sender had tried to send. I instantly singled out one that I felt strongly he had *not* used. It was a golden Aztec mask that I found repulsive. In actuality, it was the one he had tried to send. On the basis of this result, the experiment was judged a resounding failure.

But two other totally unexpected and unforeseeable experiences gave me pause. At two of the three times when the sender was concentrating on the picture, I began to talk about how much I hated a certain city. Moreover, on one of these occasions the diffuse dim orange light in the room where I sat suddenly seemed to became bright yellow for a short period, an experience so surprising that I mentioned it in my remarks to the tape recorder. (The experimenter later assured me that the intensity of the light had been constant throughout.) By any conventional criteria, the sender had failed to transmit anything to me. But why did I twice talk about dislike of a certain city—the same response that the picture evoked when I saw it? And why did the light in the room seem to brighten to the color of the mask? If these experiences have any implication at all, it is that one source of failure in telepathic experiments may be that the researcher attends to the wrong variables. There is no way of knowing in advance what aspects of a stimulus will be telepathically transmitted.

Two other examples of possibly relevant but often neglected factors in experiments on telepathy merit our acknowledgment. One is that many findings suggest that believers in a parapsychological phenomenon are more apt to experience it than skeptics, and that emotional involvement also increases the success rate. Yet out of legitimate concern for scientific rectitude, experimental designs regularly seek to exclude observer bias and emotional states as potential contaminants. The second is that many experiments in parapsychology, such as repeatedly guessing sequences of cards, are deadly dull, and often deliberately exclude subjects who believe in the phenomenon being studied, thereby weighting the odds against success.

Despite the methodological and conceptual problems they present, parapsychological phenomena deserve continuing efforts to investigate them. Such study might cast light on many aspects of human functioning and could have profound metaphysical implications. More specifically, phenomena lying within the domain of clairvoyant reality may suggest promising new modes of psychotherapy. LeShan (1974) suggests that through suitable meditation exercises, both therapist and patient can enter this domain in which boundaries between individuals dissolve, thus enhancing therapy. This position is close to that of existential psychotherapists who talk of therapist and patient "merging" (Havens 1974).

Summary

This chapter has examined the influencing and healing features of the psychotherapeutic encounter from the standpoints of the therapist, the patient, and the therapeutic situation itself. The therapist's training and expertise affect the therapist's self-image and the patient's attitude toward him or her, and thereby the therapist's effectiveness as a healer. With respect to sociocultural factors, the extent of the social and educational distance between therapist and patient may affect their acceptance of each other. Although the therapeutic outcome may be somewhat related to the therapist's ability to adhere consistently to a particular technique, personal attributes of the therapist and patient seem to be more important.

The personal qualities that predispose patients to a favorable therapeutic response are similar to those that heighten susceptibility to methods of healing in nonindustrialized societies, religious revivals, experimental manipulation of attitudes, and administration of a placebo. One personal characteristic, locus of control, may determine the patient's relative openness to influence by different forms of therapy.

When psychotherapy is viewed as a system, its success seems related not only to aspects of the patient-therapist interaction that affect the therapist's zeal and the patient's confidence but also to a convergence of the therapist's and patient's values, which involves a greater shift in the values of the patient than in those of the therapist. Such considerations lead to the conclusion that the psychotherapeutic alliance differs in a fundamental respect from legal and business contracts in that the patient's impaired autonomy imposes greater responsibility on the therapist.

The chapter closes by touching on the possibility that important therapeutic interactions might sometimes be telepathic.

NINE

Evocative Individual
Psychotherapies

"Would you tell me, please, which way I ought to go
from here?"
"That depends a good deal on where you want to get
to," said the Cat.
"I don't much care where — so long as I get *somewhere*,"
Alice added as an explanation.
"Oh, you're sure to do that," said the Cat, "if you only
walk long enough."
— *Alice's Adventures in Wonderland*

Introduction

Our review of rhetoric, religious revivals, cults, faith healing, and other
persuasive activities related to healing has suggested that all psychotherapies are meant to help patients reduce or overcome distress, function better in personal relationships and at work, and concomitantly
increase self-esteem and heighten patients' sense of control over themselves and their surroundings. The personal troubles amenable to psychotherapy are manifestations of disharmonies within patients or between patients and others close to them. Psychotherapy tries to help
patients resolve these disharmonies by increasing their ability to cope
with problems of life created by the interaction of genetic determinants,
past history, and current social environment. Psychotherapeutic pro-

185

cedures enhance morale as they challenge maladaptive patterns of behavior and encourage more successful ones. Successful treatment helps patients achieve an increased sense of inner freedom, self-efficacy (Bandura 1982), and satisfaction with life.

While a comprehensive review of current psychotherapies is well beyond our powers, we now turn to representative examples of some current American psychotherapies in search of the factors that account for their effectiveness in helping certain types of patients or relieving certain symptoms. In keeping with our central focus, we will examine these factors in relation to the features that all psychotherapies have in common. We shall confine our discussion to psychotherapies based on naturalistic theories of human distress, prescinding from "transpersonal" therapies — those involving various rituals of meditation, prayer, and, sometimes, mind-altering drugs — that are intended to provide experiences of direct contact with transcendental healing powers. For reasons given earlier, we can offer little personal insight into these forms of religious healing, but we acknowledge that they may be immensely helpful to some persons suffering from certain types of distress.

Classification of Psychotherapies

The remainder of this book focuses on particular forms of psychotherapy in the contemporary United States. The following crude scheme of classification orients the reader to the various therapies we propose to review in detail.

Classifying psychotherapies is a daunting task. It was not always thus. For many decades, dyadic interview therapies based on psychoanalysis and its modifications dominated the field. Though these therapies differed in their conceptualizations, all relied primarily on patient-therapist conversations that focused on the patient's past history as related to current problems. Adherents of Freud, Jung, Adler, Rank, and others debated violently about what the emphasis or topic of the therapeutic conversation should be, but they never questioned the method itself.

Developments since World War II have progressively disrupted this relatively tidy state of affairs. Conceptualizations and accompanying procedures based on modifications of psychoanalysis have mushroomed. Various behavioral techniques transposed to humans from the animal researches of Pavlov and Skinner have proliferated, as have group methods. Founders of allegedly new therapeutic methods continue to emerge, each with a band of disciples, a rationale, and new claims for therapeutic effectiveness. These claims range from reasonably modest assertions to extravagant boasts of having at last discovered the royal road to mental health for everyone. All flourish simultaneously because all have something to offer; none has yet displaced any of the others, because none has found the ultimate answer. According to a recent survey, there are more than 400 distinguishable schools of psychotherapy (Karasu 1986).

The thirst for novelty, which is perhaps stronger in the United States than elsewhere, fuels this explosion of psychotherapies. Americans typically assume the new is better than the old until proven otherwise. It is a medical truism that all forms of treatment work best just after they are introduced. The power of new therapies derives in part from the enthusiasm of the inventor and in part from patients' pleasurable emotional reaction to the prospect of a new remedy, especially when recommended by an authority. Thus, all new remedies foster emotional states analogous to those aroused by placebos. In addition the emotional investment of both healer and patient may lead both of them to overestimate the effectiveness of a new treatment and make overly optimistic claims for it.

In any case, the wild profusion of contemporary therapies could be classified in many different ways. For the purposes of exposition, we have chosen to describe therapies first by their targets and by the settings in which they occur, then by the techniques by which therapists try to influence patients' cognitive, emotional, or behavioral states.

The target of treatment is, of course, the person seeking help, who may be seen alone, with customary associates (usually the immediate family, but sometimes also colleagues and friends), or with complete strangers. In group and family therapies the focus can be on the members as individuals, on their interactions in the group, or on the emergent properties of the group itself as it may aid its members (see Chapter 11).

Therapies that focus on the individual typically assume that symptoms amenable to psychotherapy arise primarily from the interaction of life events with patients' intrinsic vulnerabilities. These weaknesses, caused by inner conflicts, destructive ways of conceptualizing experience, or maladaptive habitual patterns of behavior, lead to disturbed communications with others.

By contrast, many group approaches attribute the patient's symptoms to the pathology of the communication system of which the patient is a part. From the group therapist's perspective, individual therapy is really a group of two. Analysis of communications between patient and therapist is equivalent to study of a stress-producing interpersonal communication system, and internalized reference groups in both patient and therapist affect what transpires in therapy. In this sense, all therapy is group therapy.

Treatment settings range from offices or clinics, where people are seen briefly, to hospitals, where patients live for days, months, or years. In between are various settings such as day hospitals or halfway houses, where the patient spends the major part of each day. A residential setting creates the possibility for milieu therapy or the creation of a therapeutic community. Though most controlled settings include individual, group, or family therapy, much of their therapeutic value is presumed to lie in their organizational rules and value systems and in the types of activities they foster. The boundaries between different settings and levels of care are not fixed. Ideally, patients move freely among them, depending on how much environmental protection and support they require at various times.

Because they are clearly distinguished from daily life, all therapeutic settings provide a relatively protected environment where patients can feel free to express forbidden thoughts, release pent-up emotions, or experiment with new ways of behaving without fear of consequences. As a result, the ultimate test of the success of any form of treatment is whether the patient can sustain in daily life the beneficial changes achieved in therapy. Follow-up sessions and efforts to involve the patient's intimates in the therapeutic process are two common ways of reinforcing these changes.

The variety of psychotherapeutic procedures precludes any neat classification, especially since their aims and methods overlap. For purposes of exposition, however, we will divide psychotherapies into three crudely defined and overlapping categories — evocative (Whitehorn 1959), directive, and mixed. The central aim of evocative therapies is to provide a relationship or a setting that facilitates the patient's total personality development. Focal symptom relief or problem resolution is expected to occur as the patient overcomes general difficulties such as internal conflicts, faulty assumptive systems, or emotional blocks. In directive therapies, the therapist remains firmly in charge, prescribing certain activities or rituals for solving specific problems or alleviating certain symptoms. Directive therapies assume that general improvement in personal functioning will follow automatically from the resulting increase in patients' self-confidence and sense of inner freedom. Mixed forms of psychotherapy include those in which evocative or facilitative techniques are used to relieve focal symptoms, those in which therapists direct patients' activities in the service of evocative ends, and eclectic treatments that blend the goals and techniques of purer forms.

Whether the therapist is overtly directive or uses a more facilitating approach, all psychotherapeutic procedures involve cognitive, emotional, and behavioral components. Psychotherapies differ, however, in their relative emphasis on these aspects of personal functioning. In keeping with their goal of inducing focal changes, directive therapies in particular tend to emphasize certain of these aspects over others. Cognitive therapies (Beck 1976), for example, are designed to provide patients with new information about themselves and new ways of conceptualizing their experiences. Since all mental illnesses have behavioral manifestations and behavioral change is a major criterion of therapeutic success, cognitive and other forms of directive psychotherapy also focus explicitly on helping patients change troublesome behaviors. Such methods all fall under the generic term "behavior modification" (O'Leary and Wilson 1975).

Both evocative and directive therapies produce strong emotional reactions. Particularly in evocative therapies, the therapeutic relationship itself may mobilize strong feelings. Emotional reactions accompany significant attitudinal shifts, and an optimal level of arousal facilitates learning of all sorts. In addition, as considered in the next chapter, intense emotional reactions in therapy sometimes seem to be followed by cognitive reorganization and marked relief of certain forms of distress. Certain directive therapies make such arousal their primary focus by prescribing techniques to trigger "abreaction," the reexperiencing of early traumatic experiences that are presumed to lie at the root of patients' current symptoms. Although the aim of abreactive procedures is evocative, the method is strictly directive, so we have chosen to discuss them in the next chapter as examples of mixed psychotherapy.

Finally, certain therapies move on all fronts at once with equal vigor, trying to elicit new behaviors, evoke emotional discharges, and change conceptualizations simultaneously. Psychodrama is the prototype of this mixed approach (Moreno 1971).

The emotional, cognitive, and behavioral changes that psychotherapy seeks to effect are closely intertwined. If all goes well, each reinforces the others. A more workable assumptive world based on a more accurate cognitive appraisal of self, other persons, and life events leads to behavior that is more successful and less frustrating. Success in turn reduces the patient's anxiety, heightens self-confidence, and fosters positive emotions that increase flexibility of thinking. The resulting behavioral changes further strengthen the patient's new assumptive systems. This happy state of affairs is rarely, if ever, fully achieved, but it affords a useful model for thinking about the methods and goals of different forms of treatment.

Though dyadic evocative and directive therapies may achieve similar results, they differ in many important respects. Cognitive, behavior, and abreactive therapies are discussed in the next chapter as examples of directive or mixed therapy. The balance of this chapter deals with evocative approaches, particularly psychoanalytic, existential, and client-centered psychotherapy.

Schools of Evocative Therapy

Evocative therapies assume that all humans are fulfilling only a small part of their potential for productivity, self-actualization, joy, and harmonious relationships with others. Psychoanalytic therapies attribute such limitations to the painful or frightening experiences we have all suffered in the course of growing up. To guard against further hurts, analytic theory postulates that people resort to more or less unconscious self-protective or avoidance maneuvers. Some of these prove to be maladaptive solutions that impede personality growth and integration, creating the distress and disability that bring patients to treatment.

"Existential" psychotherapy, an influential form of evocative psychotherapy, shares the assumption that distress results from concerns that patients fear to bring to awareness. Existential therapists, however, believe that pain results not from early traumatic experience but "from the individual's confrontation with the givens of existence" (Yalom 1980, p. 5), such as death, freedom, isolation, and meaninglessness.

Both psychoanalytic and existential psychotherapies are rooted in pessimistic European philosophies of life. Evocative therapies that aim to promote "self-actualization" reflect a more optimistic, American view of human nature. Maslow (1970) termed these therapies the "Third Force," to distinguish them from psychoanalysis and behavior therapies. An influential version is the client-centered therapy associated with Carl Rogers (Rogers and Sanford 1985).

Therapies of self-actualization assume that humans are basically good, and that anger, destructiveness, and other unattractive qualities are responses to or manifestations of damaging life experiences. Such approaches give greater weight than do psychoanalytically oriented therapies to the effects of patients' current or recent experiences, while minimizing the possible role of fixed, unchangeable deficits or vulnerabilities. They also focus more on patients' conscious mental experiences and the contradictions between patients' real and ideal selves than on uncovering and resolving unconscious conflicts.

Whatever their underlying theory, evocative therapies are fundamentally person centered rather than problem or symptom oriented. Thus, particular manifestations of patients' underlying difficulties that are of interest to evocative therapists may or may not correspond to the symptoms and focal behaviors addressed by directive therapists.

Whether the goal is to bring repressed memories to awareness, to help patients verbalize and master existential dilemmas, or to promote self-actualization, the evocative therapist maintains an attitude of serious, respectful, noncritical interest no matter how shameful or shocking the patient's revelations. This "unconditional positive regard," to use Rogers' term, makes patients feel accepted by an admired and trusted person. In response, they dare to reveal more and more humiliating, frightening, or otherwise upsetting experiences they have previously pushed out of awareness. In the process, they usually become aware of undervalued positive qualities.

While fully recognizing that the most important part of this process occurs as the patient actually tries out new insights in daily life, evocative therapists, in accordance with their philosophy, seldom explicitly try to instigate changes in patients' behavior. They reason that such changes will occur naturally as patients develop progressively greater self-understanding and self-acceptance, qualities that enable them to become more spontaneous and to engage in more successful and satisfying interactions with others.

From a sociological perspective, evocative psychotherapies are probably applicable to a narrower range of patients than are directive ones. Some patients may be unable to cope with the upsetting memories or feelings unearthed by evocative techniques. Except in skillful hands, such approaches are not suitable for patients whose emotional stability is fragile or who are so disorganized that they require hospitalization.

Moreover, evocative therapies require that patients be highly motivated toward self-understanding and be at least minimally able to sense and communicate their inner feelings through words (Sloane et al. 1975). In consequence, suitable patients must also have some verbal skill. This requirement can be partly circumvented by the use of drawings, paintings (Siegel 1988), or dancing and other bodily exercises that enable persons to gain access to and communicate inner states.

Psychoanalysis and Psychodynamic Psychotherapies

All evocative approaches are derived in part from psychoanalysis, which was historically the first and is still the dominant paradigm for this type of treatment. As mentioned above, Freud attributed patients' distress and disability mainly to unresolved unconscious internal conflicts dating from painful or frightening infantile and early life experiences with members of their families. He postulated that the repressed memories of these experiences were the sources of symptoms and disturbances in intimate relationships. The goal of therapy was to bring these emotionally charged memories back to consciousness and loosen their hold, thereby permitting the patient to resume emotional growth.

Like every other form of psychotherapy, psychoanalysis was and is a cultural enterprise, best understood in the context of its particular cultural and historical setting. Freud developed psychoanalysis within a competitive, male-dominated society that placed a high value on individual integrity and achievement. Women, although possessing many endearing qualities, were considered physically and morally frailer than men. That society's ideal person was an inner-directed man who, guided by high moral principles, strove for success and resisted social pressures that might compromise his principles and ideals. Such men often feared that too much openness could expose weaknesses that others could exploit. Furthermore, too much concern with the welfare of others might hamper a man in pursuing his personal goals, which necessarily involved hindering others from reaching theirs. Success in this context depended on maintaining a righteous, self-confident façade, which required denying or suppressing inner impulses that could create self-doubts if admitted to consciousness.

Freud's great achievement was his recognition that damage might result from such self-deception or the repression of unacceptable impulses and his creation of a method for bringing disavowed parts of the self into awareness. Another crucial Freudian insight was that in an intimate treatment relationship, patients eventually feel and act toward the therapist in ways that re-create troublesome interactions with parents and other important figures from the past. Most psychoanalytic therapies put great weight on the mutual exploration by patient and therapist of these "transference reactions" as the major route to increased self-knowledge, and thereby therapeutic gain.

Freud shared the nineteenth-century faith that science held the solution to all problems. He insisted that the information psychoanalysis revealed about the patient's subjective state had the status of scientific fact. Such material was valid, he argued, because it was elicited by an impartial, trained observer, using the method of "free association." This procedure involved encouraging the patient to report absolutely everything that came to mind, including dreams and fantasies, no matter how humiliating or irrelevant. The therapist listened with an attitude of free-floating attention, occasionally offering interpretations of the meanings of the patient's productions. In theory, the analyst did not influence the course of the associations but, to use Freud's metaphor, functioned simply as a mirror. To minimize distractions and encourage relaxation, which fosters the free flow of thought, Freud had the patient lie on a couch while he sat in a chair out of the patient's line of vision.

As a cultural offshoot of Europe, with more stress on competition and an even greater faith in science, America was highly sympathetic to both the goals and the scientific pretensions of psychoanalysis. The theory and technique were readily transplanted to American soil, where they have undergone numerous modifications (Cooper and Sacks 1988). In particular, psychodynamic therapies in the United States have come to diverge from the original model in two directions that seem related to cultural differences between twentieth-century America and nineteenth-century Europe.

The European family structure was authoritarian — father knew best. Furthermore, though children were expected to have no secrets from their parents, the reverse emphatically did not hold. The traditional psychoanalytic session mirrors this pattern in that it is conducted in the strictest privacy. All the confiding is done by the patient, and, although he or she may choose not to exert it directly, the analyst holds all the authority.

Reflecting the antiauthoritarian element of American thought and the looser, less hierarchical organization of the contemporary American family, the American therapist practicing dynamic psychotherapy often descends from this pedestal. Instead of lying on a couch, the patient may sit up and conduct a face-to-face conversation with the therapist, symbolizing the changed power relationship. American psychodynamic therapies, furthermore, conceptualize the therapeutic interview as an encounter in which both participants actively engage and in which the therapist should be somewhat self-revealing, especially of feelings evoked by the patient. The therapist is also expected to be overtly supportive. In short, the American therapist has ceased to be an aloof European parent and become a knowledgeable, friendly, and accessible American one (Greben 1984).

The second feature of American culture that has influenced psychoanalysis is its pragmatic, action-oriented philosophy. While this philosophy achieves its fullest expression in directive therapies, it has also stimulated the creation of time-limited psychodynamic ones. These have become an increasingly important form of treatment in response to social and economic pressures to reduce the costs of care.

Although psychoanalysis initially often lasted no longer than today's brief therapies, the average duration of psychoanalytic therapy soon stretched to years. Since the potential number of supposedly pathogenic, repressed memories is virtually limitless, analysts and patients agreed that people could continue in this form of treatment as long as they found it rewarding and could afford it. To be expensively psychoanalyzed became a status symbol in some circles, and for some persons regular visits to the analyst became an integral feature of their lifestyle, like going to church.

More recently, however, American therapists in the psychoanalytic mode have sought to speed up the therapeutic process by creating a variety of time-limited approaches. These therapies focus on identifying and correcting the current maladaptive feelings, thoughts, and behavior that perpetuate patients' difficulties, rather than on unearthing their origins. To this end, time-limited therapies seek to keep the therapeutic conversation focused on helping patients uncover, verbalize, and resolve certain overriding, conflict-laden issues. Examples of such issues are the "core conflict relationship" (Luborsky 1984) or feelings for the parent of the opposite sex (Sifneos 1989). Since all "brief dynamic therapy . . . [is] primarily rooted in psychodynamic principles" (Sifneos 1989, p. 1563), we shall not consider different time-limited techniques separately, beyond this brief mention of their appeal in the context of American culture.

Evocative Therapies as Methods of Persuasion

Patients, especially if properly prepared, are as readily influenced by evocative therapies as by directive ones. As noted in Chapter 8, patients in Rogerian client-centered therapy follow the therapist's unwitting leads, and the patient's values shift toward those of the therapist in the course of successful treatment. Psychoanalysts, similarly, unwittingly influence patients' free associations. Fish's linguistic analysis (1986) of Freud's account of his psychoanalysis of the Wolf-Man (1953) documented the extent of this influence. Fish demonstrated how Freud, by his choice of words, implicitly guided the patient's responses while simultaneously denying to the patient and himself that he was doing so.

Similarly, as an example of what has been termed "doctrinal compliance" (Ehrenwald 1966), psychoanalytic patients may produce dreams "in a form that will best please the analyst" (Stekel, quoted in Wolff 1954, p. 466). One study, for example, compared reports of dreams told immediately on awakening with those told to a psychiatrist in a subsequent interview. The investigators found the dreamers failed to report to the therapists material they anticipated would not win the therapist's interest or approval (Whitman, Kramer, and Baldridge 1963). This finding reminds us that patients' attitudes toward their therapists influence everything they report, even when they are recounting such apparently personal experiences as dreams or memories.

Another example of doctrinal compliance is that the kind of improvement patients report tends to confirm their therapists' theories. Patients in psychoanalysis, which relates mental health to the extent of the patient's self-knowledge, express increasing awareness of unconscious material as therapy progresses. Those who report improvement in client-centered therapy report that the discrepancy between their perceived and ideal selves has been reduced (Rogers and Dymond 1954). Therapists who consider that the ability to sense and directly express feelings is a sign of progress find that their patients are better able to do this as therapy progresses (Murray 1956). To pile up further examples would merely belabor the point that evocative therapies influence patients' productions. Indeed, in view of the experimental studies showing that evaluation apprehension, high in all patients, is a major source of responsiveness to the experimenter's expectations, it would be surprising if this were not so.

Although the information elicited by evocative therapies may not satisfy the criteria of scientific validity, the scientific method is not the only path to truth. As Thomas Huxley put it, "Nature is not a mechanism but a poem" (Irvine [1955] 1963, p. 44).

With all their potential sources of error, psychoanalysis and similar therapies have greatly enlarged our understanding of human nature and have benefited many patients. Consideration of some of the persuasive and therefore healing features of psychoanalytic therapies will increase both our ability to evaluate them fairly and our understanding of the processes at work in all psychotherapies. The features we shall discuss are modeling, the therapist's neutrality, verbal exploration of the past, and interpretations.

Modeling or Identification

Many of the sources of the therapist's influence in evocative therapy are present in any relationship in which one person feels dependent on another. A particularly important one has been termed *identification*, or, to avoid unnecessary theoretical implications, *imitation* or *modeling*. Modeling has been shown to be a powerful mechanism of learning, especially in children (Bandura 1977).

Evocative psychotherapies resemble parent-child relationships in that patients enter into emotionally charged interactions with a therapist on whom they depend for guidance or advice. At the most superficial level, some patients unconsciously mimic their therapists' mannerisms, but the identification is often broader and deeper. The patient may imitate the therapist's way of approaching problems or adopt aspects of the therapist's values. The therapist's ability to be tolerant and flexible may influence patients to become more so; the therapist's willingness to accept and openly admit limitations without becoming insecure may help patients accept personal shortcomings. To the extent that the therapist serves as a model, it is important that his or her own emotional house be in order — a major stated reason for the requirement of psychoanalytic schools that the therapist undergo their version of psychoanalysis (see Chapter 8).

The "Neutrality" of the Therapist

In considering the remaining persuasive and healing features of evocative therapies, we shall use orthodox psychoanalysis as the prototype. Although today's evocative therapies differ from it in various ways, classical psychoanalysis most clearly highlights the issues involved.

Paradoxically, one of the more persuasive features of psychoanalysis is its insistence that the analyst does not influence the patient's productions. All of us try to gain support for our assumptive systems by getting others to confirm them (Festinger 1954), and others' confirmation of the validity of our opinions is more convincing if they appear to have reached their conclusions independently. Since patients provide the major source of confirmation of psychotherapeutic doctrines, therapists' belief in their own objectivity may paradoxically increase their motivation to get patients to produce confirmatory material.

From the patients' standpoint, the apparent objectivity of the psychoanalyst may enhance his or her influencing power. Patients for whom science carries high prestige may have more confidence in a therapist who appears to be scientifically open-minded than in one who is dogmatic. A therapist's manifestation of a scientific attitude can be viewed as a rhetorical device to increase his or her ethos, particularly in the eyes of the many Americans who value science highly.

Most practitioners of psychoanalysis do not openly claim infallibility, which would be incompatible with a scientific attitude. Despite this disclaimer, psychoanalysis and many other evocative therapies have retained certain characteristics of the self-consistent, irrefutable conceptual schemes underlying religious healing. To be sure, many psychotherapists acknowledge that their concepts are scientifically unproven and display a detached, critical attitude toward them in academic discussions. For the purposes of therapy, however, basic concepts are not open to question. In the actual therapeutic situation, the patient's feelings and behavior are interpreted in terms of the therapist's particular view of human functioning, and treatment is expected to continue until the patient somehow acknowledges the correctness of this view. For example, a particular theory may attribute patients' troubles primarily to repressed intrapsychic conflicts or to an unrealistic self-image. Therapy is not complete until the patient produces information confirming this assumption and, presumably as a result, modifies his or her behavior in the direction deemed to represent improvement. The therapist does not even entertain the possibility that such information may be irrelevant to the patient's particular illness. Freud put it bluntly: "It is, of course, of great importance for the progress of the analysis that one should always turn out to be in the right vis-à-vis the patient" (Breuer and Freud 1957, p. 281).

Similarly, in keeping with a scientific attitude, the analyst typically concludes the initial interview by offering the patient an opportunity to explore problems further, while refraining from making explicit claims that this exploration will be helpful. Patients nevertheless maintain an expectancy of help, as shown by their willingness to persist in treatment, even at the cost of considerable time, money, effort, and emotional distress. Mere curiosity about one's inner life would not supply sufficient motivation for this tenacity. As Karl Menninger, a leading psychoanalyst, wrote: "The essence of psychoanalytic treatment is intellectual honesty, and no one in honesty can predict with definiteness what the future will bring. Yet if the analyst did not *expect* to see improvement, he would not start, so taking the case *is* an implied prediction. . . . The patient who submits himself for psychoanalytic therapy begins with a certain blind faith in the psychoanalyst, regardless of the disclaimers he may profess. He begins, too, with various hopes and expectations, regardless of the skepticism he may express" (Menninger and Holzman [1958] 1973, pp. 30, 38; italics in the original).

In the early phases of analysis, the patient's expectation of help (see Chapter 2) is aroused by the analyst's steady attention and by the symptomatic improvement that so often occurs at the start of treatment. If, as is characteristic of all but the most rigidly orthodox psychoanalyses, the analyst takes a history that is not too dissimilar from a medical one, this invokes the culturally induced healing image of the physician.

As therapy progresses, the analyst's behavior may confound the patient's expectations in ways that enhance both influence and healing. Unlike the usual medical healer, the therapist offers no prescriptions or advice. At the same time, the therapist differs from persons familiar to the patient by failing to respond to provocation. Analysts do not display either anger or contrition in response to criticism, sympathy or impatience in the face of complaints, or amorousness, embarrassment, or rebuff if the patient is seductive. These nonresponses, by disconfirming aspects of the patient's assumptive world, motivate the patient to change.

The subtlety and unobtrusiveness of the therapist's maneuvers, coupled with the explicit denial that he or she is exerting pressure in any direction, may increase the analyst's power to influence. How can a person fight influences that apparently do not exist? The person has no target against which to direct resistance. Furthermore, people are more likely to adopt ideas they believe they have reached independently than those that seem imposed from outside.

The psychoanalyst's steadfast refusal to assume active leadership creates an ambiguous situation for patients, who have only vague ideas of what is expected, how long therapy will go on, and how they will know when they have finished. In response to the patient's attempts to gain clarification, the analyst does nothing at all, makes noncommittal encouraging sounds, or asks noncommittal questions. The resulting lack of clarity may enhance the influencing power of the situation. As pointed out in Chapter 2, everyone constantly tries to formulate stable and clear assumptions to guide behavior. Analysands' struggle to resolve the ambiguities of psychoanalysis stimulates their active participation, a process as important for the success of evocative therapies as for other forms of healing and influence.

Moreover, a person who lacks a clear set of expectations in a given situation tends to look to others for direction (Sherif and Harvey 1952). This tendency may explain why confusion increases suggestibility (Cantril 1941) (see Chapter 10). In evocative therapies, patients' belief that relief from suffering depends on doing or saying the right thing strengthens their motivation to scrutinize the therapist for clues as to what is expected. Thus the patient is likely to be acutely aware of the therapist, even the therapist who sits out of sight, as in psychoanalysis. Subtle signs such as the analyst shifting position may serve as cues that affect the patient's productions.

The senior author remembers from his own psychoanalysis attending to the slightest clues of his analyst's interest or boredom. He was acutely aware of changes in the analyst's breathing, restlessness, or sounds of writing. He wrongly assumed that these sounds indicated that the analyst was taking notes on particularly significant material. The analyst eventually admitted that he was simply doodling.

The ambiguity of the analytic situation created by the therapist's neutrality enhances its therapeutic power. Ambiguity or lack of clarity arouses strong emotions. The relation of ambiguity to anxiety is obvious. Nothing is harder to tolerate than uncertainty, especially when making the correct choice seems vital. Patients may also experience resentment and mounting feelings of frustration as the therapist consistently refuses to satisfy implicit or explicit demands for help. Such tension arises particularly in classical psychoanalysis, in which the therapist may remain virtually silent for long periods. As Menninger and Holzman put it:

> The patient's sense of frustration affords a continuing provocation to resentment. For, as the days go by, there develops in the patient a growing suspicion that there exists between him and his therapist what an economist would call "an unfavorable trade balance." The patient has "cooperated," he has obeyed instructions, he has given himself. He has contributed information, exposing his very heart, and in addition to all this he has paid money for the sessions in which he did it. And what return has he gotten from the physician? Attention, audience, toleration, yes — but no response. No "reaction." No advice. No explanation. No solution. No help. No love. [1973, pp. 53–54]

The analyst's refusal to come to the patient's rescue may serve many valuable functions. The state of mind it produces, although unpleasant, may facilitate attitudinal change, not only by arousing patients emotionally but also by helping them recognize that their expectations of the therapist are unrealistic. This recognition may be a step toward the achievement of a generally less dependent attitude toward others.

Beyond mobilizing emotion, all successful psychotherapy heightens the patient's sense of mastery. At first glance, psychoanalytically oriented therapies do not seem to offer many opportunities for experiencing success, from which the sense of mastery is largely derived. The therapist offers no overt encouragement or approval. Treatment lacks a clear structure or timetable, so the patient has no easy way of judging progress. Thus, the therapeutic "task" is a difficult one.

This very difficulty makes psychoanalysis congenial to persons who are skilled at verbalizing and conceptualizing their feelings and who have experienced successes in the past from this type of activity. In general, to persist in evocative treatment, patients must possess or develop considerable "ego strength" or frustration tolerance, which implies the capacity to derive a sense of mastery from overcoming one's own undesirable feelings.

Along the same lines, all evocative therapies seek to "evoke an awareness of self-initiated thinking and action" (Bruch 1961, p. 54). To this end the therapist maintains that patients' gains stem from their own efforts. Moreover, the increased self-awareness produced by evocative therapy inherently enhances a person's sense of self-control. Freud, in one of his brilliant metaphors, pictured the conscious self, the Ego, as a rider on a powerful and fractious horse, the Unconscious or Id, and expressed the goal of psychoanalysis with the dictum, "Where Id was there shall Ego be."

Finally, although the ultimate criterion of success, completion of therapy, may be long delayed in psychoanalysis, when it does come, it implies entry into the highly select group of the successfully analyzed, a step that greatly enhances the patient's sense of achievement.

Verbal Exploration of the Past

The weight placed on detailed verbal exploration and interpretation of the patient's psychic life, with emphasis on his or her past history, is another important influencing property of evocative therapies, particularly psychoanalytic ones. Persons influence themselves by verbalizing or writing down inner experiences.

A person experiences written or spoken thoughts or feelings through the distance receptors — the eyes or ears — rather than directly. That is, they are experienced as coming from the external world through the channels that are best equipped to make discriminations. Thus, speaking or writing down thoughts and feelings apparently helps the person organize and evaluate them.[1] The person who, when asked for an opinion, allegedly replied, "How do I know what I think until I've heard what I have to say?" may have spoken the literal truth.

The particular emphasis that psychoanalysis places on verbalizing past history resembles the procedures of some traditional healing rites, in which the sufferer repeatedly reviews the same historical material in the presence of someone who maintains a consistently receptive attitude. In these rituals, as in psychoanalysis, verbal repetition seems important for weakening old patterns of response and learning new ones. Thus therapeutic exploration of a patient's past is no mere fact-finding expedition. Rather, the patient gains insight into current maladjustments by uncovering their historical sources and thereby becomes better able to change them, as in the example of the curio shop cited in Chapter 2.

Even in prolonged therapy, patients recall only a minute fraction of their past experiences. From these fragments they construct a meaningful story or "apologia," elements of which vary according to the patient's current mood and the other aspects of the therapeutic situation (see Chapter 3). For example, the unhappy experiences and overwhelming, insoluble problems that dominate the history given by a depressed person may shrink to minor episodes after he or she is feeling better. Re-

1. Perhaps the same process operates in biofeedback, a form of therapy in which patients gain conscious control of visceral functions after they are linked to visual or auditory displays.

covered depressive patients often become aware of new, more optimistic memories or make optimistic reevaluations of those reported earlier.

Patients' feelings and expectations about the person to whom they are reporting also influence the memories they select. One may produce quite different life histories, all true, for a prospective employer, a sweetheart, or a therapist.

A study of twelve patients in group therapy dramatically illustrated the effect of the immediate situation, particularly attitudes toward the therapist, on the recall of past experiences. The patients' reported childhood memories about experiences with parents or siblings, or childhood sexual experiences, were transcribed on cards after the first sessions. The whole pack, consisting of an average of twenty-five memories from each, was given to the patients three months to four years later. All were asked to sort the cards into three piles — their own memories, not their own memories but generally true about their past lives, and false or inapplicable. Not one patient was able to identify all of his or her previously reported memories; the average number of memories correctly identified was about half. In particular, for both sexes, memories reflecting the initial effort to impress the therapist had disappeared by the time of retesting. These included memories of exhibitionistic sex play for the women and memories of rejecting or paragonlike fathers for the men. The author concluded: "It is systematically impossible to reconstruct the childhood life space from retrospective reports by adults . . . geared to the requirements of the situations in which the retrospection is made" (Bach 1952, p. 97).

In psychotherapy, review of the past inevitably mobilizes feelings of guilt or shame. In the absence of overt direction from the therapist, patients are tempted to become ever more self-revealing in the hope of eliciting a supportive response. Since patients know that they are supposed to bring up troublesome and painful experiences, they do, and many of these may induce guilt: "Sooner or later . . . the confessions and confidings . . . begin to include material which the patient had not been aware of any need to confess. . . . He soon gets into the position of 'betraying' himself and implicating others. He finds himself telling tales out of school and admitting things which he had previously denied — perhaps even to himself. So, whereas at first he had been relieved by the diminished pressure of his confessions, now new pressures develop because of them" (Menninger and Holtzman 1973, pp. 102–3). Such confessions are integral to religious healing or conversion, and also play a role in other ways of producing changes in attitudes, such as thought reform (Frank 1973).

The therapist's continued, impartial interest in the face of material that arouses guilt or shame implies forgiveness. Since the therapist in some sense represents society, such interest may make patients feel less isolated. Thus, even without the therapist's specific interventions, review of the past, while it sometimes temporarily increases demoralization, ultimately enhances morale.

Interpretations

Reworking the past may induce changes in patients even in the absence of a clear response from another person, but therapists typically increase their influence by making explicit interpretations in response to what they hear.

Interpretations vary in complexity. The simplest type consists of repeating something the patient has said, perhaps with some change in emphasis, so that the patient becomes more clearly aware of particular implications. In a roughly ascending scale of degree of inference and complexity, other forms of interpretation are: summarizing (to coordinate and emphasize certain aspects of the patient's account); verbalizing the feelings that seem to lie behind the patient's utterances; and sharply confronting unrecognized attitudes implied by particular statements. Interpretations may also suggest symbolic meanings of patients' statements, as when a therapist interprets a dream of going on a journey as a reference to death. All interpretations are guided by the therapy's particular conceptual scheme and expressed in its terms.

In psychoanalytic therapy, patients deduce implications for their conduct from the therapist's periodic interpretations of what they say. Though some interpretations may have a purely evocative function, in general they constitute an important vehicle of therapeutic influence. As Aldous Huxley wrote in another context: "'A mere matter of words' we say contemptuously, forgetting that words have the power to mold men's thinking, to canalize their feeling, to direct their willing and acting. Conduct and character are largely determined by the words we currently use to discuss ourselves and the world around us" (1962, p. 2).

As the therapist's chief means of demonstrating understanding of the patient and command of technique and theory, skillful interpretations arouse and maintain the patient's confidence in the therapist as a master of a special healing art, thereby enhancing the patient's hopes for help. Incidentally, the ability to make interpretations also reassures therapists about their own competence, tempting young and inexperienced practitioners to offer too many interpretations.

Interpretations influence the patient in what the therapist believes to be a therapeutic direction by subtly conveying acceptance or rejection of the patient's productions. By simply labeling a patient's feeling, for example, the therapist implies that he or she is not afraid of it, that it is familiar, and that he or she will continue to accept the patient in spite of it. Such an interpretation has an enabling function — it encourages the patient to continue further in the same direction. Other interpretations, especially those that point out some inappropriateness in the patient's feelings or behavior, are implicit criticisms. By indicating that an aspect of the patient's psychic life is maladaptive, the therapist also implies that the patient should feel differently or do something else. Such an interpretation differs from a conventional suggestion in that it does not tell the patient how to change, but only that change would be desirable. Its effect is to inhibit certain lines of feeling or conduct and to encourage the patient to develop more acceptable ones.

As a means of regulating the patient's emotional arousal, interpretations have both general and specific effects. Any interpretation that heightens the patient's sense of mastery or increases his or her faith in the therapist reduces tension. Interpretations indicating the therapist's acceptance of the patient's expressed feeling may induce relief and relaxation. They also encourage the patient to feel and express the emotion more fully. By contrast, interpretations that confront previously repressed fantasies or feelings that are inconsistent with a person's self-image may heighten tension.

The same type of interpretation may enhance the self-esteem of one patient and weaken that of another. People who are overwhelmed with guilt or shame may gain considerable support from interpretations implying that their behavior was an inevitable reaction to the actions of others. On the other hand, such formulations might aggravate the condition of patients who are already too prone to transfer responsibility for their difficulties to others. Such persons often feel like powerless pawns of a malignant fate, and so may gain support from interpretations that highlight their own contributions to their predicaments. The interpretation that a person's troubles are self-inflicted implies that he or she has the power to resolve them, thereby indirectly enhancing the sense of mastery. (See the example of Mr. Angelo, pp. 262–63.)

Schachter (1965) characterized an emotion as a fusion between the awareness of an internal state and the person's attribution of its cause, based on his or her own past experiences and clues in the immediate environment. This formulation helps us understand the power of an interpretation to directly influence a particular emotion. In patients, the attribution of cause creates a vicious circle. Attributing a pounding heart to incipient heart disease, or difficulty in concentrating to impending insanity, arouses anxiety and aggravates the original symptoms. A simple reassurance that supplies a convincing, less ominous alternative explanation of the symptoms may produce a marked improvement in the patient.

Beyond relieving specific symptoms, interpretations may induce far-reaching changes in aspects of patients' personalities. The apologia which patients bring to treatment justifies and supports a maladaptive self-image or otherwise contributes to their disability and distress. In general, patients have blotted out certain experiences and over-emphasized others. Since a person's self-image includes expectations about the future supported by pictures of the past, changing the person's current self-image requires changing his or her view of the future through reinterpretation of the past and present. Following the lead of the therapist's interpretations, the patient recalls repressed experiences and reinterprets them in terms of the therapist's conceptual scheme. In this way, the patient gradually constructs a new apologia that provides a more favorable view of the future and sustains a new and better self-image.

Thus, from a cognitive standpoint, interpretations produce "insight." This can be viewed as a reworking of the past that leads to the discovery of new facts, as well as a recognition of new relationships between previously known facts and a reevaluation of their significance. Analogous to the hermeneutic circle, an interpretation directs the attention of the patient and therapist toward new material that confirms the validity of the therapist's formulation. Such validation encourages the search for more confirmatory material. Over time, the assumptive systems underlying the therapist's interpretations become increasingly reinforced at the expense of the patient's original ones.

Many analytically oriented psychotherapies pay special attention to the detection and interpretation of patients' reactions to the analyst, especially those transferred from their past experiences with others. At a simple level, a patient may exaggerate suffering in the belief that the therapist, like a person encountered in the past, can be won over by arousing his or her sympathy. Another may hide material that he or she thinks might arouse the therapist's contempt. In short, transference colors patients' reports about all aspects of life. Therapists must therefore interpret patients' attitudes toward them and the treatment situation.

Transference reactions also provide valuable clues to the patient's feelings and behavior toward important persons outside of therapy. Bringing the patient to see how certain reactions result from confusing the therapist with figures from the past increases the patient's ability to detect and then correct similar inappropriate reactions to important others. For example, a man may discover that in some respects he is reacting to the therapist as if the therapist were the patient's childhood image of his father. Such insight may lead to a recognition of similar inappropriate reactions to other "father figures," such as employers.

As mentioned earlier, psychoanalysts and their critics have long recognized the possibility that interpretations may directly influence patients' productions. In keeping with their emphasis on therapeutic objectivity, psychoanalysts have sought to deny that interpretations can operate as suggestions in this sense. Evidence from psychoanalysis itself casts considerable doubt on this contention. Freud made his well-known assertion that "we are not in a position to . . . influence the products of the analysis by arousing an expectation" (Breuer and Freud 1957, p. 295) before he discovered that some patients fabricated infantile memories in accordance with his theories. A leading analyst once went to some lengths to distinguish between correct and incorrect interpretations, arguing that the latter might operate by suggestion, but offering elaborate reasons why the former did not. The following quotation, from an article written some twenty years later, suggests that he did not entirely convince himself: "Despite all dogmatic and puristic assertions to the contrary, we cannot exclude or have not yet excluded the transference effect of suggestion through interpretation" (Glover 1952, p. 405).

Close examination of the effects of a particular interpretation on a particular patient illustrates the power of interpretations and the interaction of the many ways in which they exert their healing influence. The senior author once saw a patient who was apparently relieved of recurrent bouts of severe depression, preoccupation, and irritability in a single interview (Frank 1962). These symptoms had occurred at one- or two-week intervals since shortly before the patient's marriage five years earlier. Following the birth of a daughter a few months before coming to treatment, the patient was determined to be a perfect mother. This resolution provoked extreme irritability, often culminating in violent outbursts connected with fears that she was not handling the child exactly right. The patient feared she would fail the child as her mother had failed her, and the intensity of her feelings played into her fear of impending insanity. She came to see me reluctantly, at the insistence of her husband, in whose eyes I had high prestige.

A review of the patient's past history revealed that her mother had been away much of the time during her infancy and then had vanished completely when she was about three. Her few memories of her mother were scenes of tender care. After her mother left, the patient's father remarried and soon went overseas in the armed forces for a year and a half. The patient described herself as a crybaby during his absence. Following her father's return, she became apparently happy and carefree until the age of fourteen, when she discovered some of her mother's letters and a newspaper clipping in the attic. These seemed to imply that the mother had been mentally ill and had committed suicide. Finding out this information precipitated a new period of brooding and irritability. The patient was afraid to tell her father of her discovery lest she hurt his feelings. She angrily withdrew from him and began to fantasize about whether her mother had committed suicide, whether her father's insensitivity was somehow responsible, and whether she, too, would commit suicide. These feelings again lifted, apparently spontaneously, after a year or so, and she became her former self until late in her courtship. Both families opposed the marriage because the patient was Jewish and her fiancé Protestant. This opposition created tension in their relationship, which seemed to contribute to the recurrence of the young woman's depression. A final bit of information is that in the interview, the patient showed obvious conflict about whether to confide in me.

My reconceptualization of the historical cause of the patient's symptoms was that, having twice been abandoned by people on whom she felt dependent (her mother and her father), she was afraid to put her trust in anyone, including her husband. I said that she was showing this distrust in her reluctance to see me as well as in her behavior in the interview itself. I attributed her earlier periods of depression to the original desertions by her mother and father and their reactivation by her discovery of the letters.

As the patient said in the next interview, my interpretation "went off like a gong." She confirmed her acceptance of it by spontaneously attributing the recurrence of her depression and irritability during her courtship to her fiancé's periodic threats to terminate the engagement because of family opposition. She recognized that these threats had reactivated the feelings that followed her desertion by her mother and father. In the three months that I was able to follow her, during which I saw her only twice, she remained essentially symptom free. For the first time she fully accepted that her mother had committed suicide. She felt more friendly toward her father, and he seemed less reserved toward her. She no longer tried to be a perfect homemaker and mother. For example, she was able to admit to her husband sometimes that she was too tired to cook. Above all, she began to confide her feelings to him. To her astonishment, she realized that in her brooding periods she thought she had been speaking her feelings aloud but had actually been reciting them to herself.

A plausible explanation of the effect of my words is that the patient's feelings were essentially inexplicable to her. The only explanation she had been able to construct — that she was going crazy and would commit suicide like her mother — aggravated her distress. On the basis of her history and behavior in the interview, I offered a plausible and reassuring formulation. By construing her symptoms as expressions of her fear of again being abandoned by someone on whom she depended, I enabled her to relabel her feelings as "normal." The acceptability of this interpretation, which in itself sharply reduced her anxiety, was enhanced by my high prestige. Furthermore, my explanation strongly implied that she should change her behavior. Instead of trying to banish her fears by proving to herself that she did not need her husband, she should seek his reassurance by telling him about them. Fortunately, her husband was able to respond to her revelations by offering support and encouragement, which dissolved the barrier between them and reinforced the new behavior.

In short, my interpretations provided a more benign explanation of her symptoms than her own, thereby enabling her to construct a more optimistic apologia. These interpretations also implied that she had the power to correct the miscommunication with her husband that had helped perpetuate her distress. In these ways the interpretations combated her demoralization and enhanced her sense of mastery.

More generally, this example supports two different but complementary theories of psychopathology. In keeping with the view that experiences in early life are the taproot of neurosis, my interpretations made sense of the patient's current feelings in the light of her past experiences. From this perspective, the core therapeutic element of my intervention was to confront the patient's adult self with the distortions she had unconsciously carried over from childhood. Her recognition of the inappropriateness of her reactions in her current situation then allowed her to make healthy changes in her attitudes and behavior.

An alternative view is that although maladaptive neurotic patterns stem from the past, they are perpetuated by forces in the present. It is important not to confuse the cause of a symptom with its current meaning, since the current meaning can often be changed regardless of the symptom's cause (Whitehorn 1947). Without affecting the historical causes of my patient's distress, my interpretations changed the meaning she attached to her symptoms. This insight, in turn, stimulated beneficial changes in her self-image and her behavior toward her husband and her father.

This alternative conceptualization of neurotic symptoms is based on the assumption that people try to control their social environment by seeking to elicit affection, attention, respect, and other favorable responses from others. "Control" in this sense is not the same as dominance. A dependent wife controls her husband's behavior by forcing him to make all decisions for her. According to this view, a neurotic symptom may be a disguised effort to control other persons without taking responsibility for it. That is, the symptom conceals from the patient and others the real purpose of the patient's behavior. Presumably, patients resort to oblique tactics because they are too insecure to use direct ones. Since the goal of these tactics is covert, however, patients continue to experience and express the symptom because they can never be sure it has achieved its end (Haley 1963).

In terms of this framework, the aim of therapy is to make patients aware of their own contribution to the perpetuation of their symptoms and to offer support until they find the courage to take responsibility for their behavior. With such support, patients may be able to identify their covert goals. They can then either adopt new strategies to achieve these goals or modify them appropriately (Frank 1966).

Occasionally, interpretations based in this conceptualization of psychopathology will improve even deep-seated and complex symptoms. An example was provided by a young, married nurse, a patient of the senior author. She worked in a nursing home and suffered from crippling obsessions, among them fears of running over elderly people (Frank 1966). The obsessions had started at her first meeting with her future mother-in-law, who, she felt, disapproved of her. As the result of an emotionally traumatic childhood, the patient was filled with impotent resentments toward her own family, strong feelings of self-hatred, and fears of rejection by others. Her husband, a rather obsessional lawyer, was angered by any efforts his wife made to change him. He had demanded that she leave her first therapist because he felt that the therapist was trying to change him through her. He had told his wife he could not see why a woman should ever be angry at her husband. Though consciously angry at her husband for his "indifference" and for not showing her enough tenderness, the patient was unable to tell him so directly, fearing both her own anger and his rejection.

The patient was a heavy smoker, against her husband's wishes, and on one occasion he became angry when she lit a cigarette despite his protests. She said nothing, but instantly had a flare-up of obsessive fears that she had run over an old lady while driving home from work the day before.

The next day, while out for a drive with her husband, she meant to ask him to stop at the spot to make sure nothing had happened, but forgot to mention it until he had driven past it. Then, suddenly recalling her purpose, she abruptly demanded that he turn around and go back for what seemed to him a nonsensical reason. Naturally he refused, whereupon she flew into a violent rage.

My interpretation of this event was that her symptoms enabled her to vent her legitimate anger at her husband, but only on grounds that were obviously absurd, which humiliated her. He could not respond appropriately, because he did not know what she was really angry about.

After some months of treatment devoted to clarification of her own and her husband's feelings, the patient stated that she had discovered that she could "trust" her husband — that his feelings for her were genuine and that his apparent indifference was often simple preoccupation with other matters. She felt able to talk more openly with him about her feeling of neglect, and he responded with affection. Her obsessions sharply diminished, and she lost her fear of pregnancy. She remained greatly improved over a follow-up period of several years.

An important aim of the patient's therapy was to make her aware that flare-ups of her irrational fears often coincided with occasions for legitimate anger at her husband. That is, the "unconscious" purpose of her symptoms was to elicit more consideration from her husband for her as a person. To be sure, her obsessions did gain his consideration for her as a patient. His solicitousness, however, further undermined her self-esteem because it was given on the basis that she was sick, not that her demands were legitimate.

Viewing a symptom as a miscarried communication implies that others are also always involved; if the patient gives up the symptom, others also must change. This insight has led some therapists to include members of the patient's social network in treatment, as considered in Chapter 11. Here we note only the implication that if a patient recovers, someone else may get "sick." Such an event occurred in the case just described.

The husband came to see me in great distress some months after the completion of his wife's therapy. He said he had lost all interest in her. In addition, he was clinically depressed, had lost ten pounds, and complained of abdominal pains, restlessness, and inability to concentrate. He quickly recognized that when his wife was psychologically crippled, he could maintain a protective attitude toward her. This fulfilled his need to dominate the marriage and helped him contain his anger at her exasperating behavior. Her recovery made his dominance less certain and also deprived him of his defenses against his anger. His wife, in turn, aggravated his condition by trying to "help" him analyze his feelings — that is, she placed herself in a superior position by casting him in the role of patient. His symptoms subsided and his affection for his wife returned rapidly after a joint session in which all this came out into the open. The wife agreed to stop "treating" her husband and to give his spontaneous recuperative powers a chance.

It must be added that at a follow-up interview three years later, the patient did not remember any of my clever interpretations. She said she had improved because I had made her "feel like a real person." That is, the healing power of my interpretations seemed to lie more in the general attitude they conveyed than in their precise content.

Yalom eloquently reports a nearly identical experience in describing a successful psychotherapy during which patient and therapist independently wrote down their impressions of each interview: "All my elegant interpretations? She never even heard them! What she remembered and treasured were the soft subtle exchanges which to her conveyed my interest and caring" ([1970] 1985, p. 104). Many patients express a similar perception of what helps most in therapy.

Therapists who have spent much time and energy learning the exact timing and wording of interpretations, and who believe that only "correct" interpretations will lead patients to change, find it hard to accept that the attitude their words convey may contribute more to therapy than the words' precise content. Though therapists of all schools attribute improvement in their patients to their particular technical skills, the ability to raise morale through conveying to patients that they are valued as persons may be more important.

In addition to conveying certain therapeutic attitudes, interpretations link the patient's personal troubles to the therapist's conceptual scheme. This connection to an established set of concepts diminishes the patient's sense of isolation, especially when the same concepts are also applied to normal persons. Such interpretations enable patients to reconceptualize problems in terms that enhance feelings of closeness to others. Moreover, the aesthetic or dramatic qualities of some conceptual frameworks, notably those in the Freudian or Jungian tradition, heighten their effectiveness. The colorful metaphors and images of these forms of psychoanalysis imply that the patient, far from being an insignificant creature, is a battleground of titanic forces or a storehouse of the accumulated myths and wisdom of the ages. In a sense, these concepts link the individual to suprapersonal forces, echoing the ideas that are so important in cults and religious healing. In any case, such interpretations heighten a patient's sense of importance and thus may bolster morale.

Paradoxically, interpretations based on existentialist philosophies, which view individual existence as objectively meaningless, can also strengthen morale. The view that neurotic symptoms are failed attempts to cope with universal, existential dilemmas helps the patient overcome demoralizing feelings of uniqueness. Furthermore, interpretations in an existential framework are intended to help patients withstand the realization that life is meaningless by enabling them to discover their own capacity to infuse it with meaning. While people cannot control many external events that affect their welfare, they are free to determine what position to take toward them. This realization helps the person preserve a sense of inner freedom by finding meaning even in suffering and despair (Frankl 1984).

Summary

Psychotherapies can be classified according to whether they deal primarily with the individual patient, with the patient as a member of a group, or with the patient's total milieu in a controlled setting. They can also be roughly classified as person- or problem-centered and as evocative, directive, or mixed.

This chapter has examined the persuasive and healing properties of evocative, person-centered, individual psychotherapy, using classical psychoanalysis as the chief example. The evocative therapist is a model with whom the patient can identify. In psychoanalysis, the analyst's refusal to offer overt guidance creates emotionally arousing ambiguity that fosters dependency and suggestibility in patients. Over time, the analyst's neutrality allows patients to attribute progress to their own efforts, thereby increasing their sense of mastery. Detailed therapeutic review of the patient's past life results in confessions that arouse guilt, shame, and other destructive emotions, while the therapist's steady, nonjudgmental interest implicitly conveys forgiveness and reacceptance into society. Repetitive review of the past also helps patients rediscover neglected assets and reconstruct their histories to support a better self-image.

Interpretations, the overtly influencing interventions of psychoanalysis, affect patients emotionally, cognitively, and behaviorally. They convey approval or disapproval, thereby shaping patients' reports. Healing interpretations reduce the patient's cognitive confusion by naming inchoate feelings and ordering them within a conceptual framework. Interpretations may stir patients emotionally by confronting them with disavowed aspects of the self; those that change patients' perceptions of the causes of their distress may bring profound relief. Interpretations of symptoms as oblique efforts to control others may lead to beneficial changes in behavior. Finally, interpretations implicitly convey the therapist's theory of human nature and philosophy of existence. Adopting the therapist's philosophy may reduce or mitigate patients' suffering by placing it in a broader context that gives it significance. A major therapeutic function of all interpretations, regardless of their specific content, is to convey the therapist's interest and support.

TEN

Directive Individual Psychotherapies

"Where do you come from?" said the Red Queen.
"And where are you going? Look up, speak nicely, and
don't twiddle your fingers all the time."
— *Through the Looking Glass*

As we have seen, evocative, person-centered therapies seek to improve patients' total psychological functioning by providing a supportive, accepting therapeutic relationship in which previously unconscious experiences or issues can emerge into full awareness. Evocative therapists further assume that any therapeutic experience fosters general personality growth and integration, and that as this occurs, particular symptoms and psychological disabilities resolve themselves. That is, evocative therapies foster favorable conditions for change but leave specific changes up to the patient. To this end, the therapeutic situation is largely unstructured, although time-limited evocative therapies direct patients' attention to specific personal issues.

By contrast, directive therapies attack discrete symptoms or problems in a highly structured, systematic, narrowly focused way. They further assume that helping patients overcome particular symptoms may stimulate more profound improvements in their general state. This strategy is the obverse of producing symptomatic improvements through the fostering of basic reorganization or general personality growth.

The techniques of these two types of therapy also seem fundamentally dissimilar. Unlike evocative therapists, who use examination of the therapeutic relationship itself as an integral feature of therapy, directive therapists use the relationship primarily as the source of therapeutic leverage. Eschewing neutrality, they readily employ such familiar forms of persuasion as exhortation, advice, instruction, and setting a good example. With the exception of abreactive therapies, furthermore, directive therapies typically keep patients firmly rooted in the present, ignoring the historical bases of their problems. Finally, these therapies seem more scientifically oriented than the avowedly humanistic, evocative ones. Broad, imprecise concepts like the unconscious or the structure of personality, central to evocative therapies, are anathema to directive therapists, at least those in the behavioral tradition. Behavior therapists are committed to dealing with phenomena that can be observed, quantified, and studied according to methodologically rigorous designs.

Despite these differences, evocative therapies rooted in metapsychological speculations about the meaning of life may have the same effects, and operate by the same mechanisms, as those apparently derived from laboratory experiments on the behavior of lower animals. Existential psychotherapy and Jungian psychoanalysis have more in common with the "deconditioning" of a simple phobia than their proponents recognize. In Chapter 9 we suggested that an unstructured therapy conducted by an apparently neutral therapist may exert its healing influence in part through covert behavior modification.

Similarly, directive psychotherapies, even those theoretically grounded in research on animal behavior, share the healing components of evocative ones. Like every form of psychological healing, directive psychotherapies improve patients' morale by offering them a therapeutic relationship and a rationale that inspires hope, fosters mastery, and relieves confusion. No less than evocative therapies, directive ones mobilize humans' symbolic capacity in the service of personal growth and beneficial changes in attitude.

To be sure, such directive techniques as exposure for phobias and guided abreaction for the resolution of trauma may have specific effects on particular symptoms or conditions. The meanings patients attach to these and other directive procedures, however, contribute importantly to their success.

Though directive and evocative therapies may have similar healing components and similar outcomes, they do differ importantly in their target populations. Not all directive therapies require that patients have a good frustration tolerance, strong motivation, and an ability to verbalize feelings. Thus, some forms are useful with patients who are not suited to an evocative approach — for example, people who are psychotic or mentally retarded.

This broad applicability may create ethical problems. Certain directive therapies have been applied to patients who are unwilling to cooperate because their behavior is grounded in assumptions not shared by the wider society. Examples include addicts, antisocial personalities, sex offenders, and even members of religious cults who are subjected to "deprogramming" (see Chapters 1 and 4). Whether efforts to change the attitudes and behavior of involuntary patients should be termed therapy is a matter of ethical debate. Our discussion of directive therapy dodges this important but peripheral issue by considering only those treatments that are used with patients who share the same goals as the therapist, seek treatment voluntarily, and are able to follow instructions.

Though all directive therapies simultaneously affect patients' thought, behavior, and emotions, we follow conventional usage in classifying particular approaches as cognitive, behavioral, or abreactive. Cognitive and behavior therapy are historically and conceptually linked, so we will discuss them together before examining examples of each in greater depth. We will then turn to abreactive treatments and their implications for understanding the role of emotional arousal in therapy. In emphasizing the persuasive and healing features that these therapies share with other approaches, we leave open the question of how much the distinguishing features of particular methods contribute to their success.

An Overview of Cognitive and Behavior Therapy

Cognitive and behavior therapies assume that the patient's presenting symptom or maladaptive behavior is itself the problem, not merely the manifestation of underlying unconscious motives or conflicts. In keeping with this assumption, the therapist first identifies the symptoms or behaviors for which the patient seeks help and the environmental conditions that initiate, sustain, or exacerbate them. The therapist then prescribes a therapeutic program comprising specific procedures. He or she guides and encourages the patient's efforts to carry out the procedures in treatment sessions and then in daily life. Therapeutic procedures may be applied to specific symptoms, such as suicidal ideation or compulsive hand washing, and to more general aspects of patients' adaptation, such as the inability to openly express feelings or a lack of assertiveness (Black and Bruce 1989).

If treatment enables the patient to overcome a troublesome symptom or change a problematic behavior, the patient experiences a general increase in self-efficacy, competence, or mastery. As a result, the patient is able to encounter and master situations that he or she previously avoided. This "ripple effect" affects areas far removed from the initial complaint. Spiegel and Linn (1969), for example, described a patient who regained his sexual potency through hypnosis. This success made him able for the first time to protect himself from exploitation by business partners and to discharge dishonest employees. Similarly, Bandura (1982) found that patients who overcame simple phobias through modeling with guided participation (see pp. 219–20) experienced feelings of mastery that contributed to general therapeutic gains.

Although most cognitive and behavior therapists would scorn such terms, these examples suggest that successful cognitive or behavior therapy indirectly fosters personality growth, self-realization, or some of the other nebulous but highly desirable goals of evocative approaches.

Cognitive and behavior therapies are apparently backed by a large body of psychological experiments on humans and animals. Conforming to the model of applied sciences, the goals, procedures, and outcomes of these therapies are expressed in objective terms. Progress in overcoming a snake phobia, for example, is determined by the patient's ability to come progressively closer to a snake under standardized conditions. Such rigorous measurement of patients' responses enables researchers to monitor patients' progress and to compare the relative success rates of different therapies. The experimental attitude thus fosters innovativeness and flexibility. A researcher knows whether a procedure has achieved its stated goal and will try new approaches if it has failed. To their credit, cognitive and behavior therapists have conducted investigations that have exposed the limitations and inadequacies of their own conceptualizations. These studies have led to the development of progressively more adequate theories and procedures. Such demonstration that psychotherapy can be studied experimentally is a permanent contribution.

Cognitive and behavior therapies have flourished in the United States for many reasons. They reflect the American pragmatic world-view that distrusts theories, encourages experimentation, and advocates using any method that works. In addition, their apparent scientific rigor serves the interests of diverse groups. Psychologists have found in these therapies fodder for innumerable Ph.D. theses. Though much of this research is of doubtful relevance to actual therapeutic practice, it allows psychologists to view themselves as applied behavioral scientists, with all the cachet this implies. The methods of cognitive and behavior therapists also appeal to third-party payers, who demand objective standards by which to determine the cost-effectiveness of various procedures.

Many patients find cognitive and behavior therapies more appealing than evocative, person-centered ones. Cognitive and behavior therapists focus on the particular symptoms or behaviors that bring the patient to therapy and not on early memories, fantasies, and dreams. Behavioral and cognitive techniques are therefore less likely to arouse guilt or shame and may incur less resistance than evocative techniques. Moreover, the cognitive-behavioral focus on particular problems resembles the familiar medical model, in which patients generally have confidence. Since these therapies are usually time-limited, they require a much smaller commitment of time and money than open-ended, evocative approaches. Moreover, as therapy proceeds, tangible signs of progress in overcoming target symptoms enhance patients' acceptance of treatment.

Cognitive and behavior therapists are as optimistic as evocative ones about the effectiveness of their methods. Directive approaches clearly surpass others, however, only in relieving anxieties that are linked to particular stimuli, situations, or persons. The findings of a survey of a random sample of members of the Association for the Advancement of Behavior Therapy suggest that for other conditions, cognitive and behavior therapies are no more effective than other therapies. Reporting on all their patients, not merely those presenting discrete anxiety, respondents in this survey claimed a median success rate of 70.5 percent, which is equivalent to that of person-centered therapies (Swan and MacDonald 1978).

Despite fundamental similarities, cognitive and behavior therapies differ from each other in the nature and extent of their research base, their particular rationales, and the conditions they treat. Because human cognitive capacities are unique, cognitive therapies derive from applied research in human subjects, rather than from the basic animal research that supports many behavioral approaches. In general, behavioral approaches are best suited to such circumscribed problems as phobias or the awkward social behavior of chronically psychotic patients. Cognitive therapy, by contrast, can improve broad syndromes such as generalized anxiety or depression. In light of these differences, we shall examine each approach in more detail before commenting further on their common effects.

Cognitive Therapies

All cognitive therapies postulate that persons' behavioral and emotional states are responses to internalized sentences (Ellis 1962) or automatic thoughts (Beck 1976) about the meanings of their experience, not to situations or events per se. Patients' symptoms or maladaptive behaviors are considered to be responses to inappropriate interpretations of events, interpretations which cognitive therapies seek to change. Thus, cognitive therapists may legitimately be characterized as rhetoricians, and their procedures as rhetorical arguments.

In many cases, cognitive therapists seek to change meanings that are unconscious, though they do not use the term in the psychoanalytic sense of "defensively repressed." Rather, cognitive therapists assume that automatic thoughts are unnoticed because they are fleeting and habitual, like eye blinks. Beck (1970) cited as an example a man who felt anxious every time he saw a dog, even a chained one or a puppy, because he had the fleeting, barely conscious thought, "He is going to bite me." Bringing this automatic thought to the forefront of consciousness allowed the man to recognize its absurdity with respect to most dogs and relieved his fear.

"Rational emotive" therapy is a complete system of cognitive therapy based on the assumption that neurotic distress and maladaptive behavior are caused by internalized sentences. The sentences targeted by this system are more general than the one in Beck's vignette and represent a pervasive attitude toward life. The belief that one must be loved at all times to survive is a typical example. The therapist unearths these hidden postulates, assumed to be limited in number, and then helps the patient recognize their illogicality and act on new-found understanding, "to un*do* (as well as to un*think*) his self-defeating indoctrination" (Ellis 1962, p. 123; italics in the original).

To achieve this end, the rational-emotive therapist uses any appropriate means of persuasion, including exhortation, argument, browbeating, and instructing patients to engage in behaviors that would expose the falsity of their assumptions. An example of successful treatment of a subjective symptom and a behavioral problem by rational-emotive psychotherapy follows (Ellis 1959). The unusually favorable outcome of this case should not be regarded as typical. Many homosexuals have no wish to change their sexual preference, and of those who do, many do not respond to this or any other form of psychotherapy.

The patient was a thirty-five-year-old, exclusively homosexual man who had experienced periodic attacks of chest pain and palpitations. His homosexual activities had been going on for sixteen years. In addition, he was emotionally overdependent on his parents, having reluctantly and resentfully abandoned a teaching career to take over the family business after his father suffered a stroke. The therapist first attacked the patient's homosexuality, the patient's most pressing concern. The therapist's goal was not to cause the patient to surrender his homosexual desires but to overcome his irrational block against heterosexual behavior. After determining that the patient had not once made an initial homosexual advance, the therapist told him that his outstanding motive for remaining homosexual was fear of rejection, springing from his illogical belief that being rejected, especially by a woman, was a terrible thing. "His fear of rejection, of losing approval, of having others laugh at and criticize him was examined in scores of its aspects, and revealed to him again and again . . . [and] scornfully, forcefully *attacked* by the therapist" (Ellis 1959, p. 341; italics in the original).

Concomitantly, the patient was encouraged to date women in order to overcome his fears by actually interacting with them. The therapist told him how to behave on a date, what to expect, how to avoid being discouraged by rebuffs, and when to make sexual advances. After completing seven weekly sessions, the patient had heterosexual relations that were satisfying to him and his partner. By the twelfth week of treatment he was "virtually a hundred percent heterosexual. All his waking and sleeping fantasies became heterosexually oriented and he was almost never interested in homosexual outlets" (Ellis 1959, p. 342).

The therapist attacked the patient's psychosomatic symptoms and vocational problems in a similar manner. As the man overcame each one, he was able to resume his interrupted academic career. It should be noted that the therapist virtually ignored such basic issues in the patient's life as his resentful overattachment to his mother and his probable jealousy of his father's hold over her.

The patient discontinued treatment after nineteen sessions. A letter from him three years later revealed that he was married and teaching in a university. His interest in homosexual activity had vanished, and his cardiac symptoms had not recurred.

Beck's cognitive therapy (1976) and Bandura's therapy based on principles of social learning (1977) are two other influential and widely practiced cognitive approaches. Beck, like Ellis, attributes distress and disability to the automatic thoughts that intervene between environmental events and a person's particular emotional responses to them. Beck asserts that these thoughts become codified into schemas, similar to the present authors' assumptive systems. These schemas provide standards by which people evaluate, steer, or inhibit their own behavior and judge the behavior of others. Therapy is a set of procedures designed to modify dysfunctional thoughts and schemas in a systematic way.

The most sophisticated and well-researched applications of cognitive therapy have been in the treatment of depression (Burns 1980) and, more recently, anxiety disorders (Beck, Emery, and Greenberg 1985). A review of its use in depression illustrates the basic principles of this approach and the status of current research.

According to cognitive theory, the essence of depression is a cognitive triad: a negative view of the self, of current life experiences, and of the future (Burns 1980). Therapy helps the patient ferret out these negative thoughts and schemas and substitute more adaptive ones. For example, a depressed patient who voices the thought, "I always feel miserable," might be instructed to keep an hourly activity schedule. At the end of the day, the patient would rate each event in accordance with its effect on his or her sense of mastery and the pleasure it yielded. Depressed patients regularly discover that they have been systematically underrating their positive experiences and overrating their negative ones. As patients come to recognize the discrepancy between self-evaluation and actual experience, their need to reduce cognitive dissonance (Festinger 1957) may cause them to adopt a more balanced view. Other negative cognitions are exposed, confronted, and revised in a similar manner.

This theoretically plausible, well-articulated program has proved quite effective in alleviating depressions, including some that are quite severe. Like so many other innovations, cognitive therapy yielded impressive early successes. The National Institute of Mental Health Treatment of Depression Collaborative Research Program comparing two modes of psychotherapy and the administration of an antidepressant accompanied by minimal supportive therapy for depression, however, revealed that cognitive therapy was no more effective than the other modes (Elkin et al. 1989).

Furthermore, a detailed analysis revealed only scattered and insubstantial evidence of mode-specific differences in outcome among the three therapies. That is, the type of improvement following antidepressant medication was indistinguishable from the improvement following cognitive therapy. The researchers concluded that core processes operating across treatments (in the present authors' terms, common factors) override differences among techniques (Imber et al. 1990). In light of these and other findings, the inventor of this therapy himself concluded that "proponents of cognitive therapy for depression must still demonstrate that something beyond nonspecific processes . . . produce[s] the changes noted" (Hollon and Beck 1986, p. 454).

Like cognitive therapy, the therapy-based social learning theory of Bandura (1977) has generated an impressive body of elegant research. While giving appropriate weight to biomedical factors, social learning theory emphasizes that humans' extraordinary symbolic powers are major determinants of the formation and regulation of their thoughts, affects, and actions. This theory postulates that people regulate their behavior by envisaging its consequences and can learn vicariously by observing what happens to others.

Applied to psychotherapy, social learning theory has led to the successful use of modeling with guided participation to help patients overcome strongly established fears of specific objects. A patient may quickly overcome a deep-seated fear of dogs, for example, after a few demonstrations by a model who shows pleasure patting a dog and then shows the patient how to do the same while offering encouragement and reassurance. Bandura also stresses the fact that success in conquering any one fear contributes to self-efficacy, which in turn may produce general therapeutic gains (Bandura 1982).

The success of this or any other therapy does not necessarily prove the validity of the theory that guides it. For example, Bandura stresses the role of imagined consequences in generating fears, and of corrective learning by example in overcoming them. Research on other treatments for phobia, however, suggests that any treatment that keeps patients in contact with the feared situation or object long enough for the fear reaction to extinguish itself will be effective. From this perspective, the main therapeutic value of Bandura's theory is its plausibility or rhetorical power, which moves patients to expose themselves to the situations they fear. To further illustrate this point, we now turn to behavioral treatments for phobia and related conditions.

Behavior Therapies

The term "behavior therapy" is conventionally used to characterize therapies that apply the conditioning theories of Pavlov and Skinner to human beings. In Pavlovian or respondent conditioning, behavior is shaped by the stimuli preceding it. For example, if a bell is repeatedly sounded before a hungry dog is offered food, the dog will eventually salivate to the sound of the bell. In Skinnerian or operant conditioning, behavior is shaped by its consequences. For example, a pigeon will learn to peck a particular spot if this initially random act is regularly followed by the presentation of food. Both types of conditioning have engendered enormous quantities of research on animals and humans, leading to extraordinary gains in understanding animal and, to a lesser degree, human behavior.

Although animal research provides an inviting conceptual and methodological bridge to research in psychotherapy, animal studies have one serious and inescapable limitation. The chief forces motivating human behavior are symbolic. One need only consider the incredible feats motivated by bits of colored cloth in the form of national flags to realize the overriding role of meanings in human affairs. The healing power of all psychotherapies rests on symbolic communication. In animals, the capacity to symbolize is rudimentary at best. Thus, extrapolating from animal studies to human psychotherapy may bypass the essential elements that make therapy effective.

A large but indeterminate part of the results of human behavioral research may likewise be invalid because researchers have failed to take subjects' interpretations of their experiments into account. This caution applies particularly to so-called analogue research on persons with mild complaints who have not sought therapy but have been induced by various incentives to volunteer for treatment. College students provide a tempting and inexhaustible pool for analogue studies. Students are relatively plentiful (which facilitates setting up control groups), cooperative, and intelligent. Since most are not seriously handicapped, they can be assigned to different experimental conditions without concern that one may prove less effective than another. On the other hand, since students are induced to volunteer by pay or by such incentives as being excused from an examination, their motive for participation may be more to please the teacher or get the reward than to gain relief from symptoms. Hence their reports and behavior are especially subject to contamination by compliance with the experimenter's expectations and other demand characteristics of the situation. Such considerations raise serious questions as to how far one can apply the findings of analogue studies to bona fide patients. For this reason, the following discussion omits results of analogue research.

The forms of behavior therapy that we shall consider fall into two main groups: reinforcement and counterconditioning. In technical terms, a positive reinforcement is a stimulus, the appearance of which after a bit of behavior increases the probability of that behavior's occurring again. A negative reinforcement increases the probability of the behavior by ceasing or failing to occur following it. Though these categories include many more classes of stimuli than rewards and punishments, for the sake of stylistic simplicity we shall use the term "reward" for positive reinforcement and "punishment" for negative reinforcement.

As we have seen (Chapter 8), such subtle rewards and punishments as small signs of approval or disapproval can shape a patient's verbal behavior even when the therapist is apparently completely neutral. The use of token economies to shape the behavior of severely handicapped persons in mental hospitals and institutions for the mentally retarded is a more obvious therapeutic application of behavioral reinforcement (Paul and Lentz 1977). This procedure rewards or punishes certain behaviors by giving or withholding tokens that patients can exchange for candy or increased privileges. Although in theory the effects of token economies result mechanically, the actual success of these programs largely depends on close relations between patients and staff, and additional reinforcement of the desired behaviors through praise.

In reinforcement paradigms, rewards and punishments are delivered after the subject has shown the behavior in question. Counterconditioning stimuli are delivered simultaneously with the behavior. Like reinforcement, counterconditioning can be either positive or negative. Positive counterconditioning involves pairing an event that normally provokes avoidance with a pleasant stimulus of sufficient strength to overcome the avoidant response. Thus, offering candies in the doctor's office may help a child overcome fear of going to the doctor. An application to psychotherapy is discussed at length below.

Negative or aversive counterconditioning inhibits undesirable behavior by linking it to an unpleasant stimulus. An example would be trying to cure alcoholics by repeatedly giving them drinks mixed with drugs that induce vomiting. Another illustration is the effort to eliminate sexual responses to homosexual stimuli or fetish objects by coupling the presentation of the stimulus with a painful shock (Marks and Gelder 1967).

Aversive counterconditioning may help eliminate undesirable behaviors in patients who cannot be reached by verbal communication. It has been used, for example, to discourage self-mutilation in brain-damaged children. In general, however, the use of aversive counterconditioning in psychotherapy has fallen into disfavor. Punishment as a form of treatment can too readily lead to abuse. Furthermore, patients who are so strongly motivated to change that they will voluntarily submit to aversive therapy can usually be helped by more positively oriented procedures.

The treatment of phobias — that is, of anxiety linked to specific situations, persons, or objects — has been the most general psychotherapeutic application of behavior modification. Behavioral techniques have also been used to treat generalized anxiety and panic attacks.[1]

Joseph Wolpe's "reciprocal inhibition" or "systematic desensitiza-

---

1. American researchers generally separate panic attacks from other forms of anxiety, whereas British researchers are more likely to espouse the position that panic represents the extreme of a continuum of severity. As the British researcher Isaac Marks put it, "No one yet has shown that the distinction between mild anxiety and severe panic is more categorical than the distinction between mild pain and severe agony" (1987a, p. 1161). This curious cultural cleavage may exist because panic attacks, being temporarily controllable by medication, are a bonanza for drug manufacturers. In America these companies conduct aggressive advertising campaigns, sponsoring and publicizing research in favor of the position that panic is a distinct illness responsive to their particular remedy. At the time of writing, the issue is unsettled.

tion" provides an example of a treatment for anxiety based, at least in the mind of its founder, upon the principles of positive counterconditioning. As briefly described in Chapter 3, Wolpe's experiments with cats showed that if anxiety is evoked simultaneously with a physiologically incompatible response such as eating, the anxiety gradually disappears (1958).

Application of this theory to humans is based on the assumption that people cannot be relaxed and anxious at the same time. Treatment by reciprocal inhibition involves three steps: training in progressive, deep muscle relaxation; the construction of anxiety hierarchies; and the counterpoising of relaxation to the anxiety evoked by imagining progressively more frightening levels of the hierarchy. For example, if the patient is afraid of snakes, the lowest level of the hierarchy may be imagining a glimpse of a snake across a field; the highest, fantasizing a snake wrapping itself around the patient's neck. Patients first relax, then repeatedly imagine the scene at the lowest level of the hierarchy until they can stay relaxed. They then move up the hierarchy, pausing at each step until they can stay relaxed at that level. Eventually the patient can imagine the most frightening scene without feeling anxiety. Throughout, the therapist is at the patient's side offering encouragement.

At this point, a linguistic purist may object that applying the term "behavior therapy" to a method that employs fantasy considerably stretches the meaning of the term "behavior." Be that as it may, a more substantive criticism of reciprocal inhibition is that implosion and flooding therapies are equally or more effective. These therapies, in sharp contrast to reciprocal inhibition, seek to create and maintain maximal anxiety by exposing the patient, in fantasy or reality, to the phobic stimulus for a prolonged period. The theory behind implosion and flooding, supported by animal experiments, is that repeated escape from an anxiety-arousing stimulus actually reinforces the anxiety. Hence, researchers have been able to extinguish an animal's anxiety by forcing it to remain in contact with an anxiety-provoking stimulus for a sufficient period of time with no possibility of escape.

Applied to humans, implosive and flooding therapies are based on the hypothesis that all effective treatments for phobias work by exposing patients to prolonged real or fantasied contact with the anxiety-producing stimulus or situation until the anxiety is extinguished. Consistent with the findings from animal experiments, such exposure eventually extinguishes the anxiety (Klein et al. 1983; Marks 1987b).

Implosive therapy seeks to arouse prolonged, overwhelming anxiety as the patient fantasizes contact with the phobic stimulus at maximal intensity until he or she is exhausted (Stampfl 1976). The therapist evokes and guides the patient's frightening fantasies and pushes them to extremes. For example, a man with a fear of snakes is encouraged to imagine ever more frightening encounters with snakes, culminating in the snake's biting his tongue, crawling into his stomach, and laying eggs there which hatch into thousands of slimy little snakes, which then shred his lungs, and so on. The success of implosive therapy obviously depends in part on such rhetorical skills as the therapist's gift for evoking vivid imagery and his or her capacity to gauge the intensity of patients' reactions.

Implosive therapy differs from abreactive therapy, considered presently, in that it typically seeks to extinguish emotional response to a circumscribed stimulus rather than to an overwhelming traumatic situation. To this end, implosive therapy seeks to intensify an emotion rather than simply to elicit it. It is unclear to what extent the underlying physiological processes in the two therapies resemble or differ from one another.

Like implosive therapy, flooding therapy seeks to arouse and prolong maximal emotional response to a specific phobic stimulus, but does so by exposing the subject to the feared stimulus in reality rather than in fantasy, when this is possible. Exposure therapy works mainly for specific phobias that are unaccompanied by other symptoms. Phobic patients who also experience generalized anxiety or depression may require anti-anxiety or antidepressant medication (Marks 1987a, 1987b).

The success of implosion and flooding therapies calls into serious question Wolpe's assumption that the patient's level of anxiety must be increased gradually and extinguished at every step by association with a stronger stimulus inhibiting anxiety.

The sometimes successful treatment of compulsions by preventing the patient from carrying out the compulsive ritual is another example of a therapy that relieves anxiety by prolonging it to the point of exhaustion. The function of many compulsive rituals is to ward off anxiety. Thus, soiling the hands of a compulsive hand washer and preventing the person from washing until the resulting emotional distress subsides may eliminate the behavior. Reciprocal inhibition, implosion, and flooding can be viewed as forms of rhetoric in the sense that they depend on the therapist's power to persuade patients to participate in rituals that require them to remain in real or fantasied contact with the source of their anxiety.

Reports of psychoanalytic success with phobias can be explained in the same way. A patient in psychoanalysis is persuaded that the source of a phobic symptom is not the apparent stimulus, but some repressed conflict the stimulus represents. Prolonged efforts to unearth the conflict and its ramifications keep the patient psychologically in contact with the stimulus long enough for the anxiety to extinguish itself. Insight-oriented therapies, however, have been found to be much less efficient than cognitive-behavioral ones in achieving this end.

In addition to their rhetorical power, behavioral treatments share the effective elements of other forms of psychotherapy, especially the ability to arouse strong emotions and the enhancement of feelings of self-efficacy or mastery. In this connection, exposure is not as easy as it sounds. Returning to the treatment of phobias, we note that for exposure to be effective, the patient must "engage" with the feared stimulus: "The experience of fear must pass all our defenses which try to stop it from reaching our awareness so that the emotion can be processed to the point of becoming habituated" (Marks 1978b, p. 477). Thus, patients' discovery that they can learn to endure exposure is a powerful demonstration that they can master distressing feelings through their own efforts. Similarly, with compulsive patients, "response prevention works well when self-imposed, and imposing external constraints achieves little in the long run" (Marks 1978b, p. 493). This formulation implies that the technique works best when patients can take credit for their success, thereby enhancing their sense of mastery.

Indeed, one research study highlights the importance of an increased sense of mastery to the success of exposure. In a carefully designed comparison of exposure and mastery therapy for persons fearful of driving or heights (Williams, Dooseman, and Kleifield, 1984), researchers excluded persons whose phobias were so mild that they might respond to any treatment, and accepted only those who could not drive more than ten blocks on a major thoroughfare or climb above the sixth floor. All subjects were asked to rate their level of perceived self-efficacy, anxiety, and other subjective states before entering treatment and then were assigned randomly to exposure or mastery treatment. Both exposure and mastery treatments were brief, consisting of three one-hour sessions unless the patient overcame the phobia before that.

In the exposure treatment, the experimenter, who remained on the ground, simply encouraged the height phobics to go to higher floors, progressing as rapidly as possible. Driving phobics were taken to the route on which they had failed in the previous behavioral test and were encouraged to drive as far as they could, noting the cross street of the farthest point reached. The experimenter did not accompany them.

The guided mastery treatments were presented as a collaborative enterprise in which the therapist's role was to help the patients learn to master fear. The experimenter stayed with the patients throughout the tasks, constantly encouraging them and suggesting various means for attaining their goals.

To summarize the findings, the level and strength of perceived self-efficacy pre- and posttest was a significantly more accurate predictor of performance attainment than was anxiety either before or during performance of the feared tasks. Furthermore, a change in self-efficacy correlated significantly with the degree of success in overcoming the phobia, whereas a change in anxiety did not. These findings support the view that a heightened sense of self-efficacy or mastery contributes importantly to the success of exposure therapies.

Confidence in this conclusion must be qualified by the fact that the researchers were proponents of self-efficacy therapy. Their vested interest in the results again raises the specter of possible subtle biases introduced by the demand characteristics of the experimental situation. In this connection, a meta-analysis by Smith, Glass, and Miller revealed that those who conduct research on their own brands of therapy find them to be more effective than do impartial investigators (1980). Nevertheless, the findings of Williams, Dooseman, and Kleifield (1984) support the view that a heightened sense of self-efficacy or mastery contributes importantly to the success of exposure therapies.

Morale-building Effects of Cognitive and Behavior Therapies

Though directive cognitive and behavior therapies emphasize the role of specific procedures in relieving particular conditions, we conclude this section with a reminder that a large part of their effectiveness may lie in the morale-building components they share with all psychotherapies.

All cognitive and behavior therapies enhance morale by providing detailed explicit descriptions of what the patient must do and how he or she is to evaluate progress. Therapists typically give patients this information at the start of therapy, review it during therapy, and often supplement it with reading materials. In this way the therapies implicitly create and reinforce positive expectations. These actions also quickly reduce the demoralizing initial confusion of many patients and keep it minimized throughout treatment. Explicit instructions also facilitate the development of a therapeutic relationship by providing a continuing task or series of tasks which the therapist monitors. The procedures are so simple and clear that they may be taught through manuals, such as that of Burns for cognitive therapy of depression (1980) and that of Marks for exposure therapy of phobias (1978). Marks (1987b) reported that after his manual had become widely known, some patients bought it and cured themselves without visiting a therapist at all. Others, however, still needed personal support and guidance. At this writing, the personality characteristics that determine patients' ability to make do with a symbolic rather than a live therapist remain to be clarified.

In any case, in most cognitive and behavior therapies, the patient's trust in the therapist is as important as it is in all other forms of psychotherapy. Thus, Sloane et al. (1975) found that patients in behavior therapy who reported more improvement also experienced their therapists as more warm, genuine, and empathic, a finding that is similar to the perceptions of patients who improved in psychoanalytically oriented treatment. More than a decade later, an extensive review of the field concluded: "It is . . . increasingly clear that the quality of the therapeutic relationship may be influential in determining success or failure of behavioral therapies" (Emmelkamp 1986, p. 432).

Patients who treat themselves according to a manual lack an actual therapeutic relationship, but their faith in the authority of the person writing the program implies a fantasied relationship that provides important support.

Aversion therapies that require the patient to be strongly motivated highlight the importance of the therapeutic relationship to successful outcome. Marmor (1971), for example, reported that two homosexual patients who had been responding well to aversive conditioning suffered serious relapses immediately after becoming angry with him. One, who had been free not only from homosexual contacts but even from homosexual urges, relapsed because he believed that the therapist had violated his confidence. He immediately sought a homosexual partner to see "how really good" the treatment was. Despite much more treatment, he was never again completely free of homosexual urges and activities. The other patient indulged in a series of homosexual acts immediately after expressing his irritation at the therapist for seeming more interested in results than in him as a person.

The procedures of cognitive and behavior therapies heighten patients' hopes by providing incremental experiences of success in overcoming their distress. Such experiences, furthermore, contribute powerfully to the sense of mastery because they result from the patients' active participation in the therapeutic task, both in the treatment sessions and in the homework done between them. In consequence, patients can rightly attribute their improvement in part to their own efforts.

Thus, behavior and cognitive psychotherapies create a therapeutic relationship and provide patients with new information, incentives, and opportunities for learning, as well as encouragement to practice what they have learned. All forms of cognitive and behavior therapy arouse emotions by requiring patients to face situations or perform actions that provoke anxiety or other unpleasant emotions. These features also enhance patients' sense of mastery.

Our analysis suggests that directive and evocative therapies have much in common. Recognition of their shared features has contributed to the development of approaches that mix evocative and directive elements for maximal effect (Lazarus 1989). Two of these approaches, implosion and flooding, which are designed to evoke and resolve the emotions linked to anxiety-arousing stimuli, have already been considered. Posttraumatic stress disorders and their treatment by abreactive methods deserve more extended consideration because they highlight what is known, and what remains to be learned, about the psychological and neurophysiological effects of extreme emotional arousal and how these effects may be counteracted by procedures that include the common features of all psychotherapies.

Emotional Arousal, Abreactive Therapy, and Posttraumatic Stress Syndromes

Cross-cultural and historical studies of psychological healing suggest that strong emotional arousal often contributes importantly to the success of any psychotherapy. In Chapters 4 and 5 we noted the emotional intensity of traditional healing rituals and religious revivalism. The historical importance of emotionally shocking procedures in the treatment of mentally ill patients is equally striking. In the first century A.D., Celsus wrote of a patient who showed abnormal behavior: "When he has said or done anything wrong, he must be chastised by hunger, chains and fetters. . . . It is also beneficial in this malady, to make use of sudden fright, for a change may be effected by withdrawing the mind from the state in which it has been" (Zilboorg 1941, p. 70). Brutal methods of arousing emotion in mentally ill persons continued during subsequent centuries, often in the guise of exorcising demons. Even Pinel, the great nineteenth-century humanitarian who struck the chains from the insane, believed that fright was an effective remedy. Early "scientific" treatments of disturbed patients included submerging them until they nearly drowned or spinning them in a chair until they lost consciousness. Pinel's American contemporary Benjamin Rush asserted: "Terror acts powerfully on the body through the medium of the mind and should be employed in the cure of madness" (Blain 1970, p. 80). A modern proponent of Zen similarly described the therapeutic use of emotional shock "in the case of a student who attempted suicide several times and was awakened and cured by a thundering cry of a master" (Sato 1958, p. 214).

Since the days of Mesmer, certain forms of psychotherapy in the West have mobilized intense emotions. In mesmeric sessions, female patients sat about the *baquet* (a container filled with "magnetized" water) holding hands and pressing their knees together to facilitate the flow of magnetic fluid. From time to time, they touched the diseased parts of their bodies with iron rods that had been dipped into the baquet. Then the assistant magnetizers entered, strong handsome young men who massaged the ladies in various ways and stared intently into their eyes, to the accompaniment of "a few wild notes on the harmonica . . . or the piano-forte, or the melodious voice of a hidden opera singer. . . . Gradually the cheeks of the ladies began to glow, their imaginations became inflamed; and off they went, one after the other, in convulsive fits" (Schwitzgebel and Traugott 1968). Some of the convulsions lasted more than three hours. Finally, Mesmer, dressed in an elegant silk robe, would solemnly enter and touch each patient with his magnetic white wand, quickly restoring the ladies "to sensibility and sometimes to health."

While disdaining such dramatic methods, Freud initially strove to produce similarly intense states of arousal by encouraging patients, with the aid of hypnosis, to "abreact" early traumatic experiences in their full intensity (Breuer and Freud 1957). Although this "cathartic" technique sometimes produced dramatic improvement, the results often proved transitory, and Freud soon abandoned it for free association and interpretation. His experience may explain why abreactive therapies seem to wax and wane in popularity. Their ability to produce change seems to be continually rediscovered, only to be followed by disillusionment when the change does not persist.

Experiments on Emotional Arousal and Attitudinal Change

Inspired by historical and cross-cultural evidence of the importance of intense emotion in psychological healing, the senior author and his colleagues conducted a series of experiments on the relationship of emotional arousal to attitudinal change (Hoehn-Saric et al. 1978). A brief review of the findings of these experiments may cast some light on the effects of implosion and flooding, and of contemporary therapies based on abreaction, which are considered below.

The subjects in these experiments were all psychiatric outpatients. Ether was administered to them in subanesthetic doses, a procedure which produces excitement in most people. Ether is essentially safe in these doses, and rapid exhalation of the drug facilitates regulation of the subjects' level of arousal. A person's consciousness in the excited state is somewhat clouded.

In the initial experiment, patients participated in conventional interview therapy for several sessions. On the basis of these interviews, and in consultation with the research staff, the therapist, one of two senior psychiatrists participating in the experiments, selected a focal concept that he would try to shift and several control concepts (selected by criteria that need not concern us here) that he would not try to change. The research team looked for a focal concept that was related to the patient's internal conflicts. The concept selected was one the therapist thought could be shifted in a few interviews, but was not so linked to events in the patient's current life that it might change from day to day. Examples of focal concepts were "my mother's influence on me" and "my tolerance of imperfections in persons close to me."

Subjects were asked to rate the focal and control concepts on a widely used self-reporting instrument, the Osgood Semantic Differential (Osgood, Suci, and Tannenbaum 1957), before and after one regular therapy session without ether. They then repeated these ratings before and after three weekly, one-and-a-half-hour sessions in which ether was administered. During the ether sessions, the therapist guided the patients toward emotionally charged experiences in their lives. Whenever the patients seemed emotionally aroused or just afterward, the therapist tried to persuade them to change their attitudes toward the focal concept. The therapist embedded his suggestion in a dynamic interpretation that offered an explanation of the origin of the attitude, indicated its inappropriateness to the patients' present life situation, and suggested a more constructive alternative.

The researchers found that the focal concepts showed significantly more variability—that is, shifts in either direction—than the concepts that served as controls. As Figure 4 shows, the focal concepts shifted cumulatively in the direction encouraged by the therapist. Compared with the shift that occurred before and after the session without ether, the magnitude of the shift reached statistical significance by the third arousal session. Between sessions it drifted back toward its initial level, but on the average the gains were partially preserved. Patients differed markedly in the extent to which their attitudes could be shifted and in the persistence of these changes. The experimental design did not allow the team to determine the personal and situational factors that might have contributed to these differences between subjects.

In the original experiments, the adequacy of the control condition was open to question for several reasons. Preparation for the ether sessions involved considerable fuss, such as going without breakfast and not wearing wool. The sessions themselves were dramatic procedures, and the researchers all knew the purpose of the study. A combination of the placebo response, compliance with the demand character of the situa-

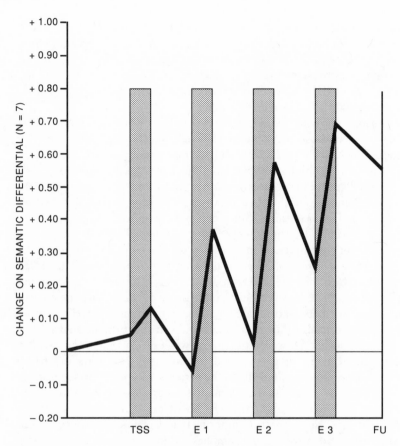

Figure 4.

Change of Focal Concept during and between Ether Arousal Sessions

Note: Positive values denote a change in the predicted direction. *TSS* = therapy session with suggestion; *E1,2,3* = ether arousal sessions with suggestion; *FU* = follow-up session.

tion, and unwitting transmission of the researchers' expectations may thus have influenced the team's findings.

To try to rule out these alternatives, the researchers repeated the experiment with the most rigorous controls they could devise. They created a low-arousal control group that received a tranquilizing pill before the experimental sessions and no ether during them. Patients in the high-arousal condition received an inert pill before the sessions in addition to the ether. The therapists who conducted regular therapeutic interviews before the experimental sessions and selected the focal concepts did not know to which group their patients were assigned. During the experimental sessions, outside consultants, who did not know the design or purpose of the study, made the suggestions. A strong ether odor pervaded the experimental room for all the patients, so the consultants thought all were receiving ether.

As might be expected, the findings of the second experiment were less striking than those of the preliminary one, but they did confirm it. The focal concepts showed more lability and shifted more in the desired direction in the high-arousal than in the low-arousal condition.

A further set of experiments was needed to control for another possible confounding variable. In addition to promoting arousal, low doses of ether cloud consciousness. Since perceptual confusion is known to increase susceptibility to influence, this effect may have increased the patients' suggestibility to an unknown extent. To pursue this issue the researchers designed another experiment, too complex to be described here, in which they induced arousal by means of an inhalant containing adrenalin, which does not cause confusion. Compared with the control group of patients who inhaled a vapor containing only saline, those receiving adrenalin showed a significantly stronger directional shift in the focal concept. However, the change was less than that found in either ether experiment, suggesting that the cognitive confusion caused by ether contributed significantly to the patients' receptivity to suggestion.

In both the ether and the adrenalin studies the exact wording of the suggestion was very important. To be effective, the therapist had to conceptualize the suggestion in terms that explained the source of the patient's maladaptive attitude, emphasized the beneficial consequences of the suggested change, and conveyed the conviction that the patient had the power to change. Often the therapist had to change the wording of the suggestion several times, until quite suddenly the patient accepted it.

The results of these experiments leave many questions unanswered. A crucial unresolved question is whether arousal itself increases suggestibility, or whether the relaxation or exhaustion that follows arousal is more important. In neither of the ether experiments could the timing of the suggestion be controlled exactly. At times the suggestion was made when patients were maximally aroused, and at others it was offered after the peak of arousal had passed. The researchers' impression was that patients were more susceptible to suggestion in the relaxed or exhausted state, when they seemed eager to talk and were receptive to the therapist's comments. Thus, suggestions given during periods when patients were relaxed may have accounted for the positive findings.

Clinically, this is not surprising, since methods like systematic desensitization and hypnosis rely on relaxation to heighten suggestibility. From a theoretical point of view, however, the similar effects of two such apparently different states as relaxation and arousal suggest that they may have unrecognized physiological or psychological qualities in common. Two clinical observations support this speculation. As noted earlier, reciprocal inhibition and implosion achieve similar results, though one aims to produce deep calm and the other, maximal anxiety. Second, as will be seen below, sudden emotional storms in the form of abreaction may occur spontaneously in states of relaxation. Only further research can elucidate the relationships between arousal, relaxation, and suggestibility more precisely.

Despite their limitations, the above-mentioned experimental studies together support two clinical impressions concerning emotional arousal in relation to attitudinal change. First, the increased lability of the focal concepts in the aroused condition shows that, when accompanied by cognitive confusion, emotional arousal or its aftermath shakes the psychic structure. Second, the direction of the shift in the focal concept during arousal supports the clinical impression that intense emotional states heighten patients' susceptibility to therapists' influence.

Nevertheless, it is important to recognize that the long-term therapeutic effects of intense emotion may be limited. The psychologist Kurt Lewin distinguished three phases in changing ingrained attitudes (Lewin 1958). First, the attitude must be "unfrozen"; then it must be changed; and finally the changed attitude must be "refrozen." The experiments of Hoehn-Saric et al. (1978) suggest that emotional arousal, especially when accompanied by cognitive confusion, facilitates the first two stages. However, since these experiments did not determine why subjects' new attitudes tended to drift back to baseline between sessions, they cast no light on the factors that refreeze changed attitudes.

In any event, these findings confirm the importance of distinguishing between aspects of psychotherapy that cause attitudinal change and those that maintain it. A form of treatment should not be lightly discarded simply because its benefits are short-lived. The first task is to produce change; the problem of maintaining it is methodologically and conceptually distinct. Abreactive therapies, to which we now turn, address these issues in a clinical context.

Abreactive Psychotherapies and Posttraumatic Stress Disorder

Abreactive treatments cause patients to reexperience emotionally traumatic events from the past, accompanied by maximal emotional discharge continued to the point of exhaustion. Abreaction can be accomplished in a variety of ways, but all require a highly supportive setting, a therapist who takes full charge, and various methods of encouraging the patient to remember or re-create the events in fantasy.

Interest in abreaction has increased in the United States in recent years because of its role in the treatment of posttraumatic stress disorder (PTSD), a common sequela of the battle experiences of American troops in World War II, Korea, and Vietnam. As described in *DSM III-R* (American Psychiatric Association 1987), patients with PTSD have developed both intrusive and avoidance symptoms following an extraordinary trauma. Intrusive symptoms include the inability to suppress thoughts of the trauma, unpleasant physical reactions to reminders of it, irritable outbursts, nightmares, and flashbacks. These positive symptoms may alternate with or be overshadowed by negative or dissociative ones, including amnesia for some or all of the traumatic events, efforts to avoid all reminders of the trauma, and loss of interest and pleasure in normal relationships and activities.

The stressful experiences that may cause PTSD are not confined to the battlefield. According to Horowitz, an authority on traumatic stress disorders, events that may lead to this syndrome create a feeling of "sudden helplessness and shocking perceptions" (1988, p. 6). These are features of such civilian catastrophes as car accidents, factory explosions, and toxic spills, increasingly common events in complex technological societies. Some victims of rape or family violence also develop clear-cut PTSD. Indeed, the widespread prevalence of PTSD is far from surprising, given the worldwide dramatic increase in social disorganization, violence, migrations of refugees, and other severe social stresses.

Moreover, evidence is mounting that the posttraumatic stress disorder described in *DSM III-R* represents only the extreme end of a continuum of pathological stress reactions. The list of other disorders in which trauma may be a causal or exacerbating factor is long and growing. Horowitz stated that about 60 percent of persons diagnosed as having any mental disorder have experienced a severe life event in the weeks preceding onset, compared with only 20 percent of persons in a control group not suffering from a mental disorder (1988). Struck by the similarities between features of borderline personality disorder and posttraumatic stress disorder, Herman, Perry, and van der Kolk (1989) specifically explored histories of borderline patients for childhood trauma and found that no fewer than four-fifths of them reported such traumas, primarily physical and sexual abuse and witnessing domestic violence. Similarly, histories of severe childhood trauma have been elicited in 98 percent of cases of multiple personality disorder (Putnam 1989).

Andreasen (1985) noted that children are more vulnerable to stress than adults. For example, after being burned, 80 percent of young children continue to show such posttraumatic symptoms as intrusive memories, nightmares, and numbing of responsiveness for one to two years, as compared with only 30 percent of adults. In short, responses to stressful experiences, especially in early life, probably contribute more to psychological disturbances in adulthood than has generally been recognized.

Though Freud's early writings show that he was clearly aware of the role of childhood trauma in the development of adult symptoms, later psychotherapists may have underestimated its importance for several reasons. What may be devastating to a baby, such as being left neglected, cold, or hungry for a few hours, may be a minor stress to an adult, who therefore underestimates its importance. Patients may forget these experiences or be unable to verbalize them because they occurred in a preverbal stage of life. If such traumas are remembered, the patient may conceal them out of shame or embarrassment. Finally, by the time patients reach a therapist, their reactions have been integrated into so many aspects of their personalities that the traumatic origin of particular symptoms or attitudes is no longer obvious. In any case, as Herman and van der Kolk (1987) reported, information about early trauma has not been routinely sought, or if obtained, has been disbelieved.

Further evidence suggesting the pathogenic role of trauma is that symptoms of many disorders overlap those of PTSD. Reminders of trauma may trigger panic attacks. Other neurotic symptoms such as free-floating anxiety or depression may be part of patients' long-term posttraumatic adaptation. Borderline personalities may display outbursts of rage, dissociation, and unstable relations with others, for example, while blunted affect and restricted expression of emotion are characteristics of schizoid and schizotypal personality disorders.

These observations lend plausibility to therapeutic schools that analogize most mental illness to posttraumatic states and therefore stress the unearthing and reexperiencing of very early emotional experiences. Two such schools, dianetics (Hubbard 1987) and reevaluation counseling (Jackins 1978), were created and have been conducted entirely by laypeople. Both have large followings. Primal therapy, an example of an abreactive treatment created by professionals (Janov 1970; Rosen 1977), is based on the hypothesis that neurotic symptoms result from chronic suppression of unbearably painful feelings created by the "Primal Scene,"[2] the moment in childhood when a person experiences the devastating realization "that he cannot be himself and expect to be loved by

2. Janov has misappropriated this term from Freud, who coined it to refer to children's actual or fantasied witnessing of parents' sexual intercourse.

his parents" (Janov 1970, p. 24). Treatment involves creating conditions that enable patients to relive these feelings in their full intensity, thereby freeing themselves from the emotionally crippling consequences of these childhood traumas.

Primal therapy deliberately intensifies patients' dependency on the therapist by demanding that they first undergo one or two days of total isolation, a method also used in Japanese Morita therapy (Kora 1965). Isolated patients hunger for the stimuli provided by human contact, and the therapist is the only one to whom they can turn. Prolonged isolation also forces the patient into self-examination, which is often accompanied by considerable psychic distress. Thus, even before the actual therapy starts, the patient is emotionally aroused.

While each therapeutic school that focuses on emotionally reexperiencing the past has its own rationale and terminology, all are essentially modifications of Freud's initial conceptualizations and procedures. In general, their practitioners maintain that emotionally painful or threatening traumatic experiences in early life lead persons to banish the original experience from consciousness and to avoid stimuli that are reminiscent of it. Cues closely linked with the event are avoided first, followed by progressively more distant cues that become associated with them. If persons cannot avoid the stimulus, they protect against the associated painful feelings by blunting them. As a result, such persons experience a progressive loss of spontaneity, restriction of activities, and impoverishment of personal relationships. For obvious reasons, they are apt to suffer from anxiety, anger, depression, and similar feelings.

Repression, avoidance, and defensive maneuvers prevent the traumatized person from correcting the initial distortions or discovering that the original source of trauma no longer threatens them. In addition, these self-protective maneuvers may lead to what might be called self-alienation. One of the patients in the ether experiment described above (pp. 229–32) dramatically demonstrated this phenomenon. He had sought treatment for chronic mild depression and anxiety, which were brought to a head by his inability to feel close to his girlfriend. After a few whiffs of ether, he suddenly became agitated, shouting that he had to kill himself and struggling so violently that it took three persons to restrain him. Later, in recalling the experience, he said that he felt as if he were going crazy because there were two of him — one on the outside to whom we were relating and one on the inside that we couldn't reach: "That me once removed. . . . It was a horrible empty feeling — the gap between what I am to myself and others. I just couldn't live that way. That's the way crazy people feel." His initial complaints seemed related to early experiences involving intense guilt over sex and defecation. These also emerged vividly during the ether sessions.

Abreaction seems to be a crucial element of therapies that promote healing after trauma. Certain abreactive techniques involving the neuromuscular system are based on the theory of Wilhelm Reich. According to this view, emotions created by early trauma or conflicts are locked into what Reich called character armor, which is expressed in postural sets, characteristic facial expressions, and chronic muscular tensions (Reich 1972). Releasing these tensions by means of manipulations or exercises (Lowen 1975) brings the buried emotions to consciousness and full expression, with recovery of the memories attached to them, thereby freeing the patient to resume emotional growth.

All abreactive therapies seem to invoke altered states of consciousness, states as diverse as intense arousal, extreme fatigue, hypnotic trance, and mystical transcendence. Though apparently different, each of these states seems to make patients hypersuggestible by shaking up existing psychic structures. When aroused or entranced, patients experience reduction of their critical faculties, coupled with feelings of loss of control over mental functions. This leads them to seek support and clarification from some compelling source — an authority figure, a religious or political dogma, or even an inner voice. Dependency increases in such a state; the person feels in the power of this strong force and accepts ideas proceeding from it as ultimate truth. These effects may account for the observation, described in Chapter 4, that altered states of consciousness typically precede religious conversions.

Sometimes merely discussing the past in the context of an emotionally intense therapeutic relationship is sufficient to produce abreaction. Therapists can also facilitate the process by hypnosis or narcosynthesis, the use of small doses of intravenous barbiturates to put patients in a trancelike state. Stimuli associated with past trauma, such as recordings of battle sounds played to combat veterans (Kolb 1985), also may trigger abreaction, either alone or in conjunction with an altered state of consciousness.

Many severely traumatized persons experience repeated spontaneous abreactions in the form of nightmares, flashbacks, and other dissociative states. These can be crippling symptoms that repeat or even intensify the effects of the original traumatization. By contrast, abreactions purposely evoked in the context of therapy may contribute to healing. The therapist's ability to initiate and terminate the abreaction helps patients feel less out of control. Furthermore, an understanding therapist who repeatedly analyzes the experience in terms of a therapeutic rationale helps patients reintegrate the recaptured memories into their current self-concept and world-view. Finally, the therapist helps patients resolve the adjustment problems resulting from the original trauma and from their efforts to cope with it.

In treating victims of combat trauma, for example, Kolb tapes their abreactions and after each one reviews the tape with the patient and offers therapeutic interpretations. Treatment also always includes having the patient join a group of persons who have undergone similar stressful experiences. Members of these mutual support groups, which meet regularly for months or years, share their battle experiences and support each other in learning to cope with the psychological and interpersonal consequences.

As the ether experiments (Hoehn-Saric et al. 1978) demonstrated, emotional release followed by relaxation facilitates changes in patients' attitudes by disorganizing habitual ways of responding. In addition, as patients discover that they can survive the dreaded emotions at full intensity, the initial trauma and all the cues that have become linked to it lose their power to elicit anxiety, anger, or depression. Patients no longer have to avoid them or defend against their impact. Thus, successful abreactive therapy frees patients from crippling emotional inhibitions, enlarges their repertoire of behavior, and enhances their ability to enjoy life.

While emotional flooding, implosion, or abreaction may well have specific healing effects for particular disorders, the focus of our interest remains the therapeutic features these techniques share with other approaches.

The ability of abreactive methods to arouse patients' hopes hardly needs elaboration. The therapist's willingness to work intensively with the patient for long periods and the highly dramatic nature of the procedures involved foster the expectation of benefit. The therapist's ability to alter a patient's subjective state by any method is an impressive demonstration of power that further heightens credibility and enhances hope. All in all, these therapies must appear to the patient to be powerful remedies.

As an extreme form of the arousal mobilized by all forms of psychotherapy, abreaction highlights the social-bonding features of intense emotion. Any strong emotion, whether pleasant or unpleasant, may strengthen affectional bonds. Children are often devoted to cruel, brutal parents, as prisoners are to harsh jailers. Shared intense emotional experiences also bind members of groups to each other. Mobs swayed by strong emotions fuse into a single entity in which individual members are completely submerged. Military units that have undergone battle experiences become closely knit, and the bonds may last well after the members are scattered in civilian life.

Abreactive methods excel in their ability to change the patient's self-image from that of a person who is at the mercy of emotions to one who can withstand and eventually control them. This sense of heightened mastery is fostered by patients' discovery that they can survive the real or fantasied feared situation at maximal intensity, sometimes even exceeding what could possibly occur in real life, as in the example of the treatment for snake phobia.

Finally, posttraumatic stress disorders and their resolution through abreaction exemplify the close interaction of bodily and mental states discussed in Chapter 6. Arousal is by definition a psychophysiological state. The overwhelming emotions associated with both the instigating traumas and their resolution during treatment involve neurophysiological processes that have triggered much speculation. Sargant, for example, likened them to ecstatic states produced by spirit possession and religious revivals (1957). He considered them all to be forms of Pavlovian protective transmarginal inhibition resulting from prolonged over-stimulation of the central nervous system. Such states, among other effects, make the organism hypersensitive to any external stimuli. New research suggests that PTSD involves dysregulation in the autonomic nervous system (Giller 1990). These findings open up exciting possibilities for enhancing treatment through drugs. Kolb, for example, showed that the constant irritability, startle reactions, and explosive rages seen in severe posttraumatic disorders may be attenuated by adrenergic blocking agents (1985). Antidepressant drugs, which have a host of physiological effects, improve a variety of posttraumatic symptoms (Frank et al. 1990).

The physiological correlates of arousal suggest that some of the benefits of abreaction may be neurological rather than symbolic. The repeated observation that abreaction may be effective even when it is induced by a false memory of a traumatic experience that never actually occurred (Marks 1987b) supports this possibility. That is, the benefits of abreaction seem to depend in part on the state of arousal itself in a therapeutic context, regardless of how it is induced.

Abreaction may also involve state-dependent learning, another neurophysiological process relevant to psychotherapy. "State-dependent learning" is a term referring to the fact that persons more readily remember experiences occurring in a particular mood state when that state is recreated (Reus, Weingartner, and Port 1979). For example, rapidly cycling manic-depressive patients have better recall of information learned during the manic phase when they are manic and of information learned during depressions when they are depressed. Similarly, a person who has an experience when intoxicated by certain drugs, including alcohol, may be able to recall the experience only when in a similar state of intoxication. In *City Lights*, Charlie Chaplin used this phenomenon for comic effect. A millionaire befriends the little tramp when drunk. Much to Charlie's bewilderment, the man thereafter greets him as a bosom friend when drunk but doesn't even recognize him when sober. Similarly, it may be that traumatic events experienced in a state of extreme emotional arousal can be recalled and made accessible to change only when the patient is brought to an equivalent state.

Summary

We have classified cognitive, behavioral, and abreactive approaches as directive psychotherapies because the therapist overtly guides the therapeutic session. As in evocative therapies, the success of these methods depends on the therapist's ability to win patients' trust, inspire hope, enhance the sense of mastery, and enlist active participation in the therapeutic process.

Cognitive and behavior therapies are structured so that the immediate goals are always clear and the patient can judge his or her progress toward them. They also encourage the patient to try out therapeutic insights in real life. Because they focus on the conquest of specific symptoms, cognitive and behavior therapies may be more effective than evocative ones in heightening the sense of mastery and in generally increasing self-confidence. They teach patients to confront situations and inner feelings they have previously avoided, thereby opening up renewed opportunities for learning and growth. These therapies seem effective in treating depression and for such specific symptoms as panic attacks, compulsions, and phobias.

Cognitive and behavior therapies are ostensibly derived from scientifically rigorous experiments on animals and humans. In consequence, they give therapists courage to be flexible and to subject their methods to objective evaluation. In these respects their effects on the field of psychotherapy have been salutary. Clinically, however, the apparently scientific aspects of these therapies may function primarily as rhetorical devices that persuade patients to change maladaptive attitudes or to remain in contact with a phobic stimulus until it no longer arouses anxiety.

Abreactive therapies combine evocative and directive elements in the treatment of posttraumatic states, ranging from certain neurotic symptoms and personality disorders to classical PTSD. The central feature of abreactive therapies is reevocation of patients' intense emotional responses to past stressors. These emotional states heighten the patient's dependence on the therapist and promote transient attitudinal changes. For the changes to endure, prolonged support from the therapist and others must follow the abreactions. With this support, patients may learn to reintegrate their experiences into current patterns of living. The healing of posttraumatic stress disorders through abreaction may cast light on the interaction of neurophysiological and psychological states.

ELEVEN

Group and Family Psychotherapies

"I'm glad they've come without waiting to be asked," she thought; "I should never have known who were the right people to invite!"

— *Through the Looking Glass*

The personalities of individuals are shaped by the groups into which they are born or which they join. People construct their assumptive worlds by checking their own perceptions and feelings against those of others. Young children are influenced mainly by parents and other elders whom they perceive as possessing superior power and knowledge. In many societies, as children grow older, age-mates who share experiences unknown to the older generation exert increasing influence.

As life goes on, a person acquires some group memberships by virtue of his or her position in society and others by voluntary adherence. Groups of both types validate the individual's feelings, perceptions, and self-esteem. People dread ostracism by the groups to which they aspire and experience a powerful surge of relief and joy when they feel accepted. The standards, expectations, and emotional contagion of a group can sometimes produce striking and permanent shifts in values and behavior, as in religious conversions. Similar forces may inspire members to extraordinary acts of heroism, self-sacrifice, or villainy, acts of which they would be incapable alone. One thinks of the atrocities perpetrated by the staffs of the Nazi extermination camps, or the martyrdom of the early

Christians. Indeed, the phenomenon of martyrdom shows that group standards can override even such powerful personal needs as self-preservation. Many followers of Gandhi and Martin Luther King, Jr., for example, held themselves to nonviolent action even in the face of danger to their lives.

Large, highly structured organizations dedicated to particular interests or goals may strongly influence members' attitudes relevant to these interests. The National Rifle Association influences members' views toward gun control laws, and the American Medical Association affects physicians' attitudes toward health maintenance programs. Though such organizations may represent and play upon members' general worldview, their primary influence is limited to particular issues. By contrast, small, face-to-face groups like the family exert a powerful, pervasive influence on many aspects of members' assumptive worlds. Therapy groups share this quality.

Americans have always been great joiners of voluntary social, political, and fraternal organizations (Tocqueville [1835] 1945). Such gregariousness is not, however, an uncomplicated expression of desire for human company. A brief look at United States history and the nation's current culture suggests that Americans hunger for group membership in part to compensate for feelings of suspicion, competitiveness, and isolation.

The North American continent was settled by people who rejected, or were rejected by, their own societies. Separated from their parent cultures, immigrants struggled to maintain a sense of community as they confronted first the openness and isolation of the frontier and later the hostility of established groups of earlier settlers. These struggles involved both coming together with like-minded individuals and excluding others labeled as deviants or undesirables (Erikson 1966). Indeed, the noted social historian John Roche (1963) described early nineteenth century America as a society in which outcasts of established communities were free to form new communities in which they could be intolerant of others.

Political scientists have noted that small, face-to-face groups flourish whenever a society is in transition, as they did before the revolutionary eras in France, the United States, and Russia. The extensive, rapid, and unprecedented changes taking place in present-day life (Frank 1979) make this another such unstable era. In the 1920s, the philosopher Alfred North Whitehead remarked to his students that they were the first generation in human history that could not rely on the precepts of their grandfathers. Since then, the pace of change has accelerated to the point that a youth can scarcely rely on the precepts of an older sibling. Projections of the future depend on the assumption that past conditions will continue to hold, so disconnection from the past implies disconnection from the future. Today, Americans are, so to speak, marooned on an island in time, living in an uncertain present, unable to make plans and plagued by feelings of insecurity.

No one can predict how instantaneous worldwide mass communication, nuclear weapons, ecological damage, or trips to the moon and planets will ultimately affect human beings' habits and values. Certainly they will erode many time-hallowed rules of conduct, including those governing human relations. Rapid change and social mobility have seriously weakened such sources of emotional security as extended families, enduring marriages, and small, stable work groups. The shallow and shifting sociability of the residential development, the office, the committee, and the club, being tainted with undercover competition for popularity, power, and prestige, offers no adequate substitute.

James Thurber summed up the prevailing state of mind in one of his "Fables for Our Time," which tells of a "fairly intelligent" fly who wisely refused to land on a spiderweb because no other flies were in it. The fly then lit on a piece of flypaper crowded with flies, because he assumed they were dancing. The moral is: "There's no safety in numbers, or in anything else" (1939, p. 13).

The shifting boundaries of accepted and outcast groups in American society creates an inexhaustible pool of those considered deviant because of illness, oddity, different beliefs, or unacceptable behaviors. Mirroring the group affiliations of the wider society, supportive groups of every sort form to buffer these social outcasts from discrimination and neglect. Such groups provide them, in their turn, with a place to experience mutual support and validation.

Small groups provide the illusion, if not the substance, of safety. They may prove to be the most promising means of counteracting certain damaging features of contemporary life, especially alienation from the past and from one's fellow humans. Small groups form oases of the like-minded against the buffeting of the outside world, forums in which members feel that they have some power to influence one another, and nuclei of a counterculture that hammers out the new values and political forms that eventually supersede the old ones. In this sense, any group activity that provides members with a coherent system of values and relieves alienation and despair is a form of psychotherapy.

Classifying Group Therapies

Adequate discussion of any type of therapy group would include consideration of membership, leadership, the goals of the therapy, and the methods used to achieve these goals. Each of these interrelated categories can be subdivided in several different ways. For our purposes we shall make only the following distinctions:

1. *Members:* Participants may be strangers or intimates — that is, family members or others in a person's social network. Therapeutic groups of strangers may be open to any distressed person. Encounter groups, for example, require only that participants be seeking an enriching experience. Membership in other therapy groups is sometimes limited to persons with specific clinical disorders such as addiction, phobia, or chronic bodily illness.

2. *Leaders:* Leaders of therapy groups range from professional members of established mental health disciplines to nonprofessionals trained only to conduct a particular kind of group. Self-help groups are led by fellow sufferers, with or without training beyond their experience in the program.

3. *Goals:* The goals of group therapy range from relieving specific forms of distress or disability to providing personally enriching experiences. Though conceptually distinct, these goals overlap in practice. Overcoming specific disabilities enriches a person's life, and life-enriching experiences promote changes that diminish symptoms.

4. *Methods:* As with individual therapies, methods of group therapies are hard to classify. Therapy groups embody the common elements of all psychotherapies, including an identified healer, a particular therapeutic setting, and a procedure that promises beneficial change (see Chapter 2). These elements account for much of any therapy group's effectiveness. Moreover, though group leaders may rigidly adhere to specific techniques for research purposes, in practice, experienced therapists typically employ whatever techniques they think may help in a given situation.

In keeping with our analysis of individual therapy, we shall crudely classify group therapies as directive, evocative, or mixed. In directive groups, interactions follow a format specified by either the leader or a manual. In evocative, free-interaction groups the therapist tries to facilitate spontaneous interactions that enable members to become more comfortable with their own feelings and to relate more intimately with others. In a mixed group therapy such as psychodrama, directive methods are used to achieve evocative ends.

We begin with a passing look at encounter groups, nonprofessionally led evocative groups designed to provide enriching experiences for non-specifically distressed people. Such groups exemplify the role of cultural forces in generating new forms of healing experience. Then we turn briefly to directive groups aimed at particular conditions, especially the growing movement of peer self-help psychotherapy groups. The bulk of the chapter is a detailed look at professionally run, evocative psychotherapy groups, still the predominant form of group therapy in this country and the one most familiar to the authors. We close with a discussion of family therapy. This field encompasses a variety of directive and evocative therapies applied to the families of patients with specific disorders and to people whose distress seems rooted in family interaction.

Encounter Groups

Masserman suggested that all humans struggle against three basic fears — fear of loss of health, fear of alienation from others, and fear that life is meaningless (1971). Since cosmic despair and social alienation are often two sides of the same coin, methods that seek primarily to relieve one also affect the other. Religious revivals foster a strong sense of fellowship; persons may emerge from any mystical experience feeling a greater sense of unity not only with a meaningful universe but also with their fellow humans (see Chapter 4). Similarly, intense, intimate interactions may enhance or restore faith that existence has meaning and that life is good.

Encounter groups exemplify the healing properties of such interactions. Their history begins during the turbulent 1960s. Attempting to cope with the widespread cultural dislocations and proliferating new ideologies of that period, hundreds of people flocked to "personal growth" centers, exemplifying the "human potential" movement (Appelbaum 1979). Though the popularity of these organizations has waned, those that are still active seek to enrich participants' lives through a variety of group experiences designed to promote spontaneity, joy, and feelings of intimacy. In addition to encouraging members' open, verbal confrontations with one another, these groups use physical activities and sensory stimulation to arouse emotion and heighten members' self-awareness.

As their name suggests, encounter groups focus on the present moment, the immediate group interaction. This focus may appeal strongly to those who feel alienated from the past and from their fellow humans. Encounter groups attract both people who do not define themselves as ill and others who also seek classical psychotherapy. Lieberman, for example, found that half to four-fifths of the people attending growth centers or encounter groups had been or were currently in psychotherapy (1977).

The effects of encounter groups overlap with those of other healing groups. Responding to encouragement to drop their social masks and enter into open, honest, emotionally intense interactions with one another, encounter-group members gain a more complete and accurate awareness of the effects of their own actions and reactions. Concomitantly, they learn to recognize and accept their inner feelings. Members of traditional therapy groups may make similar gains. Some encounter groups go beyond therapy groups in seeking to engender peak experiences, not unlike those of a religious revival or the psychedelic experience sometimes produced by consciousness-altering drugs (Appelbaum 1979). Therapy, encounter, or religious groups all help members achieve greater self-acceptance and acceptance of others, with a resulting increase in spontaneity and happiness (Rogers 1971).

Encounter groups pioneered certain techniques that more classical therapy groups have begun to employ. Two particular features of encounter groups are filtering into the armamentarium of mainstream group therapy. The first is the use of "marathon" sessions to speed up group formation and facilitate emotional arousal (Stoller 1968). The second is the rediscovery of the human body. The value system of encounter groups reminds professionals that full communication involves more than talk, and affirms the legitimacy and value of sensuous pleasures. Touching and caressing are powerfully consoling forms of human interaction that need not always have sexual connotations (Schutz 1967). Recognizing that mental states are reflected in bodily postures (see Chapters 6 and 10), encounter-group pioneers developed exercises and techniques that reduce bodily and psychic tensions. Mental health professionals may draw on similar techniques in treating certain overly inhibited psychiatric patients who seem alienated from their bodies and rejecting of bodily experience (Lowen 1975).

The ultimate value of encounter groups remains uncertain. Many members come away from a successful encounter group program with a sense of having had a rewarding experience, and some function better socially afterward. There is little evidence, however, that encounter groups produce any deep or long-term changes in the personalities of most participants. Moreover, on leaving an encounter group, some participants, like some members who leave cults (see pp. 83–84), may experience reentry problems created by conflicts between the attitudes and behavior fostered by the counterculture of the group and the expectations of family and friends.

A more serious concern is that the group sessions themselves can seriously upset some members, and their bad effects may endure for some time (Yalom and Lieberman 1971). Encounter groups' potential for causing distress raises an important point of differentiation between them and mainstream therapy groups. Leaders of encounter groups come from a variety of backgrounds. Some are untrained or trained only in the particular technique they use, and so are ill-equipped to deal with members who react adversely. By contrast, most therapy groups are conducted or overseen by members of the established mental health professions.

Professional and nonprofessional group leaders, furthermore, may differ significantly in their acceptance of responsibility for members' general welfare. The ethics of the established mental health professions obligate therapists to warn patients about the risks of treatment and to assume responsibility for dealing with any harmful consequences of therapy. Some encounter-group leaders, on the other hand, disclaim any responsibility for the untoward effects of their groups. They maintain that members come as free agents and are free to leave if they wish. This position is untenable for two reasons. First, although members join voluntarily, they may do so with the unrealistic expectation that the encounter group will evoke only pleasurable and growth-promoting experiences. Indeed, the leader may foster these expectations in order to attract participants. Actually, encounter groups may be intensely stressful, especially for persons who are emotionally fragile. Second, the freedom to leave at will is largely illusory. Encounter groups generate strong pressures for members to see the experience through. These forces may produce deep feelings of rejection and failure in those who leave or try to leave. For these reasons, people who are emotionally unstable or clinically ill are well advised to join only professionally led therapy groups.

Group Therapy

Group and individual treatments share many common effective elements. These include the relationship between socially sanctioned healer and sufferer in a therapeutic setting, the effort to relieve confusion and isolation, and the mobilization of hope. Group treatment magnifies the healing power of the acceptance that every type of therapy grants the sufferer. Therapy groups accept patients without regard to success or achievement (Dreikurs 1951). In fact, the ticket of admission is precisely that one has failed to solve certain problems of living. When persons first enter a therapy group, they tend to evaluate one another according to the standards prevailing in the wider society. As the group continues, members gain status less on the basis of outside achievements and more on their sincerity and their ability to discuss their own and one another's problems constructively. Group members thus feel accepted because of who they are in the group rather than because of what they have accomplished outside. The therapy group, like Robert Frost's "home," is "something you somehow haven't to deserve" (Frost 1915).

In addition to these common elements of all therapies, the group format allows for such unique healing components as universality, altruism, vicarious learning, and cohesiveness. Our own analysis of these components accords with Bloch and Crouch's recent, authoritative review of the subject (1987), though we use slightly different definitions and accord particular factors different weights.

We shall first examine the function of these healing components in directive and evocative therapy groups, and then apply our conclusions to family therapy as a special case. This chapter concerns only outpatient groups. We discuss inpatient group therapy in Chapter 12 as one component of a hospital's total therapeutic program.

Directive Group Approaches

In directive therapy groups, a therapist or an established group code firmly guides the transactions of the members. Directive methods can be used with groups of any size. Directive groups teach members to relate to others in ways that combat their perceptual distortions, lift their spirits, and help them develop and practice social skills. Many large directive groups explicitly cultivate a strong sense of cohesiveness through rituals, testimonials, and formal group-recognition of members' progress.

Most professionally led directive groups treat persons who suffer from identifiable clinical disorders. Examples include rehabilitation groups for schizophrenic patients (see Chapter 12), support groups for people with such chronic physical illnesses as multiple sclerosis or rheumatoid arthritis, and, more recently, cognitive therapy groups for depression or anxiety. Psychodrama, discussed below, is a professionally led group with both directive and evocative features, and is offered both to people with discrete mental illnesses and to those suffering from nonspecific distress.

Peer self-help groups represent another rapidly expanding and widely practiced form of directive group therapy (Hurvitz 1970; Scheff 1972). The methods of two prototypical self-help programs, Alcoholics Anonymous (A.A.) and Recovery Incorporated, exemplify the therapeutic elements of directive groups in general.

Both A.A. and Recovery, Inc., being run by their members, substitute for a permanent leader a book that performs similar functions. The book, written by the founder, promulgates the movement's ideology, prescribes the structure and activities of meetings, and instructs members how to behave in the meetings as well as in daily life. The book is also a storehouse of maxims and precepts. Members are expected to familiarize themselves with its contents and frequently cite passages from it at meetings. In short, these books function much like the sacred texts of religious sects. They offer guidance and inspiration and provide a shared ideology expressed in a language that incorporates terms and images identified with the sect. This language cements the ties of members to one another and at the same time distinguishes them from outsiders, in both ways strengthening group cohesiveness.

Run solely by and for alcoholics, A.A. provides a model for many other self-help groups. Its text (Alcoholics Anonymous 1973) is called the Big Book by members, and some refer to it as "our Bible." Participants at A.A. meetings either give inspirational testimonials describing the horrors of life as an alcoholic and the benefits of sobriety achieved through A.A., or read from and discuss passages from the Big Book and other texts outlining the principles of the program (the twelve steps). Long-time members who are well versed in these principles exercise leadership on an informal and shifting basis. Alcoholics Anonymous groups meet frequently, and new members are encouraged to attend daily. The program is designed to replace the familial or social relationships that support the alcoholic's drinking with the companionship of a group whose standards support abstinence. Individual relationships between new members and experienced sponsors, who are available at times when the group is not meeting, powerfully reinforce and sustain abstinent behavior. An A.A. member in crisis can call on a sponsor for help in applying the group's general principles to the member's particular situation.

To combat the alcoholic's unrealistic feelings of omnipotence, A.A. requires drinkers to admit that their craving for alcohol is stronger than they are, and that superior forces are needed to overcome it. Thus, while not espousing any specific creed, A.A. invokes religious feelings. Members must also make restitution to those they have harmed, an activity that counteracts demoralizing feelings of guilt and remorse and helps restore self-respect. Recovering drinkers strengthen their good resolves by seeking out and trying to help other alcoholics. Such altruism both bolsters their self-esteem and reminds them vividly of the fate that awaits them if they resume drinking.

Recovery, Inc. (Wechsler 1960), is a directive self-help organization that grew out of the groups that Dr. Abraham Low conducted for his patients after their discharge from a state mental hospital. His principal tenet was that "the first step in psychotherapeutic management is to convince [patients] that the sensation can be endured, the impulse controlled, the obsession checked" (Low [1950] 1968, p. 19).

After Dr. Low's death, the movement continued autonomously, using his writings as its guide. Members now include all types of mental patients who are capable of functioning in the community; leaders are experienced members who have received special training. Meetings begin with the reading of a selection from Dr. Low's book by the leader. Active members sit on a panel, and the leader calls on each one to describe a recent situation which aroused feelings of anger, depression, or anxiety. The speaker and other members then take turns analyzing the situation. They focus on how applying the principles of Recovery Incorporated helped or could have helped the member handle the problem effectively. Comments often take the form of slogans or quotations from Dr. Low's book. Each person on the panel is allowed only a fraction of the total meeting time, so that several members can be heard at every session. A social hour follows the structured part of the meeting. Members may contact leaders or fellow participants outside of sessions, but the program mandates that these contacts be brief, limited to a description of an immediate problem and to suggestions about which of the program's principles the caller should apply in that situation.

In a recent controlled study of Recovery, Inc., Galanter (1988) found substantial increases in well-being and a diminution of psychological symptoms in members who felt themselves to be committed to the program.

Though A.A. and Recovery, Inc., have comparable procedures and rates of success, their therapeutic rationales differ to match the conditions for which each program was originally designed. Alcoholics Anonymous insists that the alcoholic person admit inability to control drinking by an act of will; the cornerstone of Recovery Incorporated is that the patient can overcome symptoms through will power. The comparable effects of these opposing rationales illustrate again that a therapeutic program must be convincing to the sufferer — that is, rhetorically persuasive — whether or not it is scientifically or universally true.

Whatever the specific problems addressed, all directive group approaches counteract demoralization. Structured programs organize members' confusion and accompanying feelings of helplessness into a coherent framework that they may apply in many situations. The cogency of the rationale and the example of the therapist or the experienced self-help leader kindle members' hopes of overcoming their difficulties. Through direct praise and acknowledgment of successes, members' feelings of mastery and self-worth are enhanced.

A common criticism of directive approaches is that members identify too strongly with the group's particular focus. Critics argue, for example, that a person who goes to daily A.A. meetings and repeatedly promotes the program may become rigidly confirmed in the deviant identity of a "dry drunk," and that this identification will stunt further personality growth. Such concerns, however, are exaggerated. Research into typical patient careers suggests that many members experience only a transient period of intense identification with the group (Powell 1987). For others, the identity they derive from group participation, though deviant, may be more functional than the sense of helpless suffering they endured before joining.

Another common criticism leveled at all types of directive therapy groups is that they oversimplify members' problems to make them conform to the group's ideology. In practice, however, the effectiveness of directive therapies depends on finding a balance between their rationale and participants' individual experiences. Members of directive groups are generally allowed to tell their stories freely and to bask in the group's acceptance and attention before any effort is made to recast the experience in the light of the group's therapeutic framework. Those who find the group's ideology overly restrictive often drop out. Indeed, a lack of fit between the individual's formulation of a problem and the group's rationale is one of the primary reasons for the failure of a self-help approach (Powell 1987).

As with individual therapies (see Chapters 9 and 10), the line between directive and evocative group methods is far from absolute. Psychodrama exemplifies a mixed approach. In psychodrama, the therapist takes an overtly directive role. He or she instructs the patient to act out, or to watch others act out, a personal problem. Other patients and therapists serve as both actors and audience. Patient and therapist collaborate to varying degrees in choosing the problem, selecting the other players, and suggesting the dialogue and action. Afterward the therapists lead a discussion in which players and audience participate (Moreno 1971).

The directive methods of psychodrama serve evocative ends. Patient and therapist select the patient's unique, emotionally salient problems. As the playlet proceeds, the actors become increasingly spontaneous and emotionally involved. Members of the audience participate vicariously. In consequence, the situation may develop an intense emotional impact for all participants, and these feelings provide the focus for the discussion following the psychodrama. Ultimately, the success of this type of therapy depends both on the structuring and limit-setting properties of the directive procedure and on such evocative elements as emotional catharsis and the patients' sense of achieving an individualized resolution of their problems. Incidentally, many features of encounter groups, including role playing, body contact, and bodily modes of expression, can be traced to psychodrama.

Evocative Group Therapies

In contrast to structured or directive approaches, evocative group therapies strive to stir emotions and promote members' self-knowledge through free discussion and honest self-revelation (Foulkes 1964; Frank and Powdermaker 1959; Yalom [1970] 1985). Professionally led evocative groups generally include up to twelve members. Participants may or may not come to the group with particular diagnoses. The leaders try to create a supportive atmosphere in which members can examine their interactions with important persons in their lives, with one another, and with the group leader. In the absence of formal structure, pressure toward candid self-expression arouses members' emotions. Evocative group standards allow considerable latitude for experimentation. Over time, members learn how they appear to one another, and are motivated to make suitable modifications in their assumptive worlds and behavior.

A particular interaction that occurred in a group of six female homemakers with neurotic difficulties illustrates the kind of experience free-interaction group therapy can produce (Frank and Ascher 1956). The group's meetings had been lively, with members freely expressing feelings toward one another and toward the male psychiatrist who conducted the group.

Mrs. Smith, the central patient of this episode, was a thirty-two-year-old member who complained of nervousness, gagging, and fullness in the stomach. She connected her symptoms directly to anger with her mother, a demanding, complaining woman who seemed to favor the patient's younger sister. The mother reportedly brought all her complaints to the patient, asked her advice, then rejected it. Mrs. Smith expressed strongly ambivalent feelings toward her mother: "I love her so much, I resent what she is doing." She could not tell her mother how she felt and was ashamed of her attitude. Her stomach cramps and jittery feelings came on when she felt anger with her mother and was unable to express it. She often had anxiety attacks when her mother criticized her. Her general attitude seemed to be that "you must not show your feelings or people will take advantage of you."

In the group, Mrs. Smith participated actively from the start, at first in a superficial way. She frequently spoke of her family problems and gradually came to identify Mrs. Jones, an older group member, with her mother. As a result of certain experiences in the group, she came to resent Mrs. Jones for not appreciating her, but she could mention this only when the older woman was not present. At the same time, Mrs. Smith wanted to help Mrs. Jones, thus practically duplicating her attitudes toward her mother.

Mrs. Smith's symptoms improved over the course of several months. Though she reached the point where she could say, "I don't get sick when [my mother] makes the same old nuisance of herself," she still could not express her resentment. In therapy sessions she took the lead in focusing the group discussion on sexual difficulties, over the protests of Mrs. Jones.

The day before the seventy-second meeting (in the nineteenth month of treatment), Mrs. Jones called Mrs. Smith and told her she wasn't coming to the group because Mrs. Smith talked about sex all the time. In reporting this to the group, Mrs. Smith said that Mrs. Jones was acting exactly like her mother and that she had felt frightened and resentful after the telephone conversation. She added that she still felt extremely guilty and could talk this way only because Mrs. Jones was absent. Scarcely had these words left her lips when Mrs. Jones walked in, looking deeply distressed. She wore no makeup, her hair was stringy, and as she collapsed in her chair, she seemed about to weep. Mrs. Smith's tension mounted visibly until suddenly she burst into tears and began screaming: "I caused it, I know it's my fault! I caused it, I caused it! I know it's my fault!"

To reduce the almost unbearable tension, the therapist asked Mrs. Smith to explain her outburst. Mrs. Smith said: "It's the way I feel about my mother. I know I caused her to feel the way she does." Mrs. Jones listened and then said calmly: "What makes you think you upset me? It's something entirely different." She then described some recent temper outbursts against her husband and son, and resentment toward her husband for his indifference. Mrs. Smith brightened up more and more as she came to see that she was not responsible for upsetting Mrs. Jones. At the following meeting, Mrs. Smith said the discovery that Mrs. Jones had not been angry with her but was upset over something else had made her feel a good deal better. The next week she indicated that she no longer felt obligated to listen to her mother's complaints or give in to her demands.

Two months later Mrs. Smith was finally able to criticize Mrs. Jones to her face. Laughingly, she told Mrs. Jones, who was complaining, that Mrs. Jones was just trying to make everyone feel bad because she was feeling bad. Some weeks later the therapist noted: "Mrs. Smith can take Mrs. Jones much better and there is a good deal of warm exchange between the two."

In this example, Mrs. Smith's experiences in the group gradually helped her feel less fearful of and guilty toward Mrs. Jones, who represented her mother. Eventually she was able to openly defy this surrogate mother by continuing to discuss details of her sexual difficulties. Mrs. Jones's emotional upset seemed to confirm Mrs. Smith's worst fears, until she made the startling discovery that Mrs. Jones was actually disturbed about something quite unconnected with Mrs. Smith. As a result, Mrs. Smith realized that her feelings were not as destructive to others as she had feared. Her criticism of Mrs. Jones became increasingly direct, leading to a much better relationship between them. Concomitantly, Mrs. Smith gained increased emotional independence from her mother.

Unique Qualities and Therapeutic Features
of Evocative Groups

Since most patients who benefit from free-interaction groups have already participated in a wide range of groups based on school, work, common interests, and social activities without losing their symptoms, evocative therapy groups must have healing features that social groups lack. These features include acceptance, encouragement of open expression of feelings, and continued communication in the face of antagonism.

Therapy groups resemble healthy families in accepting members without regard to failures and other imperfections and in provoking and permitting free expression of feeling. Unlike many families, however, they provide members with opportunities, incentives, and means for identifying and breaking up patterns of distorted communications. The first ground rule of evocative groups is that members are to engage in what Mace termed "uninhibited conversation" (Foulkes and Anthony 1957, p. 8). Participants are expected to drop their façades and reveal, as honestly as possible, feelings about themselves and one another. Openness inevitably leads to emotionally arousing confrontation and conflict. A second ground rule requires members to continue communicating in the face of antagonism. Together, these characteristics enhance opportunities for learning.

In individual therapy, the therapist is the patient's only source of information. In the group, other members also serve as sources of feedback, as models, and as guides. Moreover, patients' perceptions of professionals as being different from ordinary people limit the therapist's usefulness as a model. Other group members may provide models closer to the patients' personal condition. Each can learn from observing how others handle contingencies arising in the group and hearing how they have coped with similar problems. Although some participants become discouraged or envious upon seeing another member improve, they more typically experience a surge of hope and the desire to emulate others' success.

The perceived similarities among group members constitute what Yalom ([1970] 1985) terms "universality," a powerful therapeutic element. Many demoralized patients feel isolated and believe that their problems are unique. Practically all members of therapy groups, including those who are outwardly very successful, endorse the value of hearing from other members' own lips that they have similar problems or weaknesses. It seems that each member suspects that others see through his or her own façade of competence and poise, yet takes others' masks at face value. After the first shock, the mutual self-revelation that occurs in therapy groups can bring enormous relief.

In describing their own impressions of and reactions to others' behavior in the group, members aid others' self-understanding and provide powerful incentives for change. People can seldom afford to be totally honest with one another in daily life. Everyone conceals or distorts feelings out of such diverse motives as a desire to avoid hurting the other person, fear of retaliation, or intent to manipulate. Furthermore, people who come to psychotherapy characteristically behave in ways that bother others, often without knowing it. After chronically enduring criticism or rebuff, they often distrust others' responses.

Over time, the ground rule that feelings should be honestly expressed increases members' trust in one another. As they become more willing to accept others' statements as true reflections of their underlying attitudes, group members increasingly profit from feedback about the impression they are making.

As sources of feedback, group members may be more acceptable than the therapist. One member may be able to sense another's feelings and express them more comprehensibly than the therapist because he or she is more like fellow group members or has had similar experiences. For the same reasons, members can sometimes transmit the therapist's views to one another more effectively than the therapist.

Though more acceptable, members' feedback may be less useful than the therapist's because their own problems and preconceptions are apt to bias their perceptions. Since members lack the therapist's authority, however, other members feel freer to reject their unhelpful advice or interpretations.

Along the same lines, acceptance by peers may be more valuable to group members than acceptance by the therapist. Members often perceive the therapist as having no choice — the professional role demands such behavior. The group treatment of a nineteen-year-old Catholic man who was overwhelmed with guilt over masturbation illustrates how the professional role may diminish the impact of a therapist's responses. The young man was first treated in several individual sessions by a male therapist who tried in vain to reassure him that his guilt was unwarranted. When that approach failed, the therapist placed him in a group of older men. There, he remained mute for a few sessions, but finally, with the encouragement of other members, he "confessed" his secret. The other members, some of whom also were Catholic, showed no shock or surprise. At the same time, their serious discussion showed that they did not minimize the importance of the problem or the justification for the young man's guilt feelings. By the next session, the young man's depression had vanished, and he soon stopped coming. A follow-up interview a year later revealed that he had maintained his improvement. He attributed his cure to the group sessions and remembered an identifying feature of each member. When asked why the therapist had been ineffective, he replied: "It is good to have things come from a bunch of guys. The therapist lives in his own little world."

Criticism or even anger can also convey support. Many mental patients are accustomed to being pitied, scorned, or ignored. An angry blast from a group member may show such patients that they are taken seriously enough to arouse anger. Moreover, criticism that implies that the critic knows the person is capable of doing better can be supportive rather than destructive.

Everyone needs to feel needed. Mental patients characteristically feel, or are made to feel, that they are a burden to others. Individual therapy does not dispel this feeling, since help flows only from the therapist to the patient. The relationship is complementary, not reciprocal. All the patient can do for the therapist is pay bills promptly, report gratifying improvement, and recommend the therapist to friends. On rare occasions, the therapist may be willing to accept a present.

By contrast, therapy groups enhance morale by providing members with incentives and opportunities for altruism. Each member of a therapy group can give as well as receive help. Participants find they can aid one another by comparing experiences or giving useful information, insights, or advice. The discovery that their advice is taken seriously – a rare event for many patients – can greatly boost members' self-esteem.

As noted earlier, many forms of indigenous healing go further by requiring that the patient do something for others. Shrines like Lourdes encourage pilgrims to pray, not for themselves but for one another. Such altruistic activities enhance feelings of virtue, combat morbid self-centeredness, and strengthen the individual's feelings of kinship with others.

In addition to providing overt support, creating opportunities for learning, and enhancing self-esteem, group therapies arouse emotional tension and teach members to handle conflict. Patients often find group therapy more unsettling than private sessions because group attendance makes public the person's need for psychotherapy. Moreover, in initial group sessions, members typically feel the discomfort of strangers who are thrown together for the first time. Though initial tensions soon pass, group therapies provide many sources of tension and occasions for conflict throughout the group's life (Frank 1957a). The knowledge that they are expected to reveal intimate details of their lives to other persons whom they derogate heightens members' unease. To the extent that they feel self-loathing, members are likely to fear and dislike others they perceive as similar to themselves.

Group conflicts confront the distortions in participants' assumptive systems and increase self-assurance by teaching participants to assert themselves and to withstand antagonism (Frank 1957a). The ground rules — that members should express their feelings without holding back and that they must continue communicating despite conflict — maximize the likelihood that all will learn something from these confrontations. Similar situations in daily life are usually less helpful because antagonists ordinarily break off communication. Such ruptures prevent people from discovering the distortions that may be contributing to disputants' hostility and from finding ways of resolving it (Newcomb 1947).

In continuing conflict, protagonists will bring up more and more material to bolster their positions as they display their characteristic ways of expressing or responding to antagonism. Eventually, prolonged group conflicts teach participants to express themselves more effectively. Disputing parties gain self-confidence from being able to hold their ground in the face of opposition. As a result, they may develop more effective ways of resolving disagreements or of conducting interpersonal conflicts outside of therapy.

Furthermore, through this process each party in the conflict can gain not only increased understanding of others but also increased self-knowledge. Individual therapy helps patients develop more harmonious relations with others by resolving internal tensions; group therapy offers members the opportunity to reduce inner tensions by resolving their externalized manifestations.

To benefit from conflict, however, the antagonists must feel secure. Uncontrolled or unresolved hostility leaves group members feeling traumatized and may drive one or more members from the group. The therapist's task is to ensure that all feel supported, that everyone adheres to the ground rules, and that matters are not permitted to get out of hand. To these ends, the therapist encourages uninvolved members to support both parties in a conflict. If need be, the therapist will come to the rescue of the weaker or more vulnerable one.

Group members' different positions in society, the rivalries generated by aspects of the group situation itself, and distorted perceptions of self and others arising from individual life experiences all contribute to the conflicts that occur in group therapy. The differences in viewpoint between a southern white person and a northern black person, or between an employer and a worker, exemplify sources of conflict that are rooted in social realities. Conflicts arising from the properties of the group itself are rivalries for such group roles as the sickest, the therapist's favorite, or the group leader. These rivalries are especially provocative when the prize is a position that only one member can hold at a time.

Distortions based on members' personal life histories provide the most therapeutically useful sources of conflict. Two common categories are the so-called mirror and transference reactions. In individual therapy, only the therapist can evoke transference and mirror reactions, while a group affords multiple stimuli for such responses.

The term "mirror reaction" refers to the tendency of people to detect and disapprove in others traits they dislike in themselves before they recognize the source of the dislike. For example, two Jewish members of a group run by the senior author expressed intense mutual antagonism (Powdermaker and Frank 1953, pp. 237–39). One ostensibly gloried in his background and the other tried to deny it. After bitterly criticizing each other for months, each recognized that he secretly entertained the same feelings he was attacking in the other.

Transference connotes the tendency of patients to inappropriately transfer feelings previously attached to important persons in their past lives to people in the present. In a group, members' reactions to other members and to the therapist may duplicate their reactions to persons playing analogous roles in real life.

The example cited earlier — Mrs. Smith's reactions to Mrs. Jones — illustrates this phenomenon. In a different group, transference created a heated interchange between two group members, one of whom described his pleasure in fantasizing different roles, especially after he had had a few drinks. The other became furious with him for "living in a dream world." It soon turned out that for years the angry man had been vainly trying to reform his alcoholic mother, who, he felt, lived in a dream world. She was the real target of his feelings (Powdermaker and Frank 1953, pp. 245–48).

As the central figure of the group, the therapist arouses transference reactions that are at least as strong as those that occur in individual therapy. These reactions may be especially helpful in illuminating group members' attitudes toward authority figures or help-givers. Patients seem able to experience and express angry or fearful feelings toward the therapist more promptly in a free-interaction group than in individual treatment. The presence of other members seems to provide protection and support. A member who attacks the therapist may be a spokesperson for others, and the public character of the proceedings is a good guarantee against the feared retaliation of the therapist.

In two different groups, for example, a patient whose parents had been brutal and unpredictable never sat next to the therapist. Each always made sure that at least one other patient intervened. When asked about this behavior, each patient said he did it to preclude the therapist's striking him. One added that he thought the therapist kept a loaded revolver in his desk drawer! Neither had dared to mention these feelings in individual sessions.

In short, free-interaction groups engender crises. Patients discover that their habitual ways of coping are inadequate to the occasion, a realization that is accompanied by strong emotional arousal. Such events sometimes disrupt patients' habitual patterns and provide the impetus for new solutions.

All types of therapy groups have an additional therapeutic element, which is probably the most essential to their success. Known as group cohesiveness, it is a property that individual therapy cannot possess (Frank 1957b; Yalom [1970] 1985). Group cohesiveness, which can be most simply described as the attraction of a group for its members, develops out of members' shared history of such supportive and tension-arousing experiences as those just outlined. In circular fashion, increased cohesiveness enhances members' tolerance of further disturbing events and confrontations.

Group cohesiveness both contributes to and reflects group morale. Strongly cohesive groups invariably also possess high morale, and demoralized groups tend to fragment. Furthermore, the morale of a group as a whole goes hand in hand with the morale of its members, as religious cults and military combat units strikingly demonstrate. Since psychotherapy focuses on individuals, we shall consider group cohesiveness only as it affects the group's members.

The more cohesive a group is, the stronger the morale of its members will be, and the more its standards will influence members, both during and between group sessions. For these reasons, the deliberate efforts of therapists to speed the development of group cohesiveness have been shown to accelerate both symptomatic improvement and desired personality change in group members (Liberman 1971).

Since psychiatric patients typically derogate themselves, a puzzling question is why evocative therapy groups become cohesive at all. Like Groucho Marx, mental patients would be expected to reject any group that accepted them as members. Especially in initial meetings, members' tolerance for one another may be relatively low. Nevertheless, membership in groups of their peers enhances patients' morale in several ways. Some derive self-esteem from the belief that joining a therapy group shows their superiority to patients who lack the good sense to do the same. In addition, membership in a cohesive group enhances each member's feeling of personal power, for the group in some way represents an extension of the self. Each member influences the group's functioning, if only because his or her absence makes a difference. Shared responsibility for the group's activities enhances feelings of competence. For this reason, dependence on a therapy group seems less potentially demoralizing to patients than a similar degree of dependence on a therapist.

Humans are social creatures who cannot prosper or even survive in isolation. People — however diverse and for whatever reasons brought together — soon form mutually supportive ties. This tendency is not universal, of course, and an uncongenial member often quickly drops out of a therapy group. In an appropriate context, however, the drive to affiliate may overcome extreme intrapsychic or social barriers. In one instance, an outpatient therapy group fostered an unlikely friendship between two women — one a demure, white, suburban homemaker and the other a black, lower-class slum dweller who had a violent temper and a history of alcoholism and prostitution. One could not imagine two persons more different in background and temperament. In the group, however, the slum dweller displayed an exceptional ability to articulate her own feelings and reflect those of others in a supportive way. She was the star of the group, though none of the other members remotely resembled her. She and the suburban homemaker became so friendly that they would go out for a meal after the group session.

Since therapy groups are composed of emotionally ill persons, it is also surprising that evocative groups seldom if ever become cohesive on the basis of unhealthy group standards. Foulkes speculated that "the deepest reason why [group] patients can reinforce their normal reactions and correct each other's neurotic reactions is that *collectively they constitute the very Norm from which, individually, they deviate*" (1964, p. 297; italics in the original).

It is likely that groups become cohesive only by accepting and incorporating the standards of the therapist. Though cohesiveness based on shared antagonism to the therapist may sometimes be a phase of group formation, members cannot afford to demolish the person on whom they depend for help. A therapy group, therefore, will not remain unanimously hostile to its leader for long. Invariably some members will come to the therapist's defense, and therapeutic group standards will prevail.

The standards developed by therapy groups contribute heavily to the long-term beneficial effects of this kind of therapy. People tend to internalize the standards of emotionally salient groups. When group members must make decisions in their daily lives, these internalized values exert a powerful influence. The process may occur outside of awareness, or it may reflect a person's conscious desire not to disappoint fellow group members. The anticipation of having to confess a lapse at the next meeting enhances the pressure to conform to the group's expectations.

Indeed, group therapy may be superior to individual therapy with respect to maintaining improvement in other contexts. In many respects the therapy group is society in miniature. Other members' reactions teach a person what to expect outside the group in ways the therapist cannot. Groups thus provide a good testing ground for new behavior. The more closely the group mirrors the patient's ordinary social contacts, the more readily a member can transfer behavior that was successful in the group to daily life. When friends or family oppose patients' efforts to apply what they have learned in therapy, the patients' ability to maintain improvement may depend upon how well group participation has taught them to deal with conflict and withstand antagonism.

For all these reasons, some people make permanent shifts in their assumptive systems and behavior following group discussions after individual sessions have had no effect. The young man with masturbation guilt clearly illustrates the point. We conclude this section with another example, one that ties together many therapeutic aspects of groups. The protagonist is Mr. Angelo, a thirty-year-old married man who entered group therapy after three years of individual treatment. Mr. Angelo's major complaint was that he had "no urge to live" because he knew that he suffered from a progressive, inherited loss of hearing. Several members of his family were already severely affected. It soon appeared that the main source of his distress was not the disability itself but the attitude he and his family adopted toward it. All of them regarded deafness as a disgrace to be concealed from others. Their resulting inattentiveness often provoked teasing or scorn, reactions they interpreted as proof that their affliction was disgraceful.

Mr. Angelo had discussed this problem repeatedly in individual therapy. Though he had learned a lot about himself, his chronic depression did not lift, and he continued to try to conceal his handicap. In the group his reticence diminished very gradually. At the group's thirty-sixth meeting he finally overcame his fears sufficiently to reveal the whole story. In the process he mentioned a new fear, one he had not disclosed in individual sessions. He was convinced that when he became completely deaf he would be helpless and his wife would abandon him. As he spoke, he burst into tears. No one in the group mocked him, and no one saw his affliction as disgraceful. Instead, they were supportive and reassuring. The next day he left on vacation (the imminence of a break in treatment may have precipitated his self-revelation). In sharp contrast to previous occasions, he immediately told some new-found acquaintances about his disability. To his surprise, he enjoyed his vacation as never before. Thereafter, Mr. Angelo gained ground steadily as he accepted the idea of dealing with his deafness like any other handicap. Despite obvious deterioration in his hearing, his long-standing depression lifted almost completely, and he soon terminated therapy. Except for infrequent, transient flurries of depression, each relieved by one or two interviews, he has maintained his improvement for many years.

Apparently the attitudes of the group convinced Mr. Angelo, as his psychiatrist could not, of the falsity of his conviction that others regarded his loss of hearing as a disgrace. His changed attitude allowed him to risk revealing his disability outside the group, and the success of this experiment facilitated his progressive recovery.

Why did a group succeed after an individual therapist had failed? We speculate that Mr. Angelo felt free to reveal his handicap because experience in the group had convinced him that the others did not derogate admissions of weakness. Moreover, the group code, which stressed honest revelation of feelings, enabled him to trust the responses of his fellow members. Since group members represented the larger society, Mr. Angelo could easily generalize this experience to other situations. As in all psychotherapy, this patient further benefited from realizing that he was contributing to a problem he had previously attributed to malign fate. As a result, he recognized that he had the power to do something about his difficulties. Finally, drawing an analogy to religious healing, Mr. Angelo's experience illustrates the power of confession of a guilty secret followed by reaffirmation of a group's acceptance. All these factors contributed to a major beneficial change in Mr. Angelo's assumptive world.

Drawbacks and Disadvantages of Evocative Groups

Evocative group therapies are not automatically acceptable to everyone. As many as 40 percent of public clinic outpatients referred for group therapy fail to show up for the first meeting (Klein and Carroll 1986). A major reason for their reluctance may be fearful anticipation of having to reveal themselves before strangers. In fact, this anticipation is not necessarily unjustified. Patients' censorious reactions may give early meetings the quality of a "peer court," or a few members' unremitting complaints may demoralize the rest. These occurrences contribute to the high drop-out rate in early group meetings (Bach 1954).

In directive groups, the structured activities, insistence on members' giving only favorable reports, and early indoctrination of patients into a therapeutic program foster cohesiveness. Lacking these techniques, the therapist of a free-interaction group cannot always establish therapeutic group standards early enough to forestall destructive or discouraging interactions. Moreover, cohesiveness may not be strong enough to hold patients in treatment long enough for them to experience the benefits of group therapy.

Such considerations are reminders that in evocative group therapies, as in individual ones (see pp. 105–52), "preparation . . . is an absolutely essential task of the therapist" (Yalom [1970] 1985, p. 286). Explicitly telling patients what to expect from a group and how to participate improves many aspects of group functioning in early meetings.

Though anticipated invasion of privacy seems to be a significant disadvantage of free-interaction group therapy, it has proved to be relatively unimportant, at least for patients who are willing to remain in this form of treatment. To be sure, members initially often hesitate to reveal feelings or experiences of which they are ashamed, but such reticence also occurs in individual therapy. Many patients actually find it easier to confess their transgressions before a group of peers than to open up to a therapist of high status behind closed doors. In any case, in a mature group, no topic is too "hot" to handle.

Another potential disadvantage of group as compared to individual therapy for some patients is that in individual therapy, patients are assured of the undivided attention of the therapist for the duration of the treatment session. They have the freedom to go into detail describing past history, dreams or fantasies, secure in the knowledge that nothing will stimulate someone else to interrupt with his or her own preoccupations. Some patients seem to need the opportunity to retreat from others and solve their problems through unhurried introspection or indulgence in fantasy in the presence of an understanding listener.

In therapy groups, by contrast, each patient must continuously cope with the real or anticipated reactions of others. Each member speaks while aware that others want the floor, and he or she must always be prepared for a variety of responses. Groups typically have little patience with private worlds; members prefer to discuss topics in which all have an interest. As a result, group therapies may be unduly strenuous for patients who are easily hurt by criticism or who have difficulty holding their own in a competitive atmosphere. Such patients may do better in individual treatment or in directive groups where the leader assumes an overtly guiding or protective role.

Indeed, the ability of a free-interaction group to engender strong emotion is at once its strongest asset and its most important potential drawback. Intense arousal does not always inspire patients to rise to new solutions. Patients may deteriorate or, more commonly, drop out when group support is insufficient to buffer the anxiety, resentment, guilt, and similar distress aroused by group participation.

An example illustrates the power of an evocative group to stimulate disturbing feelings without offering the emotional support that enables the patient to deal with them. The patient was a middle-aged woman who had devoted her life to caring for other family members at considerable emotional cost to herself. She dealt with resentment and frustration indirectly, by complaining constantly about her health. Her complaints helped make her life more tolerable by eliciting some attention and concern from her relatives. In her therapy group, however, such martyr-like behavior was unacceptable; group members persistently criticized this woman or ignored her. At the same time, the group's discussions stimulated her repressed hostile and sexual feelings. Her anger with her mother reached such a pitch that she struck the senile old lady on two occasions. This created intense guilt, which the group did not assuage. At this point the patient needed an operation, which enabled her to stop group treatment without loss of face. Her group experience could scarcely have been considered helpful.

The negative features of free-interaction group therapy are by no means absolute. Appropriate measures may circumvent them or even turn them to advantage. As suggested by a massive study of various leadership styles in encounter groups, a skillful leader can avert possible misadventures once a group is under way. Encounter groups are sufficiently similar to free-interaction groups to permit tentative generalizations from one to the other. In the study of leadership styles, the best outcomes were achieved by leaders who displayed a high degree of caring and who frequently attributed meanings to members' behavior. The effective leaders were moderately controlling, to keep things moving without deadening spontaneity, and sufficiently confrontational to stir members emotionally without evoking more tension than members could integrate (Yalom [1970] 1985).

It may be that the ideal form of psychotherapy would utilize both individual and group methods. To be sure, group and individual sessions may interfere with each other under some circumstances. For example, patients may withhold material in one setting, knowing that they can bring it up in the other. On the other hand, the two modalities can supplement each other. Individual therapy allows patients to explore in detail subjective experiences for which groups have little tolerance; groups provide feedback and support that individual therapy cannot duplicate. For this reason, when time and resources permit, many group therapists also see group members individually from time to time (Bieber 1971). Similarly, group religiomagical healing rituals may include private sessions between patient and shaman.

Family Therapy

Family therapy encompasses a host of activities ranging from individual treatment focused on understanding the patient's family relationships to staged meetings of all the significant others in a person's social network (Haley 1971). At the center of this continuum lie therapies that treat individual symptoms and behavior as manifestations of current and historical problems within the person's most intimate social network, the family.

The psychodynamic, behavioral, and existential traditions described earlier (Chapter 1) have all contributed to the development of family therapy. Many family theorists also draw upon sociological and sociopsychological concepts concerning small groups and social systems. In the treatment of eating disorders, for example, one family therapist might explore the internal and interpersonal dynamics that lead a person to pursue unhealthy thinness, while another might teach parents to use behavior modification to promote a child's weight gain.

Existential family therapists, who do not claim to treat specific disorders, use evocative metaphors to communicate to family members the common pain of the human condition. Their technique is intended to disrupt entrenched dysfunctional patterns of interaction. Such interventions encourage family members to recognize and support one another in facing their common suffering. Existential family therapists believe that learning to deal with the emotions aroused in therapy improves the participants' ability to tolerate painful feelings without lapsing into neurosis or maladaptive behavior (Whitaker 1976).

The richness and diversity of family theory reflect the several professional traditions that have coalesced into a single, though still fragmented, therapeutic domain (Broderick and Schrader 1981). Early in this century, hospital and community social workers were the first professionals to focus on the family as the unit to be served. Initially they considered family members' symptoms to be responses to the overwhelming stresses of poverty, immigration, or chronic illness in one family member. After psychoanalysis popularized the concept of trauma and emotional repression as the source of symptoms, many social workers became interested in family interactions as causes of neurosis and delinquency, especially in children.

Interest in the psychodynamics of family life gained widespread popular and professional acceptance in the 1950s, when society redefined some forms of delinquency as psychiatric illness. The decriminalization of some antisocial behavior brought psychologists, psychiatrists, and even sociologists into the field. They in turn began to articulate various theories about the social and familial roots of delinquency, and to propose remedies.

Concurrently, in the years after World War II, the direct study of human sexual physiology, behavior, and dysfunction provided a body of information that was applied in the developing fields of marriage counseling and sex therapy. The same period saw an explosive growth of interest in mental health and mental illness, particularly in the social and possibly remediable causes of psychosis. Members of all the mental health professions began developing family-systems concepts in an effort to understand and redefine the problems of severely disturbed, hospitalized psychiatric patients. Some family theorists became convinced that faulty communication within the family caused patients' illnesses and that altering these supposed pathogenic processes would lead to recovery. These psychiatrically based practitioners coined the term "family therapy" to describe what they believed was a specific treatment for major mental illnesses.

Although a growing body of epidemiological and neurophysiological data calls into question the notion of disturbed communication as a major cause of psychotic illness, family therapy remains important within psychiatry. New evidence confirms that many psychiatric patients (including neurotic and psychosomatic ones) have seriously disturbed families and that family processes contribute to the degree of disability and frequency of breakdown in patients (Leff and Vaughn 1985).

Reflecting this diverse history, contemporary family therapies include the treatment of families whose members have been subjected to unusual social stresses; families with disturbed or misbehaving children or adolescents; couples whose marriage and sexual relationship have been unhappy or unfulfilling; and families of the mentally ill. Each school offers its own theory of the role of family processes in the particular problems it seeks to treat. Here, in our search for the common features and effects of all psychotherapies, we shall highlight a few of the principles that guide many family therapies, recognizing that the field is more sophisticated and diverse than our generalizations may imply.

Some Principles of Family Therapy

Most family theories embody a concept of "healthy" family functioning. Healthy families have a clear structure in which members assume complementary roles. Adult members share decision-making power and agree on clear lines of authority in particular situations. Parents behave like parents, and children are not burdened with inappropriate confidences or responsibilities. The emotional climate of the healthy family is one of affection, confidence to handle life's challenges, and tolerance for the needs and behavior of all members (Beavers 1976). Family therapies seek to change the structure or emotional tone of disturbed families, thereby helping them achieve this healthy ideal.

Family theorists believe that all family members contribute to the symptoms and behavior of individuals, and that individual difficulties disturb others' functioning (Fogarty 1976). Even when the most symptomatic member is diagnosed as having an identifiable disease, such as a major psychosomatic syndrome (asthma, ulcerative colitis), mental illness (depression, schizophrenia), or behavior disorder (alcoholism, anorexia nervosa), the therapist views the symptoms as being in part forms of manipulation or communication within the family. Family therapists typically direct attention away from the primary sufferer to the family as a whole and to the function the "identified patient" is serving for others (Haley 1971, pp. 227–36).

For example, in seeing a family of a child recurrently hospitalized for asthma, the therapist assumes that the child's illness performs certain essential functions for other family members. The asthma may absorb one parent's attention and desire to be nurturing, thereby eclipsing marital dissatisfactions or postponing the anticipated sadness of having the child grow up and leave home. Acting on this formulation, the therapist may try to disconnect the child and the most concerned parent and to elicit the peripheral parent's response to the child's illness. When successful, such an intervention strengthens the marital relationship, with the result that the child's illness is no longer needed to fill one parent's emotional needs. Striking reductions in the frequency and severity of the child's relapses may follow (Minuchin et al. 1979).

The reciprocity between patients' problems and the family's responses suggests that modifying family interactions can increase a patient's motivation to improve. For example, family therapy for alcoholism may focus on changing the spouse's "enabling" behavior rather than on the drinker's drinking. As the spouse's involvement diminishes, the drinker is no longer protected from the consequences of intoxication. Various crises then occur, forcing the alcoholic to recognize the need for change. Like group therapy, family therapy thus seems a promising alternative for substance abusers, young delinquents, and other persons whose value system or social network supports their deviant or disruptive behavior (Gurman and Kniskern 1981). Such people are typically refractory to individual approaches (see Chapter 1).

Family therapists who believe that the patient's apparent illness is really an effort to help other family members may explicitly share this formulation with the family (Aponte and VanDeusen 1981). Such "reframing" of illness as helpfulness is a rhetorical therapeutic device. By implying that the patient has altruistic motives and the power to help others, such an intervention may significantly relieve the sufferer's feelings of guilt and impotence.

Like any powerful therapeutic technique, reframing is a double-edged sword. In one moving case report, a psychiatrist with a neurologically impaired, autistic child described the destructive impact of an evaluation team which rediagnosed the child as schizophrenic. The team referred the family to a therapist who considered schizophrenia to be a manifestation of disturbed communication within the family, especially communication between the parents and between mother and child. The psychiatrist and his wife were encouraged to accept responsibility for the child's symptoms, which were in fact beyond their control. As they embarked on a fruitless search to identify the ways in which their communication might be damaging their son, the couple's anxiety, guilt, and level of disagreement increased. The father was driven into individual therapy, the parents contemplated divorce, and the child became more asocial and disruptive. In a vicious circle, the simultaneous deterioration of the child's behavior and the parents' relationship seemed to confirm the therapist's formulation of the problem as primarily one of familial communication. Finally, an outside neurological reevaluation confirmed the original diagnosis. Instead of continuing to try to cure their son's illness by changing their own behavior, the parents joined several other families to found a school with a supportive program for retarded children, with excellent results (Kysar 1968).

This example further illustrates the complex relationship that exists between truth and the healing power of a therapeutic rationale. Though a therapeutic principle need not be true to be effective, a false one may have sufficient persuasive power to do great harm. The family therapist raised false hopes that were not fulfilled. His apparently authoritative formulation disconfirmed the parents' perception of their son's illness and replaced their understanding with confusion. The couple's ensuing demoralization made them less able to exert control over their circumstances, precipitating a cycle of failure and further unhelpful treatment.

Family Therapy and Demoralization

To the extent that a patient is demoralized, he or she typically feels isolated from others. Family therapy restores morale by mobilizing the figures who are of greatest emotional significance to the patient. Bringing in the family reverses isolation and demonstrates to the patient that others care enough to make an effort on his or her behalf.

While techniques vary widely, all family therapies attempt to improve communication between family members, and all teach individuals to handle conflict. In disturbed families, rules are communicated obliquely, and no one has the authority to enforce them. Conflicts continue endlessly, engendering a climate of hopelessness and frustration. Successful family therapy teaches members to communicate directly and to resolve conflicts in ways that appear fair and understandable. Disputants learn that they can increase their power to get what they want by following the family's rules. As in group therapy, an improved ability to handle conflict thus enhances the individual's feelings of mastery.

The construct of demoralization is particularly useful in arriving at an understanding of the effects of "structural" family therapy, as illustrated by the case of the asthmatic child above. Tactics such as disrupting overly close bonds between one parent and a child and encouraging closer bonding between the marital pair normalize generational boundaries and roles within the family. Established social roles embody clearly defined expectations. When a family member's behavior conforms to a particular social role, others are better able to predict his or her behavior. Demoralizing confusion and uncertainty diminish as a result. Moreover, a normal family role structure means that each member has clear responsibilities, tailored to his or her own developmental level. In consequence, each person can successfully fulfill others' expectations, and all derive self-esteem from participation in family life.

In recent years the most salient finding in family research has been the demonstration that high levels of expressed emotion in the families of chronic schizophrenic patients contribute to the frequency and severity of the patients' relapses. When family therapy succeeds in reducing this high level of expressiveness, patients experience fewer acute episodes and require less psychotropic medication (Kanter, Lamb, and Loper 1987). A more detailed examination of these findings further supports our hypothesis that much apparent mental illness is a form of demoralization, and that successful psychotherapy enhances morale.

"Expressed emotion" is defined as a composite of family members' level of hostility, criticism, and overinvolvement with the schizophrenic member. Though the researchers who coined the term believed that such expressiveness could exist independent of the patient's behavior (Leff and Vaughn 1985), others maintain that this negative emotional climate may be the family's understandable reaction to a disruptive or withdrawn person (Brown, Birley, and Wing 1972). Thus, family members become angry and blame the patient for incapacity or misbehavior because they do not understand that the patient is actually ill. Believing that the patient has the power to change, family members persist in ineffective efforts to improve his or her behavior. Everyone suffers from the resulting cycle of disappointment, anger, and frustration. In our terms, critical overinvolvement reflects the family's demoralization at being trapped in a situation over which they feel they have lost control.

Family therapy that aims to reduce expressed emotion involves educating all members about the patient's condition, helping them formulate realistic expectations about its course, suggesting techniques for coping with its most troublesome aspects, and improving family communication and problem solving generally (Anderson, Hogarty, and Reiss 1980; Falloon et al. 1982). Thus, addressing family members' confusion, despair, and isolation — three essential elements of demoralization — may produce or maintain symptomatic improvement even though the patient's underlying disease persists.

Family Therapy in Perspective

Though there are many different models of family intervention, no particular approach has proved unquestionably superior to any other. As with many other forms of psychotherapy, the therapist's particular technique or theory seems to have less impact on the outcome of family therapy than do his or her personal qualities and the severity of the case. Predictably, mild-to-moderate family problems are more responsive to treatment than severe ones. The therapist's personality attributes, timing in raising major issues, and respect for family members' defenses also seem to exert significant influence on the success of treatment (Gurman and Kniskern 1981).

As we have said, family therapy may be effective for some conditions that are difficult to treat individually, including substance abuse, adolescent delinquency, eating disorders, and psychosomatic illnesses. Despite many claims for the superiority of a family approach, however, systematic proof that family therapy surpasses group or individual treatment exists for only one condition. When the presenting problem is marital disharmony, conjoint therapy with the partners together is preferable to concurrent individual therapy for each spouse (Gurman, Kniskern, and Pinsof 1986; Gurman and Kniskern 1981). As with self-help programs, the importance of this finding may not be that particular techniques are specifically effective. Rather, conjoint treatment may be more effective because its rationale best accords with the patients' view of the problem and its potential solution.

The major difference between family therapy and other forms of group therapy, obviously, is that family members constituted a group before entering therapy, remain together between sessions, and expect to be linked for an indefinite future. The implications for therapy are both unfavorable and favorable. The major unfavorable aspect is that when family members' psychopathologies reinforce each other, the family system as a whole resists change. In such situations, working with individuals separately may be more effective. Another hazard is that unskillfully led family sessions may trigger destructive interactions that continue between sessions. Family members, in contrast to the strangers composing other therapy groups, cannot escape one another.

On the favorable side, if therapy succeeds in changing a pathological family system, the change is apt to last because the reinforcement operates continuously instead of only during therapy sessions. Indeed, an important question for future research is the possibility that family therapy provides the best vehicle for maintaining therapeutic gains over the long term. Individuals terminate therapy, groups disband, but the family remains a force in a person's life long after treatment has ended.

Summary

After briefly describing the encounter-group movement and citing examples of directive group therapies and self-help programs, this chapter focuses on the dynamics of free-interaction groups comprised of strangers. The persuasive power of these groups probably resides in the tendency of each person to look to others for validation of feelings and attitudes. Therapy groups differ from ordinary social groups by encouraging the honest expression of feelings, requiring members to continue communicating despite conflict, and granting status for reasons other than social standing or achievement. These factors help group members discover unsuspected similarities, common ground that counteracts their sense of isolation. The multiple models provided by group members promote cognitive and behavioral change in individuals.

Therapy groups arouse patients emotionally. Pressures toward self-revelation, members' conflicts rooted in differences in outlook, differences in life experiences, and members' distorted perceptions of one another based on mirror and transference reactions all contribute to the group's intense emotional climate. Such arousal fosters cohesiveness, which in turn increases members' hopes, combats their demoralization, and heightens their self-confidence by offering mutual support.

Family therapy, though historically distinct from group therapy, embodies many of the same effective elements. Family therapy may bolster morale by relabeling problems, directly mobilizing emotionally salient support, and replacing chaos and despair with order and hope. Like group therapy, family therapy offers individuals multiple sources of feedback and new learning. Family therapy may be particularly valuable in helping patients maintain their improvement over time by teaching family members to reinforce rather than oppose changes made in therapy.

Like any powerful remedy, group and family therapies can produce harm as well as benefit. Their greatest potential drawback is their failure to supply — especially in early meetings — sufficient support to enable members to cope with the stresses that these therapies generate. Suitable combinations of group or family and individual therapy may overcome these disadvantages.

TWELVE

Psychotherapy in a
Controlled Environment

<hr>

"We're all mad here. I'm mad. You're mad."
"How do you know I'm mad?" said Alice.
"You must be," said the Cat, "or you wouldn't have
come here."
Alice didn't think that proved it at all.
— *Alice's Adventures in Wonderland*

Up to this point we have focused on forms of healing and persuasion that are brought to bear on patients intermittently, in the setting of their daily lives. We now propose to glance briefly at the forces influencing patients who live in special environments for much or all of their day, highlighting those aspects that involve principles of psychotherapy already considered. Disruption of usual activities and relationships is a basic condition of all treatment in controlled settings. Similar disruptions are part of the influencing process that occurs on pilgrimages to healing shrines, or upon joining and living in a religious cult.

We shall first examine the problems for which patients are typically hospitalized and give a brief, historical review of the different philosophies that guide institutional treatment for the mentally ill. This history provides a context for considering three types of treatment: the traditional state mental hospital, milieu therapy, and community care.

274

Social Breakdown Syndromes and Demoralization

Though patients admitted to mental hospitals often have some diagnosable disease, the reason for admission is frequently what Gruenberg (1974) termed the "social breakdown syndrome," a crisis of adaptation to the environment followed by identifiable patterns of disturbed behavior. This condition, which may be acute or chronic, is seen not only in hospitalized patients but also in former mental patients who are living in the community, in never-hospitalized persons with various genetic or biological vulnerabilities, and in people who have no underlying illness but are facing major disruptions in their lives.

In brief, the social breakdown syndrome is one possible reaction to "a discrepancy between what the person can do and what he is expected to do" (Gruenberg 1974, pp. 703–4). The person is initially considered responsible for failing to meet some external demand — for example, the requirements of a new job or a family member's requests for change. This failure undermines the person's self-concept, and as a result, he or she comes to depend increasingly upon the immediate external world for cues as to how to think and behave. People in this state may become indecisive, impulsive, or both, producing a downward spiral of action and reaction that culminates in their being extruded from normal social interaction or withdrawing from it. According to Gruenberg, "withdrawal, self-neglect, dangerous behavior, shouting, self-harm, failure to work and failure to enjoy recreation" are among the particular problematic behaviors that may occur and lead to hospitalization, and "either troublesome behavior or functional performance deficit may predominate" (1974, p. 703).

Clearly, the social breakdown syndrome is a form of demoralization. The isolated, confused person on the verge of hospitalization is in a uniquely suggestible state. Entry into the hospital removes conflicting role expectations and assigns the person the role of being sick or disabled. This new role absolves patients of blame at the cost of being considered abnormal or incompetent. When the sick role is conferred in the context of a well-articulated program for recovery, which may involve the "constructive use of medical authority . . . and valuable clinical rituals" to modify the social and personal expectations that precipitated the crisis, the outcome may be favorable (Gruenberg 1974, pp. 706–7). Incarceration of the suggestible person in a hopeless or chaotic environment, however, is likely to make matters worse, leading to the chronically disturbed behavior of the "back ward" patient.

An Overview of Controlled Settings and Their Rationales

State hospitals and private sanitariums were once the only alternatives for patients needing more than outpatient care. Today such patients may be treated in a state hospital, a freestanding psychiatric hospital, a residential treatment school, a psychiatric ward in a general hospital, or the inpatient service of a community mental health center. Controlled settings that are more integrated into the community but that offer some form of mental health treatment include group homes, halfway houses, sheltered workshops, and partial hospitals. Treatment is sometimes offered in shelters, such as those for runaways or battered women. Mentally ill persons are also housed and sometimes treated (or mistreated) outside the mental health system in prisons and nursing homes. While these institutions serve many purposes, from the standpoint of their power to influence or change people, their salient quality is that each embodies some fundamental concept of dysfunction and treatment which patients are encouraged to internalize. Thus, a battered wife hospitalized for anxiety and depression is treated as an ill person and sees herself that way, while the same woman in a shelter would be encouraged to view herself as the victim of her partner and to change the conditions of her life.

Despite their apparent diversity, most treatment sites embody either the psychosocial or the organic view of the causes, and therefore the appropriate treatment, of social breakdown syndromes. Proponents of the psychosocial approach to treatment attribute patients' breakdowns primarily to intrapsychic or environmental stresses. Practitioners of the organic approach blame pathological states of the central nervous system. In the nineteenth century, these two perspectives generated two distinct types of institutions: the facility offering "moral treatment," and the traditional mental hospital. Psychosocial treatment later developed two different but complementary emphases. The first, embodied in the "psychotherapy hospital" (Almond 1974), focused on resolving patients' internal psychological conflicts. The second attempted to address the pathogenic social forces affecting the patient by creating a "therapeutic community." In recent years, mental health professionals have tried to integrate the organic, intrapsychic, and psychosocial conceptualizations of illness into "milieu therapy," which we shall discuss at length later in this chapter.

Asylums offering "moral treatment" were the first American institutions designed to treat rather than merely segregate the mentally ill. Their programs reflected the then widely held American belief that the pressures of an increasingly open and chaotic society lay at the root of many mental illnesses (Rothman 1971). The essence of moral treatment was compassion and forbearance toward the ill. The approach was designed to foster patients' recovery by treating them as much as possible as if they were not disturbed (Almond 1974). Patients in moral-treatment institutions were removed from their home environments, cared for by a staff committed to humanitarian principles, and urged to follow a simplified schedule of activities centered around farming or some other routine occupation. The theory linking social change to individual distress suggested that the key to recovery lay in following a well-ordered, undemanding routine derived from such traditional values as subjection to benign authority and agrarian work. This kind of treatment derived legitimacy not from scientific evidence but from the cultural values of a particular class of citizens at a particular period in history. Much of its success depended upon the consensus of belief between doctor and patient. The massive numbers of immigrants with different values and allegiances who flooded mental health institutions in the middle and late nineteenth century eventually made the moral-treatment model impossible to sustain. Nevertheless, until moral-treatment institutions became overcrowded and unable to restrict their patients to those with moderate or recent-onset illness, their rates of cure were impressive, even taking into account some inflation of their claims to success (Rothman 1971; Almond 1974).

During the middle of the nineteenth century, the moral-treatment model and its associated institutions gradually gave way to the large custodial asylum. The traditional state mental hospital embodied the belief that mental illnesses were untreatable brain diseases and that the best that could be done for patients was to provide for their basic needs and apply controls to their disturbed or disruptive behavior (Rothman 1971).

In the twentieth century, the popularity of the psychoanalytic assumption that persons' internal psychological conflicts cause their social breakdown sparked the creation of the private "psychotherapy hospital." In these institutions, which were far too expensive for public funding, patients received intensive psychotherapy for a few hours each week, usually along psychoanalytic lines. These programs adhered to the psychoanalytic values of permissiveness and acceptance of disruptive behavior, intense transference to the individual therapist, focus on past trauma, and open-endedness of treatment. In other ways these institutions maintained the quasi-medical structure of the public hospital. Reflecting their greater affluence, psychotherapy hospitals also provided comfortable living arrangements and attractive recreational facilities, which were viewed primarily as a means of filling patients' time between therapy sessions (Caudill 1958). Recently, these features have received more attention as aspects of a generally therapeutic environment.

The next important ideological development in the history of mental institutions was the creation of the "therapeutic community" in the 1940s. This type of program harkened back to the moral-treatment model, in which the social causality of illness predominated and illness could be reversed by social intervention. Proponents of the therapeutic community radically questioned the legitimacy of the concept of mental illness. According to this view, the label "mental illness" permits society to extrude or control persons who display a particular form of social deviance characterized by the persistent breaking of "residual rules." Residual rules are principles of decent behavior that cannot be formally specified, because they are virtually innumerable and depend on specific situations. For example, behavior that would be considered boorish (and in violation of a residual rule) at a dinner party might be perfectly acceptable at a picnic.

Most behavior that violates residual rules is only mildly disturbing to others, so society can ignore such behavior or explain it away. Flagrant and persistent breaking of residual rules, however, may become intolerable. Examples of violations that frighten or anger others would be talking loudly to oneself in public or claiming to get messages from Mars. The initial rule-breaking behavior may have diverse causes, but it is the reactions of family, friends, and society to the rule-breaker that socialize him or her into the role of mental patient. These reactions include rejection, stigmatization, and treatment of the patient by mental health personnel as if he or she were mentally ill. In short, according to social labeling theory, a goodly portion of the suffering and behavior of the disturbed person is created by the stigma and other untoward consequences that result from being labeled mentally ill. Mental illness is not an innate property of the individual but the product of interactions between the person and the social environment (Scheff 1966). This formulation accords with Gruenberg's discussion of the social breakdown syndrome.

Therapeutic communities were designed to reverse the damaging effects on persistent residual rule-breakers of society in general and of other types of institutional treatment in particular. These communities sought to replace the rigid medical hierarchy of the asylum and the psychotherapy hospital with a tolerant and egalitarian social structure. Individual psychotherapy or biomedical treatment administered by a physician gave way to intense levels of patient-patient and patient-staff interaction. To prevent dependency and regressed behavior, patients were given significant responsibility for the functioning of the community. Such responsibility usually involved patient-staff government or community meetings in which patients decided their own and one another's privileges and even, in extreme cases, regulated the use of medication or electroshock (Baker et al. 1953; Jones 1953; Greenblatt, York, and Brown 1955).

These communities further required complete openness on the part of all members, a focus on immediate problems, and dynamic group therapy to identify and change the attitudes and behaviors that made patients vulnerable to social breakdown (Gutheil 1985). Group and community participation was the essential therapeutic activity, with other modalities of treatment either not offered or used only to facilitate such involvement.

In their extreme forms, the programs of the psychotherapy hospital and the therapeutic community have major structural and conceptual flaws (Wilmer 1981). In both, the devaluation of organic etiological factors may deprive seriously ill patients of appropriate biomedical treatment. The psychotherapy hospital, vividly portrayed in Joanne Greenberg's autobiographical novel, *I Never Promised You a Rose Garden* (1965), seems prone to relatively high levels of impulsive or disruptive patient behavior, covertly conflicting staff attitudes that can increase patients' distress (Stanton and Schwartz 1954), prolonged lengths of stay, and difficulties with reentry into the outside world. In the therapeutic community, lack of privacy, blurring of staff roles, and reluctance to acknowledge any apparent illness as legitimate may damage patients who cannot fit in with the group, especially those who are psychotic, confused, or in need of diminished stimulation. As with the psychotherapy hospital, therapeutic communities require relatively long stays for patients to become involved and to internalize the community's values. Long periods away from home and the emphasis on the destructive aspects of patients' families and social networks can erode patients' outside support. In either institution, the patients' adjustment to a particular therapeutic culture may not transfer easily to the outside world.

The true therapeutic community, moreover, is difficult to sustain. Both patients and staff are continually tempted to return to the older, more comfortable arrangement in which the staff assume virtually total responsibility for the patients' welfare. Only aggressive staff training and support can prevent such lapses. Therapeutic communities are currently also threatened by the erosion of their financial bases of support (Adler 1988).

This historical review provides a context for examining the processes by which hospitals or other controlled environments shape thought and behavior. These processes have been studied most extensively in traditional state mental hospitals, usually with emphasis on their negative effects. In the rest of this chapter, we shall discuss some of the principles highlighted in these classic cautionary examples and then look at how some of the same principles have been turned to better account in various contemporary therapeutic environments. We should note that our description of the traditional state hospital is based on work done before the current wave of deinstitutionalization and hospital reform, so few current institutions fit the model exactly.

The Traditional Mental Hospital

The extensive direct control that the traditional mental hospital exerts over patients' lives is perhaps their most powerful means of influence. Many patients are placed in such hospitals by court order or other legal proceeding. Once confined, they must obey explicit rules governing dress, activity, acceptable social behavior, and so on. While patients typically conform in order to avoid trouble or from a desire to please, many forms of coercion are applied when necessary. These range from the staff's authority to grant or deny privileges (including discharge) to physical or chemical restraints that both subdue and punish transgressors.

The degrading and coercive aspects of the traditional asylum program — which may be present to a lesser degree in any closed or involuntary setting — bear uncomfortable resemblances to the processes of "thought reform" (Goffman 1962). Thought reform is the effort totalitarian regimes make to shift the moral and political values of political prisoners. What distinguishes these activities from simple repression are the methods used to modify a person's internal world. In addition to punishment and deprivation, these methods include an intense, dependent personal relationship between the prisoner and some representative of the authority structure, prolonged isolation from normal sources of validation and support, and the repeated challenging of previously held beliefs. Similar conditions were once present in many hospitals. Patients were confined indefinitely, forbidden contact with outsiders, and forced to depend completely on the staff, who interpreted all of their current and past behavior as proof of incompetence or illness. Though mental institutions employing some or all of these techniques still exist, the steady decline in the number of involuntary patients, increased awareness of patients' rights, and shorter lengths of stay across the board make the analogy to thought reform less pertinent than it once was, and we will not pursue it here.[1]

It is, moreover, easy to overestimate the power of coercion to promote psychological change. Merely forcing patients to accept hospital rules and routines does not necessarily affect their thoughts and attitudes, any more than simple imprisonment turns political prisoners into criminals or criminals into law-abiding citizens. The power of a total institution, to use Goffman's phrase, to change persons' inner lives depends in part on the processes at work in psychotherapy generally.

The overriding coherence of the theory that guides the treatment program of a traditional mental hospital is the key to the institution's influence. Everything about a controlled setting — the architecture (Rothman 1971), the structure of the staff, the nature of patients' activities — reflects a particular view of what is wrong and how to correct or respond to it. Thus, these aspects of hospital settings have great symbolic power (Lennard and Gralnick 1986). They are, moreover, internally consistent, so patients everywhere meet confirmation of the model guiding their treatment, even if its principles are never made explicit.

For example, as we have said, designers of state mental hospitals believed that the insane were victims of mysterious brain diseases that made them incompetent, irresponsible, and prone to violence. Moreover, these diseases were apt to be chronic, even lifelong. As a result, insane patients, for their own protection and that of others, had to be shielded from harm in settings geared to long-term care. These assumptions led to the building of mental hospitals in isolated areas, far from the communities they served. Patients were kept behind locked doors in wards or rooms generally stripped of all but the minimum of furniture. Such conditions reflected both the view that patients had little appreciation of their environment and the mandate that care be as economical and safe as possible.

In keeping with the analogy between mental and physical illness, the staff of a traditional mental hospital resembled that of a general hospital. Personnel formed a complex hierarchy with physicians at the apex, aided by clinical psychologists. Beneath them were professionally trained ancillary staff members, such as nurses and social workers, with aides or attendants at the bottom. Since it was assumed that patients were incapable of knowing, much less asserting, what was in their own best interest, their role was to submit to treatment and take orders without question.

Like psychoanalysis or a religious creed, the self-contained theoreti-

1. For a fuller discussion of the parallels between thought reform and psychotherapy, see Frank 1973.

cal system that creates such a setting cannot be disproved by countervailing examples. Staff members subscribe to an irrefutable conceptual scheme that views any nonconforming behavior as evidence of mental illness and everything they do as therapeutic, even though patients may rightly perceive many of the staff's acts as done for their own convenience or as punishment for misbehavior.

A classic, though controversial, study (Rosenhan 1973) underscored the power of the internally consistent assumptive world of hospitals that subscribe to the illness model, even those with adequate material resources. In this naturalistic experiment, various healthy researchers presented themselves to hospital admission facilities complaining of having recently heard voices, though otherwise giving accurate personal histories and acting normally. All were admitted, and over the course of hospitalizations ranging from seven to fifty-two days, hospital staff members failed to identify a single pseudopatient. Indeed, the staff often cited the normal aspects of the pseudopatients' past history and current behavior as evidence of psychopathology. For example, the chart of one pseudopatient who was observed making notes in the dayroom read, "patient engages in writing behavior" (p. 253). Interestingly, other patients did sometimes identify the impostors.

Rosenhan's findings confirmed Goffman's (1959) observations of life in a state mental hospital — in particular, the self-reinforcing quality of staff-patient interactions. As Goffman noted, the depersonalizing quality of the hospital environment strengthens its ability to alter patients' attitudes about themselves and others. Thus, patients are assumed from the outset to be irresponsible. Goffman described how any protest is met by bland condescension, the "institutional smirk" that implies that the staff knows best. Similarly, Rosenhan's pseudopatients found that in large and small matters — ranging from having little or no privacy to being casually slighted or ignored when they initiated contact with a staff member — they were treated as nonpersons owing to their supposed illness. This process — similar to what Goffman termed the "mortification of the self" — closely resembles the way cults render members more amenable to the ideas of the group by systematically undermining their individuality and capacity for independent thought.

Moreover, if demeaning treatment drives the patient to covert or open rebellion — becoming mute, refusing to eat, tearing up clothing, or attacking the furniture — such behavior merely confirms that the patient is mentally ill and belongs in the hospital. Patients who persist in rebelling are transferred to ever more simplified and restrictive quarters, which forces them to resort to ever more primitive ways of revolting. If one is thrown naked into a bare room which is then locked, among the few remaining means of protest are urinating on the floor or smearing feces on the wall. Such behavior, of course, serves only to convince the staff that the decision to put the patient in seclusion was correct. Over prolonged periods of time, patients may internalize the staff's attitudes, so that they become as hopelessly ill as others believe them to be.

So far we have stressed the psychonoxious influences of the traditional state mental hospital, but some of its features may be beneficial. Though research suggests that active treatment of any kind is generally better than custodial care (Cournos 1987), it is not rare for patients to improve upon transfer from a private hospital to a state institution. Such improvement suggests that what some need most is to be left alone. It is unfortunate that the word "asylum" has fallen into disuse, since providing asylum from overwhelming buffetings of life may be the first step toward restoring a psychotic patient's capacity to function. The traditional mental hospital's geographical isolation, authoritarian organization, simple, structured environment, and lack of challenges requiring decisions may help patients recover psychological balance or stimulate their spontaneous recuperative powers. Its monotony or unpleasantness may bolster patients' motivation to "pull themselves together" and gain release.

Moreover, in keeping with their belief in the organic basis of mental illness, state hospitals were among the first to offer patients effective psychopharmacological treatments. More relevant for our discussion is that within the limits of their resources, many hospital programs encourage healthy patient behaviors. Patients who exhibit some degree of self-control often participate in supervised, organized, goal-directed activities, including housekeeping or maintenance chores, occasional social or recreational functions, and occupational therapy. These activities may be coupled with a systematic scale of privileges and penalties, sometimes in the form of token economies that explicitly attempt to mold patients' behavior (pp. 221–22). "Social skills training" (Paul and Lentz 1977), another behavioral method for improving the coping skills of chronically ill patients, is a growing area of psychotherapeutic activity (Liberman et al. 1985). The directive methods of most psychosocial rehabilitation programs fit well into the existing structure of the traditional hospital.

Milieu Therapy

Recognition of the powerful, though often negative, influence of the hospital setting has inspired various efforts to create controlled environments that enhance the treatment of both the psychosocial and the organic aspects of mental illness. In such programs, the treatment milieu includes responsible participation in a patient-staff community, a focus on concrete problems and current interactions, and various group activities. Gunderson (1983) has described the beneficial elements of milieu therapy, including its power to engage patients' attention, contain disruptive behavior, support morale, and validate progress (see also Tucker and Maxmen 1973).

The core of milieu therapy, in all its forms, is the socialization of patients to well-defined norms in a controlled setting. A much-studied therapeutic program that one of us (J.B.F.) knows well (Almond 1974) illustrates how this approach may support or restore patients' morale while fostering beneficial changes in attitude.

The program is a twenty-bed inpatient psychiatric unit in a university teaching hospital. Incoming patients are screened to exclude those who need only brief evaluation and treatment, those who are unwilling to participate and do not fulfill legal criteria for involuntary commitment, and those who have been through the program several times without benefit. In this, as in other successful milieu programs, careful screening of patients is essential; hospitals that must take all comers are at a great disadvantage in implementing a milieu approach (Shore and Shapiro 1979).

The ward accepts chronic or involuntary patients, but in limited numbers. Though many patients are suicidal, withdrawn, or otherwise seriously disturbed, most are able to handle basic self-care and to interact with others. Those who are initially too psychotic or confused to participate are quickly given psychotropic drugs to bring florid symptoms under control, a precondition for involvement in a busy and socially stimulating program.

Unlike patients on general medical wards or in traditional asylums, patients on this unit wear street clothes, as do staff members. Rather than being isolated in private or semiprivate rooms, patients sleep together in rooms where the beds can be used as couches during the day. While each patient has an individualized treatment plan, members of the patient community spend most of their time in activities with one another. These include communal meals, various modalities of group therapy and recreation, and participation in decision-making meetings about one another's privileges and about issues affecting the whole ward. Examples of whole-ward issues include schedules, cleanliness, and disruptive events. Many normally private interactions take place in public, as when senior psychiatrists make rounds and speak with patients individually in front of other patients. Most patients attend weekly individual psychotherapy sessions, but therapists are not permitted to keep the content of these sessions confidential from the rest of the staff.

Patients on this ward are granted different levels of supervision and responsibility depending on their condition. The lowest status is one of constant observation by a staff member; the highest, permission to leave the ward with another patient during any period of free time. A patient committee reviews each request for promotion to a higher, more responsible status. The request is then publicly granted or denied in a twice-weekly "community meeting" of patients and all staff members (psychiatrists, nurses, social workers, trainees, activities therapists, and aides). The decision is made contingent on whether or not the patient has shown improvement in symptoms, behavior, or attitude. Though staff members retain ultimate decision-making power, they follow patients' advice or suggestions whenever possible. In many ways, the ward is a small society, with traditions, particular uses of language, and stylized patterns of interaction that have built up over the years of its existence.

Almond described the core psychotherapeutic element of this program as "communitas, . . . a sense of being part of a group of essentially equal members who are important to one another" (1974, p. 25). All participating members of the community take responsibility for others as well as themselves, so all acquire merit by being altruistic. In fulfilling their responsibilities, moreover, patients and nonmedical staff perform such traditional medical functions as analyzing or diagnosing a problem, relieving the sufferer of responsibility (demotion in status), and suggesting a remedy (giving advice or even recommending an adjustment in medication). The sense of being aligned with the healing forces of medicine combats patients' sense of powerlessness and isolation, much as feeling close to transcendental healing forces improves the condition of those at a revival meeting or religious shrine. By being forced to actively think and behave like a physician or therapist, patients learn to see things from the therapist's point of view. This helps them internalize the therapist's values. Similar processes occur in any group therapy where members are encouraged to help each other rather than rely solely on the therapist for aid.

In this program and others like it, such sharing of healing powers, though embedded in the social structure, also requires the active involvement of a committed leader or group of leaders to model and teach the approach. Indeed, charismatic leadership seems to be a feature of many healing communities. This quality, similar to the ethos of the rhetorician and the spiritual power of the cult leader, derives from many sources in the ward setting. These sources include the leader's warmth, energy, and persuasive skill; the prestige of the institution as a whole; and the staff's belief in the leader's powers. When the leader is a physician, his or her ability to control the fearful and disorganizing symptoms of illness through drugs provides additional therapeutic leverage that many shamans would envy.

Patients entering any treatment setting are often confused and suggestible by virtue of having failed to meet others' expectations and their own. Upon admission to a therapeutic milieu, they encounter a set of conflicting expectations that may further confuse them and thereby heighten their openness to therapeutic influences. The fact of hospitalization confirms for the patient that he or she is sick, yet the doctors, nurses, and other patients do not behave in typical medical ways. Patients are simultaneously granted the sick role and expected to assume responsibility for themselves and for others in the community. When patients approach the staff for help — for instance, to ask for information about the unit or request assistance with daily activities — they are encouraged to turn to other patients first. These paradoxical expectations initially provoke distress in the form of angry outbursts and escalating demands for control or staff attention, or, at the other extreme, withdrawal. Often, however, such discomfort motivates patients to try to understand and conform to the rules and values guiding their treatment. Mastering the complex social demands of the setting helps rebuild patients' sense of self-efficacy and competence.

From the moment of entry, patients experience a ward routine that embodies many of the effective features of other forms of psychotherapy. All but the most severely disturbed patients are "specialed" on admission by more experienced patients, who relieve confusion by orienting newcomers to the schedule and philosophy of the unit. New patients are asked repeatedly in different settings to say what problems brought them to the hospital. Their days are filled with different activities, so that they have little time alone in which to brood. Almond calls this process social and sensory saturation, likening it to the chanting, music, and dancing that may engage people in traditional healing rituals.

Sources of hope abound in the therapeutic milieu. Most powerful is the testimony of the experienced patients who have achieved independent status and are moving out into the community. As these patients explain the program to newcomers, they reinforce their own understanding and acceptance of its principles, much as members of religious cults deepen their faith by proselytizing.

A further beneficial quality of a therapeutic milieu is that participation involves healthy behaviors, which may precede internal change. In the early stages of membership, patients may trek dutifully from one meeting to another, speak when called on, but remain inwardly aloof. Gradually, however, patients' inner lives may come to mirror their outward behavior as cooperative, caring, responsible members of the group. This process is a form of the reduction of cognitive dissonance. Moreover, the patients' inward change in attitude is contingently reinforced by their gradual progression through the status system and attainment of greater freedom of movement. Each move to a higher status confirms progress and enhances the sense of mastery.

Group Therapy within the Milieu

Participation in the ward community is not the only therapeutic element of the milieu program. Both pharmacological treatment and individual psychotherapy contribute to patients' improvement, as they would in any outpatient setting. In keeping with their emphasis on communal participation, however, milieu therapy units tend to downplay these modalities and to emphasize various forms of group and family therapy. Groups within the milieu share the core therapeutic features of outpatient therapy groups in mobilizing hope, engendering a sense of belonging in isolated people, promoting universality by exposing patients to others with problems like their own, and encouraging altruism (Yalom [1970] 1985).

Inpatient groups also present special problems that require some modification of outpatient group techniques. The membership of inpatient groups fluctuates constantly due to admissions and discharges, and most patients begin with major barriers to trusting and interacting with others. Such groups may meet several times per week, and they require directive leadership to prevent complete fragmentation. Inpatient groups typically focus on the present. Much group time is taken up with orienting new members, discussing and trying to resolve problems that contributed to patients' being hospitalized or that have arisen in the hospital, and bidding farewell to members who are leaving (Beeber 1988). Given the constant struggle to maintain continuity, psychodrama groups, in which a particular problem can be identified, acted out, and analyzed in a single meeting, may be particularly appropriate to the inpatient setting. Yalom, similarly, has suggested that every session of an inpatient group be conducted as a complete therapeutic experience in itself (1983).

In contrast to members of outpatient groups, members of inpatient units interact in many contexts. This feature may be helpful; members can draw on knowledge from other experiences on the ward as they interact in the group and can continue to pursue helpful interactions with one another between meetings. On the other hand, anticipating facing other group members throughout the day may make some patients reluctant to reveal embarrassing or shameful concerns. Furthermore, the fear of such consequences as loss of status or privileges may inhibit confrontation and honest self-disclosure.

Inpatient units tend to be heterogeneous with respect to both diagnosis and level of impairment. Having an actively psychotic patient in a free-interaction group may be disorganizing to the patient and inhibiting to other members. A depressed but socially intact patient may feel demeaned in a group aimed at helping chronic schizophrenic patients handle simple social transactions. In consequence, some inpatient units offer specialized groups to deal with particular problems or to address the needs of patients at different levels of functioning. Actively or recently psychotic patients, for example, may be assigned to directive groups focusing on handling day-to-day ward activities, coping with symptoms, rehearsing everyday social interactions with others, and so on. These behaviorally oriented directive approaches hold great promise for the social rehabilitation of chronic patients (Paul and Lentz 1977). Inpatient behavior modification and social rehabilitation groups have also been used successfully with anorexic patients (Levandusky and Dooley 1985).

Various creative arts therapies — music, art, poetry, and dance — may be a specialized part of a milieu program. Beyond the aesthetic pleasures of artistic expression and the manipulation of symbols for therapeutic purposes (Fleshman and Fryrens 1981), these modalities are often especially helpful for patients who are not verbally skilled or who are too disturbed to participate in a free-interaction group.

Another increasingly popular form of inpatient group therapy is "psychoeducation." Patients attend a lecture or video program about some aspect of their illness and afterward discuss the main points of the presentation and how these apply to the individual case (Adler 1988). This approach may also be used for family members of hospitalized or seriously ill patients. Outcome studies suggest that psychoeducation is of particular benefit in changing some of the family attitudes that are associated with early relapse (Falloon et al. 1982).

Other forms of family therapy also play a crucial role in milieu treatment. In keeping with the psychosocial model of social breakdown, inpatient family therapy encourages family members to examine their role in precipitating hospitalization and in smoothing the patient's return to the outside world (Anderson 1977). Families, with or without patient members present, may also participate in programs or groups with the families of other patients. Such activities give them direct experience of the ward's treatment approach while assuaging some of the guilt, isolation, and sense of failure that accompany placing a parent, spouse, or child in a mental institution.

The Effects of Milieu Therapy

Milieu therapy clearly improves patients' morale while they are hospitalized. An early illustration was the post–World War II transformation of the admissions ward of a naval hospital, where acutely disturbed patients had previously been controlled by heavy sedation, seclusion, and physical restraints. These measures implicitly encouraged patients to abandon all self-control by intoxicating and terrifying them and by conveying the staff's expectation that they could not control themselves. A new ward administrator was determined to establish powerful group expectations, shared by patients and staff, that patients could exert self-control and that restraints would not be needed. He achieved this through daily community meetings of patients and staff followed by a meeting of the staff alone. In the course of ten months, during which nearly a thousand patients were admitted to the service, not one required restraints or seclusion (Wilmer 1958). A more recent study compared patients randomly assigned to a medical model unit or milieu therapy unit that also dispensed medical treatment. The investigators noted a significant reduction in elopements and suicidal behavior in patients participating in milieu therapy (Oldham and Russakoff 1982).

Another clear benefit of milieu therapy is its impact on the staff. Though some professionals find it difficult to deal with the nontraditional roles and diffusion of responsibility that characterize this approach, those who find such work congenial are able to maintain their morale even in the face of alienating or frightening patient behavior. Training and ongoing group work for the staff are essential to the functioning of a milieu program. As a result, staff members learn to treat patients as persons rather than objects, and to feel like human beings rather than functionaries. These effects, usually ignored in outcome studies, are not trivial, in light of the stress of inpatient work and the abuse of patients that may occur when caretakers are untrained, alienated, or demoralized.

The long-term effects of milieu treatment are difficult to measure, given the variety of programs that exist, the heterogeneity of patients in them, and the fact that a patient's mere conformity within a therapeutic milieu is no proof that he or she has changed or internalized its values. The little that is known suggests that milieu therapy does not specifically remedy any discrete illness, but combats the demoralization that either precedes hospitalization or occurs as a result of it. Participation in a milieu program may also help correct certain maladaptive attitudes or behaviors, though these effects are subtle. While patients' participation in milieu therapy (often quantified in research studies merely by the length of the hospital stay) does not reduce the number of subsequent hospitalizations or clearly improve long-term social adjustment in work or relationships, it may improve participation in outpatient treatment and bring a consequent reduction in symptoms (Mattes 1982). Almond (1974) found that milieu treatment enhanced patients' use of follow-up care, but only for those who appeared to have adopted the ward's values at the time of discharge. Paul and Lentz (1977) noted that when specialized behavior-modification programs are incorporated into a therapeutic milieu, their effectiveness for targeted problems exceeds that of the milieu alone.

While milieu therapy seems to have only modest and nonspecific effects on most of the severe mental illnesses for which people are hospitalized, it may play a more specific role in such problems as substance abuse (Brook and Whitehead 1980) and eating disorders (Levandusky and Dooley 1985). Central to such problems are patients' minimization or denial of their condition and adherence to deviant attitudes that sustain their behavior. Intensive pressure from peers seems to be one of the few effective tools for overcoming entrenched denial. A high-intensity program combining education, confession, behavior modification, and commitment to a new set of values may be needed to shift longstanding attitudes. A controlled environment is often necessary to prevent dysfunctional behavior and its rewards — that is, to make patients uncomfortable enough to want help.

The prototype for such a program is Synanon, a therapeutic community for drug addicts. Participation involves repeated confession of addiction, mutual confrontation of denial, and other activities that enable members to progress through a hierarchy of statuses from novice to therapist (Deissler 1970). In many respects, the members' routine parallels that of a medieval monastery, with members living and working together, pooling their resources, and supporting the organization through mendicant activity (Frank 1973).

Synanon's ultimate or general efficacy has proved to be quite limited (Brook and Whitehead 1980), probably because addiction involves physiological dysfunctions as well as maladaptive or deviant attitudes. Nevertheless, confession and other elements of the Synanon approach remain important in the treatment of addictions and behavioral disorders of many kinds. The testimony of those who have persisted with Synanon or related approaches indicates that a specialized milieu may sometimes have a powerful impact on disorders for which other types of psychotherapy are generally ineffective.

From Therapeutic Community to Community Care

Recognition of the high cost and limited benefits of inpatient milieu therapy has, in its turn, been one of many factors contributing to the development of community care for the mentally ill. Many studies document its benefits, but the community-care movement, like previous mental health reforms, is rooted as much in ideology as in scientifically proven therapeutic advances (Gutheil 1985). Community programs have proliferated since the 1960s, though they are still far from sufficient to meet the needs of the deinstitutionalized chronically ill or the never-institutionalized person seeking help (Mollica 1983). Important questions exist about the long-term viability of community services and about their actual costs and limitations. Our interest, however, is confined to the ways community services resemble or improve upon the psychotherapy offered to similar patients in controlled settings.

Community programs encompass living arrangements for mental patients as well as the treatments that are designed to sustain or rehabilitate them. A recent American Psychiatric Association report classified residential settings by their level of intensity of treatment and degree of restrictiveness or supervision (Arce and Vergare 1985; Talbott 1985). At the most intensive level of care one finds group homes and skilled nursing facilities. The least restrictive level of community care is that of the patient who lives alone or with family and attends an outpatient clinic. Patients from a variety of residential settings may attend programs that meet for only part of the day, including intensive, time-limited, partial hospitalization programs designed as substitutes for inpatient care, rehabilitation programs for those with social or vocational deficits, and open-ended day programs for maintaining chronic patients in the community (Parker and Knoll 1990).

In general, the availability of a broad spectrum of community facilities and treatment programs increases therapeutic leverage by allowing for some separation of patients based on their functional abilities (Arce and Vergare 1985). The more homogeneous the patient group, the more readily patients identify with one another and feel that the treatment program specifically addresses their individual needs. As in other forms of psychotherapy, this sense of being treated as an individual in accordance with an appropriate rationale is in itself a healing influence.

Intensive community programs that are intermediate between inpatient and ambulatory settings — for example, partial or day hospitals and nonhospital residential facilities with on-site treatment — enjoy at least three further advantages over round-the-clock inpatient care. The first is that such programs favorably change the meanings patients attach to their problems. While hospitalization conveys to a person that he or she is sick, not fully responsible, and obliged to depend on others for help, community programs imply that even an obviously ill person is still partly functional. Second, intermediate treatment enhances continuity between therapy and a person's usual social roles and activities. Third, treatment in nonhospital settings allows patients to assume real responsibilities. These may have a greater effect on morale and a greater carry-over into posttreatment life than the important but still artificial duties imposed in the hospital.

A Veterans Administration study comparing the long-term effects of partial hospitalization to those of inpatient treatment illustrates the different meanings patients attach to the two modalities of care. The patients were their own controls in the sense that, before participating in the partial hospitalization program, all had had extensive inpatient treatment. The study showed that those who did well in the day hospital program — and presumably adopted some of its values — were less likely to be admitted to psychiatric inpatient units in the two years following their treatment than in the two years preceding it. Even more striking was the finding that these patients also made significantly fewer requests for medical or surgical assistance in the posttreatment period. At least one explanation is that day hospital treatment discouraged participants from seeing themselves as patients needing care whenever they ran into difficulty (Comstock et al. 1985). Similarly, in a review of studies in which patients were randomly assigned to community or inpatient programs, Kiesler (1982) found that patients who were initially treated in a hospital were more likely to be readmitted than comparable patients in community care.

Many proponents of community care stress the value of patients' being able to partially maintain their usual roles even while in intensive treatment (Pang 1985). When patients are treated at the hospital during normal working hours but remain at home on evenings and weekends, families have little incentive to extrude them or to form barriers to their reentry into the family. Such events are common when people are institutionalized for long periods. Another, frequently unstated advantage of partial hospitalization is that patients experience less sexual deprivation than occurs during inpatient stays. Ongoing interaction between patients and their families has also been a stimulus to the heartening growth of such advocacy and support groups as the National Alliance for the Mentally Ill and Families of the Mentally Ill. These organizations provide education and emotional support for patients and their families and represent the political interests of both groups.

Being able to do real work as a part of treatment has important advantages. Programs that meet only in the evenings allow patients to work or continue their schooling. This buffers patients from the financial hardship of intensive treatment and reduces the stigma of disability or of not having meaningful responsibilities. Patients in halfway houses may hold regular daytime jobs. Unemployed residents cook and share household responsibilities, important survival skills for independent living. In their description of a therapeutic work farm, Knobloch and Knobloch (1977) stressed the power of genuinely taxing work to increase the cohesiveness of the patient community and enhance patients' confidence and self-esteem. They noted that during periods of bad weather, when work was impossible, patients experienced a marked drop in morale and a diminished capacity to participate in the program's many therapeutic activities other than work.

Finally, the repeated and easy movement of patients between community-based treatment programs and their normal environments may facilitate the transfer of learning between settings. Patient have the opportunity to bring immediate, real-life problems into the treatment setting and can readily apply skills learned in treatment to situations in the outside world.

Some aspects of community treatment may be less advantageous than treatment in the hospital. For example, family caretakers may experience overwhelming stress when forced to assume the burden of caring for very ill, violent, or disruptive members over the long term. The permeability of the boundary between the treatment program and the patient's life may defuse the strength of the emotional arousal and diminish the intensity of interaction that occurs in a controlled setting. Patients in more open settings are better able to keep some of their maladaptive behavior out of the therapeutic spotlight and may be less open to group influences if they have other sources of gratification or self-esteem (Knobloch and Knobloch 1977). For addicts and alcoholics in open settings, the opportunity to continue to drink or use drugs during the hours they are not in treatment can subvert the therapy entirely.

In sum, while some severely disturbed or uncontrollable patients need long-term inpatient care (Shore and Shapiro 1979; Sharfstein 1985), many can be treated with in open settings with programs of varying intensity. Some patients in the community require supervision and treatment indefinitely; others may be able to move through a hierarchy of settings toward progressively more independent functioning. In one study of long-term outcomes, patients who were managed in the community reported better quality of life and higher self-esteem than those treated in hospitals. They also showed somewhat improved readmission and relapse rates (Talbott 1985). At minimum, when treatment in open settings is matched to patients' level of impairment, its impact seems to be less depersonalizing and demoralizing than that of comparable inpatient programs.

Summary

This chapter describes the forces that operate for good or ill in controlled therapeutic settings. Patients typically enter these settings in a state of crisis or social breakdown that makes them uniquely vulnerable to the conditions and expectations they encounter. Most controlled settings embody a powerful, internally consistent view of the nature of patients' difficulties. Patients in large, custodial asylums encounter an unshakable assumptive system according to which they are incompetent and everything that happens to them is treatment. The depersonalizing and restrictive hospital environment encourages passivity and dependency. The isolation, simplified life, and authoritarian atmosphere of the hospital may mobilize recuperative forces in certain patients, but for many who do not respond promptly, these features retard recovery.

Recognition of the antitherapeutic influences of the conventional mental hospital and increasing awareness of the psychosocial forces fostering hospitalization have led to the development of three types of inpatient programs: those that employ individual psychoanalytic psychotherapy; those that stress therapeutic group forces; and, finally, those that integrate both into milieu therapy. The primary target of milieu treatment is the social breakdown that precipitates or prolongs hospitalization. Patients and staff participate in a variety of group activities aimed at restoring self-respect, encouraging patients to assume responsibility for themselves and others, and teaching new behaviors or attitudes.

Although milieu therapy has beneficial effects on patients' morale while they are in the hospital, these effects do not necessarily persist after discharge. A variety of open settings in the community provide alternative forms of treatment. Community programs allow for individualized treatment based on patients' level of disability, minimize disruption of patients' usual activities, and facilitate the transfer of learning from the treatment setting into daily life.

Epilogue
Some Personal Reflections on the
Intellectual History of This Book

Do all that you know, and try all that you don't.
— *The Hunting of the Snark*

In many ways, the successive editions of this book represent a diary of the intellectual journey that constitutes a professional career. The interested reader may be curious to know more about the people, events, and ideas that have shaped my thinking during this long and fascinating voyage. As must be apparent, in the course of my intellectual journey I have been influenced by more people and in more ways than I can possibly identify. The extent of this influence is especially great since, far from being a solitary thinker, I have always been open to and stimulated by the ideas of others. This brief acknowledgment, therefore, must serve to express my deep gratitude to the many forgotten helpers who are not mentioned in this note or in the book itself.

The journey may be said to have begun when I was a graduate student in psychology and my imagination was fired by the writings of Kurt Lewin, a brilliant German psychologist. His central assumption was that the major determinants of behavior, feeling, and thinking lie in the person's "life space" — that is, his or her current social environment. The life space includes the person's conscious thoughts, feelings, and values. Past events affect psychological functioning only as they shape current attitudes (Lewin 1935). Using this framework, Lewin succeeded in devising ingenious experiments directly relevant to human motivation, an area that at that time was almost totally ignored by academic departments of psychology.

Another of Lewin's powerful concepts was "action research," the premise of which was that the best way to discover the causes of any phenomenon is to try to change it. His successful projects reinforced my later interest in doing research in psychotherapy as a procedure devoted to changing patients' attitudes.

Under Lewin's aegis or actual supervision I conducted two experimental projects that have influenced my thinking ever since. The first explored how experiences of success or failure, determined by the relation of actual performance to expected performance, affected a person's estimates of future performance as well as self-esteem (Frank 1935). The second experiment showed that it was possible to construct a crude scale of social pressure, and to identify some of the factors determining the level at which the experimental subject would yield (Frank 1944). The relevance of these studies to psychotherapy, in which a therapist seeks to change a patient's attitudes toward self and others, is apparent.

While conducting these studies, I encountered psychoanalysis, initially an orthodox therapeutic analysis, and some years later, while briefly a candidate in a psychoanalytic training institute, a training analysis. My training analyst, Benjamin Weininger, was a maverick who focused on current problems and did not hesitate to suggest ways of dealing with them. While both analyses, especially the second, were instructive and beneficial, in neither did I experience convincing subjective evidence of the validity of psychoanalytic theories. It was, however, easy to reconcile Lewin's concepts with those of Harry Stack Sullivan, whose theories dominated the training institute. Sullivan emphasized the important role of interactions with "significant others" in shaping personality (Sullivan [1953] 1968). For many reasons, including the unscientific dogmatism and contentiousness of many psychoanalytic schools, I never completed psychoanalytic training.

Psychiatric training at the Johns Hopkins Hospital under Adolf Meyer and John C. Whitehorn instilled a nondogmatic outlook, a respect for facts, and a conviction that systematic observation of individuals in their social context could yield worthwhile insights into human functioning. Consistent with this background as well as with the dominant teachings of the time, I conceptualized psychiatric symptoms as persistent maladaptive attempts to resolve intrapersonal and interpersonal conflicts arising from traumatic early life experiences. Psychotherapy enabled patients to develop more appropriate solutions by bringing the more or less unconscious past and present sources of symptoms to full awareness in the context of a supportive relationship with a therapist. Although, as the text of this book makes clear, I came to recognize and appreciate the contributions of psychotherapies based on cognitive, behavioral, and existential conceptualizations, therapies grounded in psychodynamic theory, broadly defined, have maintained a dominant place in my thinking.

After completing psychiatric training, I joined the psychiatric staff of the army hospital in the Philippines organized by Johns Hopkins. In this congenial environment I was able to conduct a study of delayed convalescence from schistosomiasis in American soldiers. The findings demonstrated the considerable contributions of psychological stress to symptoms of illness. This experience later resurfaced as part of an ongoing secondary interest in the so-called holistic view of health and disease, considered in Chapters 5, 6, and 7.

After discharge from the armed services, I took the natural step of applying my clinical and research background to research in psychotherapy. The immediate post–World War II years were particularly favorable for such work. Numerous wartime psychiatric casualties had created widespread public support for psychotherapy research, and private and public funding agencies poured money into it. Above all, countless able young psychiatrists, psychologists, and social workers released from uniform were looking for opportunities to start or resume interrupted careers in the field of mental health.

While I was working at a Veterans Administration psychiatric clinic and trying to decide what to do next, a gifted psychoanalyst, Florence Powdermaker, offered me a position as her principal assistant in a large-scale, empirical, qualitative study of group psychotherapy with inpatient and outpatient veterans (Frank and Powdermaker 1959). Working intensively with psychiatrists, psychologists, and psychiatric social workers provided invaluable preparation for subsequent collaborative research and its inevitable interdisciplinary tensions. These years also created an enduring interest in group methods of therapy and respect for their power, as reflected in Chapters 4, 5, and 11.

At the conclusion of the group therapy project I returned to Johns Hopkins, taking along some of the research staff. My position as director of the hospital's psychiatric outpatient department provided easy access to ambulatory patients as subjects for research. Our team initially hoped to move from qualitative to quantitative studies of group therapy, but the complexities of group interaction defeated our attempts to develop an adequate research strategy. Accordingly, we shifted to individual psychotherapy.

After much cogitation we eventually decided to use very simple quantitative measures to evaluate patients' responses to therapy. We chose a global rating of improvement by the patient, the therapist, and the research staff, a symptom checklist filled out by the patient, and an estimate of changes in social functioning based on a structured interview by a research social worker. As described in Chapter 7, we used these measures to compare three forms of therapy as different as we could make them within our theoretical framework. These were weekly individual therapy, weekly group therapy, and minimal individual therapy (one half-hour session every two weeks for a period of four to six months).

To our astonishment and chagrin, patients in all three conditions showed the same average relief of symptoms. This relief appeared before any differences in the components of the three therapies had time to make themselves felt. In retrospect, considering the crudeness of our improvement measures, the heterogeneity of the patient samples, and other inadequacies of the design, differences in the results of the three therapies would have had to be very large to be detectable. Nevertheless, this failure to find any differences in symptom relief from these widely different forms of therapy led us to conclude, perhaps rashly, that the features shared by different psychotherapies account for much of their effectiveness.

This conclusion, which has stood the test of time, encouraged us to shift the focus of our research from differences in therapies to their similarities. We studied three of these common features: hope or positive expectation, emotional arousal, and enhancement of the sense of mastery.

A Hopkins colleague, David Rosenthal, inspired our interest in the study of hope. He suggested that all forms of psychotherapy produced placebo responses in addition to whatever effects might follow from their specific techniques. Though at first I resisted this idea as devaluing psychotherapy, the results of the first studies convinced me that he was right. In accordance with the precept, "If you can't lick 'em, join 'em," I coauthored a paper with him (Rosenthal and Frank 1956), and our research team went on to compare the effect of psychotherapy with that of the administration of a placebo, as described in Chapter 7.

At this point in my journey, I had the great good fortune to receive a fellowship at the Center for Advanced Study in the Behavioral Sciences in Palo Alto, where I drafted the first edition of this book. While I was there, many informal discussions with cultural anthropologists greatly enlarged and enriched my knowledge of indigenous healing, incorporated in Chapter 5. These discussions also deepened my understanding of the holistic perspective alluded to earlier.

Back at Johns Hopkins, as we were concluding the placebo studies,

Martin Orne urged us to do a controlled test of an "anticipatory social-ization interview" he had devised to improve the effectiveness of psycho-therapy (Orne and Wender 1968). We seized this opportunity. Using a version of his interview modified according to our needs, we were able to show that shaping patients' expectations to accord with the particular form of psychotherapy they received led to improved outcome, as de-scribed in Chapter 7.

We next turned to the emotional arousal shared by all forms of psy-chotherapy, using first subanesthetic inhalation doses of ether and later adrenalin to eliminate the perceptual confusion caused by ether. The findings supported our clinical impression that emotional arousal in-creased patients' susceptibility to therapists' efforts to change their atti-tudes, at least temporarily (Chapter 10).

In a final research project, we sought to explore the relation of thera-peutic outcome to increased sense of mastery. We set up two conditions: "mastery," in which patients were led to attribute their improvement to their own efforts; and "placebo," in which they were led to attribute their improvement to an inert pill. The most intriguing finding was that patients who felt themselves to be predominantly in control of their lives improved more in the mastery condition, while patients who felt their lives to be primarily controlled by external circumstances improved more in the placebo condition (Chapter 8). This was the only finding in any of our studies that strongly linked a personality attribute to differ-ential responses to different forms of therapy.

Emphasis on the shared healing features of all psychotherapies has been the unifying theme of all the editions of this book. For mysterious reasons, it took me a decade or so to draw the obvious conclusion that the presence of shared effective features of psychotherapy implied a shared source of distress and disability in patients. For want of a better term, I called this condition "demoralization." This insight came just in time to be shoehorned into the last chapter of the second edition. In the present edition we have been able to introduce it near the start (Chapter 2), where it properly belongs, and to consider it more fully throughout.

Over the years I became increasingly puzzled by the contrast between the methodological sophistication of the research conducted by many outstanding psychotherapy researchers and the triviality of most of their findings. Most of the relationships found, while statistically significant, have been too weak to influence clinical practice. Moreover, many un-necessarily elaborate experimental designs have merely examined minor variations in methods or concepts or confirmed common-sense conclu-sions.

While I was sporadically thinking about this issue, Michael J. Mahoney asked me to write a comment on a contribution to a book he was editing. The article pointed out resemblances between psychotherapy and rhetoric (Glaser 1980). Suddenly the light dawned. As a type of persuasion, psychotherapy might be more closely allied to rhetoric and its close relative, hermeneutics, than to behavioral science!

A powerful reinforcement for this unsettling insight was hearing a seminar presentation by a linguistic analyst, Stanley Fish. In his talk, Fish brilliantly developed the thesis that the meaning of a text is determined by interaction with the reader, and therefore differs with each reader and on each occasion (1982). Whether emphasizing past experiences or current symptoms, a patient's clinical history resembles a text, and psychotherapy a collaborative effort of patient and therapist to discern its meaning. Could the fundamental limitation of psychotherapy research be that researchers have been trying to apply to the realm of meanings methods created to elucidate facts?

The resemblance of psychotherapy to rhetoric and hermeneutics generates many disturbing questions. If therapists' healing powers depend more on personal qualities such as persuasive talent and innate warmth than on a mastery of techniques, how should therapists be selected and trained? In what sense, if any, can one evaluate the truth of a patient's history? What are the ethical implications of using scientific authority to endorse one or another form of therapy if none of the underlying theories can be true in an objective sense? Although to do adequate justice to many such questions requires more knowledge than I possess, I believe the relation of psychotherapy to rhetoric and hermeneutics to be of fundamental importance, as discussed in Chapter 3 and elsewhere throughout the book.

These, then, were some of the way stations I visited in more than fifty years of studying and practicing psychotherapy. In the course of my journey, I have reached the following conclusions. The shared morale-enhancing properties of all forms of psychotherapy contribute importantly to their favorable outcomes. The interaction between particular therapists and patients, determined by the personal qualities, values, and expectations of both, contributes more to outcome than does therapeutic technique. Two probable exceptions to this general rule seem to be emerging. The first is that sufficiently prolonged exposure to an anxiety-provoking stimulus may relieve the anxiety linked to the stimulus. The second is that abreaction of an original trauma in a therapeutic context may be essential to alleviating posttraumatic stress disorders, a category whose ultimate boundaries are still unknown. These conclusions imply that in most cases, therapists should feel free to use whatever techniques are most congenial, and that therapists should not hesitate to adapt their techniques to accord with the personality, values, and expectations of particular patients.

Obviously, more territory remains to be explored. So my intellectual journey ends, not with conclusions but with questions, as all such journeys should.

JEROME D. FRANK

References

Abram, H. S.; Moore, G. L.; and Westervelt, F. B. 1971. Suicidal behavior in chronic dialysis patients. *Amer. J. Psychiatry* 127:1199–1204.

Abramson, L. Y.; Seligman, M. E .T.; and Teasdale, A. D. 1978. Learned helplessness in humans: Critique and reformulation. *J. Abnorm. Psychol.* 87:49–74.

Adler, W. N. 1988. Milieu therapy. In *Modern hospital psychiatry*, edited by J. R. Lion, W. M. Adler, and W. L. Webb, Jr., pp. 109–28. New York: W. W. Norton.

Adland, M. L. 1947. Review, case studies, therapy, and interpretation of the acute exhaustive psychoses. *Psychiatr. Q.* 21:38–69.

Alcoholics Anonymous. 1953. *Alcoholics Anonymous: Twelve steps and twelve traditions.* New York: Alcoholics Anonymous Publishing Co.

Almond, R. 1974. *The healing community: Dynamics of the therapeutic milieu.* New York: Jason Aronson.

American Psychiatric Association. 1987. *Diagnostic and statistical manual — IIIR.* Washington, D.C.: American Psychiatric Press.

Anderson, C. M. 1977. Family intervention with severely disturbed inpatients. *Arch. Gen. Psychiatry* 34:697–702.

Anderson, C. M.; Hogarty, G. E.; and Reiss, D. J. 1980. Family treatment of adult schizophrenic patients: A psychoeducational approach. *Schizophr. Bull.* 6:490–505.

Andreasen, N. C. 1985. Post-traumatic stress disorder. In *Comprehensive textbook of psychiatry*, edited by H. I. Kaplan and B. J. Sadock. 4th ed., pp. 918–24. Baltimore: Williams & Wilkins.

Aponte, H. J., and VanDeusen, J. M. 1981. Structural family therapy. In *Handbook of family therapy*, edited by A. S. Gurman and D. P. Kniskern, pp. 310–60. New York: Brunner/Mazel.

Appelbaum, S. A. 1979. *Out in inner space: A psychoanalyst explores the new therapies.* Garden City, N.Y.: Anchor Press/Doubleday.

Arce, A. A., and Vergare, M. 1985. An overview of community residences as alternatives to hospitalization. *Psychiatr. Clin. North Amer.* 8:423–36.

Argyle, M. 1958. *Religious behaviour.* London: Routledge & Kegan Paul.

Aristotle. 1941. Rhetorica. In *The basic works of Aristotle*, edited by R. McKeon, pp. 1325–1451. New York: Random House.

Bach, G. 1952. Some diadic functions of childhood memories. *J. Psychol.* 33:87–98.

———. 1954. *Intensive group psychotherapy*. New York: Ronald Press.

Bahnson, M. B., and Bahnson, C. B. 1969. Ego defenses in cancer patients. *Ann. NY Acad. Sci.* 164:546–47.

Baker, A. A.; Jones, M.; Merry, J.; and Pomryn, B. A. 1953. A community method of psychotherapy. *Brit. J. Med. Psychol.* 26:222–44.

Bandler, R., and Grinder, J. 1979. *Frogs into princes*. Moab, Ut.: Real People Press.

Bandura, A. 1977. *Social learning theory*. Englewood Cliffs, N.J.: Prentice-Hall.

———. 1982. Self-efficacy mechanism in human agency. *Amer. Psychologist* 37:122–47.

Bandura, A.; Lipsher, D. H.; and Miller, Paula E. 1960. Psychotherapists' approach-avoidance reactions to patients' expressions of hostility. *J. Consult. Psychol.* 24:1–8.

Barber, T. X. 1961a. Death by suggestion: A critical note. *Psychosom. Med.* 23:153–55.

———. 1961b. Physiological effects of "hypnosis." *Psychol. Bull.* 58:390–419.

Barlow, D. H.; Craske, M. G.; Cerny, T. A.; and Klosko, J. S. 1989. Behavioral treatment of panic disorder. *Behav. Ther.* 20:261–82.

Beavers, W. R. 1976. A theoretical basis for family evaluation. In *No single thread: Psychological health in family systems*, edited by M. Lewis and J. T. Gossett, pp. 3–46. New York: Brunner/Mazel.

Beck, A. T. 1970. Cognitive therapy: Nature and relation to behavior therapy. *Behav. Ther.* 1:184–200.

———. 1976. *Cognitive therapy and the emotional disorders*. New York: International Universities Press.

Beck, A. T.; Emery, G.; and Greenberg, R. L. 1985. *Anxiety disorders and phobias*. New York: Basic Books.

Beck, A. T.; Rush, A. J.; Shaw, B. F.; and Emery, G. 1979. *Cognitive therapy of depression*. New York: Guilford Press.

Beeber, A. R. 1988. A systems model of short-term, open-ended group therapy. *Hosp. Comm. Psychiatry* 39:537–42.

Beecher, H. K. 1956. Relationship of significance of wound to pain experience. *J. Amer. Med. Assoc.* 161:1609–13.

———. 1961. Surgery as placebo. *J. Amer. Med. Assoc.* 176:1102–7.

Begbie, H. 1909. *Twice-born men: A study in regeneration*. New York: Fleming H. Revell.

Beitman, B. D.; Goldfried, M. R.; and Norcross, J. C. 1989. The movement toward integrating the psychotherapies: An overview. *Amer. J. Psychiatry* 146:138–46.

Bennett, M. I., and Bennett, M. B. 1984. The uses of hopelessness. *Amer. J. Psychiatry* 141:559–62.

Benson, H. 1975. *The relaxation response*. New York: William Morrow & Co.

Benson, H., and Proctor, W. 1984. *Beyond the relaxation response*. New York: New York Times Books.

Berger, P. L., and Luckman, T. 1966. *The social construction of reality: A treatise in the sociology of knowledge*. Garden City, N.Y.: Doubleday, Anchor Books.

Berrigan, L. P., and Garfield, S. L. 1981. Relationship of missed psychotherapy appointments to premature termination and social class. *Brit. J. Clin. Psychol.* 20:239–42.

Beutler, L. E. 1981. Convergence in counseling and psychotherapy: A current look. *Clin. Psychol. Rev.* 1:79–101.

Beutler, L. E.; Arizmendi, T. G.; Crago, M.; Shanfield, S.; and Hagaman, R. 1983. The effects of value similarity and clients' persuadability on value convergence and psychotherapy improvement. *J. Soc. Clin. Psychol.* 1:231–45.

Beutler, L. E.; Crago, M.; and Arizmendi, T. G. 1986. Research on therapist variables in psychotherapy. In *Psychotherapy and behavior change*, edited by S. L. Garfield and A. E. Bergin, pp. 213–56. New York: John Wiley & Sons.

Bieber, T. B. 1971. Combined individual and group psychotherapy. In *Comprehensive group psychotherapy*, edited by H. I. Kaplan and B. J. Sadock, pp. 153–69. Baltimore: Williams & Wilkins.

Binswanger, L. 1956. Existential analysis and psychotherapy. In *Progress in psychotherapy*, edited by F. Fromm-Reichmann and J. L. Moreno, pp. 144–48. New York: Grune & Stratton.

Black, J. L., and Bruce, B. K. 1989. Behavior therapy: Clinical update. *Hosp. Comm. Psychiatry* 40:1152–58.

Blain, D. 1970. Benjamin Rush, M.D. *Transactions & Studies of the College of Physicians of Philadelphia* 38:61–98.

Bliss, K. 1988. LSD and psychotherapy. *Contemp. Drug Probl.* 15:519–54.

Bloch, S., and Crouch, E. 1987. *Therapeutic factors in group psychotherapy*. New York: Oxford University Press.

Bok, S. 1974. The ethics of giving placebos. *Sci. Amer.* 231, no. 5:17–23.

Bolin, R. 1988. Response to natural disasters. In *Mental health response to mass emergencies: Theory and practice*, edited by M. Lystad, pp. 22–51. New York: Brunner/Mazel.

Bootzin, R. R. 1985. The role of expectancy in behavior change. In *Placebo: Theory, research, and mechanisms*, edited by L. White, B. Tursky, and G. E. Schwartz, pp. 196–210. New York: Guilford Press.

Bootzin, R. R., and Lick, J. R. 1979. Expectancies in therapy research: Interpretive artifact or mediating mechanism? *J. Consult. Clin. Psychol.* 47:852–55.

Bowlby, J. 1980. *Attachment and loss*. New York: Free Press.

Brecher, E. M. (and the Consumer Reports Book editors). 1973. *Licit and illicit drugs: The Consumers Union report on narcotics, stimulants, depressants, inhalants, hallucinogens, and marijuana, including caffeine, nicotine, and alcohol*. Boston: Little, Brown & Co.

Brenner, C. [1955] 1973. *An elementary textbook of psychoanalysis*. Rev. ed. New York: International Universities Press.

Breuer, J., and Freud, S. 1957. *Studies on hysteria*. Vol. 2 of *The complete psychological works of Sigmund Freud,* edited and translated by J. Strachey. New York: Basic Books.

Broderick, C. B., and Schrader, S. S. 1981. The history of professional marriage and family therapy. In *Handbook of family therapy,* edited by A. S. Gurman, and D. P. Kniskern, pp. 5–38. New York: Brunner/Mazel.

Brook, R. C., and Whitehead, P. C. 1980. *Drug-free therapeutic community: An evaluation.* New York: Human Sciences Press.

Brown, G. W.; Birley, J. L. T.; and Wing, J. K. 1971. Influence of family life on the course of schizophrenic disorders: A replication. *Brit. J. Psychiatry* 121:241–58.

Bruch, H. 1961. Conceptual confusion in eating disorders. *J. Nerv. Ment. Dis.* 133:51–67.

Budd, M. A., and Zimmerman, M. E. 1986. The potentiating clinician: Combining scientific and linguistic competence. *Advances* 3:40–45.

Burke, K. 1969. *A rhetoric of motives.* Berkeley: University of California Press.

Burns, David D. 1980. *Feeling good.* New York: William Morrow & Co.

Cannon, W. B. 1957. "Voodoo" death. *Psychosom. Med.* 19:182–90.

Cantril, H. 1941. *The psychology of social movements.* New York: John Wiley & Sons.

———. 1950. *The "why" of man's experience.* New York: Macmillan.

———. 1957. Perception and interpersonal relations. *Amer. J. Psychiatry* 114:119–26.

Caplan, G. 1964. *Principles of preventive psychiatry.* New York: Basic Books.

Caplan, P. 1987. The psychiatric association's failure to meet its own standards: The dangers of "self-defeating personality disorder" as a category. *J. Pers. Disorders* 1:178–83.

Carkhuff, R. R. 1969. *Helping and human relations: A primer for lay and professional helpers.* Boston: Houghton Mifflin.

Carr, J. E. 1970. Differentiation similarity of patient and therapist and the outcome of psychotherapy. *J. Abnorm. Psychol.* 76:361–69.

Cassem, N., and Hackett, T. P. 1971. Psychiatric consultation in a coronary care unit. *Ann. Intern. Med.* 75:9–14.

Caudill, W. A. 1957. Problems of leadership in the overt and covert social structure of psychiatric hospitals. In *Symposium on preventive and social psychiatry,* pp. 345–63. Washington, D.C: Walter Reed Army Institute of Research.

———. 1958. *The psychiatric hospital as a small society.* Cambridge, Mass: Harvard University Press.

Chappell, M. N.; Stefano, J. J.; Rogerson, J. S.; and Pike, F. H. 1936. The value of group psychological procedures in the treatment of peptic ulcer. *Amer. J. Diges. Dis. Nutrition* 3:813–17.

Chodoff, P. 1987. Effects of the new economic climate on psychotherapeutic practice. *Amer. J. Psychiatry* 144:1293–97.

Christensen, C. W. 1963. Religious conversion. *J. Nerv. Ment. Dis.* 9:207–23.

Clark, D. M.; Salkovskis, P. M.; and Chalkley, A. J. 1985. Respiratory control as a treatment for panic attacks. *J. Behav. Ther. Exp. Psychiatry* 16:23–30.

Clark, E. T. 1929. *The psychology of religious awakening.* New York: Macmillan.

Clark, J. G., Jr. 1979. Cults. *J. Amer. Med. Assoc.* 242:279–81.

Cluff, L. E.; Canter, A.; and Imboden, J. B. 1966. Asian influenza: Infection, disease, and psychological factors. *Arch. Intern. Med.* 117:159–63.

Cohen, L. H.; Sargent, M. M.; and Sechrest, L. B. 1986. Use of psychotherapy research by professional psychologists. *Amer. Psychologist* 41, no. 2:198–206.

Comstock, B. S.; Kamilar, S. M.; Thornby, J. I.; Ramirez, J. P.; and Kaplan, H. B. 1985. Crisis treatment in a day hospital: Impact on medical care seeking. *Psychiatr. Clin. North Amer.* 8:483–99.

Cooper, A. M.; Frances, A.; and Sacks, M. 1988. The psychoanalytic model. In *Psychiatry*, edited by J. O. Cavanar, vol. 1, pp. 1–16. Philadelphia: J. B. Lippincott.

Cournos, F. 1987. Hospitalization and outcome studies: Implications for the treatment of the very ill patient. *Psychiatr. Clin. North Amer.* 10:165–76.

Cousins, N. 1983. *The healing heart: Antidotes to panic and helplessness.* New York: W. W. Norton.

———. 1989. *Head first: The biology of hope.* New York: E. P. Dutton.

Cranston, Ruth. [1955] 1957. *The miracle of Lourdes.* Reprint. New York: Popular Library.

Crasilneck, H. B., and Hall, J. A. 1985. *Clinical hypnosis: Principles and applications.* New York: Grune & Stratton.

Davidson, J. R. T.; Kudler, H. S.; and Smith, R. D. 1990. Assessment and pharmacotherapy of posttraumatic stress disorder. In *Biological assessment and treatment of posttraumatic stress disorder*, edited by E. L. Giller, pp. 203–21. Washington, D.C.: American Psychiatric Press.

Davis, J. M. 1985. Antidepressant drugs. In *Comprehensive group psychotherapy*, edited by H. I. Kaplan and B. J. Sadock, 4th ed., pp. 1513–2537. Baltimore: Williams & Wilkins.

deFigueiredo, J. M., and Frank, J. D. 1982. Subjective incompetence, the clinical hallmark of demoralization. *Compr. Psychiatry* 23:353–63.

Deissler, K. J. 1970. Synanon: Its concepts and methods. *Drug Alcohol Depend.* 5:28–35.

Delgado, R. 1977. Religious totalism: Gentle and ungentle persuasion under the first amendment. *S. Cal. Law Rev.* 51:1.

Dent, J. K. 1978. *Exploring the psycho-social therapies through the personalities of effective therapists.* Rockville, Md.: U.S. Department of Health, Education, and Welfare.

Deren, Maya. 1953. *Divine horsemen: The living gods of Haiti.* London: Thames & Hudson.

Deutsch, A. 1980. Tenacity of attachment to a cult leader: A psychiatric perspective. *Amer. J. Psychiatry* 137:1169–77.

Deutsch, R. M. 1977. *The new nuts among the berries: How nutrition nonsense captured America.* Palo Alto, Calif.: Bull Publishing.

DiMascio, A.; Weissman, M. M.; Prusoff, B. A.; Nev, C.; Zwilling, M.; and

Klerman, G. L. 1979. Differential symptom reduction by drugs and psychotherapy in acute depression. *Arch. Gen. Psychiatry* 36:1450–56.

Docherty, J. P. 1985. Afterword to Section V. *American Psychiatric Association annual review*, vol. 4. Washington, D.C.: American Psychiatric Press.

Dohrenwend, B. P., and Crandall, D. L. 1970. Psychiatric symptoms in community, clinic, and mental hospital groups. *Amer. J. Psychiatry* 126:1611–21.

Dohrenwend, B. P.; Shrout, P. E.; Egri, G.; and Mendelsohn, F. S. 1980. Nonspecific psychological distress and other measures for use in the general population. *Arch. Gen. Psychiatry* 37:1229–36.

Dreikurs, R. 1951. The unique social climate experiences in group psychotherapy. *Group Psychother.* 3:292–99.

Ehrenwald, J. 1966. *Psychotherapy: Myth and method.* New York: Grune & Stratton.

———, ed. 1976. *The history of psychotherapy: From healing magic to encounter.* New York: Jason Aronson.

Eisenbud, J. 1970. *PSI and psychoanalysis.* New York: Grune & Stratton.

Elkin, I.; Shea, M. T.; Watkins, J. T.; Imber, S. D.; Sotsky, S. M.; Collins, J. F.; Glass, D. R.; Pilkonis, P. A.; Leber, W. R.; Docherty, J. P.; Fiester, S. J.; and Parloff, M. B. 1989. NIMH treatment of depression collaborative research program: General effectiveness of treatments. *Arch. Gen. Psychiatry* 46:971–82.

Ellis, A. 1959. A homosexual treated with rational psychotherapy. *J. Clin. Psychol.* 15:338–43.

———. 1962. *Reason and emotion in psychotherapy.* New York: Lyle Stuart.

Emmelkamp, P. M. G. 1986. Behavior therapy with adults. In *Handbook of psychotherapy and behavior change*, edited by S. L. Garfield and A. E. Bergin, 3rd ed., pp. 385–442. New York: John Wiley & Sons.

Encyclopaedia Britannica. 1972, 19:278. 1986, 4:629.

Erikson, E. H. 1968. *Identity, youth, and crisis.* New York: W. W. Norton.

Erikson, K. T. 1966. *Wayward puritans.* New York: John Wiley & Sons.

———. 1978. *Everything in its path.* New York: Touchstone Books.

Evans, D. A.; Block, M. R.; Steinberg, E. R.; and Penrose, A. M. 1986. Frames and heuristics in doctor-patient discourse. *Soc. Sci. Med.* 22:1027–34.

Evans, F. J. 1974. The power of a sugar pill. *Psychol. Today*, April, pp. 55–59.

———. 1985. Expectancy, therapeutic instructions, and the placebo response. In *Placebo: Theory, research, and mechanisms*, edited by L. White, B. Tursky, and G. E. Schwartz, pp. 215–28. New York: Guilford Press.

Everson, T. C., and Cole, W. H. 1966. *Spontaneous regression of cancer.* Philadelphia: W. B. Saunders.

Falloon, I. R. H.; Boyd, J. L.; McGill, C. W.; Razani, J.; Moss, H. B.; and Gilderman, A. M. 1982. Family management in the prevention of exacerbation of schizophrenia. *N. Engl. J. Med.* 306:1437–40.

Farber, B. A., and Geller, J. D. 1977. Student attitudes toward psychotherapy. *J. Amer. Coll. Health Assoc.* 25:301–7.

Favazza, A. R. 1987. *Bodies under siege: Self-mutilation in culture and psychiatry.* Baltimore: Johns Hopkins University Press.

Feierman, S. 1985. Struggles for control: The social origin of health and healing. *Afr. Stud. Rev.* 28:73–147.

Festinger, L. 1954. A theory of social comparison processes. *Hum. Relat.* 7:117–40.

———. 1957. *A theory of cognitive dissonance.* Evanston, Ill.: Row, Peterson & Co.

Festinger, L.; Riecken, H. W.; and Schachter, S. [1956] 1964. *When prophecy fails.* Reprint. New York: Harper & Row, Torch Books.

Fiedler, F. E. 1953. Quantitative studies on the role of therapists' feelings toward their patients. In *Psychotherapy: Theory and research,* edited by O. H. Mowrer, pp. 296–315. New York: Ronald Press Co.

Field, M. J. 1955. Witchcraft as a primitive interpretation of mental disorder. *J. Ment. Sci.* 101:826–33.

Fish, S. 1982. *Is there a text in this class? The authority of interpretive communities.* Cambridge, Mass.: Harvard University Press.

———. 1986. Withholding the missing portion: Power, meaning, and persuasion in Freud's "The Wolf-Man." *Times Literary Supplement,* August 29, pp. 935A–938A.

Fleshman, B., and Fryrens, J. L. 1981. *The arts in therapy.* Chicago: Nelson-Hall.

Fogarty, T. P. 1976. Systems concepts and the dimensions of self. In *Family therapy: Theory and practice,* edited by P. J. Guerin, pp. 144–53. New York: Gardner Press.

Foon, A. E. 1987. Review: Locus of control as a predictor of outcome of psychotherapy. *Brit. J. Med. Psychol.* 60:99–107.

Ford, E. S. C. 1963. Being and becoming: The search for identity. *Amer. J. Orthopsychiatry* 17:472–82.

Foulkes, S. H. 1948. *Introduction to group analytic psychotherapy.* London: Heinemann.

———. 1964. *Therapeutic group analysis.* New York: International Universities Press.

Foulkes, S. H., and Anthony, E. J. 1957. *Group psychotherapy: The psycho-analytic approach.* Baltimore: Penguin Books.

Fox, J. R. 1964. Witchcraft and clanship in Cochiti therapy. In *Magic, faith, and healing,* edited by A. Kiev, pp. 174–200. New York: Macmillan.

Frank, J. B.; Kosten, T. R.; Giller, E. L., Jr.; and Dan, E. 1990. Antidepressants in the treatment of posttraumatic stress disorder. In *Posttraumatic stress disorder: Etiology, phenomenology, and treatment,* edited by M. Wolf, pp. 107–83. Washington, D.C.: American Psychiatric Press.

Frank, J. D. 1935. Individual differences in certain aspects of the level of aspiration. *Amer. J. Psychol.* 47:119–28.

———. 1944. Experimental studies of personal pressure and resistance. *J. Gen. Psychol.* 30:23–41, 43–46, 57–64.

———. 1946. Emotional reactions of American soldiers to an unfamiliar disease. *Amer. J. Psychiatry* 102:631–40.

———. 1952. Group therapy with schizophrenics. In *Psychotherapy with schizophrenics,* edited by E. B. Brody and F. C. Redlich, pp. 216–30. New York: International Universities Press.

————. 1957a. Some aspects of cohesiveness and conflict in psychiatric outpatient groups. *Bull. Johns Hopkins Hospital* 101:224–31.

————. 1957b. Some determinants, manifestations, and effects of cohesiveness in therapy groups. *Int. J. Group Psychother.* 7:53–63.

————. 1962. The role of cognition in illness and healing. In *Research in psychotherapy*, edited by H. H. Strupp and L. Luborsky, 2:3–12. Washington, D.C.: American Psychological Association.

————. 1966. Treatment of the focal symptom: An adaptational approach. *Amer. J. Psychother.* 20:564–75.

————. 1973. *Persuasion and healing: A comparative study of psychotherapy*. Rev. ed. Baltimore: Johns Hopkins University Press.

————. 1974. Psychotherapy: The restoration of morale. *Amer. J. Psychiatry* 131:271–74.

————. 1977. Nature and functions of belief systems: Humanism and transcendental religion. *Amer. Psychologist* 32:555–59.

————. 1978a. Expectation and therapeutic outcome: The placebo effect and the role induction interview. In J. D. Frank, R. Hoehn-Saric, S. Imber, B. L. Liberman, and A. R. Stone, *Effective ingredients of successful psychotherapy*, pp. 1–47. New York: Brunner/Mazel.

————. 1978b. Psychotherapy and the healing arts. In *Healing: Implications for psychotherapy*, edited by J. L. Fosshage and P. Olsen, pp. 31–47. New York: Human Sciences Press.

————. 1979. Mental health in a fragmented society: The shattered crystal ball. *Amer. J. Orthopsychiatry* 49:397–408.

————. 1981. Holistic medicine: A view from the fence. *Johns Hopkins Med. J.* 149:222–27.

————. 1983. The placebo is psychotherapy. *Behav. Brain Sci.* 6:291–92.

————. 1985. Further thoughts on the anti-demoralization hypothesis of psychotherapeutic effectiveness. *Integrative Psychiatry* 3:17–20 (plus commentary on pp. 21–26).

————. 1986. Psychotherapy: The transformation of meanings. *J. Roy. Soc. Med.* 79:341–46.

————. 1987. Psychotherapy, rhetoric, and hermeneutics: Implications for practice and research. *Psychotherapy* 24:293–302.

————. 1989. Non-specific aspects of treatment: The view of a psychotherapist. In *Non-specific aspects of treatment*, edited by M. Shepherd and N. Sartorius, pp. 95–114. Toronto: Hans Huber.

Frank, J. D., and Ascher, E. 1956. Therapeutic emotional interactions in group treatment. *Postgrad. Med.* 19:36–40.

Frank, J. D.; Gliedman, L. H.; Imber, S. D.; Nash, E. H.; and Stone, A. R. 1957. Why patients leave psychotherapy. *Arch. Neurol. Psychiatry* 77:283–99.

Frank, J. D.; Gliedman, L. H.; Imber, S. D.; Stone A. R.; and Nash, E. H. 1959. Patients' expectancies and relearning as factors determining improvement in psychotherapy. *Amer. J. Psychiatry* 115:961–68.

Frank, J. D., and Powdermaker, F. B. 1959. Group psychotherapy. In *American Handbook of Psychiatry*, edited by S. Arieti, pp. 1362–74. New York: Basic Books.

Frankl, V. E. [1955] 1986. *The doctor and the soul: From psychotherapy to logotherapy.* Reprint. New York: Random House.

———. 1960. Paradoxical intention, a logotherapeutic technique. *Amer. J. Psychother.* 14:520–35.

———. 1984. *Man's search for meaning: An introduction to logotherapy.* New York: Simon & Schuster.

Freud, S. 1920. *A general introduction to psychoanalysis.* New York: Liveright.

———. 1953. From the history of an infantile neurosis. In *The complete psychological works of Sigmund Freud,* edited and translated by J. Strachey, vol. 7. London: Hogarth Press and Institute of Psychoanalysis.

———. 1964. Dreams and occultism. In *The complete psychological works of Sigmund Freud,* vol. 22, edited and translated by J. Strachey. Toronto: Hogarth Press.

Friedman, H. J. 1963. Patient expectancy and symptom reduction. *Arch. Gen. Psychiatry* 8:61–67.

Friedman, M. J. 1988. Toward rational pharmacotherapy for posttraumatic stress disorder. *Amer. J. Psychiatry* 145:281–85.

Frost, R. 1915. *North of Boston.* New York: Henry Holt.

Fujita, C. 1986. *Morita therapy: A psychotherapeutic system for neurotics.* Tokyo and New York: Igaku-shoin.

Gabbard, K., and Gabbard, G. O. 1987. *Psychiatry and the cinema.* Chicago: University of Chicago Press.

Gadamer, H. G. 1982. *Truth and method.* New York: Crossroad.

Galanter, M. 1978. *Currents in alcoholism: Psychological, psychiatric, sociological, anthropological, and epidemiological topics,* vol. 4. San Diego: Grune & Stratton.

———. 1982. Charismatic religious sects and psychiatry: An overview. *Amer. J. Psychiatry* 139:1539–48.

———. 1988. Zealous self-help groups as adjuncts to psychiatric treatment: A study of Recovery, Inc. *Amer. J. Psychiatry* 145:1248–53.

———. 1989. *Cults: Faith, healing, and coercion.* New York: Oxford University Press.

Galassi, J. P., and Galassi, M. D. 1973. Alienation in college students: A comparison of counseling seekers and non-seekers. *J. Counseling Psychol.* 20:44–49.

Garfield, S. L. 1986. Research on client variables in psychotherapy. In *Handbook of psychotherapy and behavior change,* edited by S. L. Garfield and A. E. Bergin, 3rd ed., pp. 213–56. New York: John Wiley & Sons.

Garfield, S. L., and Bergin, A. E., eds. 1986. *Handbook of psychotherapy and behavior change.* 3rd ed. New York: John Wiley & Sons.

Gazzaniga, M. S. 1985. *The social brain: Discovering the networks of the mind.* New York: Basic Books.

Geertz, C. 1973. *The interpretation of cultures.* New York: Basic Books.

Gevitz, N., ed. 1988. *Other healers: Unorthodox medicine in America.* Baltimore: Johns Hopkins University Press.

Giller, E. L., Jr., ed. 1990. *Biological assessment and treatment of posttraumatic stress disorder.* Washington, D.C.: American Psychiatric Press.

Gillin, J. 1948. Magical fright. *Psychiatry* 11:387–400.

Glaser, S. 1980. Rhetoric and therapy. In *Psychotherapy process: Current issues and future directions*, edited by M. J. Mahoney, pp. 313–34. New York: Plenum Press.

Gliedman, L. H.; Nash, E. H., Jr.; Imber, S. D.; Stone, A. R.; and Frank, J. D. 1958. Reduction of symptoms by pharmacologically inert substances and by short-term psychotherapy. *Arch. Neurol. Psychiatry* 79:345–51.

Glik, D. C. 1952. Research methods in psychoanalysis. *Int. J. Psychoanal.* 33:403–9.

―――. 1986. Psychosocial wellness among spiritual healing participants. *Soc. Sci. Med.* 22:579–86.

Glover, E. 1952. Research methods in psychoanalysis. *Int. J. Psychoanal.* 33:403–9.

Goffman, E. 1959. The moral career of the mental patient. *Psychiatry* 22:123–42.

―――. 1962. *Asylums: Essays on the social situations of mental patients and other inmates.* Chicago: Aldine.

Goleman, D. 1985. *Vital lies, simple truths: The psychology of self-deception.* New York: Simon & Schuster.

Gordon, J. S. 1980. The paradigm of holistic medicine. In *Health for the whole person: The complete guide to holistic medicine*, edited by A. C. Hastings, J. Fadiman, and J. S. Gordon, pp. 3–27. Boulder, Colo.: Westview Press.

―――. 1987. *The golden guru: The strange journey of Bhagwan Shree Rajneesh.* Lexington, Mass.: Stephen Green Press.

Greben, S. E. 1982. Some sources of conflict within psychoanalytic societies. *Int. J. Psychoanal. Psychother.* 9:658–78.

―――. 1984. *Love's labor: Twenty-five years of experience in the practice of psychotherapy.* New York: Pantheon, Schocken Books.

Greenberg, J. 1965. *I never promised you a rose garden.* New York: New American Library.

Greenberg, L. S., and Safran, J. D. 1989. Emotion in psychiatry. *Amer. Psychologist* 44:19–29.

Greenberg, R. P., and Staller, J. 1981. Personal therapy for therapists. *Amer. J. Psychiatry* 138:1467–71.

Greenblatt, M.; York, R. H.; and Brown, E. L. 1955. *From custodial to therapeutic patient care in mental hospitals.* New York: Russell Sage Foundation.

Griffith, E. H.; Adams, A. A.; and Young, J. L. 1988. Nally II: Further clarification of clergy malpractice. *Hosp. Comm. Psychiatry* 39:1041–43.

Grinspoon, L., and Bakalar, J. B. 1985. Drug dependence: Non-narcotic agents. In *Comprehensive textbook of psychiatry*, edited by H. I. Kaplan and B. J. Sadock, 4th ed., pp. 1003–15. Baltimore: Williams & Wilkins.

Grof, S. 1975. *Realms of the human unconscious: Observations from LSD research.* New York: Viking Press.

Gross, M. L. 1978. *The psychological society.* New York: Random House.

Gruenberg, E. M. 1974. The social breakdown syndrome and its prevention. In *American handbook of psychiatry*, edited by G. Caplan, pp. 697–711. New York: Basic Books.

Grünbaum, A. 1984. *The foundations of psychoanalysis: A philosophical critique.* Berkeley: University of California Press.

Gunderson, J. G. 1983. An overview of modern milieu therapy. In *Principles and practice of milieu therapy*, edited by J. G. Gunderson, O. A. Will, Jr., and L. R. Mosher, pp. 1–13. New York: Jason Aronson.

Gurman, A. S. 1977. The patient's perception of the therapeutic relationship. In *Effective psychotherapy: A handbook of research*, edited by A. S. Gurman and A. M. Razin, pp. 503–43. New York: Pergamon Press.

Gurman, A. S., and Kniskern, D. P. 1978. Deterioration in marital and family treatment: Empirical, clinical, and conceptual issues. *Fam. Process* 17:3–21.

———. 1981. Family therapy outcome research: Knowns and unknowns. In *Handbook of family therapy*, edited by A. S. Gurman and D. P. Kniskern, pp. 742–76. New York: Brunner/Mazel.

Gurman, A. S.; Kniskern, D. P.; and Pinsof, W. 1986. Research on marital and family therapy. In *Handbook of psychotherapy and behavior change*, edited by S. L. Garfield and A. E. Bergin, 3rd ed., pp. 565–625. New York: John Wiley & Sons.

Gutheil, T. G. 1985. The therapeutic milieu: Changing themes and theories. *Hosp. Comm. Psychiatry* 36:1279–85.

Hackett, T. P., and Cassem, N. H. 1975. Psychological management of the cardiac infarction patient. *J. Hum. Stress* 1, no. 3:25–38.

Haley, J. 1963. *Strategies of psychotherapy.* New York: Grune & Stratton.

———. 1969. *"The power tactics of Jesus Christ" and other essays.* New York: Avon Books.

———. 1971. A review of the family therapy field. In *Changing families: A family therapy reader*, edited by J. Haley, pp. 1–12. New York: Grune & Stratton.

Hankoff, L. D.; Freedman, N.; and Engelhardt, D. M. 1958. The prognostic value of placebo response. *Amer. J. Psychiatry* 115:549–50.

Havens, L. L. 1974. The existential use of the self. *Amer. J. Psychiatry* 131:1–10.

Heine, R. W. 1953. A comparison of patients' reports on psychotherapeutic experience with psychoanalytic, nondirective, and Adlerian therapists. *Amer. J. Psychother.* 7:16–23.

Henderson, S. 1981. Social relationships, adversity, and neurosis: An analysis of prospective observations. *Brit. J. Psychiatry* 138:391–98.

Henry, W. E. 1966. Some observations on the lives of healers. *Hum. Dev.* 9:47–56.

———. 1977. Personal and social identities of professional psychotherapists. In *Effective psychotherapy: A handbook of research*, edited by A. S. Gurman and A. M. Razin. New York: Pergamon Press.

Herman, J. L., and van der Kolk, B. A. 1987. *Psychological trauma.* Washington, D.C.: American Psychiatric Press.

Herman, J. L.; Perry, J. C.; and van der Kolk, B. A. 1989. Childhood trauma in borderline personality disorder. *Amer. J. Psychiatry* 146, no. 4: 490–95.

Herz, F. M., and Rosen, E. J. 1982. Jewish families. In *Ethnicity and family therapy,* edited by M. McGoldrick, J. K. Pearce, and J. Giordano, pp. 364–92. New York: Guilford Press.

Hillman, J. 1983. *Healing fiction*. Barryton, N.Y.: Station Hill.

Hilts, P. J. 1980. Psychotherapy put on couch by government. *Washington Post*, September 14, pp. A1, A12.

Hinkle, L. E.; Plummer, N.; Metraux, R.; et al. 1957. Studies in human ecology: Factors relevant to the occurrence of bodily illness and disturbances in mood, thought, and behavior in three homogeneous population groups. *Amer. J. Psychiatry* 114:212–20.

Hoehn-Saric, R.; Frank, J. D.; Imber, S. D.; Nash, E. H., Jr.; Stone, A. R.; and Battle, C. C. 1964. Systematic preparation of patients for psychotherapy: I. Effects on therapy behavior and outcome. *J. Psychiatr. Res.* 2:267–81.

———. 1978. Emotional arousal, attitude change, and psychotherapy. In J. D. Frank, R. Hoehn-Saric, S. Imber, B. L. Liberman, and A. R. Stone, *Effective ingredients of successful psychotherapy*, pp. 73–106. New York: Brunner/Mazel.

Hollingshead, A. B., and Redlich, F. C. 1958. *Social class and mental illness*. New York: John Wiley & Sons.

Hollon, S. D., and Beck, A. T. 1986. Cognitive and cognitive-behavioral therapies. In *Handbook of psychotherapy and behavior change*, edited by S. L. Garfield and A. E. Bergin, 3rd ed., pp. 443–82. New York: John Wiley & Sons.

Holmes, O. W. [1861] 1911. Currents and counter-currents in medical science. In *Medical essays, 1842–82*, pp. 173–208. New York: Houghton Mifflin.

Honorton, C. 1977. Psi and internal attention states. In *Handbook of parapsychology*, edited by B. B. Wolman, pp. 435–72. New York: Van Nostrand & Reinhold.

Horowitz, M. 1988. Stress-response syndrome. In *Psychiatry*, edited by J. V. Cavernan, vol. 1, chap. 41, pp. 1–16. Philadelphia: J. B. Lippincott.

Housman, A. E. 1922. *Last poems*. London: Richards Press.

Hubbard, L. R. 1987. *Dianetics: The modern science of mental health*. Los Angeles: Bridge Publishers.

Hughes, C. W.; Stein, E. A.; and Lynch, J. J. 1978. Hopelessness-induced sudden death in rats: Anthropomorphism for experimentally induced drownings? *J. Nerv. Ment. Dis.* 166:287–401.

Hurvitz, N. 1970. Peer self-help psychotherapy groups and their implications for psychotherapy. *Psychotherapy* 7:41–49.

Huxley, A. 1959. *Heaven and hell*. Baltimore: Penguin Books.

———. 1962. Words and their meanings. In *The importance of language*, edited by M. Black, pp. 1–12. Englewood Cliffs, N.J.: Prentice-Hall, Spectrum Books.

Hyman, H. H., and Singer, E., eds. 1968. *Readings in reference group theory and research*. New York: Free Press.

Imber, S. D.; Pande, S. K.; Frank, J. D.; Hoehn-Saric, R.; Stone, A. R.; and Wargo, D. G. 1970. Time-focused role induction: Report of an instructive failure. *J. Nerv. Ment. Dis.* 150:27–30.

Imber, S. D.; Pilkonis, P. A.; Sotsky, S. M.; Elkin, I.; Watkins, J. T.; and Colins, J. F. 1990. Mode-specific effects among three treatments for depression. *J. Consult. Clin. Psychol.* 58:352–59.

Imboden, J. B. 1957. Brunswick's theory of perception: A note on its applicability to normal and neurotic personality functioning. *Arch. Neurol. Psychiatry* 77:187–92.

Imboden, J. B.; Canter, A.; Cluff, L. E.; and Trevor, R. W. 1959. Brucellosis, III: Psychological aspects of delayed convalescence. *Arch. Intern. Med.* 103:406–14.

Inglis, B. 1965. *The case for unorthodox medicine.* New York: G. P. Putnam's Sons.

Irvine, W. [1955] 1963. *Apes, angels, and Victorians: Darwin, Huxley, and evolution.* New York: Time, Inc.

Jackins, H. 1978. *The human side of human beings: The theory of re-evaluation counseling.* 2nd ed. Seattle: Rational Island Publishers.

Jacobs, D.; Charles, E.; Jacob, S. T.; Weinstein, H.; and Mann, D. 1972. Preparation for treatment of the disadvantaged patient: Effects on disposition and outcome. *Amer. J. Orthopsychiatry* 42:666–74.

Jacobson, G. 1968. The briefest psychiatric encounter. *Arch. Gen. Psychiatry* 18:718–24.

Jaffe, D. T., and Bresler, D. E. 1980. The use of guided imagery as an adjunct to medical diagnosis and treatment. *J. Hum. Psychol.* 20:45–59.

James, W. [1936] 1989. *The varieties of religious experience.* Reprint. New York: Macmillan.

Janov, A. 1970. *Primal therapy: The cure for neurosis.* New York: G. P. Putnam's Sons.

Jaspers, K. 1963. *General psychopathology.* Translated by J. Hoenig and M. W. Hamilton. Manchester: Manchester University Press.

———. 1964. *The nature of psychotherapy: A critical appraisal.* Translated by J. Hoenig and M. W. Hamilton. Chicago: University of Chicago Press, Phoenix Books.

Johnson, D. 1977. *The protean body: A Rolfer's view of human flexibility.* New York: Harper & Row.

Jones, B. A. 1983. Healing factors of psychiatry in light of attachment theory. *Amer. J. Psychother.* 37:235–43.

Jones, K. R., and Vischi, T. 1979. The impact of alcohol, drug abuse, and mental health treatment on medical care utilization: Review of the research literature. *Med. Care [Suppl.]* 17:1–82.

Jones, M. 1953. *The therapeutic community.* New York: Basic Books.

Jospe, M. 1978. *The placebo effect in healing.* Toronto: D. C. Heath.

Kadushin, C. 1969. *Why people go to psychiatrists.* New York: Atherton.

Kanter, J.; Lamb, H. R.; and Loper, C. 1987. Expressed emotion in families: A critical review. *Hosp. Comm. Psychiatry* 38:374–80.

Karasu, T. B. 1982. Personal communication.

———. 1986. The specificity versus nonspecificity dilemma: Toward identifying therapeutic change agents. *Amer. J. Psychiatry* 143:687–95.

Kelley, H. H. 1967. Attribution theory in social psychology. In *Nebraska symposium on motivation, 1967,* edited by D. Levine, pp. 192–238. Lincoln: University of Nebraska Press.

Kellner, R., and Sheffield, B. F. 1973. The one-week prevalence of symptoms in neurotic patients and normals. *Amer. J. Psychiatry* 130:102–5.

Kelly, G. A. 1955. *The psychology of personal constructs*, vol. 2, *Clinical diagnosis and psychotherapy*. New York: W. W. Norton.

Kelman, H. 1969. Kairos: The auspicious moment. *Amer. J. Psychoanal.* 29:59–83.

Kiesler, C. A. 1982. Mental hospitals and alternative care: Noninstitutionalization as potential public policy for mental patients. *Amer. Psychologist* 37, no. 4:349–60.

Kiev, A., ed. 1964. *Magic, faith, and healing*. New York: Macmillan.

Killip, T. 1988. Twenty years of coronary bypass surgery. *N. Engl. J. Med.* 319:366–68.

Kinkead, E. 1959. *In every war but one*. New York: W. W. Norton.

Klein, D. F., and Rabkin, J. G. 1984. Specificity and strategy in psychotherapy research. In *Psychotherapy research: Where are we and where should we go?* edited by J. B. W. Williams and R. L. Spitzer, pp. 306–29. New York: Guilford Press.

Klein, D. F.; Zitrin, C. M.; Woerner, M. G.; and Ross, D. C. 1983. Treatment of phobias: Behavior therapy and supportive psychotherapy. Are there any special ingredients? *Arch. Gen. Psychiatry* 40:139–45.

Klein, M. H.; Dittman, A. T.; Parloff, M. R.; and Gill, M. W. 1969. Behavior therapy: Observations and reflections. *J. Consult. Clin. Psychol.* 33:259–66.

Klein, R. H., and Carroll, P. A. 1986. Patient characteristics and attendance patterns in outpatient groups. *Int. J. Group Psychother.* 36:115–32.

Kleinman, A. 1980. *Patients and healers in the context of culture: An exploration of the borderland between anthropology, medicine, and psychiatry*. Berkeley: University of California Press.

———. 1988. *Rethinking psychiatry: From cultural category to personal experience*. New York: Free Press.

Kleinman, A., and Good, B. 1985. *Culture and depression: Studies in the anthropology and cross-cultural psychiatry of affect and disorder*. Berkeley: University of California Press.

Klerman, G. L. 1972. Psychotropic hedonism vs. pharmacological Calvinism. *Hastings Cent. Rep.* 2:1–3.

———. 1985. Psychoneurosis: Integrating pharmacotherapy and psychotherapy. In *Successful psychotherapy*, edited by J. L. Claghorn, pp. 69–91. New York: Brunner/Mazel.

Klosko, J. S.; Barlow, D. H.; Tassinari, R.; and Cerny, J. A. 1990. A comparison of alprazolam and behavior therapy in treatment of panic disorder. *J. Consult. Clin. Psychol.* 58:77–84.

Knauth, P. A. 1975. *A season in hell*. New York: Harper & Row.

Knobloch, F., and Knobloch, J. 1977. Recent advances in residential and day-care treatment of neurotic patients: Concept of integrated psychotherapy. In *New dimensions in psychiatry: A world view*, edited by S. Arieti and G. Chrzanovski, vol. 2, pp. 466–89. New York: John Wiley & Sons.

———. 1979. *Integrated psychotherapy*. New York: Jason Aronson.

Koch, S. 1981. The nature and limits of psychological knowledge: Lessons of a century qua "science." *Amer. Psychologist* 36:257–69.

Kolb, L. C. 1985. The place of narcosynthesis in the treatment of chronic and delayed stress reactions of war. In *The trauma of war: Stress and recovery in Viet Nam Veterans*, edited by S. M. Sonnenberg et al., pp. 211–26. Washington, D.C.: American Psychiatric Press.

———. 1987. A neuropsychological hypothesis explaining post-traumatic stress disorder. *Amer. J. Psychiatry* 144:989–95.

Komrad, M. S. 1983. A defence of medical paternalism: Maximising patients' autonomy. *J. Med. Ethics* 9:38–44.

Korchin, S. J. 1975. *Modern clinical psychology: Principles of intervention in the clinic and community*. New York: Basic Books.

Koss, M. P., and Butcher, J. N. 1986. Research on brief psychotherapy. In *Handbook of psychotherapy and behavior change*, edited by S. L. Garfield and A. E. Bergin, 3rd ed., pp. 627–70. New York: John Wiley & Sons.

Kraines, S. H. 1943. *The therapy of neuroses and psychoses*. Philadelphia: Lea & Febiger.

Krippner, S., and Ullman, M. 1970. Telepathy and dreams: A controlled experiment with electroencephalogram-electro-oculogram monitoring. *J. Nerv. Ment. Dis.* 151:394–403.

Krippner, S., and Villoldo, A. 1976. *The realms of healing*. Milbrae, Calif.: Celestial Arts.

Kubie, L. 1936. *Practical aspects of psychoanalysis*. New York: International Universities Press.

Kurland, A. A.; Savage, C.; Pahnke, W. N.; Grof, S.; and Olsson, J. E. 1971. LSD in the treatment of alcoholics. *Pharmakopsychiatrie Neuro-Psychopharmakologie* 4:83–94.

Kushner, H. S. 1981. *When bad things happen to good people*. New York: Pantheon, Schocken Books.

Kysar, J. 1968. The two camps in child psychiatry. *Amer. J. Psychiatry* 125: 103–9.

Lambert, M. J.; Shapiro, D. A.; and Bergin, A. E. 1986. The effectiveness of psychotherapy. In *Handbook of psychotherapy and behavior change*, edited by S. L. Garfield and A. E. Bergin, 3rd ed., pp. 157–211. New York: John Wiley & Sons.

Lasagna, L.; Mosteller, F.; von Felsinger, J. M.; and Beecher, H. K. 1954. A study of the placebo response. *Amer. J. Med.* 16:770–79.

Lazarus, A. A. 1973. "Hypnosis" as a factor in behavior therapy. *Int. J. Clin. Exp. Hypn.* 21:25–31.

———. 1989. *The practice of multimodal therapy: Systematic, comprehensive, and effective psychotherapy*. Baltimore: Johns Hopkins University Press.

Leff, J., and Vaughn, C. 1985. *Expressed emotion in families: Its significance for mental illness*. New York: Guilford Press.

Lennard, H. L., and Bernstein, A. 1960. *The anatomy of psychotherapy: Systems of communication and expectation*. New York: Columbia University Press.

Lennard, H. L., and Gralnick, A. 1986. *The psychiatric hospital: Context, values, and therapeutic process*. New York: Human Sciences Press.

LeShan, L. 1965/1966. An emotional life history associated with neoplastic disease. *Ann. NY Acad. Sci.* 125:780–93.

———. 1974. *The medium, the mystic, and the physicist: Toward a general theory of the paranormal.* New York: Viking Press.

Levandusky, P. G., and Dooley, C. P. 1985. An inpatient model for the treatment of anorexia nervosa. In *Theory and treatment of anorexia nervosa and bulimia: Sociocultural and psychological perspectives,* edited by S. W. Emmett, pp. 211–34. New York: Brunner/Mazel.

Levine, S. V. 1981. Cults and mental health: Clinical conclusions. *Can. J. Psychiatry* 26:534–39.

Levinson, S. 1982. Law as literature. *Texas Law Rev.* 60:373–403.

Lévi-Strauss, C. 1958. *Anthropologie structurale.* Paris: Librairie Plon.

Levy, N. B. 1981. Psychological reactions to machine dependency: Hemodialysis. *Psychiatr. Clin. North Amer.* 4:351–63.

Lewin, K. 1935. *A dynamic theory of personality.* New York: McGraw-Hill.

———. 1958. Group decisions and social change. In *Readings in social psychology,* edited by E. E. Maccoby, T. M. Newcomb, and E. L. Hartley, 3rd ed., pp. 197–211. New York: Henry Holt.

Liberman, B. L. 1978a. The maintenance and persistence of change: Long-term follow-up investigations of psychotherapy. In J. D. Frank, R. Hoehn-Saric, S. Imber, B. L. Liberman, and A. R. Stone, *Effective ingredients of successful psychotherapy,* pp. 107–29. New York: Brunner/Mazel.

———. 1978b. The role of mastery in psychotherapy: Maintenance of improvement and prescriptive change. In J. D. Frank, R. Hoehn-Saric, S. Imber, B. L. Liberman, and A. R. Stone, *Effective ingredients of successful psychotherapy,* pp. 35–72. New York: Brunner/Mazel.

Liberman, R. P. 1964. An experimental study of the placebo response under three different situations of pain. *J. Psychiatr. Res.* 2:233–46.

———. 1971. Behavioural group therapy: A controlled study. *Brit. J. Psychiatry* 119:535–44.

Liberman, R. P.; Massel, H. K.; Mork, M. D.; and Wong, S. E. 1985. Social skills training for chronic mental patients. *Hosp. Comm. Psychiatry* 36:396–403.

Lieberman, M. A. 1977. Problems in integrating traditional group therapies with new group forms. *Int. J. Group Psychother.* 27:19–32.

Lieberman, M. A.; Yalom, I. D.; and Miles, M. B. 1973. *Encounter groups: First facts.* New York: Basic Books.

Liebowitz, M. R.; Fyer, A. J.; Gorman, J. M.; et al. 1984. Lactate provocation of panic attacks. *Arch. Gen. Psychiatry* 41:764–70.

Link, B., and Dohrenwend, B. P. 1980. Formulation of hypotheses about the true prevalence of demoralization in the United States. In *Mental illness in the United States: Epidemiological estimates,* edited by B. P. Dohrenwend et al., pp. 114–32. New York: Praeger.

Linn, L., and Schwarz, L. W. 1958. *Psychiatry and religious experience.* New York: Random House.

Lipton, M. A.; DiMascio, A. D.; and Killam, K. F. 1978. *Psychopharmacology: A generation of progress.* New York: Raven Press.

London, P. 1986. *The modes and morals of psychotherapy.* New York: Hemisphere Publishing.

Lorion, R. P. 1974. Patient and therapist variables in the treatment of low income patients. *Psychol. Bull.* 81:344–54.

Low, A. [1950] 1968. *Mental health through will-training.* 16th ed. Boston: Christopher Publishing House.

Lowen, A. 1975. *Bioenergetics.* New York: McCann & Geoghegan.

Lowinger, P., and Dobie, S. 1969. What makes the placebo work? A study of placebo response rates. *Arch. Gen. Psychiatry* 20:84–88.

Luborsky, L. 1976. Helping alliances in psychotherapy. In *Successful psychotherapy,* edited by J. L. Claghorn, pp. 92–118. New York: Brunner/Mazel.

————. 1984. *Principles of psychoanalytic psychotherapy.* New York: Basic Books.

Luborsky, L.; Crits-Christoph, P.; McLellan, A. T.; et al. 1986. Do therapists vary much in their success? Findings from four outcome studies. *Amer. J. Orthopsychiatry* 56:501–11.

Luparello, T. J.; Leist, N.; Lourie, C. H.; and Sweet, P. 1970. The interaction of psychologic stimuli and pharmacologic agents on airway reactivity in asthmatic subjects. *Psychosom. Med.* 32:509–13.

McGuire, M. B. 1989. *Ritual healing in suburban America.* New Brunswick, N.J.: Rutgers University Press.

McHugh, P. R., and Slavney, P. R. 1983. *The perspectives of psychiatry.* Baltimore: Johns Hopkins University Press.

Maeder, T. 1989. Wounded healers. *Atlantic,* January, pp. 37–47.

Mandell, W. 1983. Types and phases of alcohol dependence illness. *Recent Dev. Alcohol.* 1:415–47.

Marks, I. M. 1969. *Fear and phobias,* pp. 203–23. New York: Academic Press.

————. 1978. *Living with fear: Understanding and coping with anxiety.* New York: McGraw-Hill.

————. 1987a. Behavioral aspects of panic disorder. *Amer. J. Psychiatry* 144, no. 9:1160–65.

————. 1987b. *Fears, phobias, and rituals: Panic, anxiety, and their disorders.* New York: Oxford University Press.

Marks, I. M., and Gelder, M. G. 1967. Transvestism and fetishism: Clinical and psychological changes during faradic aversion. *Brit. J. Psychiatry* 113:711–29.

Markush, R. E.; Schwab, J. J.; Farris, P.; Present, P. A.; and Holzer, C. E. 1977. Mortality and community mental health: The Alachua Co., Florida, mortality study. *Arch. Gen. Psychiatry* 34:1393–1400.

Marmor, J. 1971. Dynamic psychotherapy and behavior therapy: Are they irreconcilable? *Arch. Gen. Psychiatry* 24:22–28.

————. 1976. Common operational factors in diverse approaches to behavior change. In *What makes behavior change possible?* edited by A. Burton, pp. 3–12. New York: Brunner/Mazel.

Marnham, P. 1980. *Lourdes: A modern pilgrimage.* New York: Coward, McCann & Geoghegan.

Maslow, A. H. 1970. *Motivation and personality.* New York: Harper & Row.

Mason, R. C.; Clark, G.; Reeves, R. B.; and Wagner, B. 1969. Acceptance and healing. *J. Rel. Health* 8:123–30.

Masserman, J. H. 1971. *A psychiatric odyssey.* New York: Science House.

Mattes, J. A. 1982. The optimal length of hospitalization for psychiatric patients: A review of the literature. *Hosp. Comm. Psychiatry* 33:824–28.

May, P. R. A. 1976. Rational treatment for an irrational disorder: What does the schizophrenic patient need? *Amer. J. Psychiatry* 133:1008–11.

Meichenbaum, D. 1984. The nature of the unconscious process: A cognitive-behavioral perspective. In *The unconscious reconsidered*, edited by K. S. Bowers and D. Meichenbaum, pp. 273–98. New York: John Wiley & Sons.

———. 1986. What happens when the "brute data" of psychological inquiry is meaning? Nurturing a dialogue between hermeneutics and empiricism. In *Hermeneutics and psychological theory: Interpretive perspectives on personality, psychotherapy, and psychopathology*, edited by S. B. Messer, L. A. Sass, and R. L. Woolfolk, pp. 116–30. New Brunswick, N.J.: Rutgers University Press.

Mendel, W. M. 1964. The phenomenon of interpretation. *Amer. J. Psychoanal.* 24:184–89.

Menninger, K. A., and Holzman, P. S. 1973. *Theory of psychoanalytic technique*. 2nd ed. New York: Basic Books.

Merton, R. K. 1948. The self-fulfilling prophecy. *Antioch Rev.* 8:193–210.

———. 1957. *Social theory and social structure*. Glencoe, Ill.: Free Press.

Migier, B., and Wolpe, J. 1967. Automated self-desensitization: A case report. *Behav. Res. Ther.* 5:133–35.

Miller, J. B. 1976. *Toward a new psychology of women*. Boston: Beacon Press.

Miller, T. W. 1988. Advances in understanding the impact of stressful life events on health. *Hosp. Comm. Psychiatry* 39:615–22.

———. 1989. *Stressful life events*. New York: International Universities Press.

Mills, M.; Mimbs, D.; Jayne, E. E.; and Reeves, R. B. 1975. Prediction of results in open heart surgery. *J. Rel. Health* 14:159–64.

Minuchin, S.; Baker, L.; Rosman, B. L.; Liebman, R.; Milman, L.; and Todd, T. C. 1979. A conceptual model of psychosomatic illness in children: Family organization and family therapy. In *Advances in family psychiatry*, edited by J. G. Howells, vol. 1, pp. 316–38. New York: International Universities Press.

Mollica, R. F. 1983. From asylum to community: The threatened disintegration of public psychiatry. *N. Engl. J. Med.* 308:367–73.

Mollica, R. F., and Milic, M. 1986. Social class and psychiatric practice: A revision of the Hollingshead and Redlich model. *Amer. J. Psychiatry* 143, no. 1:13–7.

Molling, P. A.; Lochner, A. W.; Sauls, R. J.; and Eisenberg, L. 1962. Committed delinquent boys: The impact of perphenazine and of placebo. *Arch. Gen. Psychiatry* 7:70–76.

Moreno, J. L. 1971. Psychodrama. In *Comprehensive group psychotherapy*, edited by H. I. Kaplan and B. J. Sadock, pp. 460–500. Baltimore: Williams & Wilkins.

Morley, P., and Wallis, R., eds. 1979. *Culture and curing: Anthropological perspectives of traditional medical beliefs and practice*. Pittsburgh: University of Pittsburgh Press.

Mosteller, F. 1981. Innovation and evaluation. *Science* 211:881–86.

Mumford, E.; Schlesinger, H. J.; and Glass, G. V. 1982. The effects of psychological intervention on recovery from surgery and heart attacks: An analysis of the literature. *Amer. J. Public Health* 72:141–51.

Mumford, E.; Schlesinger, H. J.; Glass, G. V.; Patrick, C.; and Cuerdon, T. 1984. A new look at evidence about reduced cost of medical utilization following mental health treatment. *Amer. J. Psychiatry* 141:1145–58.

Murphy, J. 1976. Psychiatric labeling in cross-cultural perspective. *Science* 191:1019–28.

Murray, E. J. 1956. A content-analysis method for studying psychotherapy. *Psychol. Monogr.* 70:420.

Murray, E. J., and Jacobson, L. I. 1971. The nature of learning in traditional and behavioral psychotherapy. In *Handbook of psychotherapy and behavior change: An empirical analysis*, edited by A. E. Bergin and S. L. Garfield, pp. 909–50. New York: John Wiley & Sons.

Naranjo, C. 1980. *The techniques of Gestalt therapy.* Berkeley, Calif.: SAT Press.

Nardini, J. E. 1952. Survival factors in American prisoners of war of the Japanese. *Amer. J. Psychiatry* 109:241–47.

Ness, R. C., and Wintrob, R. M. 1981. Folk healing: A description and synthesis. *Amer. J. Psychiatry* 138:1477–81.

Newcomb, T. M. 1947. Autistic hostility and social reality. *Hum. Relat.* 1:69–86.

Nicholli, A. M. 1974. New dimensions of the youth culture. *Amer. J. Psychiatry* 131:396–401.

O'Connell, R. A., and Mayo, J. A. 1988. The role of social factors in affective disorders: A review. *Hosp. Comm. Psychiatry* 39:842–51.

Olden, J. 1977. Four taboos that may limit the success of psychotherapy. *Psychiatry* 40:197–204.

Oldham, J. M., and Russakoff, L. M. 1982. The medical-therapeutic community. *J. Psychiatr. Treat. Eval.* 4:337–43.

O'Leary, K. D., and Wilson, G. T. 1975. *Behavior therapy application and outcome.* Englewood Cliffs, N.J.: Prentice-Hall.

Orlinsky, D. E., and Howard, K. I. 1975. *Varieties of psychotherapeutic experience: Multivariate analyses of patients' and therapists' reports.* New York: Teachers College Press.

———. 1980. Gender and psychotherapeutic outcome. In *Women and psychotherapy*, edited by A. Brodsky and R. T. Hare-Mustin, pp. 3–34. New York: Guilford Press.

———. 1986. Process and outcome in psychotherapy. In *Handbook of psychotherapy and behavior change*, edited by S. L. Garfield and A. E. Bergin, 3rd ed., pp. 311–81. New York: John Wiley & Sons.

Orne, M. T. 1969. Demand characteristics and the concept of quasi-controls. In *Artifacts in behavioral research*, edited by R. Rosenthal and R. L. Rosnow, pp. 143–79. New York: Academic Press.

———. 1970. Hypnosis, motivation, and the ecological validity of the psychological experiment. In *Nebraska symposium on motivation*, edited by W. J. Arnold and M. M. Page, pp. 187–265. Lincoln: University of Nebraska Press.

Orne, M. T., and Dingus, D. F. 1989. Hypnosis. In *Comprehensive textbook of psychiatry*, edited by H. I. Kaplan and B. J. Sadock, 5th ed., pp. 1501–16. Baltimore: Williams & Wilkins.

Orne, M. T., and Wender, P. H. 1968. Anticipatory socialization for psychotherapy: Method and rationale. *Amer. J. Psychiatry* 124:1202–11.

Osgood, C. H.; Suci, G. J.; and Tannenbaum, P. H. 1957. *The measurement of meaning*. Urbana: University of Illinois Press.

Oursler, W. 1957. *The healing power of faith*. New York: Hawthorne Books.

Pande, S. K. 1968. The mystique of "Western" psychotherapy: An Eastern interpretation. *J. Nerv. Ment. Dis.* 146:425–32.

Pande, S. K., and Gart, J. J. 1968. A method to quantify reciprocal influence between therapist and patient in psychotherapy. In *Research in psychotherapy*, edited by J. Schlien et al., vol. 3, pp. 395–415. Washington, D.C.: American Psychological Association.

Pang, J. 1985. Partial hospitalization: An alternative to inpatient care. *Psychiatr. Clin. North Amer.* 8: 587–95.

Park, L. C., and Covi, L. 1965. Non-blind placebo trial: An exploration of neurotic patients' responses to placebo when its inert content is disclosed. *Arch. Gen. Psychiatry* 12:336–45.

Parker, S., and Knoll, J. L. 1990. Partial hospitalization: An update. *Amer. J. Psychiatry* 147:156–160.

Parkes, C. M.; Benjamin, B.; and Fitzgerald, G. 1969. Broken heart: A statistical study of increased mortality among widowers. *Brit. Med. J.* 1:740–43.

Parloff, M. B. 1986. Placebo controls in psychotherapy research: A sine qua non or a placebo for research problems? *J. Consult. Clin. Psychol.* 54:79–87.

Parloff, M. B.; Goldstein, N.; and Iflund, B. 1960. Communication of values and therapeutic change. *Arch. Gen. Psychiatry* 2:300–304.

Parloff, M. B.; Kelman, H. C.; and Frank, J. D. 1954. Comfort, effectiveness, and self-awareness as criteria of improvement in psychotherapy. *Amer. J. Psychiatry* 3:343–51.

Parry, H. J.; Balter, M.B.; Mellinger, G. D.; Cisin, I. H.; and Manheimer, D. I. 1973. National patterns of psychotherapeutic drug use. *Arch. Gen. Psychiatry* 28:769–83.

Pattison, E. M.; Lapins, N. A.; and Doerr, H. A. 1973. Faith healing: A study of personality and function. *J. Nerv. Ment. Dis.* 157:397–409.

Pattison, E. M., and Pattison, M. L. 1980. "Ex-gays": Religiously mediated change in homosexuals. *Amer. J. Psychiatry* 137:1553–62.

Paul, G. L. 1966. *Insight versus desensitization in psychotherapy*. Stanford, Calif.: Stanford University Press.

Paul, G. L., and Lentz, R. J. 1977. *Psychosocial treatment of chronic mental patients*. Cambridge, Mass.: Harvard University Press.

Peale, N. V. [1952] 1985. *The power of positive thinking*. Reprint. New York: Walker & Co.

Piper, W. E. 1979. The status of role induction in group psychotherapy. *Arch. Gen. Psychiatry* 36:1250–56.

Popper, K. R. 1959. *The logic of scientific discovery*. New York: Basic Books.

Posthuma, A. B., and Carr, J. E. 1975. Differentiation matching in psychotherapy. *Can. Psychol. Rev.* 16:35–43.

Powdermaker, F. B., and Frank, J. D. 1953. *Group psychotherapy.* Cambridge, Mass.: Harvard University Press.

Powell, T. J. 1987. *Self-help organizations and professional practice.* Silver Spring, Md.: National Association of Social Workers.

Prince, R. 1968. Contribution to the therapeutic process in cross-cultural perspective: A symposium. *Amer. J. Psychiatry* 124:1171–76.

Prusoff, B. A.; Weissman, M. M.; Klerman, G. L.; and Rounsaville, B. J. 1980. Research diagnostic criteria subtypes of depression: Their role as predictors of differential response to psychotherapy and drug treatment. *Arch. Gen. Psychiatry* 37:796–801.

Putnam, F. W. 1989. *Diagnosis and treatment of multiple personality disorder.* New York: Guilford Press.

Rado, S. 1956. *Psychoanalysis of behavior.* New York: Grune & Stratton.

Randi, J. 1980. *Flim-flam.* New York: Harper & Row.

Rashkis, H. A. 1960. Cognitive restructuring: Why research is therapy. *Arch. Gen. Psychiatry* 2:612–21.

Reed, L. S. 1932. *The healing cults: A study of sectarian medical practice — its extent, causes, and control.* Chicago: University of Chicago Press.

Rehder, H. 1955. Wunderheilungen, ein Experiment. *Hippokrates* 26:577–80.

Reich, W. 1972. *Character analysis.* Translated by Vincent T. Carfagro. New York: Simon & Schuster.

Reiser, M. F. 1984. *Mind, brain, body: Toward a convergence of psychoanalysis and neurobiology.* New York: Basic Books.

Reus, V. I.; Weingartner, H.; and Port, R. M. 1979. Clinical implications of state dependent learning. *Amer. J. Psychiatry* 136, no. 7:927–30.

Rhinehart, L. 1976. *The book of EST.* New York: Holt, Rinehart & Winston.

Rhodes, J. T.; Ford, T.; and Dickstein, L. 1989. Professional peer group counselling in the management of rheumatoid arthritis: A clinical trial. In *Advances in psychiatric medicine,* edited by R. C. W. Hall, pp. 122–41. Longwood, Fla.: Ryandic.

Richardson, J. T. 1980. Brainwashing. *Society* 17:19.

Richter, C. P. 1957. On the phenomenon of sudden death in animals and man. *Psychosom. Med.* 19:191–98.

Rickels, K. 1967. Anti-anxiety drugs in neurotic outpatients. In *Current psychiatric therapies,* edited by J. H. Masserman, 7:121. New York: Grune & Stratton.

Ricoeur, P. 1977. The question of proof in Freud's psychoanalytic writings. *J. Amer. Psychoanal. Assoc.* 25:835–71.

Riessman, F.; Cohen, J.; and Peari, A., eds. 1964. *Mental health of the poor: New treatment approaches for low income people.* New York: Free Press of Glencoe.

Rioch, M. J. 1967. Pilot projects in training mental health counselors. In *Emergent approaches to mental health problems,* edited by E. L. Cohen, E. A. Gardner, and M. Zax, pp. 110–27. New York: Appleton-Century-Crofts.

Robbins, I. 1988. Cults, converts, and charisma: Sociology of new religious movements. *Curr. Sociol.* 36:1–250.

Roche, J. P. 1963. *The quest for the dream: The development of civil rights and human relations in modern America.* Chicago: Quadrangle Paperbacks.

Rodin, J. 1986. Aging and health: Effects of the sense of control. *Science* 233:1271–76.

Rodin, J., and Langer, E. J. 1977. Long-term effects of a control-relevant intervention with the institutionalized aged. *J. Pers. Soc. Psychol.* 35:897–902.

Rogers, C. R. 1957. The necessary and sufficient conditions of therapeutic personality change. *J. Consult. Psychol.* 21:95–103.

———. 1971. The process of the basic encounter group. In *The proper study of man: Perspectives on the social sciences,* edited by J. Fadiman, pp. 211–27. New York: Macmillan.

Rogers, C. R., and Dymond, R., eds. 1954. *Psychotherapy and personality change.* Chicago: University of Chicago Press.

Rogers, C. R., and Sanford, R. C. 1985. Client-centered psychotherapy. In *Comprehensive textbook of psychiatry,* edited by H. I. Kaplan and B. J. Sadock, 4th ed., vol. 2., pp. 1374–88. Baltimore: Williams & Wilkins.

Rogow, A. A. 1970. *The psychiatrists.* New York: Dell.

Rokeach, M. 1968. *Beliefs, attitudes, and values.* San Francisco: Jossey-Bass.

Rolf, I. 1977. *Rolfing: Integration of human structures.* Santa Monica, Calif.: Dennis-Landman.

Rosen, D. 1977. A primal primer for psychiatrists. *Amer. J. Psychiatry* 134:445–46.

Rosen, J. C., and Wiens, A. N. 1979. Changes in medical problems and use of medical services following psychological intervention. *Amer. Psychologist* 34:420–24.

Rosenberg, M. J. 1969. The conditions and consequences of evaluation apprehension. In *Artifact in behavioral research,* edited by R. Rosenthal and R. L. Rosnow, pp. 280–350. New York: Academic Press.

Rosenhan, D. L. 1973. On being sane in insane places. *Science* 179:250–58.

Rosenheck, R.; Frank, J.; and Graber, M. 1987. Hospital treatment of patients with pending criminal charges: An ecological approach. *Psychiatr. Q.* 58:255–68.

Rosenman, R. H.; Brand, R. J.; Jenkins, C. D.; Friedman, M.; Straus, R.; and Wurm, M. 1975. Coronary heart disease in the western collaborative group study: Final follow-up experience of eight and one-half years. *J. Amer. Med. Assoc.* 233:872–77.

Rosenthal, D. 1955. Changes in some moral values following psychotherapy. *J. Consult. Psychol.* 19:431–36.

Rosenthal, D., and Frank, J. D. 1956. Psychotherapy and the placebo effect. *Psychol. Bull.* 53:294–302.

Rosenthal, R. 1969. Interpersonal expectations: Effects of the experimenter's hypothesis. In *Artifact in behavioral research,* edited by R. Rosenthal and R. L. Rosnow, pp. 181–277. New York: Academic Press.

Rosenzweig, S. 1936. Some implicit common factors in diverse methods of psychotherapy. *Amer. J. Orthopsychiatry* 6:412–15.

Ross, R. S. 1976. Ischemic heart disease: An overview. *Amer. J. Cardiol.* 36:496–505.

Rothman, D. J. 1971. *The discovery of the asylum: Social order and disorder in the new republic.* Boston: Little, Brown & Co.

———. 1980. *Conscience and convenience: The asylum and its alternatives in progressive America.* Boston: Little, Brown & Co.

Rotter, J. B. 1966. Generalized expectancies for internal versus external control of reinforcement. *Psychol. Monogr.* 80, no. 1.

Rounsaville, B. J. 1980. Research diagnostic criteria subtypes of depression: Their role as predictors of differential response to psychotherapy and drug treatment. *Arch. Gen. Psychiatry* 37:796–801.

Rounsaville, B. J.; Chevron, E. S.; Prusoff, B. A.; et al. 1987. The relation between specific and general dimensions of the psychotherapy process in interpersonal psychotherapy of depression. *J. Consult. Clin. Psychol.* 55:379–84.

Rounsaville, B. J.; Weissman, M. M.; and Prusoff, B. A. 1981. Psychotherapy with depressed outpatients: Patient and process variables as predictors of outcome. *Brit. J. Psychiatry* 138:67–74.

Rusk, T. N. 1971. Opportunity and technique in crisis psychiatry. *Compr. Psychiatry* 12:249–63.

Sachs, W. 1947. *Black anger.* Boston: Little, Brown & Co.

Salzman, L. 1953. The psychology of religious and ideological conversion. *Psychiatry* 16:177–87.

Sargant, W. 1957. *Battle for the mind: A physiology of conversion and brainwashing.* Garden City, N.Y.: Doubleday & Co.

Sato, Koji. 1958. Psychotherapeutic implications of Zen. *Psychologia* 1:213–18.

Schachter, S. 1959. *The psychology of affiliation: Experimental studies of the sources of gregariousness.* Stanford, Calif.: Stanford University Press.

———. 1965. The interaction of cognitive and physiological determinants of emotional state. In *Psychobiological approaches to social behavior,* edited by P. H. Leiderman and D. Shapiro, pp. 138–73. London: Tavistock Publications.

Scheff, T. J. 1966. *Being mentally ill: A sociological theory.* Chicago: Aldine.

———. 1972. Reevaluation counselling: Social implications. *J. Hum. Psychol.* 12:58–71.

Schleifer, S. J.; Keller, S. E.; Siris, S. G.; Davis, K. L.; and Stein, M. 1985. Depression and immunity: Lymphocyte function in ambulatory depressed patients, hospitalized schizophrenic patients, and patients hospitalized for herniorrhaphy. *Arch. Gen. Psychiatry* 42:129–33.

Schoenfeld, P.; Halevy, J.; van der Velden, E. H.; and Ruhf, L. 1985. Long-term outcome of network therapy. *Hosp. Comm. Psychiatry* 37:373–76.

Schofield, W. 1964. *Psychotherapy, the purchase of friendship.* Englewood Cliffs, N.J.: Prentice-Hall, Spectrum Books.

Schreiber, F. R. 1973. *Sybil: The true story of a woman possessed by sixteen separate personalities.* New York: Henry Regnery.

Schutz, W. C. 1967. *Joy: Expanding human awareness*. New York: Grove Press.

Schutz, W., and Turner, E. 1976. *Evy: An odyssey into bodymind*. New York: Harper & Row.

Schwitzgebel, R. K., and Traugott, M. 1968. Initial note on the placebo effect of machines. *Behav. Sci.* 13:267–73.

Seguin, C. A. 1965. *Love and psychotherapy*. New York: Libra Publishers.

Shader, R. I.; Goodman, M.; and Gever, J. 1982. Panic disorders: Current perspectives. *J. Clin. Psychopharmacol.* 2 (supplement): 2S–9S.

Shapiro, A. K. 1959. The placebo effect in the history of medical treatment: Implications for psychiatry. *Amer. J. Psychiatry* 116:298–304.

Shapiro, D., and Shapiro, D. A. 1987. Change processes in psychotherapy. *Brit. J. Addict.* 82:431–44.

Sharfstein, S. S. 1985. Financial incentives for alternatives to hospital care. *Psychiatr. Clin. North Amer.* 8:449–60.

Sherif, M., and Harvey, O. J. 1952. A study in ego functioning: Elimination of stable anchorages in individual and group situations. *Sociometry* 15:272–305.

Sherman, A. R. 1969. Therapeutic factors in the behavioral treatment of anxiety. Ph.D. dissertation, Yale University.

Shlien, J. M.; Hunt, H. F.; Matarazzo, J. D.; and Savage, C., eds. *Research in psychotherapy*, vol. 3. Washington, D.C.: American Psychological Association.

Shlien, J. M.; Mosak, H. H.; and Dreikurs, R. 1962. Effect of time limits: A comparison of two psychotherapies. *J. Counseling Psychol.* 31:24.

Shore, M. F., and Shapiro, R. 1979. The effect of deinstitutionalization on the state hospital. *Hosp. Comm. Psychiatry* 30:605–8.

Siegel, B. S. 1988. *Love, medicine, and miracles*. New York: Harper & Row.

Sifneos, P. E. 1989. Brief dynamic and crisis therapy. In *Comprehensive textbook of psychiatry*, edited by H. I. Kaplan and B. F. Sadock. 5th ed., pp. 1562–67. Baltimore: Williams & Wilkins

Sifneos, P. E.; Apfel-Savitz, R.; and Frankel, F. H. 1977. The phenomenon of alexithymia. *Psychother. Psychosom.* 28:47–57.

Simon, B. 1978. *Mind and madness in ancient Greece*. Ithaca, N.Y.: Cornell University Press.

Simon, J. 1978. Observations on sixty-seven patients who took Erhard Seminars Training. *Amer. J. Psychiatry* 135:686–91.

Simons, A. D.; Lustman, P. J.; Wetzel, R. D.; and Murphy, G. E. 1985. Predicting response to cognitive therapy of depression: The role of learned resourcefulness. *Cognitive Ther. Res.* 9:79–89.

Simonton, O. C., and Simonton, S. S. 1975. Belief systems and management of the emotional aspects of malignancy. *J. Transpersonal Psychol.* 7:29–47.

Sinclair-Gieben, A. H. C., and Chalmers, D. 1959. Treatment of warts by hypnosis. *Lancet* 2:480–82.

Singer, M. T. 1979. Coming out of the cults. *Psychol. Today* 12:72–82.

Skipper, J. K., Jr., and Leonard, R. C. 1968. Children, stress, and hospitalization: A field experiment. *J. Health Soc. Behav.* 9:275–87.

Slade, M. 1979. New religious groups: Membership and legal battles. *Psychol. Today* 12:81.

Slavney, P. R., and McHugh, P. R. 1987. *Psychiatric polarities: Methodology and practice.* Baltimore: Johns Hopkins University Press.

Sloane, R. B.; Cristol, A. H.; Pepernik, M. C.; and Staples, F. R. 1970. Role preparation and expectation of improvement in psychotherapy. *J. Nerv. Ment. Dis.* 150:18–26.

Sloane, R. B., and Staples, F. R. 1984. Psychotherapy versus behavior therapy: Implications for future psychotherapy research. In *Psychotherapy research: Where are we and where should we go?* edited by J. B. W. Williams and R. L. Spitzer, pp. 203–15. New York: Guilford Press.

Sloane, R. B.; Staples, F. R.; Cristol, A. H.; Yorkston, N. J.; and Whipple, K. 1975. *Psychotherapy versus behavior therapy.* Cambridge, Mass.: Harvard University Press.

Smith, M. L.; Glass, G. V.; and Miller, T. I. 1980. *The benefits of psychotherapy.* Baltimore: Johns Hopkins University Press.

Snyder, S. 1974. *Madness and the brain.* New York: McGraw-Hill.

Solomon, G. F.; Temochok, L.; O'Leary, A.; and Vich, J. 1987. An intensive psychoimmunologic study of long-surviving persons with AIDS: Pilot work, background studies, hypotheses, and methods. *Ann. NY Acad. Sci.* 496:647–55.

Spiegel, H., and Linn, L. 1969. The "ripple effect" following adjunct hypnosis in analytic psychotherapy. *Amer. J. Psychiatry* 126:53–58.

Spiegel, H., and Spiegel, D. 1978. *Trance and treatment: Clinical uses of hypnosis.* New York: Basic Books.

Spillane, R. 1987. Rhetoric as remedy. *Brit. J. Med. Psychol.* 60:217–24.

Spiro, M. G. 1967. *Burmese supernaturalism: A study in the explanation and reduction of suffering.* Englewood Cliffs, N.J.: Prentice-Hall.

Stampfl, T. G. 1976. Implosive therapy. In *Emotional flooding*, edited by P. Olsen, pp. 62–79. New York: Human Sciences Press.

Stanton, A. H., and Schwartz, M. 1954. *The mental hospital.* New York: Basic Books.

Steidl, J. H.; Finkelstein, F. O.; Wexler, J. P.; Feigenbaum, H.; Kitsen J.; Kliger, A. S.; and Quinlan, D. M. 1980. Medical conditions, adherence to treatment regimens, and family functioning: Their interactions in patients receiving long-term dialysis treatment. *Arch. Gen. Psychiatry* 37:1025–27.

Steiner, L. 1945. *Where do people take their troubles?* New York: International Universities Press.

Steinglass, P.; Weisstaub, E.; and Kaplan De-Nour, A. 1988. Perceived personal networks as mediators of stress reactions. *Amer. J. Psychiatry* 145:1259–64.

Sternberg, D. E., and Jarvik, M. E. 1976. Memory functions in depression. *Arch. Gen. Psychiatry* 33:219–24.

Stoller, F. H. 1968. Marathon group therapy. In *Innovations to group psychotherapy*, ed. G. M. Gazda, pp. 42–95. Springfield, Ill.: Charles C Thomas.

Stone, A. R.; Imber, S. D.; and Frank, J. D. 1966. The role of nonspecific factors in short-term psychotherapy. *Aust. J. Psychol.* 18:210–17.

Stotland, E. 1969. *The psychology of hope.* San Francisco: Jossey-Bass.

Strupp, H. H. 1976. The nature of therapeutic influence and its basic ingredients. In *What makes behavior change possible?* edited by A. Burton, pp. 96–112. New York: Brunner/Mazel.

——. 1986. The nonspecific hypothesis of therapeutic effectiveness: A current assessment. *Amer. J. Orthopsychiatry* 56:513–20.

——. 1988. Effectiveness of time-limited dynamic psychotherapy: Progress report. NIMH Research Grant # MH 20369. Available from H. H. Strupp, Vanderbilt University, Department of Psychology, Nashville, Tenn. 37240.

Strupp, H. H., and Hadley, S. W. 1979. Specific versus nonspecific factors in psychotherapy: A controlled study of outcome. *Arch. Gen. Psychiatry* 36:1125–36.

Strupp, H. H.; Wallach, M. S.; Wogan, M.; and Jenkins, J. W. 1963. Psychotherapists' assessments of former patients. *J. Nerv. Ment. Dis.* 137:222–30.

Stunkard, A. 1961. Motivation for treatment: Antecedents of the therapeutic process in different cultural settings. *Compr. Psychiatry* 2:140–48.

Sullivan, H. S. [1953] 1968. *The interpersonal theory of psychiatry.* Edited by H. S. Perry and and M. L. Gawel. New York: W. W. Norton.

Swan, G. E., and MacDonald, M. L. 1978. Behavior therapy in practice: A national survey of behavior therapists. *Behav. Ther.* 9:799–807.

Szasz, T. C. 1988. *The myth of psychotherapy: Mental healing as religion, rhetoric, and repression.* Syracuse, N.Y.: Syracuse University Press.

Talbott, J. A. 1985. Community care for the chronically ill. *Psychiatr. Clin. North Amer.* 8:437–48.

Talmon, M. 1990. *Single session therapy.* San Francisco: Jossey-Bass.

Thomas, C. B. 1982. Stamina, the thread of human life. *Psychother. Psychosom.* 38:74–80.

——. 1988. Cancer and the youthful mind: A forty-year perspective. *Advances* 5:42–58.

Thomas, C. B., and Dzubinski, K. R. 1974. Closeness to parents and the family constellation in a prospective study of five disease states: Suicide, mental illness, malignant tumor, hypertension, and coronary artery disease. *Johns Hopkins Med. J.* 134:251–70.

Thomas, L. 1981. Medicine without science. *Atlantic* 247:40–42.

Thompson, C. 1950. *Psychoanalysis: Evolution and development.* New York: Heritage House.

Thurber, J. 1939. *Fables for our time.* New York: Harpers.

Tiger, L. 1979. *Optimism: The biology of hope.* New York: Simon & Schuster.

Titchener, J. L. 1988. Clinical intervention after natural and technological disasters. In *Mental health response to mass emergencies,* edited by M. Lystad, pp. 160–80. New York: Brunner/Mazel.

Tocqueville, A. de. [1835] 1945. *Democracy in America.* Edited by P. Bradley. New York: Vintage Books.

Torrey, E. F. 1972. *The mind game: Witchdoctors and psychiatrists.* New York: Emerson Hall.

——. 1986. *Witchdoctors and psychiatrists: The common roots of psychotherapy and its future.* New York: Harper & Row.

Truax, C. B., and Carkhuff, R. R. 1967. *Toward effective counseling and practice.* Chicago: Aldine.

Tsuang, M. T.; Woolson, R. F.; and Fleming, J. F. 1980. Premature deaths in schizophrenia and affective disorders: An analysis of survival curves and variables affecting the shortened survival. *Arch. Gen. Psychiatry* 37:979–83.

Tucker, G. J., and Maxmen, J. S. 1973. The practice of hospital psychiatry. *Amer. J. Psychiatry* 130:887–91.

Tyhurst, J. S. 1957. The role of transition states — including disasters — in mental illness. In *Symposium on preventive and social psychiatry*, pp. 149–72. Washington, D.C.: Walter Reed Army Institute of Research.

Ungerleider, J. T., and Wellisch, D. K. 1979. Coercive persuasion (brainwashing), religious cults, and deprogramming. *Amer. J. Psychiatry* 136:279–82.

Vaillant, G. E. 1972. Why men seek psychotherapy. I: Results of a survey of college students. *Amer. J. Psychiatry* 129:645–51.

———. 1975. Sociopathy as a human process: A viewpoint. *Arch. Gen. Psychiatry* 32:178–83.

van der Kolk, B. A. 1983. Psychopharmacological issues in post-traumatic stress disorder. *Hosp. Comm. Psychiatry* 34:683–84.

Volgyesi, F. A. 1954. "School for patients" hypnosis-therapy and psychoprophylaxis. *Brit. J. Med. Hypno.* 5:8–17.

Wallace, E. R. 1988. What is "truth": Some philosophical contributions to psychiatric issues. *Amer. J. Psychiatry* 145:137–53.

Wallerstein, R. S. 1986. *Forty-two lives in treatment: A study of psychoanalysis and psychotherapy: The report of the psychotherapy research project of the Menninger Foundation, 1954–1982.* New York: Guilford Press.

Warner, W. L. 1937. *A black civilization: A social study of an Australian tribe.* New York: Harpers.

Weatherhead, L. D. 1951. *Psychology, religion, and healing.* New York: Abingdon-Cokesbury Press.

Weber, S. J., and Cook, T. D. 1972. Subject effects in laboratory research: An examination of subject roles, demand characteristics, and valid inference. *Psychol. Bull.* 77:273–95.

Webster, H. 1942. *Taboo: A sociological study.* Stanford, Calif.: Stanford University Press.

Wechsler, H. 1960. The self-help organization in the mental health field: Recovery, Inc., a case study. *J. Nerv. Ment. Dis.* 130:297–314.

Weingartner, H.; Cohen, R. M.; Murphy, D. L.; Martello, J.; and Gerdt, C. 1981. Cognitive processes in depression. *Arch. Gen. Psychiatry* 38:42–47.

Weininger, B. 1955. The interpersonal factor in the religious experience. *Psychoanalysis* 3:27–44.

Weinsheimer, J. C. 1988. *Gadamer's hermeneutics: A reading of "Truth and method."* New Haven, Ct.: Yale University Press.

Welkowitz, J.; Cohen, J.; and Ortmeyer, D. 1967. Value system similarity: Investigation of patient-therapist dyads. *J. Consult. Psychol.* 31:48–55.

West, D. J. 1957. *Eleven Lourdes miracles.* London: Helix Press.

Whitaker, C. 1976. The hindrance of theory in clinical work. In *Family therapy: Theory and practice*, edited by P. J. Guerin, pp. 154–64. New York: Gardner Press.

White, J. B. 1985. *Law as rhetoric, rhetoric as law: The arts of cultural and communal life*. Chicago: University of Chicago Press.

White, L.; Tursky, B.; and Schwartz, G. E., eds. 1985. *Placebo: Theory, research, and mechanisms*. New York: Guilford Press.

Whitehorn, J. C. 1947. The concepts of "meaning" and "cause" in psychodynamics. *Amer. J. Psychiatry* 104:289–92.

———. 1959. Goals of psychotherapy. In *Research in psychotherapy*, edited by E. A. Rubinstein and M. B. Parloff, pp. 1–9. Washington, D.C.: American Psychological Association.

Whitehorn, J. C., and Betz, B. J. 1975. *Effective psychotherapy with the schizophrenic patient*. New York: Jason Aronson.

Whitman, R. M.; Kramer, M.; and Baldridge, B. 1963. Which dream does the patient tell? *Arch. Gen. Psychiatry* 8:277–82.

Wilkins, W. 1979. Expectancies in therapy research: Discriminating among heterogeneous nonspecifics. *J. Consult. Clin. Psychol.* 47:837–45.

———. 1984. Psychotherapy: The powerful placebo. *J. Consult. Clin. Psychol.* 52:570–73.

Williams, R. B. 1989. Biobehavioral factors in cardiovascular disease. In *Psychiatry*, edited by J. O. Cavenar, vol. 2, chap. 126, pp. 1–9. Philadelphia: J. B. Lippincott.

Williams, S. L.; Dooseman, G.; and Kleifield, E. 1984. Comparative effectiveness of guided mastery and exposure treatments of intractable phobias. *J. Consult. Clin. Psychol.* 52:508–18.

Wilmer, H. A. 1958. *Social psychiatry in action: A therapeutic community*. Springfield, Ill.: Charles C Thomas.

———. 1962. Transference to a medical center. *Calif. Med.* 96:173–80.

———. 1981. Defining and understanding the therapeutic community. *Hosp. Comm. Psychiatry* 32:95–99.

Wilson, G. T., and Evans, I. M. 1977. The therapist-client relationship in behavior therapy. In *Effective psychotherapy: A handbook of research*, edited by A. S. Gurman and A. M. Razin, pp. 544–65. New York: Pergamon Press.

Wolf, S. 1950. Effects of suggestion and conditioning on the action of chemical agents in human subjects: The pharmacology of placebos. *J. Clin. Invest.* 29:100–109.

Wolf, S., and Pinsky, R. H. 1954. Effects of placebo administration and occurrence of toxic reactions. *J. Amer. Med. Assoc.* 155:339–41.

Wolff, W. 1954. Fact and value in psychotherapy. *Amer. J. Psychother.* 8:466–86.

Wolpe, J. 1958. *Psychotherapy by reciprocal inhibition*. Stanford, Calif.: Stanford University Press.

Wright, S. A. 1987. *Leaving cults: The dynamics of defection*. Washington, D.C.: Society for the Scientific Study of Religion.

Yalom, I. D. [1970] 1985. *The theory and practice of group psychotherapy*. 3rd ed. New York: Basic Books.

———. 1980. *Existential psychotherapy*. New York: Basic Books.

———. 1983. *Inpatient group psychotherapy*. New York: Basic Books.

———. 1989. *Love's executioner*. New York: Basic Books.

Yalom, I. D.; Houts, P. S.; Newell, G.; and Rand, K. H. 1967. Preparation of patients for group therapy. *Arch. Gen. Psychiatry* 17:416–27.

Yalom, I. D., and Lieberman, M. A. 1971. A study of encounter group casualties. *Arch. Gen. Psychiatry* 25:16–30.

Yochelson, S., and Samenow, S. E. 1977. *The criminal personality*. Vol. 2, *The change process*. New York: Jason Aronson.

Young, A. 1988. Unpacking the demoralization thesis. *Med. Anthropol. Q.* 2:3–16.

Zilberfeld, B. 1983. *The shrinking of America*. Boston: Little, Brown & Co.

Zilboorg, G. 1941. *A history of medical psychology*. New York: W. W. Norton.

Index

Abreactive therapies, 47, 189, 213, 214, 224, 229, 240, 300; effects of, 237–38; group support in, 238–39; nature of, 233–34; and posttraumatic stress disorder, 234–40; and Wilhelm Reich, 237; state-dependent learning in, 239–40

Adjustment disorder, 13

Adler, Alfred, 42, 186

AIDS (acquired immune-deficiency syndrome), and demoralization, 120–21, 124

Alcoholics Anonymous, 9, 16, 25, 78, 249–52; "religious" aspects of, 250; techniques of, 250. *See also* Recovery, Inc.

Alcoholism, 8–9, 13, 117, 222, 293; and family therapy, 268–69

Alexithymia, 169

Alienation, and encounter groups, 247

Altered states of consciousness. *See* Emotional arousal; Hypnosis; Meditation

Ambiguity, and anxiety, 198–99

American Psychiatric Association, 10, 291

Analogue research, 221

Analysis. *See* Psychoanalysis

Anticipatory socialization interview. *See* Role-induction interview

Antidepressant drugs, 116–17, 239; compared to psychotherapy, 56, 219. *See also* Drug therapy

Antisocial behavior, and the therapeutic relationship, 169. *See also* Deviant behavior

Anxiety, 48–49, 64, 72, 111, 120, 169–70, 203, 253, 300; and ambiguity, 198–99; and assumptive systems, 25; and behavior modification therapies, 223–25, 226

Apologia: modification of, by psychotherapy, 71–73, 204; patient's history as, 71, 200–201, 207

ARC (AIDS-related complex), 120

Aristotle, on rhetoric, 66

Association for the Advancement of Behavior Therapy, 216

Assumptive systems: and anxiety, 25; and behavior, 25–26, 50, 189, 206–7, 262–63; and psychoanalytic interpretation, 204, 210; and psychotherapy, 30–34, 50; resistance to change, 30–32, 34, 51; and validation, 27, 28–29, 31

Assumptive world: and childhood experiences, 27–29, 32; of controlled environments, 282–83; and cultural values, 29–30; formation of, 26–30, 50; nature of, 24–26, 33; and religion, 24

Asylums. *See* Controlled environments (therapeutic)

Attitudes. *See* Assumptive systems; Behavior

Attitudinal change: and abreaction, 237–38; and cognitive dissonance, 46, 179; and emotional arousal, 29, 31–32, 186, 189, 229–33, 241; experiential learning in, 46; as goal of psychotherapy, 33, 296; in group therapy, 258, 262–63; Lewin on, 233; maintenance of, 81–82,

About the Authors

JEROME D. FRANK, PH.D., M.D., received his psychological training at Harvard University and at the University of Berlin in Germany, followed by medical training at Harvard and the New York Hospital. He then joined the psychiatric staff of the Johns Hopkins Medical School and Hospital, where, except for three years in the United States Army Medical Corps followed by three years with the United States Veterans Administration, he has spent the rest of his career. He has authored or coauthored some 250 professional articles and five books. His main professional interests have been psychotherapy viewed in the context of the larger society, represented by *Persuasion and Healing*, and psychological aspects of the nuclear arms race, discussed in *Sanity and Survival in the Nuclear Age*, first published by Random House in 1967 and reissued in 1982. He lives in Baltimore with his wife, Elizabeth, a mental health counselor, and they enjoy occasional visits from their four children, all of whom are connected with academic institutions, and their six grandchildren.

Jerome Frank's daughter, JULIA B. FRANK, M.D., received her undergraduate degree in social studies from Harvard University and her medical degree from the Yale University School of Medicine. Following an internship in internal medicine, she completed psychiatry residency and a fellowship in diagnostic evaluation at Yale. For five years, she was on the Yale faculty as staff psychiatrist and then ward chief at the West Haven Veterans Medical Center. Her previously published work includes light verse, articles in the history of medicine and psychiatry, a book for young people on Alzheimers disease, and articles related to research on the pharmacological treatment of posttraumatic stress disorder. She and her husband, Mark Graber, now live in Austin, Texas, where Dr. Frank works in student mental health at the University of Texas. She is taking time from an academic career to raise three daughters, the third of whom was born between revisions of Chapters 7 and 8 of *Persuasion and Healing*.

Persuasion and Healing

Designed by Ann Walston

Composed by The Composing Room of Michigan
in Janson Text

Printed by Edwards Brothers, Inc.,
on 50-lb. Glatfelter B-16
and bound in Holliston Roxite